Prologue

This is an account of my experiences in the Vietnam War starting with my assignment to Fox Company, 2nd Battalion, 27th Marine Regiment, in February 1968. My story is not complete, since many memories have faded or been blocked from my mind, nor is it a comparison between my experiences and those of any others who served in Vietnam. If anything, my experience could be classified as "common." We weren't in the "big battles" that everyone knows about, but we weren't taking it easy either. We participated in some major operations, but mostly we just slugged it out day and night for 13 months - one month more than an Army tour, one extra month for the Corps. Oorah!!! We did the job we were called to do. All Marines gave that one extra step. Some displayed real heroism beyond the sight of cameras or officers. Some suffered horrible wounds and some died. This was *war*.

However, this is not just an account of Marines in combat, it's also a look at changes in men affected by war. Those who served in combat in the jungles of Vietnam, regardless of service, experienced much of what is written here; in their own way and in their own time. We are all Brothers in Arms. In order to write this, I'm relying on my letters home, Official Declassified Marine Corps monthly reports, the memories of others and my own memories.

This is a true account, at least as true as forty odd years allows me to be. I've struggled long and hard with the dilemma of being true and accurate against the sorrow of those family members who were affected by the loss of loved ones in Vietnam. I have chosen to be real, to be honest, and pray that anyone affected in a negative way by these events will forgive me for my sometimes brutal accounts. Also, by the request of some families, I have omitted the actual names of their loved ones. It has been said that the men in combat in Vietnam commonly went by nicknames. This was not the case in the units I served with. It was more common to call men by their last name which was the norm throughout the Corps. The names listed here are accurate. Those who died can be visited on "The Wall" and given the salute they so richly deserve. Vietnam was a real war, not just a movie or television war. Men fought and men died, God bless their souls. May God grant me the ability to tell it like it was, so that those who read this will know, at least in some small way, the effects of that war in a faraway place called Vietnam. Forgive the foul language, but accuracy requires that I tell it like it was.

I dedicate this to Our Lord and Savior, Jesus Christ, the Son of God: without whom I would not be alive to tell this tale. To all the members of 2nd Platoon, Fox Company, 2nd Battalion, 27th Marines and 2nd Platoon, Golf Company, 2nd Battalion, 5th Marines who were there with me, I say, "I am proud to have served with you." To my family who lived with the threat that I might not return alive; to my children who grew up with a mixed-up dad; to my wife Debra for her encouragement and constant support in writing this account; and to all the families who had their young men in harm's way, I say, "Thank you for your care, patience and understanding." To all who fought in Vietnam, I say, "Thank you for your service in the jungles of Vietnam." This may conjure up unpleasant memories for some or lead to a deeper understanding for others. If so, I hope those memories and realizations are healing. My thanks to Josh Klaaren, my good friend and advisor for his friendship and valuable input.

Lastly, to all who served our country in the Vietnam War and to Marines everywhere, I say, "Semper Fi."

Chapter 1

It was Valentine's Day, Wednesday, February 14, 1968, the day that the advance elements of the 27th Marine Regiment left Camp Pendleton, California for Vietnam. 2nd Battalion, 27th Marines (2/27) had been designated RLT (Regimental Landing Team) Alpha, leading the Regiment into Vietnam. My Company, Fox 2/27, would spearhead this movement.

In February of 1968, the 27th Marine Regiment was conducting training exercises aimed at combat readiness and possible orders to Vietnam. The Regiment had little time to prepare before the actual movement of troops and supporting units was ordered. On February 12, 1968, the Regiment received a Verbal Warning Order to deploy to Vietnam and on February 13, the actual Warning Order was issued. Advance elements were to deploy on February 14, 1968.

From February 12 – 20, 1968, the Regiment experienced a personnel turnover of about 3400 officers and men. After a review of the criteria for deployment, only 33 officers and 643 enlisted were eligible for deployment. Fifteen hundred non-deployables were transferred out of the Regiment, and nineteen hundred personnel were joined to the regiment in order to deploy at full strength, which in February was 139 Officers and 3647 Enlisted. These additional personnel were taken from the 5th Marine Division and were to a large degree non-infantry types, with MOS's (Military Occupational Specialty) other than those required by an infantry regiment. The Regiment was manned to fill the billets, but this renewed Regiment had no training as a unit prior to deployment to the combat zone in Vietnam, and contained few combat experienced grunts.

A regiment consisted of the regimental headquarters (H&S – headquarters and service personnel) and three Battalions. Each Battalion consisted of four rifle companies a Weapons company and an H&S Company. Each rifle company consisted of a command group, three rifle platoons and a weapons platoon. Weapons Platoon consisted primarily of the M-60 machine gun, 60mm mortar and rockets sections. The three rifle platoons consisted of a command group, three rifle squads, a machine gun squad and 60mm mortar and rocket teams.

It was my last week of training in Staging Battalion at Camp Pendleton, scheduled to go to Vietnam with other replacements. My friend and fellow machine gunner, Dan Nordmann – a tall, slim eighteen year old - and I had been together since machine gun school. We spent our last weekend on liberty enjoying the life of "Combat Ready Marines." We were full of vinegar, proud of accomplishing the goals of becoming Marines and successfully passing machine gun school. Out for a night on the town, we cruised the area and tried to decide what to do.

We spent most of our money on beer and soda. Dan drank soda because he was only 18. I had just turned 21 back in December, so I could drink beer. Finally, we decided we wanted to have a good steak before we left for Vietnam, but found ourselves short of money. Disappointed, we headed back to the base when I spied a USO building with a sign in the window that said "Pool Tournament Today, 1st Prize $50." I told Dan that I would go in there and win the tournament and then we could have our steak. He scoffed at me, knowing I was from Texas and always full of stories, but he went along with the program and followed me into the USO. He watched as I ran table after table and won the tournament. After accepting the $50 it was off to the steak house. Dan said later that even though he had doubted me at the USO, he now would believe anything I told him. It was then that I took Dan under my wing and did all I could to protect him, much to his chagrin.

Tuesday, February 13, we were in our afternoon formation in staging battalion when our Platoon Sergeant came up to us and said, "We need some volunteers. You, You, and You volunteer. Pack your sea bags." That was how Dan and I "volunteered." We were shocked to say the least. We knew we were going to Vietnam, but:

"Hey Sarge, we have a few days left in training." Oh my, don't *ever* call a Marine Sergeant "Sarge." We paid for that one.

We packed our sea bags with uniforms, toilet articles and any personal items. We had no combat gear. Arriving in the Battalion area at 2200 hours (10 p.m.) on February 13th, we were assigned according to our MOS (Military Occupational Specialty) to Fox Company, 2nd Battalion, 27th Marines (2/27). Everything was hustle and bustle. The Company was to leave on the 14th, and we needed everything! Al Decker – a more robust 19 year old - managed to make a quick call home, while the rest of us gathered our gear. We were issued all the 782 gear (Web belt, pack, helmet, metal canteens, entrenching tool, magazine pouches etc.) needed to go into combat, as well as our weapons. Riflemen were issued the M-14 rifle and Weapons Platoon personnel were issued their respective weapons, i.e. machine guns, .45 Automatic pistols, 3.5 rocket launchers, mortar tubes, etc. Tom Thomas, - tall and lanky - another friend of mine and those that remained of our unit in Staging Battalion would eventually be sent to the 27th later that night. As Tom remembers it:

"The DI (drill instructor) was frustrated and after the initial call for men, another call came down and he just threw up his hands and said, 'We're *all* going, pack your gear.' "

Where we were going, no one knew. There was a rumor (scuttlebutt) that we were headed for Korea to respond to the USS *Pueblo* incident where the ship had been boarded and captured on January 23, 1968. Being grunts, we were always the last to know what was going on. Ours was just to follow orders, and the orders were sealed for intelligence purposes.

I was assigned as the number one Gunner of 2nd Machine Gun Squad, Weapons Platoon, Fox Company, 2/27. I was issued an M-60 machine gun, Colt .45 Automatic pistol with holster, pistol magazines and Ka-Bar knife. I was loaded for bear. We were hurried off to MCAS (Marine Corps Air Station) El Toro, California to embark on a C-141 cargo plane for transit to Vietnam. My head was spinning.

"Where am I?"

"What's going on?"

"Why are we loaded up like this?"

We even had our ammo and grenades with us on the plane. Not issued yet, but ready to hand. Sitting on uncomfortable benches, laid out on the plane like pews in a church, we flew all the way to Da Nang, Vietnam, stopping once in Hawaii and once at Wake Island for fuel. We sure weren't ready for all that. Jim Seabolt, - of average build - a member of 3rd Rifle Squad, 2nd Platoon, Fox Company, remembers the flight. Looking down on Wake Island he could see a narrow strip of land shaped like a dog's hind leg, called the runway. From this altitude, the airstrip looked as thin as a shoestring.

"How can this big plane land on that little shoe string?" he wondered aloud.

Land we did, despite all the misgivings. We had a brief break from the cramped plane during refueling and took off again.

I managed to buy a post card and send it home, saying:

Dear folks,

Well, I didn't get a chance to send a post card from [Hawaii], so I am sending this one from Wake Isl. Will send another card from my next stop.

I am in the 5th Mar. Div now, the 27th Marines [Regiment]. We are now moving in regimental size to some place. We don't know where we are going, we just fly and fly. But, that's the service for you.

Write soon. Sorry I didn't get a chance to phone. Love Chuck

We landed in Da Nang, February 16, 1968, Vietnam time, with the rear echelon and other units arriving two days later. It was obvious that Korea was just a rumor after all.

True to the rush to fill necessary billets, my machine gun squad leader was a rifleman instead of a machine gunner. The others in the squad were Al Decker, Dan Nordmann, Dennis Freer, Hewett, David Lopez, James Richee and "Van" (they called me "Van" – it was easier to remember) - the name of the other man escapes me. Dennis Freer was the tallest in the squad and well built to carry the machine gun. David Lopez was short and thin but willing to do whatever it took to get the job done. James Richee was a thin dark-complected young man doing his job in the squad. My squad leader was a Lance Corporal (LCpl.) – he had a physique like a football star - and the rest of us were all either Private First Class (Pfc.), which was my rank, or Private (Pvt.). Tom Thomas was assigned as the number one gunner in 1st Squad, Machine Gun Section, Fox Company and would spend most of his time with the 1st Platoon, while my squad was assigned to the 2nd Platoon. A full complement machine gun squad would be nine men. A squad leader, and two 4-man gun teams. A gun team consisted of a team leader, a gunner, an A-gunner (assistant gunner), and one ammo humper, to help carry the machine gun ammo. The team leader would carry extra ammo and his personal rifle and ammo. The gunner would normally carry a minimum of two or three 100-round ammo belts of 7.62 ammunition and the 23 lb. M-60 machine gun as well as a .45 Auto w/ammo on his hip. The A-gunner would carry an additional two or three 100-round belts or more and a spare barrel for the M-60 plus his personal rifle and ammo. Finally, the ammo humper would carry at least four 100-round belts and the 15lb tripod which was used in stationary positions. All this and our personal gear in packs, e-tool (entrenching tool), .45 automatic, Ka-Bar knife, two canteens of water, rifles and rifle ammo etc., added to the load. All told, we humped about 80 to 100 pounds of gear.

Because of the rush to action, we carried old WWII equipment that had been issued for use in maneuvers at Camp Pendleton. This equipment consisted of a small canvas haversack and metal canteens, with WWII 782 gear (the canvas equipment that was carried into combat). We wore regular utilities (green shirt and trousers), black solid leather combat boots, helmet liners and steel pots (helmets consisted of a liner which fit "comfortably" on the head, and a steel pot that sat snugly over the liner), utility covers (cap) and flak jackets (sleeveless coats with Kevlar plates to protect against shrapnel), would round out the well-dressed Marine. Of all this gear, the haversack was the worst. It had narrow shoulder straps, which, when loaded, cut into your shoulders and hurt like crazy. It would be March before we were finally equipped to fight in the jungles of Vietnam. M-14's would be exchanged for the relatively new M-16's, requiring additional training. The M-16 never lived up to its intended purpose. It corroded easily and required frequent cleaning. Failure to clean your weapons could easily mean the end of you or your buddies. Utilities and boots were exchanged for jungle utilities (lightweight camouflaged uniforms which dried easily but didn't stand up to the rigors of the jungle), and jungle boots that were part leather and part canvas with air holes at the sole to let in air and let out water. Metal canteens were thrown away at the first opportunity and new plastic ones were "procured." Bush Marines always scrounge what they need, as we're always at the bottom of the list where resupply is concerned. However, new packs could only be obtained from the U.S. Army or the North Vietnamese Army (NVA). The Army was in the south and the NVA were out to kill you, so the humble haversack would remain to torture us. We wore our jungle utilities until they rotted on our bodies and our boots until they literally fell apart. Oorah!

It must be remembered that the Marine Corps is part of the Department of the Navy, and funding for the Corps is always much less than that of other services. That's one reason the Corps is limited to the number of personnel allowed on active duty at any one time. This was overlooked during the Vietnam War because the Corps was being used as a regular ground force rather than a naval assault force, which was the primary mission of the Corps. With limited funding, the Corps couldn't possibly maintain (material wise) a combat-ready force in the States with all the equipment necessary for jungle warfare and equally supply the troops already in Vietnam. All this said and done, it didn't help us poor grunts who bore the brunt of all these policies. Then there was the "look like Marines" mentality in the Command areas. It was not unusual to have well-dressed Marines in crisp jungle utilities and shined jungle boots, clean flak jackets and spotless helmets in our Battalion area, while Bush Marines looked like death warmed over. This was nothing new and it existed during WWII and Korea as well.

At Da Nang, our C-141 landed in a hot LZ (Landing Zone). At the time, the airfield was being rocketed and mortared. We were in combat. The 27th Marines would hold the distinct honor of being the first Marine Regiment in history to fly directly into a combat zone. Ammo and grenades were issued prior to landing and we piled out of that C-141 in true Marine Corps fashion, ready for a fight. We were loaded on a 2 1/2 ton truck, called a "deuce-and-a-half," for transport to our Battalion area and I assumed the position of a gunner with my M-60, bi-pods down, on the top of the truck's cab. On the way to our battalion area, we received small arms fire and I returned fire. We suffered a few wounded, but otherwise made it okay. They were trying to kill us! This was real! Welcome to Vietnam.

We arrived at our assigned area without further incident. Our Battalion area was the old 3rd Battalion, 5th Marines (3/5) compound located off the Anderson Trail near Phong Luc (2), southwest of Da Nang. Our Battalion, 2/27, relieved 3/5 and took on the full duties of the TAOR (Tactical Area of Operational Responsibility) on February 22, while 3/5 moved to participate in the battle for Hue City in the extreme north of South Vietnam. The 1968 Tet Offensive, which started on January 30, 1968, was in full bloom and Marines everywhere were meeting the enemy wherever they showed their faces, including the Da Nang area. With 245 casualties on January 31, 1968, that day would hold the record for the most casualties in a single day of combat throughout the history of the war.

The first thing to get our notice, besides being shot at, was the dust, a red dust that covered everything. Actually, it was more of a powder than dust and it boiled up from beneath the trucks as we left the airfield. That dust was to get in everything, our clothes, bodies, lungs, and weapons. It choked us and made us long for the jungles - that was until we got in the jungles; then we wished we were back in the dust. We had to clean our weapons often and always before going on patrol. We covered them with socks - some even used condoms - trying to keep out the dust but it was impossible, so we just stuck with cleaning. That dust was our enemy, as assuredly as the Viet Cong were.

After our arrival at the Battalion area, we were assigned quarters in tents, stored our sea bags (with dress uniforms and personal items) in huts that were set aside for that purpose. We were then put on the "lines" around the perimeter of the compound. The lines consisted of fortified trenches interspersed with machine gun positions and layers of concertina wire outside the trenches. There were about 200 yards or more of open ground from the trenches to the tree line of the jungle, plenty of space for enemy snipers to do their best, or worst, depending on your point of view. Actually, we had it pretty easy. We had a chow hall with hot meals three times a day, and if you missed a meal, the cooks would fix you up with something. We had toilets and showers, which were primitive but functional. The toilets were out-houses with half of a 50-gallon drum filled part way with diesel fuel under a basic toilet board that had modern toilet seats attached to it. The showers were 50-gallon drums filled with cold water located on wooden towers providing gravity feed through a hose to a spray head. When we weren't on the lines, we got squared away and wrote letters home. The Marine Corps always encouraged us to write home often, to let our families know that we were safe.

For most of us, fear wasn't a big factor. We operated on orders and the training we had received, which worked well enough in a fortified compound. The waiting was what got you - sitting in the trenches waiting for the enemy to attack or having a sniper suddenly shoot you in the head as you peaked over the berm. Nighttime was the worst, as we imagined all sorts of monsters coming at us out of pitch-black darkness. We still had images of war movies, where the Japs snuck up on Marines in WWII. At this time, idleness was our enemy. It gave us too much time to think and conjure up sights and sounds that we were sure were the "gooks" coming to get you. We learned about the word "gooks" denoting the VC (Viet Cong, also known as "Victor Charlie" or just plain "Charlie") and NVA (North Vietnamese Army, also called "Mr. Charles"). Even the Vietnamese people in general were referred to as gooks and from then onward, we used that term. The enemy had already become depersonalized to us. They would continue to be so as the fighting picked up. For the most part, the VC and Mr. Charles just became so many targets, targets that shot back. We had no personal experience with the enemy and so "boot camp" as we were, it just turned into one big game of who could shoot who first. That is, if you ever got a target to shoot at. Not very bright, but we had no one to teach us anything differently. We had not yet experienced the enemy first-hand, nor witnessed the destruction that warfare would inflict on our bodies, on our minds, hearts, and souls, which often outweighed and outlived the physical wounds.

One morning at dawn, Dan Nordmann and I with others from our platoon went to the chow hall tent to get some breakfast before we had to man the lines. We were excited to be in combat, and we constantly asked the guys who we were relieving, about what to expect, what it was like to be in combat and a thousand other questions, which they tried to ignore. I noticed a lone Marine sitting at a small table with his back to the kitchen wall, facing the entrance. He looked dirty but the grime was from the grease paint on his face and hands. Grease paint was a hard greasy substance in black and green colors forced into small tubes. It was used as camouflage, to break up the white of our faces and hands in the jungle, especially at night. He looked thin and worn out, with a strange look on his face. With his eyes darting at every movement around him, he would suddenly stare right through you. We later learned about that stare, which was called the "thousand mile stare." I tried to engage him in conversation, but he ignored me at first. Suddenly, "that look" centered on me and with no words spoken, I knew instinctively not to fool around with this guy. He looked and acted as if he was dangerous, and to the VC he was very dangerous. I asked one of the Marines on mess duty what that guy's problem was, and he said that the guy had just come off of a night ambush. He was also a short-timer with less than a month before he went home. No one messed with him. He came and went as he pleased and not even the senior NCO's (Non-Commissioned-Officers) went near him. A sign of things to come.

On February 19, Fox Company 2/27 was released to the control of the 1st MP Battalion in Da Nang for perimeter security of the Da Nang military complex. From February 22 to the 29th, the Battalion performed extensive patrolling of the Da Nang rocket belt. The Rocket and Mortar Belt was the area around Da Nang defined by the maximum distance from which rockets and mortars could be launched and still hit Da Nang. Patrols went out day and night in order to suppress enemy activity. This was the beginning of our combat operations. The major force of NVA and VC attackers had been repulsed during the initial Tet Offensive, so our biggest problems would be snipers and rocket/mortar attacks, which occurred routinely around Da Nang. We learned how to do patrols, how to deal with the jungle and rice paddies and how to act when attacked. The few combat experienced NCOs and officers we had were busy planning and training the troops, which left very few if any combat trained personnel to go on patrols with us. Because of that, the patrols were larger than normal, and normally led by what few experienced Marines we had.

On February 21st, I wrote my first letter home:

Dear Folks,

Well, here I am [finally], I have been quite busy lately and haven't had a chance to write. I am in Viet Nam, and have been here since Friday the 16th, which was Thursday the 15th, back in Texas.

Here's how it went; no sooner did we land at the Da Nang air base, then we were taken right out to an outpost South of Da Nang. At the [outpost], we dug in (fox holes), and were all ready to relieve the company there when (on Sunday), [they] [packed] us up again, this time armed to the teeth, and took us to a little village just east of Da Nang. That's where I am now. We are expecting a VC push into Da Nang, and are here to stop it. But so far, we haven't even had sniper fire, which is unusual for any place in Viet Nam.

Well, now you know where I am, so I guess I can start rattling on about what I have seen so far. First of all, the country itself. Here, where I am, it is very similar to south-west Texas. It is hot, but not the 100 and something that it will get this summer. It is real comfortable, except when you are out in the direct sunlight. But it is sure dusty. And it is a [choking] kind of dust. But you get used to that fast. It [hasn't] rained at all yet, but [when] it starts, I'm afraid we will have one hell of a flood. The country side has open areas, rice paddies instead of fields, and wooded areas, mostly full of bamboo. It isn't bad yet. Here is what the dirt looks like. [a dirty smudge/thumb print] [How] do you like my thumb print. Well, that is part of my natural covering of Viet Nam cure all. Yep, nothing can penetrate that armor.

Well, now a word from your friendly Vietnamese Chief. [many squiggly lines] Yep, that is exactly what their mumble-jumble sounds like to me. Of course there are a few things we understand now, like: <u>chop-chop</u> [meaning] to eat, munch, or [steal] or beg something to eat, hence to go chop chop with the mouth. Also <u>yo</u>, which as far as I can tell is short for Joe. All we [hear] from the hundreds of kids running [around] here is yo, yo, chop-chop. Oh, there is also boom-boom, for those men who can't wait to get back to their wife or girl friend. But I stay away from boom-boom, because it sounds too much like [incoming] mortar fire.

Actually though, things [aren't] bad at all. I have new jungle boots and jungle utilities, a good M-14 rifle and a certain coolness which I don't know if I deserve this early in the game. There is fresh water, and plenty of C rations. So I am getting along fine. There is only one thing I lack, and that is [cigarettes]. But it is best, that way I have to ration my butts and don't smoke as much. …

By the way, you ought to see my beard. I haven't shaved in 5 days, and I look like a beatnik. But at least the [mosquitoes] can't bite me on the face.

With all my love, Chuck

After some initial reorganization of the squad, I was reassigned as assistant gunner, carrying the M-14 rifle. Then I was once again made gunner in the number one gun team of the 2nd Squad in the machine gun section. Our squad was assigned to the 2nd Platoon, Fox Company, which consisted of a command post, three rifle squads and our machine gun squad. We were lucky to have an experienced platoon sergeant, Staff Sergeant (SSgt.) Staggs - a tall muscular man with a red handle-bar mustache - who did his best to keep us on our toes. The method for training the troops was to use what we had learned in the States followed by OJT, which in combat can be very costly. Actually, it was our attitude that needed to be "adjusted." Going from a well-trained but reasonably "human" Marine to a Real Combat Marine would not be an overnight process. It would take constant insertion, in a *real* combat environment to change us so completely. It is said that the average combat infantryman in WWII saw ten days of combat a year, and the average combat infantryman in Vietnam saw 240 days of combat a year, the difference being a result of constant exposure to enemy fire during a year in combat. Still, there really is no good comparison between combat in WWII and Vietnam. I certainly would *not* have wanted to assault the beaches in the Pacific or at Normandy or any of the other overwhelming battles that occurred. Still, it was the constant danger, constant wariness and relentless realization of no escape that affected us the most. There was no respite, no place to hide, 24 hours a day, 7 days a week, which wore down the human spirit and brought it to the primal level.

On February 23rd, I wrote again to my family:

Dear Folks,

Well, it's little old me again, writing from my mansion in the sand in this tropical paradise Viet Nam. I finally got some paper & envelopes, so I guess I will start my [novelette] on how to stay young through excitement. However, right at the moment, I am going to have to [forestall] that essay, since nothing at all has happened. Other outposts up and down our line of [defense] have been hit a little, but we haven't even received one sniper round. Now don't get me wrong, I'm not trying to hurry things, but it sure does get boring, watching all night for VC Charlie and nothing happens. Well, that's the way this war is, so I just have to make the most of it. And the easiest way I have found is to keep a good [sense] of humor.

The hardest thing though, is seeing all these hungry kids running [around] begging all day, and not being able to do [anything] about it. We give them a little food, but all that does is make more of them come [around] until we are almost driven crazy hearing chop-chop all day long, constantly. But after a while we get nice and [calloused] and it doesn't make any difference [anymore].

I can't really philosophize about this war yet, because I haven't been in it as such. But from what I have seen, we are doing the right thing. These villagers have a hard enough time making a living, without the Viet Cong to worry about. In fact, it is so bad, that these people would sell their own children for some food.

Hello, again. Today is Sunday, the [25th], and I am going to try and finish this letter. I cleaned up today, bathed in the river and half way shaved. I had a week long beard, and by the time I got to my chin, the blade just wouldn't cut it, so now [I] have a little [goatee], at least until I get ahold of another razor blade. But it sure feels good to be clean for a change.

The days here are all the same. In fact I didn't even know today was Sunday [until] someone mentioned that Church Services were going. But the nights are even worse, watching and waiting for something to happen. It sure gets boring [around] here, especially when all the action is down river from us, and we never know when it will come this way. Well enough on that.

Say, if you get a chance, I could use a few things. Like my knife, a whetstone, some candy (please no [chocolate]), and some of those plastic baggies.

With all my love, Chuck

Little did I know at the time how good I had it. Things would change quickly in March.

I remember one patrol in particular. We had a full squad patrol, with a rifle squad, machine gun team (I carried the M-60 machine gun), corpsman, radioman and squad/patrol leader. We were humping about 100 pounds each with weapons, ammo, water, chow etc. and tromping through rice paddies and villages for miles and miles. It was extremely hard for new guys unused to the heat, mud, dust, strain and real danger, which was so very different from anything we had experienced in training.

Our patrol leader stopped at the designated checkpoints, called in, and gave us a chance to rest, which helped a lot physically. Patrol routes were drawn on a map along certain coordinates, with checkpoints along the way. It was important to stick to the route given, so you didn't get mixed up with other patrols, and to provide accurate map positions of your coordinates for use when calling in fire support like mortars, artillery, or air strikes.

Being new to this business, we didn't know what was smart and what wasn't. We stopped for a break in a rice paddy while the patrol leader got his bearings. The most restful position on these breaks was to sit with your back next to a rice paddy dike and lean your pack on the dike, taking the load from those awful haversacks off your shoulders. We learned that trick early on. Well, there we were, out in the open, sitting upright along the side of a dike (like ducks in a shooting gallery), when the radioman's head slumped down on his chest. I just thought he was tired and nodded off. Someone finally noticed blood on his neck, and we realized that he had been shot. We never heard the shot, so we didn't know where it came from. Out here in the open, we were easy targets for the sniper that got the radioman. We ran out of there, seeking the nearest shelter, and carrying the body of the dead Marine. I guess you could call it a "hurried advance to the rear," since Marines never retreat. It was not a smart move to stop and rest there, or to put our backs to the enemy. With enough experience, this costly lesson could have been avoided. Lesson learned: don't make yourself a target in the rice paddies and never put your back to the enemy. If you do, someone will kill you! We also learned that people like radiomen, machine gunners, corpsmen and patrol leaders were primary targets for the enemy. Radiomen learned to pull the antenna down on their PRC-25 radios so it didn't stick up in the air, advertising who they were. Machine gunners learned to bring the heavy machine gun off their shoulders whenever possible. Corpsmen learned to hide any uniform items that would identify them as medics, and some took to carrying a rifle, which made them look like a regular grunt. Patrol leaders learned to hide their map and compass. Officers and NCOs learned not to wear insignias of rank, or anything indicating that they were in charge. All "dead" giveaways.

We were "Boot Camp". Other regiments, already in Vietnam, usually had sufficient experienced personnel to break in the "newbies." However, our entire regiment had just a fragment of the combat veterans needed to carry troops into battle. We were almost all "newbies." The influx of personnel to fill the ranks back in the States by non-combat MOSs, did nothing other than provide bodies to add mass to our unit. We had to learn, and learn quickly, the ins and outs of combat in Vietnam. In the process, men lost their lives or sustained a myriad other injuries.

We also had to learn about the Vietnamese people. As I had talked about in my letters home, our first assignment with the 1st MP Battalion positioned us in a little village just east of Da Nang. While we were there, we learned "yo" meant "Joe," and "chop-chop" meant food. There was a constant assault by hundreds of hungry children yelling:

"Yo gimme chop-chop, yo gimme chop-chop," over and over again.

At first, my reaction was one of pity and a desire to give what I could, but after days and weeks of this, we became callused and tuned it out. It was just too much to take. Then there was "boom-boom," which meant sex, and there was plenty of "boom-boom" available in the villages around Da Nang. I stayed clear of "boom-boom." There was nothing there to get excited about, with all the dirt and hunger and betel nut stained teeth. The Vietnamese chewed the betel nut, which had a mild stimulant effect and was used to fight bad breath, worms, phlegm and a many other maladies. Betel nut chewing left the teeth with a dark color and was certainly not attractive to the youth of the United States. "War is Hell," that is certain, but it's always much worse on the poor civilians caught up in the fighting. When we stopped seeing them as civilians and started to see them as possible VC. When children came up to Marines calling, "Yo gimme chop-chop," one hand extended and the other behind their back holding a grenade, our trust of them vanished. We soon learned that everyone and everything was out to get you. Between the gooks, the jungle, the snakes, rats, leeches, bacteria, heat and the monsoon rains, chances of survival were slim, and chances of being injured in one way or other were 100%.

Chapter 2

It was March 1st and my company, Fox 2/27, was again OPCON (assigned to the Operational Control) of the 1st MP Battalion, this time to the Marble Mountain Air Facility (MMAF) about five miles southeast of Da Nang. The base was located just south of the Marble Mountains, which were a series of six mountains massed in one complex. They were limestone and marble outcrops that historically had been used as a Buddhist sanctuary and were honeycombed with caves and passages that had been used for centuries. The elevation of the Marble Mountains was 8,255 feet, while the elevation of MMAF was 29 feet.

The importance of the Marble Mountains was paramount since it was the only elevated area near Da Nang and provided an excellent Observation Post (OP). Because of this height advantage, constant patrols were run to keep the area as free as possible of VC and NVA. On 31 January, 1968, the first day of the Tet Offensive, MMAF had received twenty-nine 122mm rockets, resulting in one minor injury and damage to twenty-three helicopters. Because of the constant threat to the area, there were always Marine grunt units attached to the area for security.

In a letter home on March 2nd, I wrote about our position at MMAF:

Dear Dad,

I got your letter the other day. It sure is good to hear from you. I have a little more time to write now, we are more or less finished with our bunkers and have settled down into regular night watches, patrols and ambushes. The other night this other Marine and I were volunteered to stand watch all night in this lumberyard where we had been receiving sniper fire. Well, needless to say, I was scared shitless. I couldn't have slept if I had wanted to. But, as you could guess, nothing at all happened. I was glad in a way, but it seems that all that happens around here is nothing. Nevertheless, it looks like things are going to change pretty soon. We will be moving out of these positions and might go up north to the DMZ [De-Militarized Zone]. But that remains to be seen.

It is hard to write about everything that goes on over here, especially concerning myself and what I do. But I will try to keep you all informed as to where I am and how things are. I guess I could write about all parts of this war, and I will, if you think I ought to. I leave this to your [discretion]. I know how curious everyone is about what goes on over here, especially Chris, Dan, & Billy. But how do you think Mom and Cathy would like hearing about mortar attacks and the like. I would really appreciate a word or two on the matter. (This pen has just about had it, so don't pay attention to the [writing].)

Oh, it looks like I'm the honorable coffee man. You know how I like my cup of coffee, well every morning I am usually the first one up and build myself a little fire and make some instant coffee. But finally I figured I might as well share my 'injun-newity' with my buddies, so I swiped some coffee and a couple of cans from the mess hall, made me a fire place, and am now making boiled coffee by the pot full. It really goes over big in the morning. I really surprised these guys with that bent stick trick. Nobody believed me until they saw it work. So do you have any other tricks up your [sleeve] to make life easier. Oh, I know one thing you could do, and that is send some dry wood over here. Everything is so green, that the only wood I have to burn is what I can buy from the Vietnamese people. All it takes is a little chop-chop and I get a whole fist full, and these people's fists [aren't] very big.

I asked before for my knife & whet stone, well, I sure could use them. A bayonet just isn't made for cutting wood. I might want my hand ax later on, if I can get an [okay] on it. [Machetes] are [okay], but a little [awkward] in real [dense] jungle. …

Some of these gals aren't bad looking, except when they open their mouth. I have never seen blacker and uglier teeth. Besides[,] there's no telling what kind of clap they have. From what they say, there are some kinds of V.D. here that the whores haven't even seen before. …

With all my love, Chuck

P.S. Thanks loads for the diaper rash. It goes good with the runs. (No, I don't have the runs, yet.)

My spelling was awful, as denoted by the number of words in brackets. Certainly not to glorify my writing, the purpose of these letters is to show the situation as it was, real time, and to show my transition from a "boot camp" into a Combat Marine. For now, this was a big hunting trip and we were camping out. I had learned the "bent stick trick" from my dad while making cowboy coffee over an open camp fire. Making boiled coffee was simple, just take an empty coffee can and put in the water and coffee grounds. Set it on the fire and bring it to a boil. There was only one problem: as the water boiled, it would produce a froth that would eventually run over the rim of the can. To stop this, just place a bent stick, one looking like a rocker on a rocking chair, over the mouth of the can. As the froth comes to the surface, it boils over the stick instead of the rim of the can. No sweat, no strain. Cowboy coffee.

On this "hunting trip," the only problem was that the game (gooks) shot back, which still didn't faze us that much. We were like a bunch of Boy Scouts, so ignorant of the reality of combat in Vietnam. C-rations, which contained a box of processed food with a meat/protein unit, a fruit unit, instant coffee with cream and sugar, and peanut butter with crackers were our staple diet. Included were a few cigarettes and a small roll of toilet paper. With our one hot meal a day from the nearby mess hall and time to rest and write letters between patrols, we had it pretty easy. We just didn't know about the rigors of living in the jungle yet. C-rations came with a unique can opener, one of which I still carry today, we called them our "John Wayne's." They were small metal folding can openers, which many men carried on their dog tags chain. C-rats were the staple food of combat Marines and soldiers all the way back to WWII. In fact, I often opened my C-rats and found moldy cigarettes and moldy toilet paper, no telling how old they were. We had built a dirt bunker with a tin roof and wooden sleeping platforms. We bathed in the river every other day or so and kept our bodies and our clothes as clean as possible. There were the same toilets as before, built like out-houses with metal cans cut from old 55-gallon drums partly filled with diesel fuel, which seemed to be the standard for most of the bases in Vietnam. When full, the cans were removed and the contents burned for sanitation, just one of the lovely odors of a combat area. Later we were reduced to digging "cat holes" with our entrenching tools (shovels) or just crapping on the ground off the trail somewhere and scraping a little dirt over it, like animals. SSgt. Staggs insisted on cleanliness. We could thank him forever for his understanding and insistence on staying "squared away." Shaving was a particular delight, it just made you feel good when nothing else could, and I continued this practice whenever possible. The grungy look of Marines engaged in jungle warfare may look "cool" to civilians and especially Hollywood, but it was very unpleasant for those living through it. Dirt and grime is the friend of bacteria, which we learned the hard way as our tours progressed. Infection could take you down fast and we often fought battles with bodies covered with sores called "jungle rot," pus-filled and bleeding lesions, especially on your legs. Trench Foot, a malady common to WWI, WWII and Korea, caused by feet being wet all the time, was also a problem. We carried spare socks and had the "airy" combat boots, but that only helped so much. We took off our boots and socks and aired out our feet as much as possible. But wouldn't you know it - as soon as we did that, we'd be hit by small arms fire or mortars or rockets and there we were, bootless and tender footed, as most Americans are.

Continuing with my letters, on March 4th I wrote:

Dear Mom,

I bet you have been wondering when I was going to write, especially since I already wrote to Cathy and Dad; well, I am trying to get at least one letter off to everyone while I have the chance. We will be moving out of this position in a few days, and I may have to resort to the family type letter, which is easier to write. ...

There isn't too much in the way of news. Things are pretty slow [around] here right now. About the only thing that has happened is that the Da Nang Air Base got mortared last night again, but there wasn't very much damage. Our old area is getting hit pretty hard though, and we will either be moving there or up north on the DMZ. Of course nobody knows for sure.

Oh, I don't think I told you about my house yet; well, it is a bunker about 18 feet long and 10 feet wide. We have a sleeping platform that will [accommodate] 4 people comfortably, with 3, 4'x6' compartments where we have our gear and from which we can fire, if the occasion ever arises. It looks something like this from the top. [hand drawn picture of bunker] Not bad egh! With a water tight roof and all. Yep, it is real nice, so now that we are beginning to enjoy our little home, what happens, we are moving out. Oh well, easy come easy go.

But that's not all to the life of Riley. We also get one hot meal a day at the M.P. Battalion Headquarters at the Da Nang air base, about 2 miles away. We alternate, breakfast one day, dinner the next, and supper on the third. Then we start all over again. We also bathe every other day or so in the river, and get our clothes washed. Of course, it is pretty hard to stay clean when you live in a dirt house. But I guess a dirt house is better than none.

Oh, remember you asking me about those "John Wayne" can openers we use to open C ration cans, well I am enclosing one with instructions. Let me know what you think of it.

I have a [surprise] for Cathy, and will send it as soon as I can. I will get you a [surprise] too, as soon as I find what I want. [Okay] Ma-ma-San. Eventually, I will get something for everyone. What would Dad and the boys like[?] It is pretty hard to choose things for them. …

With all my love, Chuck

From that letter it sounds like I'm a tourist, not a Combat Marine, with no cares other than finding the right souvenirs to send home. It wouldn't take long to change that attitude.

One crazy aspect of this war was the system of pay. We went to Vietnam so quickly that we hadn't been told about our options for pay. As a result, we were paid in Military Pay Currency (MPC), which is paper money only redeemable in Vietnam. It looked like Monopoly play money. There were no coins, just paper, with denominations from five cents and up. A dollar could consist of twenty pieces of paper if they were all five cents. The monthly pay for combat Marines with two years or less of service in 1968 was $109.50 for a Pvt., $113.40 for a Pfc. and $137.70 for a LCpl., plus combat pay, which varied from $50 to $65. Even though a job at $1 hr. was good in those days, and gas was $0.37 a gallon, less than $200 a month seems pretty cheap for your life.

So what do you do with your pay? You get a postal money order with your MPC and send it home, keeping out what you think you might need until the next pay day. We used the MPC to buy things we needed from the villagers, like dry wood for coffee fires, laundry, gambling debts, and also for items like cigarettes from in-country Navy Commissaries. Cigarettes in Vietnam were $1.00 a carton. We couldn't do an allotment, which would send money straight to our bank accounts, because you needed the account information to do that, and who had that information handy? We just didn't have the time to set up allotments before we left the States. Eventually we did get to set up allotments and sent the bulk of our pay home that way. Gambling debts? Yes, we bought cards at the little stores in the Battalion Area and played poker whenever possible. I did this throughout my tour and finished in the black. It was about the only way to relieve the stress that was always present. What did one WWII combat veteran say?

"Combat is a state of boredom interspersed with times of terror."

That may not be the exact quote, but it conveys the idea. That was WWII. In our case, it was more a constant state of terror interspersed with boredom. There was nowhere you could go in Vietnam that wasn't subject to some type of attack. Even when nothing happened, we knew the possibilities were there. However, at this stage, we still acted like Boy Scouts.

Around this time we got the rest of our shots to protect us from the diseases prominent in Vietnam. One of those shots was a hemoglobin shot, given to thicken the blood and help it coagulate when we were cut, scratched or otherwise wounded. I don't know how well it worked against bullet wounds. Anyway, the shot was given in the buttocks and it was awful. It was in the largest syringe and needle I ever saw and afterwards it left a large lump in your butt that felt like a basketball and hurt like crazy until the body absorbed the fluid. For a while, sitting down would be impossible, another fond memory from the war. Yuck!

On March 9, I wrote the following:

Dear Folks,

I have been out on patrols for the last 2 days, trudging through the rice paddies. Boy, let me tell you. I have never in my life seen mud like they have here in Viet Nam. I was loaded down with full pack, rifle, 5 loaded magazines, flak jacket, helmet, and 350 rounds of machine gun ammo. I am the assistant gunner. Well, I don't know how much weight that is, but I was sinking into mud up to my knees, and that's no exaggeration. One time, I actually got stuck. I had to stop and get my breath and really yank, just to get my darn leg out of that black glue called rice paddy mud. And sweat, boy I must have sweated out a ton of salt. My glasses were so fogged up, I could barely see the man in front of me, so I got disgusted and took them off. I could see real good then. My vision must be improving (ha, ha). Well, anyway, after 2 ½ hours of tromping through the worst kind of swamps I have ever seen and getting eaten up by [mosquitoes] and ants, we [came] in; not having seen one gook (Viet Cong). I guess it is good, not getting shot at; but when we go out we are ready for action, and it kinda gets [on] your nerves when you go through all that and nothing happens. But, that's this war.

There's only a couple of more pieces of news. We are moving out of this area back to [the] 2-27 area where we were at first. It seems that the Colonel's favorite company is Fox Company, and he picks us to do the hard jobs. So we are supposed to go back and secure the 2-27 area. So it looks like my days of leisure are just about over. We leave here Tues-

day. The second new development is that I will probably be the gunner when we go back to 2-27 area. They are changing our team [around] again and I have already been appointed as the next in line for gunner. So that means good-by to my rifle and I will get the machine gun and a .45 cal pistol. I'll let you know more later on. Oh, it looks like we will have 2 days out on patrol and 2 days in the area, so I will write as often as possible. …

With all my love, Your Blood & Guts Marine, Chucky Boy

With just over three weeks in Vietnam, the process that would continue throughout my tour had set in. We ran patrols forever, or so it seemed. Once again, we were learning. Good old SSgt. Staggs made sure that we trudged through the rice paddies and not on the dikes that separated them. Dikes made easy walking, but were often booby-trapped. So, we did as we were told and avoided the booby traps that were surely in place in those miles and miles of rice paddy dikes. Learning this early on saved many lives and limbs, but not all. As we got replacements we told them about the dikes, and those that listened survived, while those who ignored our advice died or went home with stumps.

Another lesson I learned was the difference between a blood trail and betel nut juice. We had been out on patrol, walking down a main trail, when I spied a large splash of dark red fluid on the ground with smaller spots around it. I called to my patrol leader, all excited, and said that I had found a blood trail. All of us being new here, he agreed and we followed the "blood trail" as it led down the lane. It didn't take long before we came upon an old woman walking along the same trail. As we passed her, someone spoke up and said to look at the ground. There it was, fresh out of her mouth, the same splash of dark red "blood" that I had seen earlier. I'm sure I blushed as the realization hit me that we had been following a betel nut juice trail and not a blood trail. I would remember that incident and avoid similar mistakes in the future. Just a dumb rooky mistake, but one not to be taken lightly, since following a wrong trail could get you in serious trouble out there in the middle of enemy territory.

I was the assistant gunner on this patrol. However, I filled whatever position necessary in our squad. Initially bouncing back and forth between gunner and A-gunner. We still carried the M-14 and wouldn't get our M-16's until we were back with our Battalion. The Battalion was still in the process of moving personnel around and it was the "senior man" that had priority. I never minded giving up the machine gun. In machine gun school, we were told that the average life span of a machine gunner in a firefight was seven seconds. I thought they were just trying to scare us, but I learned in Vietnam that it was true. Whenever the gunner would open up, all the enemy fire seemed to move, like a swarm of bees, and concentrate on that machine gun team. I experienced this more times than I care to remember. It was no fun carrying the gun, but I did it. It was my job.

Machine gunners are special people. Their job is threefold. First, protect the rifle squads. Protecting your fellow Marines is the primary goal. Second, kill as many enemies as possible. Third, provide covering fire when a movement of troops is required. I knew of few Marine machine gunners that ever thought of themselves first. It was always about your buddies. Although this attitude was not unique to machine gunners and was common among other Marines, the difference was that for machine gunners, it was part of their job. While a rifleman's job was to engage the enemy, ours was to engage and protect. Still, at this early stage, being a gunner had a certain macho feeling about it - boy was I young. We took pictures with Polaroid cameras, and smiled and showed off our muscles and our weapons. I have to laugh as I look back. Little did we know!

It was March 11, and we were returned to the control of 2/27, issued our M-16's and given a short time on the rifle range to familiarize ourselves with the weapon. Then it was off to the Ha Dong Bridge between the Battalion Area and Da Nang. The Ha Dong Bridge straddled the Song Bau Xau River. It was on the Anderson Trail about three miles east from our Battalion Area. Highway 1 was the main road between Da Nang and An Hoa to the south, and the Anderson Trail cut off of Highway 1 heading west - about ten miles or so south of Da Nang. By now my machine gun squad from Weapons Platoon was more or less permanently assigned to 2nd Platoon. Fox Company command stayed in the Battalion Area, sending out the platoons wherever they were needed. Second Platoon was assigned to the Ha Dong Bridge along with a 60mm mortar team and some assaultmen from Weapons Platoon. Assultmen carried the 3.5 rocket launcher (a Bazooka) and LAWs (Light Antitank Weapons). This bridge was pretty important, because it controlled access to the Da Nang area by road and by river from the west; farther to the west was the area around Hill 55, the A Shau Valley in the North West and the Arizona Territory in the South West, both hot spots full of VC and NVA.

In a letter home dated March 11, I wrote:

Dear Folks,

Well, I got your alls letter from the 5th and 6th, and believe you me, it was a welcome sight. …

You asked where I was now. Well, we moved back to the 2-27 area, which is about 5 miles [west] of Da Nang. The place where we were before was just across the river from Marble Mountain. That mortaring you read about was all [around] us, north, south, east, & west. We sat there and watched the shells go over us. We could even see the flashes of the enemy mortars, but there wasn't anything we could do about it. Right now, we are about 3 miles from 2-27 area on some big bridge. From what people have been saying, we will be here about a month or so. The VC are all [around] us, and we can expect rocket, mortar, or sniper fire any time of the day or night. E Company, the ones we have come to relieve, has really been hit hard. They are down to half strength already, and they have been here only 3 weeks or so. One of my buddies in E Co. already has 3 purple hearts and a Bronze Star. So you can see that my days of [leisure] are certainly over.

But enough about the war right now. I haven't been out on patrol [around] here yet, so I will wait till I go to really fill you in on all the [juicy] pieces of blood [curdling] war games. Oh, I am gunner now, at least till our gunner gets back from sick-bay. He has an infected [blister] on his foot and didn't come with us.

I am in good shape and feel pretty good despite the heat and all. …

It won't be too long till I come bopping in the front door and holler Dung Lie, I'm Home. Dung Lie means halt or stop. …

Well, it is just about dark, and time for Charlie to start acting up. …

With all my love, Your little Jungle Bunny, Chuck

The rules in Vietnam were that those with three Purple Heart Medals were sent home. Early on, those with three Hearts took advantage of this. However, soon our Command put out the word that no Purple Hearts would be issued unless you were wounded bad enough to go to the hospital, where the hospital personnel would take care of that award. Minor wounds would be ignored. They would be in your record, but no Purple Heart was to be given while in Vietnam.

I was now carrying the machine gun again, and we were housed in a bunker by the bridge, large enough to hold our entire squad. It was cramped a bit, but much better than foxholes. We had a fighting position on top of the bunker, a sandbagged firing station, to be used if the bridge was attacked.

We were on C-Rations now and soon learned the good from the bad. On the good side were: beef with spiced sauce, scrambled eggs, spaghetti with meat malls, beef stew, canned peaches (or any fruit), and peanut butter and crackers. On the bad side were ham and lima beans - which we called "ham and mother fuckers," or just "ham and mothers." The beef stew and the ham and mothers had lumps of grease or lard on the top and had to be heated to make them edible. The ham and mothers were especially bad because the lard was often a half-inch thick or more, covering the rest of the "dish." Eaten cold, they were absolutely awful, but in times of hunger, even ham and mothers looked good, cold or not. Many men found it unpalatable and discarded them or traded with the villagers for some rice. We foraged whenever we could to supplement our diet. Heating was always a problem at this stage in our tour. We were issued "heat tabs" in an aluminum package to heat our chow. They were like Sterno tabs, a flammable jelly-based tablet. They burned okay but were not very hot. It would take several of these to heat a meal, or make instant coffee. The down side of these heat tabs was the fact that they would crumble easily, especially when exposed to moisture, and there was a lot of moisture in Vietnam. Later we would learn the trick of using the plastic explosive C-4 to heat our chow, but for now, it was heat tabs or dry wood, if you could find any.

For a stove, we learned the trick of using an empty C-rat can, usually one of the small ones that carried crackers. We would cut slits along the base of the can with a "John Wayne" and push in the sides to make vent holes, then squeeze the top into an oblong to hold the round can of chow we were heating. Drop in a heat tab or a chunk of C-4 and wait for things to work. With the exception of those occasions when we were back in the Battalion Area, that was how we ate our chow the entire time we were in Vietnam.

Now, Marines being Marines, we let no opportunity go to waste to add to our meager food supply. As trucks came across the bridge, they had to be stopped and "checked." While being "checked," we took what we could from the back of the truck. Most of these trucks carried supplies to the Battalion Area, and were loaded with food or C-Rats, and occasionally ice! Yes, ice, probably slated for the Commanders' mess hall. They had to chase us away, but we got some blocks of ice from the trucks, and chopped them up with our bayonets and shared the delicious coolness. Those who had received "care packages" from home with Kool-Aid shared the wealth, and we had cold "Bugs Bunny" Kool-Aid. What a treat!

Our water was good; we had potable water from the base camp in Jerry Cans, cans used for gasoline, diesel fuel or water, marked in different colors according to their use. This was a treat too, because usually we got our water from local wells or streams, and had to add iodide tablets to make it safe to drink. Now that was some nasty water. Just imagine putting some iodine used for cuts and such into water and drinking it. We also collected rainwater at every opportunity, which proved to be the best source of water when stuck in the jungle or anywhere for that matter. I avoided bad water as much as possible by boiling my water and making coffee. Everyone thought I was crazy to drink coffee in the 100+ temperatures of Vietnam, but I never got worms or malaria that way. Many would make Kool-Aid with their nasty water so it would be drinkable. We did get some water with our resupply of "Beans and Bullets," - C-Rats and ammo - but it was usually sparse and used up quickly. When we were in a base camp, we could go to a "water buffalo," a tank on wheels that was used to store water from the water treatment plant. However, this water would often be foul and unfit to drink. We had to drink all the water we could to avoid heat exhaustion or heat stroke, and took salt tablets whenever we had them. Yet, it was never enough and many men fell from the heat. Most of the time we had to conserve our water, which meant we often suffered from dry throat and dehydration. With the dust and lack of water, our parched throats would swell enough to make us gag. I used the old Indian trick of sucking on a couple of pebbles, which would bring up the saliva and hold back the dryness. Still, like all good things, that had its drawbacks. With saliva came the swallow reflex and you know what that means, rocks in the stomach, etc. Still, it worked well enough.

Getting back to the Ha Dong Bridge, there is a little story that Dan Nordmann has told about me and one that I have told others. We had received care packages from home and one of the guys had received some Jell-O. Oh boy, Jell-O! Well, we "procured" some ice from a truck crossing our bridge - we were like Billy Goat Gruff and had to have our toll. We made up the Jell-O in a canteen cup, a metal cup that fit in your canteen pouch and used for everything like water, coffee, shaving etc. We put the cup of Jell-O in a "steel pot" (the outer portion of a helmet) and packed ice around it, put a T-shirt over it, and waited. We waited and waited and waited. Soon we ran out of patience and just drank the Jell-O. It never did gel. Oh, well, we tried. My care package contained all the goodies I craved, like canned apricots, mandarin oranges, "Bugs Bunny" Kool-Aid, jerky, candy, anchovies (I craved the salt), salted nuts, lemon drops and most of all, Camel cigarettes and baggies with rubber bands. The baggies were used to protect everything from the constant moisture and the rubber bands were used to keep the bags sealed. The rubber bands were also used as a safe way to carry grenades with the pin bent almost straight, ready to pull and throw. We would put a rubber band around the grenade and over the spoon, preventing the spoon from being released. The spoon (so called because of the shape) kept the firing device from igniting. The pin held the spoon in place, and it was normally bent on one end as a safety feature, with a loop on the other end used to pull the pin out. You had to straighten the pin, pull the pin, and release the spoon in order to ignite the internal fuse, causing the grenade to explode five to seven seconds later. The "Hollywood" version of just pulling the pin on a grenade without a straightened pin is just that, "Hollywood." Pulling a pin with your teeth is "stupid Hollywood." Carrying a grenade with a straight pin was very dangerous because the pin could fall out, which would be a disaster to say the least. It was not a good practice in combat to carry grenades that were difficult to use, when it might be necessary to throw your grenade at a moment's notice. Therefore, when on a combat patrol or ambush, we would often carry a couple of grenades ready for use. We'd bend the pins almost straight to make them easier to pull out and the rubber bands to hold the spoon as a safety feature. The rubber bands constantly rotted and had to be replaced often, so they were very valuable to us.

Well, back to the goodies. In my care package, I also received a new razor, which was great because I had a heavy beard and it was a pain to shave with a dull razor. To shave, we used our canteen cups to heat some water, and our steel pots to use as a sink. Our steel pots and canteen cups served as our sink, cook pots and even our chairs. To keep from sitting on the wet ground, we would take our helmets off and put them on the ground, with the hump down, and use that for a stool. Better than a wet butt. The best part of the goodies for me were the Camel cigarettes, a habit I had picked up as a teenager and not uncommon among the troops. However, my cigarettes were unfiltered and many of the guys would give me their Camels, Lucky Strikes or Pall Malls, and I would give them my Salems and Marlboros from the C-Rat cartons. My good friend David Lopez always remembered me as, "that crazy Texan who smoked Camels and wore his .45 slung low on his hip." Oh yeah, I had the image, but not much behind it. There was still a lot to learn.

One more goodie was the funny papers. I just loved those. I was an avid follower of the Phantom character, the "Ghost Who Walks," in the Sunday papers. My little brother Chris made it a habit to send me the funnies often and I shared them with all the guys, a real taste of normality from home. Last but not least was a real American baseball. We were overjoyed! We played with that ball until the hide wore off and the guts hung out. Sounds like a casualty I knew once.

This ingestion of "rich" foods and drink, although highly coveted, usually didn't sit well on our stomachs, or at least not mine. Shortly after all this bonanza of care packages, I was in the bunker and I turned to Dan Nordmann and said, "I gotta go." At which time I got up and left the bunker to do my business. My stomach rumbled, and after taking two steps, this watery mess came out of my rear end, ran down my legs, filling the blouse of my trousers. Blousing was a method of attaching the lower portion of the trousers to the upper part of the boot, thereby preventing the problem of tripping over your trouser leg while engaged in running and maneuvering. Continuing down, the "mess" then filled my boots. As I walked away, shit came squirting out of the air holes in the sides of my boots. WHAT A MESS! It was many steps to the river to clean up, and I squirted crap with every step. Everyone got a good laugh out of that one. Dan recalls it all by saying that as he watched me walk away from the bunker, all of a sudden the back of my trousers exploded in a patch of brown, which soon engulfed my entire lower half.

In Vietnam there was a poisonous snake nicknamed the "Two Step Snake." It was a small green viper, which would kill you before you took two steps, or so we were told. I think the real name was a Bamboo Viper. Anyway, from this snake, I took the term "The Two Step Shits," cause once you got the urge, and took two steps, it would all be down the back of your legs and into your boots. The "Two Step Shits" hit all of us at one time or another; I just had the distinction of being the first in our squad. Oh the infamy of it all! Nevertheless, it was good to laugh. We needed that. I went down to the river, stripped and washed out my trousers and boots, sat in the sun for a while and redressed. One reason the "explosion" was so noticeable, was the fact that we didn't wear underwear. We learned early on that underwear got loaded with sweat, and chaffed your thighs and private parts, causing a kind of "diaper rash." To prevent that, we did without underwear and kept things as loose as possible. The luxury of cleaning up at a river wasn't always there and when the dysentery hit while you were in the hills or mountains, you wound up with dried shit all over yourself until you could get cleaned up. Sometimes I used banana leaves, wet with dew in the morning, to clean up. Sometimes it would rain and I would collect enough water that way. However, any way you look at it, the "Two Steps" were just one of the many miseries we had to endure in the long march to the finish and Home.

The fun, if you could call it that, was soon to end. On March 14, I wrote another letter home:

Dear Folks,

Our bridge is still secure and old "Charlie" is still roaming the woods. I have been out on patrol every day so far, carrying the '60 (machine gun). We haven't had any action yet, or at least I haven't. One of our night patrols got hit by an ambush, but we didn't have any WIA's (wounded in action) luckily enough. However, yesterday, we had to really high tail it to get away from a firefight. The ARVN's (Army of the Republic of Viet Nam) were getting into it with the Cong, about 200 meters from our position in our patrol route. There were only 7 of us on the patrol, and our patrol leader decided to let the ARVN's handle it, so we moved out, catching stray rounds all [around] us. It was kinda hairy, to say the least. Oh, our gunner came back today, so I'm assistant gunner again, and get to carry my M-16 instead of that heavy old machine gun.

And another thing, guess what happened back at our Battalion Head Quarters (H. Q.). The ammo dump caught on fire and the office which was right next to it burnt down, along with our S.R.B.s (Service Record Book) and what mail they had in there. …

This bridge that we are at now, isn't too bad. We haven't had any mortar attacks, yet; nor any sniper fire, yet. The patrols are kind of rough, but the worst thing of all is the flies and mosquitoes. It's flies all day and mosquitoes all night. And these mosquitoes are really blood thirsty too. I have never seen the like. They just swarm all over you. And if you cover all the way up with your blanket, you sweat to death. So you can't win for losing. …

Well, from what I have seen and done so far in this past month, I think [it] qualifies me to say that freedom comes at high costs. But when you compare what we have to pay, for what we get in return, then freedom is well worth the price. Actually, I would much rather be any place but here, yet I know that it is here in this place that my freedom and yours is being strengthened. So with that thought in mind, I sleep pretty sound, [amidst] bombs going off all [around] me and rifle fire all over the place. So far, I haven't come real close to the one with my name on it, but every day the fighting gets closer to us and old "Charlie" gets a little braver.

Boy, you have never seen anyone so easy to wake up as me. And these patrols kinda get on your nerves, not knowing when or where you will be hit. But that's war, and like Dad said, "War is hell," or something to that effect. ...

With all my love, Your "Freedom Fighter," Chuck

I was still the optimist, looking at this war in the light of what I had been led to believe back in the States. I was still so naive about the world. On the 13th of March, the ammo dump for 2/27 caught fire and the office, which was right next to it, burnt down. Our SRBs and mail burned up with the office. Another little incident that helped make life in Vietnam a true "Hell on Earth." Fortunately, our pay records were in another location. The mosquitoes, ants, flies and leeches, just to name a few, drove us to the brink of crazy many times. We had an insect repellant we called "Bug Juice" which contained concentrated Deet, a common ingredient in insect repellant. It worked to make the leeches drop off and to repel the mosquitoes, to a point, but it was nasty. It was oily and very caustic. It would eat your clothes and melt plastic and no telling what it did to you after being absorbed by your skin. Yet, that was all we had, so we dealt with it. If you can imagine over a year of this, day in and day out, then you get the picture.

March 16th, and the war moved on. In a letter that day, I wrote:

Dear Family,

Well, here I am again. (You know, I'm going to have to think up a better introduction. That one's getting worn out.)...

There isn't a whole lot to write about, but here is what's new so far. I'm carrying the "60" again. This time with the other gun team. Their team leader went back to Regiment, and their ammo humper sprained his [ankle]. So I will be gunner for them [until] they get another man. I only have patrol every other day now, and get to swim, wash my clothes, shave, read books and write letters the rest of the time. So life isn't too bad. Our night patrol last night ran into another ambush last night, and took 2 VC. One dead and one alive. The VC that got it, got it in 3 places. In the head with a grenade and 2 slugs in the chest. Boy, that M-16 sure tears a person up. It goes in about [this] big [a circle on the paper indicating the size of an entry hole] and comes out about as big as this paper. It really tears you up. ...

With all my love, Chuck

We had become callous. Dead gooks didn't affect us much - it was still an impersonal war. Later that day, the war would become very personal. The life of Riley was over.

On March 17th I wrote home:

Dear Mom,

I got that little package you sent me. Wow! When you said that you could send 30# of [stuff], I never figured on getting 30# or rather 25# to be exact. … Really, I was never so [surprised] in all my life. Everything is in good shape in the box, except my knife. What happened, did Chris try playing [mumblety-peg] [a game where one threw a knife to stick it in the ground] on the cement or something. Seriously though, I still haven't gotten over all the nice things you sent. …

The Koolade must have been a brain storm on your part. Because we all go crazy [around] here when we get ahold of that good old "Bugs Bunny" Koolade. If you think the kids drink that [stuff] up, you ought to see mean, old, grubby, blood-thirsty Marines drink their koolade. Wild animals should act so wild. … And the fruit. That's another luxury item that is [incomparable] to anything else. We dig a hole next to the river and bury the cans in the cool, wet ground. That cool fruit sure hits the spot. … Of course, the rubber bands and [baggies] are priceless. I put [cigarettes], socks, T-shirts, shorts, matches, coffee, (pictures of barely-clad girls, he-he) and all sorts of things in the [baggies]. The rubber bands are used to hold the spoon down on grenades, close bags, to flip paper wads (he-he), etc. …

It [razor] works like a charm. You know me and my heavy, heavy beard, well, right now, it is hard to tell my face from my butt. They are both so smooth. … But the thing that tops it off, is the baseball. There is nothing in the world that means U.S.A. more than a baseball. After we wear it out, playing ball, I think I will skin it and frame the skin. What do you think of that[?] …

But right now I have something a little serious to talk about. We've had 3 missing in actions, 2 killed, and 3 wounded. It looks like old Fox company is starting to get it. I haven't been on patrol for two days now and contrary to what we were told, it looks like they are [keeping] machine guns here at the bridge in case we get hit. I'm gunner again, this time for the other team in my squad, and it looks like my position is fairly permanent now. It seems that yesterday evening, my squad leader and a couple of other friends of mine decided to go down the river in this boat we have. Well, they had been going every day about the same time of day and no one thought anything of it. But, last night they didn't come back, and here it is about 5:30 in the evening and they still aren't back. Of course, as soon as it got dark and they weren't back, we all knew what had happened, even though we still hoped for the best. So I am minus one squad leader. The way reports have it, there were some gals bathing downstream, these fellas got the word and took off. It is hard to believe sometimes how treacherous these people can be, but like they say, VC Charlie is everywhere. We are still waiting for reports from the patrols that are out looking for their bodies. It almost doesn't seem real, that one minute they are riding around in a boat and the next, they are gone without a trace. No one is really shook up, just sobered up a bit. We are Marines, and death is our business, but it is different when it is your own buddies. …

It is one thing to lose a man in a firefight, where you expect casualties, but quite another when men just disappear. Yep, this is a hell of a war. …

With all my love, Your Not-So-Hungry-Marine, Chuck

Those three men that went missing were:

My machine gun squad leader MOS 0311 Rifleman. He was 22.

Pfc David W. Erickson MOS 0351 Assultman. He was 18.

Pfc Edward L. Krausman MOS 0341 Mortarman. He was 23.

All members of Weapons Platoon, Fox Company, 2/27.

A report on the web site, *www.Marines.togetherweserved.com* states the following:

A Note from The Virtual Wall:

The 27th Marines' Command Chronology for March 1968 contains the following entry for the 16th: 2 USMC embarked in a boat to inspect bridge pilings and the banks of the river within the unit's perimeter. They exited the perimeter at 161515H. Platoon Commander knew men were missing at 1530 and sent USMC patrol to search area along west bank at 1600. Platoon returned with negative results at 1700. A 15 man USMC/ARVN patrol was sent down west bank of river at 1730 and swept area. Returned to bridge at 2200. A two-squad sized patrol was diverted at 1900 to sweep east bank of river. They secured at 2100. The two men, Pfc David W. Erickson of Minneapolis, MN, and Pfc Edward L. Krausman of Burbank, CA, were carried as Missing in Action, and promoted while in that status, until the Secretary of the Navy approved Presumptive Findings of death on 02/25/1976 and 11/28/1975 respectively. Their bodies were never recovered.

In addition, a 1968 AP article from a local military newspaper in Vietnam, reported the incident as follows:

"Beautiful Viet Girls Lure GIs to Death"

Da Nang, South Vietnam (AP) –

That beautiful Vietnamese girl, her silken black hair swirling about her fragile body as she bathes in the stream, can be an angel of death. Viet Cong terrorists around this big Marine base are now using "seduce and destroy" squads of girls, in attempts to entice Leathernecks to their deaths.

Marine sources said three Marines were missing and one was killed by the female assassination teams in three months

A captured Viet Cong confirmed that attractive girls were being recruited and trained in English and intelligence work for the assassination teams.

In one recent incident, three Marines on patrol near their camp spotted three girls swimming nude in a stream. A few minutes later, one Marine lay dead face down in the water. The other two are still missing. "It is considered probable that the females were used as lures," the sources said. The first inkling of the death-dealing decoys came in January when Marine counterintelligence units uncovered what they called a "Viet Cong suicide platoon, composed of approximately 30 females." The girls were already operating near this sprawling Marine complex.

The girls, many believed to be fresh-faced teen-agers like many Marines, work in the time-honored tradition: strike up a conversation, get the Marine talking about himself, make an appointment for a quiet rendezvous, then arrange the kill.

Marine sources said the effectiveness of the "seduce and destroy" missions – a play on the Marine combat plan of "search and destroy" – is still limited. But they are concerned enough to begin putting out warnings to the grunts, as the lower ranked men are called. The curfew, which is imposed at 8 p.m. in the once-lovely city of Da Nang, is strictly controlled.

Much of the city is completely off limits to the Leathernecks. Houses of prostitution, vermin-infested, tin-roofed shacks, stand

> less than 100 yards from the main gates of some camps. Officials are not too concerned with these. They cannot be eradicated but can be better patrolled when nearby.
>
> They are concerned, however, with the houses located deep in the twisting, dark alleys that wind away from the main streets. And now they are even more worried about the fragile-looking maidens bathing in the leaf-ringed streams near here. They may bestow the kisses of death.

So, what is the real story, and what does it mean? The Marine Corps' report was incorrect, unless there was a typo in the report, or the report was made after the discovery of my squad leader's body. There were three Marines missing on March 16, not just two. Yes, they inspected the banks of the river, and left the perimeter by boat, but that was not the reason they left the perimeter. These were three young Marines, full of testosterone and adrenaline, who had a chance to see naked girls in the river and it was just too much to ignore. To see a beautiful girl in the nastiness of combat in Vietnam would be something to entice them away from their fellow Marines and the safety of their unit. They were friends, and from all reports, knew each other at Camp Pendleton, before the unit deployed to Vietnam. They were all part of the Weapons Platoon of Fox Company, 2/27. Of course, none of this is in the official Marine Corps monthly reports, especially the aspect of the girls luring Marines to their death. The newspaper report came closer to the truth. The fact that one man was found dead, "face down in the water," was not discovered until later. It wasn't until the body was sent to Da Nang for an autopsy, that it was known for sure that it was the body of my squad leader, although we all knew it was him when we found the body.

What did this mean? It meant that things were more dangerous than anyone at that time thought. To disappear like that was spooky! In addition, this was the first time we had felt the loss of fellow Marines so deeply. My Squad Leader was my boss. I knew him. I ate with him. I joked with him. I fought the enemy with him. He was my friend and squad leader. It really struck home. Although I said in my letter home that "no one is really shook up," that wasn't true. I felt his loss to the core, and I began to build my shield, the shield of detachment, that would protect me from the pain of loss. To this day, I have not been able to dissolve that shield. The rest of my tour in Vietnam would build on this incident and build an impenetrable wall, which would only be breached twice in my life, once by the temporary loss of my children and once by divorce. However, that was much later, years after my tour in Vietnam.

The next day, March 17, we lost more men. A patrol from 1st Platoon, Fox Company, triggered a booby trap consisting of a mortar round, a 105mm artillery round and a 106 recoilless rifle round. The combined explosion took the life of two Marines and wounded two others. The KIA's (Killed in Action) were:

Pvt Mario Frank Demattio 0311, rifleman. He was 21 years old.
Cpl Edward Antone Swonke Jr. 0311, rifleman. He was 21 years old.

In a letter home on March 20, I wrote:

Dear Chrisy Boy,

Hello, Hello, Hello. I hope you forgive me for not writing you sooner. ... Really, I feel like a dog for not dropping you a line before. ...

There isn't much of anything new to tell you about life over here. Of course, you know that we lost 7 men the other day. Yep, not only that, but 2 men out of the first gun team in my squad are gone, one is transferred to another unit and the other one is out with a broken leg. And of course my squad leader is no longer with us, or among the living – so to speak. So now, there are only 2 men in the first team, me and my assistant gunner, or A-gunner as we call him; and 3 men in the other team. So out of 8 men, we only have 5 men left. I kinda wonder how many men we will have after 12 months.

Chris, this is really a hell of a war. It is not a fast moving, exciting war like the 2nd World War or even Korea. This is a slow, little, dirty war. Where you have to sit and wait for old "Charlie" to zap you. It's so hard to just sit and wait for old "Charlie" to zap you. It's so hard to just sit and wait, not knowing who is your enemy and who isn't. ...

With all my love, For my favorite little brother, Yours, Chuck

Yep, a dirty little war! On March 21st, we found the body of my squad leader. It was bloated and waterlogged. When we went to remove the body from the water, his skin peeled off, like a hog that had been scalded. We weren't exactly sure it was him, but everything we could see pointed to it.

Two days later, March 23rd, I wrote two letters home. One to my Mom talking about family matters, and in the other I wrote:

Dear Dad,

Here I am, practically [exhausted]. That letter to Mom kind of wore me out. I think I goofed, and mentioned something in a letter to the family, that should have waited till I wrote you. But I can't always sit down and write a letter to everyone individually. However, be assured that any other news of a, so to speak "bloody" nature, will be for you personally. Anyway, I figure that if it doesn't make me sick, then you might (he, he) be able to take it. We found one of the three men who went out on the boat. It was my squad leader, or rather what was left of him. He had his head shaved and his whole face blown away, like someone took a knife and split his head in two, leaving the back part. He came floating downstream the day before yesterday. Besides that, his head and body was full of maggots, and bloated to about 3 times its normal size, with the skin just hanging to the body by threads. It wasn't a very pleasant sight, to say the least. From what we could figure out, he was probably used as an example to get the other two to talk. He was the biggest of the three. Our lines have been probed almost every night since Wednesday. The way it looks, old Charlie might try to blow this bridge. There's no telling how much of a lay out he has of our defenses, but one thing is for sure, with the moon gone now, almost anything could happen. Last night, one of our patrols got chased back into our perimeter. The lead was sure flying. So now I stand watch with a grenade in each hand, my .45 on my hip and my little finger on the trigger of my ".60", the machine gun. (Ha Ha) Really, though, we really have to watch it now.

Well, that's enough for now about this dirty little war. Say, I noticed the coffee stains on your letter. We do love our coffee don't we. I finally got my foot out of the mud hole all right, but I just stepped in another one. You can't win for losing. Not only that but it rains every day here from 7:30 to 8:30 in the evening. That hour rain settles the dust and keeps the mosquitoes away, but I have the feeling that it is only a little bit of [what's] to come. …

There are a whole lot of little things I can talk about, like how I live etc. But I will wait till I write the family as a whole. We will have a lot to talk about when I get home Dad. Things happen so fast over here, that a lot of little things slip by and I don't think of them till after I have written. And then when I write again, there is a lot of new news, so quite a bit goes unsaid. But, the time goes by pretty fast over here, and It won't be long till I'm home. …

With all my love, Machine Gun Chuck.

At this point, my original 9-man squad had been whittled down to five men counting myself, but that would change to six men when James Richee returned to our squad from sick bay. I was on the gun and the list was as follows:

Myself (Gunner/Team Leader) with David Lopez (A-Gunner) and James Richee as Ammo Humper in the first gun team and Dennis Freer (Gunner/Team Leader), Allan Decker (A-Gunner) and Dan Nordmann as Ammo Humper for the other gun team.

Later, our Company Commander gathered us together and read the autopsy report he had received from Da Nang. My letter didn't quite say it all. Although I listed some of the trauma that my squad leader experienced, I was reluctant to go into more detail with my family back home, knowing how worried they were to begin with.

It was a truly devastating report and had an immediate impact on all of us in the Company. When we discovered the body floating face down in the water, we tried to pull it out of the water. However, when I reached down to do that, the skin just peeled off and we had to take a poncho and position it under the body while it was in the water and then lift the poncho out with the body in it. We tied the body in the poncho for shipment to Da Nang. I'm still haunted by that memory to this day. The other two men were listed as MIA (Missing in Action) and are still listed that way today.

The torture and death of my squad leader, as well as the loss of Pfc. Erickson and Pfc. Krausman, had a most profound impact on those of us from 2nd Platoon. The evidence of torture hardened us, galvanized our spirits and gave us the determination that we would never ever allow ourselves to be captured. For the rest of my tour this incident would stand out in my mind, it assuaged my fear of death, and gave me the certainty that I would never allow myself to be captured nor would I ever allow those under my command to be captured as long as I lived. It also affected our actions in combat. If caught in an ambush or facing superior forces, we simply got up and practiced the old Marine Corps adage, "Charge!," and this charge against an unsuspecting enemy usually saved the day. After about five weeks "in country," we had lost our innocence. We were bloodied and no longer "Boot Camp." Yes, we still had much to learn, but we had been seared in the fire of torture and death among our brothers. The war now became personal. Why some enjoy the torture of their enemy so much is still a mystery to me. Yet torture always backfires on the torturers and makes their enemies the stronger for it.

The fallout for 2nd Platoon was that our Platoon Commander was relieved from duty. His replacement was 2nd Lieutenant Barry Jones – built like a college athlete. Lt. Jones was to be a blessing to 2nd Platoon. Jim Seabolt, from 3rd Squad, remembers:

"Having Lt. Jones as our Platoon Commander was the best thing that ever happened to our Platoon. He brought the Platoon together like no one else could."

Lt. Jones' steadfast leadership, willingness to endure everything we had to endure, knowledge and coolness under fire, would enable him to forge us into a formidable fighting unit. At his right hand was SSgt. Staggs, always working for and with his "troops." Lt. Jones was a mustanger (an enlisted man who became an officer). He had already served one tour in Vietnam in 1965/66, acting as a grunt M-14 automatic rifleman and then as a platoon and company radioman. That experience would be priceless to us in 2nd Platoon. Not only did he understand platoon tactics, but he also knew how to effectively use the radio to call in fire support, medevacs, and resupply. He knew how to read a map and pinpoint our location, both of which were paramount to our operations and our safety. He trained us well, and once we had gained his confidence, he let us do our job. This was so important, because micro-management in combat can get you killed.

To sum it up, we all owed a debt of gratitude to those three men who suffered awful torture and sacrificed their lives for us. They were our heroes. They received no medals, no recognition for bravery in the face of the enemy, no acknowledgement for standing up under torture or fighting under devastating odds for their fellow Marines; yet the dreaded attempt to blow up our bridge never occurred, and I can't help but think that they held fast and did not give in to the enemy. The lessons we learned from that incident would stay with us for the rest of the time we were in Vietnam, and for the rest of our lives. It would turn us into a cohesive fighting force that was bound together by these events. We looked out after each other; we watched each other's back; we fought together as a stronger unit than before and we would "NEVER FORGET." After five weeks in Vietnam, Fox Company had suffered 4 KIA's (Killed in Action), 7 WIA's (Wounded in Action) and 2 MIA's (Missing in Action) as listed in the Official Monthly Reports for 2nd Battalion. However, the actual body count was higher due to injuries like a broken leg, malaria, the walking wounded, etc. and those wounded or killed that just slipped through the cracks. To put this in perspective, that is about the size of a full rifle squad, and easily 25% of a reinforced rifle platoon.

Counting the other types of injuries and transfers, the loss was closer to 30% of our platoon.

Chapter 3

From the official declassified Marine Corps monthly reports for March, 1968, 2nd Battalion, 27th Marines, a breakdown of the significant events for Fox Company after the events at the bridge are:

> March 18, "Fox Co., with Company G as a blocking force, swept both sides of the Song Bau Xau River." [This was the river that flowed under the Ha Dong Bridge.]
>
> March 19, "2nd Platoon, Fox Co. on combat sweep in the area of the Ha Dong Bridge, assisted by units from the 51 ARVN's."
>
> March 20:
>
> Fox Co. on a sweep, found 6 caves, captured 4 men, found another 11 caves and captured 2 men. Caves were blown. F Co. received fire from about 25 enemy wearing grey uniforms and helmets. (Probably NVA) Returned fire, swept area and observed enemy dragging and carrying wounded into thick tree line. Later that day, 1st Platoon Fox Co. came under mortar and small arms fire. During the fight a woman and child were wounded. Unsure by whom. Woman and child were evacuated by 1st Platoon for further transport to a German Hospital Ship. The witness of the event was SSGT Lucas, 1st Platoon, F-2/27.

I relate this incident to show that we were not the heartless killers that everyone made us out to be when we came home. It's true that as time wore on we were less inclined to help the civilians, because from our point of view, there were no "civilians." Everyone, even children were potential enemy combatants that could and would blow you up at every opportunity. Although I didn't witness the event myself, there were many stories of small children walking up to Marines with one hand extended, hollering:

"Yo gimme chop chop, Yo gimme chop chop", while holding a grenade in the other hand behind the back.

Once the Marines went close enough, the kid would let the spoon fly on the grenade, activating it, and blow themselves up along with the Marines. We stayed clear of civilians as much as possible because of incidents like that.

Translated from the Marine Corps Reports:

> March 21 and 22, Fox Co., 2/27, held combat sweeps in the vicinity of Duc Ky. A patrol found 7 rafts with 100 – 150 lbs of rice. The rafts were destroyed and the rice was turned over to the ARVNs.
>
> On March 22 at 11:50 a.m. local time, a squad sized combat patrol, F-2-A, from 2/27, at map coordinates 995633 was caught in an ambush. The patrol came under a heavy volume of fire on one side of the trail by 7 VC, followed by a 2nd hit from the other side by an additional 5 men. The patrol fought their way clear with no casualties. The squad returned to the Ha Dong Bridge.

We learned early on that the best way to survive an ambush was to charge, and fight your way out, a practice we employed often. It was normal to take the machine gun on some night patrols/ambushes, in order to provide that overwhelming firepower needed to spark an ambush or survive one. Our machine gun squad was pretty busy. Patrols that were meant solely for reconnaissance purposes did not carry machine guns. Hence, the former was classified as "Combat Patrol" and the latter as "Recon Patrol."

As noted above, there are many references to map coordinates in the reports. The map coordinates given in the Marine Corps records are from the military maps, handed out to all essential personnel. Later on, I would be running so many patrols, that I had a set of maps myself for each area where we operated. I literally lived – or died – by those maps. The military maps were laid out in a grid pattern with markings every 1000 meters, or clicks, as we called them. The north-south grid lines in conjunction with east-west lines formed one-kilometer square boxes across the map. The book *Where We Were in Vietnam* by Michael P. Kelley is the definitive book about this subject and a must for the serious historian.

Special grid zones (see www.marzone.com/maps/Map_Grid.htm) marked by overlays onto USGS (United States Geological Survey) maps, which added a prefix to a given set of coordinates. The areas I operated in were primarily the AT, BT and ZC zones. A very good web site for map information is in Ray's Map Room at *www.rjsmith.com*. This site also gives easy-to-follow instructions on how to find and purchase maps from the

USGS. The USGS site is http://store.usgs.gov. Three main maps cover the areas mentioned in this book. The Da Nang map (USGS #L701466413), the Dai Loc map (USGS #L701466404) and the Thruong Duc map (USGS #L701465401), available through the USGS. The Da Nang map has a zero line running north-south through Da Nang with the AT zone to the west of that line and the BT zone to the east. The Dai Loc map is adjacent to the south side of the Da Nang map and had the same AT and BT identifiers on either side of the zero line. The Thruong Duc map is the ZC zone, which is adjacent to the west side of the Dai Loc map. Lines on the maps are numbered from zero to 99 forming larger squares of 100 kilometers. An additional number is usually added, identifying points at 100 meters intervals. An example would be coordinates 995633 (found on the Dai Loc map) from the above report. The 995 is the north-south grid line 99 extrapolated in 100 meter increments out to 5 hundred meters. The 633 is the east-west grid line 63 extrapolated in 100 meter increments out to 3 hundred meters. Sometimes, map coordinates are in four digit groups, like 9952, where the last number would designate a point within 10 meters. With this information, one can follow our movements as we moved from one place to another and also used to pinpoint areas where Marines were killed or wounded. I hope this is of help to those who are interested.

One last point. The records from the 2nd Battalion, 27th Marines (2/27) often omitted the alphabetical prefixes. Since the majority of the operations undertaken by 2/27 are found on either the Da Nang or Dai Loc maps, those prefixes were not always recorded. Coordinates without prefixes are understood to have either AT or BT prefixes according to those locations on the maps.

The patrols were occurring more frequently and I found myself starting to fight two wars, one during the day and one at night. During the day we made platoon-sized sweeps or squad-sized combat patrols in the Ha Dong River area, and occasional sweeps with the Company in the Duc Ky area. At night we did night patrols/ambushes. There was some rotation going on, so we didn't have to do that every night, but we usually went out every two or three nights.

On March 27th, I wrote my brother Chris:

Dear Chrisy Boy,

Well, here I stand, fully ashamed of myself. That sure was a swell letter you wrote me. I hope you feel like doing that more often. Needless to say, I am real proud of you. You really seem to be using that head of yours, the way [you] talk about tennis and all. ...

[Okay], I quit, you can relax now, smoke a candy cigarette and drink a root beer. (Ha, Ha, He, He Aren't I mean) [and] I will show you just how brave [your] big brother is. I went out on patrol last night, and am still a little [nervous]. We had the south patrol, and had to search this little village, check out the area, and then set up an ambush. Well, I was "Tail-end-Charlie", the last man in the patrol. My job was to make sure we didn't get hit from the rear. There were only 4 of us Marines and 2 ARVN's. Six men isn't very many. I've been out on night patrols before, but this time was real different. Mainly because there are about 300 NVA's (North Vietnamese Army men) [around] this area. Well, we started out, got to the Vill, and set up an ambush to see if we could get the snipers that were harassing our perimeter. We found them all right, but not the way we wanted. They had us pinpointed. [Luckily] no one was hit. We threw grenades and lobbed M-79 rounds (the M-79 is like a shoulder mortar) and bugged out. [Okay], we figured we had shook 'em. All we are supposed to do is report enemy activity, we're not a combat patrol [as] such. Well, we continued on and everything seemed fine, then we stopped once, when an illumination flare went off and crouched down. I looked to my rear and saw something move. I figured it just might be a bush swaying in the wind. But the next time we stopped, there was this crunch crunch behind us. Oh Boy, that kinda shook me up. I let the patrol leader know that I thought we were being followed. He decided to try and shake 'em, but we couldn't. I think they have eyes like cats. Well, it was about 2:00 in the morning, (we were due back at 4:00) and we couldn't shake old Charlie. I hadn't looked behind for about 10 minutes, we were moving pretty fast, and then the man in front of me said, "Hey, I thought we only had 6 men," I looked behind me and yikes, there was a Charlie about 20 feet behind me. I whipped [around] and fired, and then all hell broke loose. We high-tailed it back to our lines, firing all the way. No one was hurt, but we were sure shook up. The way we figured it, they were out to get a prisoner and not just hit us. Boy, I won't ever forget that. ...

I'm enclosing one of the [Chieu Hoi] leaflets that are dropped by plane telling the VC to give up, and the villagers to help the Marines. Tell me if you'd like some more and maybe some different kinds. I pick 'em up on patrol. ...

With all my love, Chuck

That letter says a lot between the lines. I'm convinced that the VC didn't get any information from my squad leader, and they were out to capture another Marine to torture. I could very well have been the target for just such a scenario. However, Charlie didn't know that I was already keyed up from my squad leader's ordeal and more aware of my surroundings than most Marines. My squad leader had saved my life. Without the example of his capture and torture and death, I may well have been just another boot Marine, unaware of the dangers around me. I wish I could thank my squad leader face to face, hopefully I can in the afterlife.

The next day, our company was back at it. From the Marine Reports:

"On 28 March 1968 two platoons of Company F supported two companies of the 51st ARVN Regiment in a search and destroy operation north of the Song Bau Xau River and east of the Ha Dong Bridge. Company F set in blocking position on the south bank of the river as 4/51 elements swept southeast."

There were many lessons learned during our stay at the Ha Dong Bridge. One, of course, was, *never get captured.* With the torture and death of my squad leader, which was confirmed just a few days prior to my experience on that night patrol as tail-end Charlie, it was confirmed that the VC/NVA were out to do to me what they had done to my friend and squad leader. I just wasn't going to let that happen!

Another lesson we learned, after a few more incidents at night, was to never let them know where you are. If you set up an ambush, even at night, wait about an hour and then move again if possible. Even if the VC didn't see you set in, the villagers would and they would get the word to the VC. Turning their game against them was the only real strategy we had. We also learned not to run from the enemy. If you were taking fire and needed to move, then move deliberately. At night, once we discovered we were being followed, not attacked, we could have set a small ambush and hit them as they followed. Of course, with only six men, this would probably not have worked very well, but later, with larger night patrols, it worked like a charm. Hindsight sure is 20-20.

The 29th of March was the end of our time at the Ha Dong Bridge. We were back at the Battalion area off the Anderson Trail. We were all "saddled up," and by saddled up, I mean that we had everything we owned and all our combat gear on our backs, around our waist, in our pockets and over our shoulders. Wherever there was a space, we found something to fill it.

My pack held extra socks, T-shirts, towel, razor, soap, toilet paper, heat tabs, utility cover, writing material, wallet, deck of cards, poncho and poncho-liner, etc. It also held up to six C-ration meals, often carried inside the spare socks draped over the pack, lighter and lighter fluid, Camel cigarettes, entrenching tool (shovel), and whatever else we could stuff in them to make life in the jungle at least one step above an animal. We had two large side pockets on our trousers, which were stuffed as well. We used the plastic bags and rubber bands that we got in care packages to keep our things as dry as possible. I never was able to have a harness or pack-board. The harness would help transfer the load from the web belt onto the shoulders. The pack-board would help distribute the weight of the pack and transfer some weight to the hips. The Army had larger packs and even the NVA had better packs which were much sought after by Marines. I had a first aid kit, two canteens, Ka-Bar knife, Colt .45 Automatic, and .45 ammo, all on a web belt around my waist, with extra canteens, bayonet, and medical pouches hanging from my flak jacket. Extra toilet paper and some C-4 explosives also lived in the pockets of my trousers. The M-60 Machine Gun, with 200 rounds of belted 7.62mm (same as a .308 cal) ammo was carried on the shoulder. Then there was the piss-pot/steel-pot helmet that weighed over two pounds, including the helmet liner, which was the lightweight cover inside the steel pot. As a result my hips were always sore, as well as my back and shoulders. All that was being "saddled up," just like a pack mule.

They had us waiting on the helicopter pad for over four hours, trying to decide what to do with us. Finally, they put us in tents and we got "unsaddled." Up to this time, I had gained something of a reputation for going out on a patrol/ambush and coming back alive.

As I wrote in a letter home on the 29th:

Dear Folks,

Well, here I am and there you are. Or rather here I was and there you are. Yep, we're moving again. Where to, the good Lord only knows. I've heard everything from [Phu Bai] to [Khe Sanh] to our old area, the 2-27 area. This moving is really for the birds. You pack everything you own on your back and take off. Like the Marine Corps says, you "Saddle Up". Here I sit, waiting to leave; we've been ready since 7:00 and here it is 11:00 so there's no telling when we're going to go. …

Say, if you ever get the urge to send me another "Care Package," how's about putting in a rat trap, my sling, & some dried meat. …

You asked once about rank. Well, all I can say is that advancement is slow in the Marine Corps. Actually, I really don't care if I get rank or not. All I look forward to is getting the hell out of Viet Nam and then about a year and a half later, out of the Corps. I couldn't ever make the service my career. I'm too much of an individual. I don't know if I'll ever be much of a leader or follower. I'm just a doer. Whenever our machine gun squad has to send a man to help out the "butt platers" (ground pounders, riflemen) or whatever, the patrol leaders asked for me. Naturally, I turn them down except when it's my turn to go, but it is nice to know that [you're] wanted.

Well, here it is at 3:00 and it's hotter than hell. The sweat never stops pouring off. I'm at the 2-27 area right now. How long we will be here I don't know, but I sure wish we were back at the river. …

You all take care now, and write often.

With all my love, Chuck

I was angry so I took it out on the Corps since the enemy was nowhere to be seen. It was the kind of deep-seated anger that tears at the soul. I wasn't even aware of it then, but it was all a part of my trying to deal with the incident at the Ha Dong Bridge. The anger had to stop. Anger gets you in trouble in combat. I had to stay calm and focused in order to carry out my missions of night patrols and ambushes. Eventually the anger turned to coldness and then to complete detachment. I was also needing a rat trap – I hate rats.

I have recently learned the reason why everyone wanted me to go on patrol with them. It stemmed from an incident where I was with a patrol and the patrol leader got lost. After much consternation on his part, and mine, I agreed to lead the patrol back to our base. I easily identified our current location on the military map, and using the compass, I led the patrol back to the CP (Command Post). I seemed to have a natural instinct for direction and the jungle in general which got me and my patrols out of trouble more than once. As my reputation grew, so did my responsibilities. It wasn't long before I was leading patrols of my own and put in the platoon rotation for patrols/ambushes. That helped everyone but me, or so it seemed at the time. Normally, patrols were run by the Platoon Commander, Platoon Sergeant and/or Rifle Squad, Squad Leaders. Machine Guns were only supposed to be a support for those patrols. Using me in the patrol rotation allowed for a one in six rotation. But that wouldn't hold true once my specialty was discovered. That specialty was night patrols and ambushes. Oorah!

We were "in the rear," which meant we slept in tents and didn't have watch at night. We got hot chow and a beer call every day at 1630 hours (4:30 p.m.) – military time is calculated on a 24 hour clock. Those were the good things, but to balance it out, we had to go out on platoon sized patrols for two or three days at a time, and of course, the regular work details in the rear. This was when I assigned Dan Nordmann to mess duty. That kept him out of the jungle, at least while we were in the 2/27 area. I may have been overly protective of him, but I really did see him as a little brother. He certainly proved himself a solid fighter when called upon, but after the torture and death of my squad leader, I wasn't taking any chances with such a wonderful young man. Dan was all of 18 then.

Another common problem was the effect the "unseen enemy" had on us, which I addressed in a letter home to my dad, who was a combat veteran from WWII in the Pacific.

On March 30, I wrote:

Dear Dad,

Well, here I am, balls still intact, and I plan on keeping them that way. Not only that, but I've got my "peter" chained to my leg. It is a little uncomfortable when I have to piss, but at least I don't have to worry about it creeping into places that it doesn't belong. ...

I'm at the 2-27 area right now, and will be here until they decide to move us again. We sleep in tents, and don't have watch at night. We get hot chow and they have beer call every day at 4:30. Those are the good things. We go out on 2 and 3 day patrols, we are on work details and in general, are messed with just like back in the States. I don't guess my superiors will ever stop messing with us. That's the main reason why I don't ever want to make the service my career.

You mentioned those Japs you had to kill, well, that's bad it's true. But what's worse is when you really want to kill them. Around here, in Viet Nam, you hardly ever see your enemy. During the day, you fire into the tree line and then when it's over, you find out how many you've killed. At night, all you see is a muzzle flash, if [you're] lucky. So after a while, and after you see your buddies who get it, you really look forward to getting a "Gook" in your sights.

Oh, by the way, you remember me telling you that we found [XXX] body, he was my squad leader. Well, we found out what the [autopsy] report was. The Gooks had popped out his eyes, punctured his ear drums, and then cut off his nuts. He was probably alive during all this. Then they shot him 3 times in the back of the head. The other two who went down the river haven't shown up yet, so they might very well be [prisoners].

Say, guess what, I just found out that promotions are going to go out pretty soon, and that I'm the 4th in line for Lance Corporal in Weapons Plt. Not bad, egh. …

With all my love, Chuck

On a personal note, to show my state of mind at that time and to show the beginnings of my deterioration, I wrote the following on March 31:

Dear Mom,

Hello you old stick in the mud. I bet your ankle deep in [peat] moss and the like. Those rose bushes and other shrubs you are putting up sure sound like home life is running pretty smoothly. …

Boy, life here at 2-27 which is the Battalion Headquarters, is for the birds. Guess what we had to do just now? We had to dump all our gear out on our rack [navy word for bed] and have it searched. It seems that someone [misplaced] a pair of binoculars and the whole Company is being searched. It's things like that, that really make us mad, and fed up with Marine Corps life. I sure will be glad when I'm out.

Other than their messing [around] with us, nothing much has happened. I got to go to Mass today for the first time. I sure am glad that I went. It gave me a chance to review my thoughts about the Lord and my own life. You know, I've always been undecided about whether to enter the priesthood or not. But now, I think that for sure, I will not. Any good work I do for the Lord will be as a family man. I look forward so much to a good wife, wonderful children and a sound job. But who doesn't? Really, I am really going to save my money, so when I get home, I'll really be able to make a start. In fact, I don't even think that I'm going to go on R&R. [rest and relaxation]. All we get is 5 days, and you usually wind up spending 2 and 3 hundred dollars. Just think how much I can use that money when I get home. I plan on going back to college when I get out of the service and possibly majoring in [Psychology]. I've also thought of working part time at the police department wherever I go to college. That way, I would be making money. I would have to budget my time, which was my trouble before. I could even think of getting married. …

[Whatever] I do though, I know that I will put everything I have into it, because that is one thing I have learned. Yet, I'm real cool now, and I don't jump when an idea comes. I am really surprised at myself, the way

I can take things as they come. In fact, some people are not altogether pleased with my coolness and seeming individuality and, to build myself up a little, my seeming strength of character. Wow, how do you like that. But, nevertheless, they all respect me. I catch a little bit of guff from those ones over me, who don't like my coolness, yet I also have their respect and actually, that is all I ask. ...

With all my love, Your son, Chuck

They say that a bitching Marine is a happy Marine. That it's natural for Marines to complain about almost everything, it's just the nature of the beast. Well, I was no exception. Once the "Boy Scout" phase wore out and we learned that this was truly a life or death situation, our focus was on staying alive, not the mundane routine that existed in the States. After being removed from the Ha Dong Bridge and back in the Battalion Area, with all the Brass (high ranking officers) and office personnel, my complaining started for real. It wasn't that I didn't love the Corps, I was just tired of being messed with, or what seemed that way. Part of the problem was that we had nowhere to go to really relax. The threat of death was a constant!

These feelings would persist throughout my tour. Wanting to be back in "the rear" and out of the jungle, but hating being "in the rear," was a no win situation. It was SNAFU (situation normal all fucked up) and FUBAR (fucked up beyond all recognition) all wrapped in one, all the time.

Looking back, I think I know why Marines in combat complain so much. It wasn't anger against the Corps; it was the frustration over being in a situation where we had *no* control over our own lives. It was a way to let out the grief that we had locked in us because of the horrible wounds and death suffered by our brothers in arms. The longer we were exposed to constant combat conditions, the worse our symptoms got. Actually, it was only by the training and discipline inbred by the Corps and our camaraderie as fellow Combat Marines, that we were able to handle what came our way. Dealing with what this did to us would come later, after the war. For now, it was bitch and fight, fight and bitch. We called the Corps "Mother Crotch," or the "Crotch," because the Marine Corps had birthed us as Combat Marines and everything came from the Corps. Our dependence was total. Without the Corps we would have nothing. Actual combat was the only exception. Yes we depended on the Corps for our supplies and medevac if wounded, but in the jungle and in the fight, whether setting up ambushes or choosing a proper patrol route or taking on the enemy, our independence was allowed to come out and make us free to live or die. For the most part, the Corps couldn't protect us. We got air support, artillery support, mortar support and even Naval Gun Fire support, but even with that, it was up to us to succeed or fail, nothing was certain. Working as a group or individually, we were on our own, living by our wits and charged with adrenaline. Love it and hate it all at the same time. Yet, we loved the Corps then and we love the Corps now. Semper Fidelis. Always Faithful. Once a Marine, always a Marine. Oorah!

By the end of March, the casualty list for 2nd Battalion, 27th Marines to date was:

13 KIA 110 WIA 2 MIA (Our platoon added significantly to these numbers.)

Chapter 4

Our time in the "rear" was to be short-lived. On April 5 we were sent to an ARVN camp on Highway 1, which ran south from Da Nang down to other major bases like An Hoa. Everyone was being spread out from the 2/27 Base Area due to the transfer of the 1st Battalion, 27th Marines (1/27) up to the area around Hue. 2/27 was tasked with taking over the TAOR (tactical area of responsibility) that was covered by 1/27 plus their own TAOR. Consequently the Companies were spread thin with platoons off on their own in little camps and bases.

We had a chance to catch up on mail and care packages, which we always enjoyed immensely. I had been asking my folks to send my knife, my sling (like the one David used against Goliath) and a rat trap. My only knife was my Ka-Bar which I cherished, but it just wasn't as handy as a Buck knife. My sling was a familiar tool to me, since I used it often when hunting. I would put an oblong rock in it and sling the rock out over a draw. The rock would make a humming sound and scare the deer up to the high ground. I had intended to use it to throw grenades out farther than a man could using only his arm, but I can't remember if I ever got anyone to help me do that. A rat trap was self-defense. The rats in Vietnam were huge, with all the people to feed on, and often I would awake at night with a rat trying to get the better of me. So far, I hadn't received any of my requests but I kept asking anyway.

The short stay in the Battalion Area gave us the chance to regroup with our Company, get new replacements and renew our supplies. Among the replacements in April was George Kryicos - short and stout and usually referred to as "The Greek." He was a real nice guy and one heck of a fighter. He was readily accepted into the 2nd Rifle Squad and would prove himself many times over. He was a real joy to be with and brought a lightness to the platoon that was sorely needed. We also got a new squad leader. He wouldn't last long though. By April 26, he was transferred to Okinawa.

And I became the official squad leader. I also received the rest of the replacements for Machine Guns, which would bring my squad up to a full complement of 9 men. As squad leader, I gave up the machine gun and carried my M-16. I kept my .45 and carried that weapon with me the entire time I was in Vietnam. It became part of me and it never left my side. It had such an impact on my body that even after I was out of combat, I physically felt an emptiness on my right hip where the .45 had "lived." Years later, I could still feel the "phantom" .45 at my side.

Most replacements that arrived in April were easily assimilated into the units they were assigned to. The FNG (fucking new guy) attitude hadn't set in yet, but it would later on. After assuming the role of squad leader, I made David Lopez the Team Leader for the #1 gun team - he didn't feel comfortable carrying the M-60 because of his small physical stature. Al Decker was gunner and James Richee, Assistant Gunner (A-Gunner). Decker was a stocky young man who was the only one at that time able to assume the job of gunner for the first gun team. Richee was the only other 0331 and he was really needed as Decker's A-gunner. The #2 gun team consisted of Dennis Freer as team leader/gunner and Dan Nordmann as A-Gunner. Freer was a big young man and he had held the position of #2 gunner since the beginning of our tour. He took on the additional role as team leader and proved himself invaluable in that position. I stuck with the #1 gun team most of the time because they were all so inexperienced at that time, leaving Freer and Nordmann to carry on independently unless we were all together at the same time. We also had three Ammo Humpers (riflemen), which were divided up to provide for two four-man gun teams. One man went to Lopez's team and the other two went to Freer's team. For now though, I still carried the machine gun. Our new squad leader didn't know his job and just left my gun team and Freer's to do what was necessary for ourselves and the rifle squads who depended on our firepower.

Our stay in the Battalion Area would be short indeed, but while there we did our best to rest up a bit. When not on patrols or being messed with, we were free to do what we wanted. Free that is, after we had all our gear staged and ready to go on a moment's notice. Poker was a favorite pastime during these lags in the action and on April 3rd, I wrote:

Dear Folks,

Well, it looks like I hit a stroke of luck. First of all, some fella's around here have some [Polaroid] cameras and I'm trying to get a few pictures taken. Yep, I got them taken and am sending them to you. They turned *out real good I think and if I get a chance, I'm going to buy me one of those [Polaroid's]. You may be wondering how I can get enough money to buy one, well, that's the second bit of luck I've had. You know how I like to play poker; well since payday, just 2 days ago, I've won $200.00. I'm about ready to quit and send about $150.00 home. So if you get a money order from me, put it in my savings account [okay]? ...*

There isn't much news to give you, but I guess that's nothing new by now. Naturally, we don't know when we will get moved, or when we will be called up to go out on a operation. Like this morning, it was 2:30 am. They got us up, we saddled up and headed out to be a blocking force on a sweep. Another Company was supposed to push a bunch of "Charlies" into our position. Well, as luck would have it, they slipped by the sweeping force, so we trudged back at 11:00 this morning. That's the way it goes around here. You never know what's going to happen next. ...

With all my love, Chuck

The move was on. On April 5th I wrote:

Dear Dad,

I hate to be stereotyped, but here I am and there you are. However, you don't know where I am do you. Well, I'm in a village at an ARVN camp on highway #1. I think the name of the village is Bien Hong or something like that. It's in between the 2-27 area and Da Nang. Our plt [platoon] commander said we will be here about a month. The shit really hits the fan around here. We went on patrol this morning at 3:00 and got back at 1:30pm. And it looks like we will be doing things like that every day. (In case [you're] wondering why my writing is so neat, it is because I am writing by candle-light, and have to keep up with the flickers. How's that strike you.)

Say, let me tell you something, you thought being an engineer was rough and tough, well, you should have been a machine gunner. Then you would have had something to talk about. Besides, carrying all that lead, we also get our share in return and you better believe it. What's really bad, is when you are walking through rice paddies at night, in mud up to your knees (on a tall man) and the gooks open up on you. They can't hit much, especially at night, but they sure put the fear of the Lord into you.

But enough of that. Oh, some of the boys decided to have a knife throwing contest with these ARVN's here in camp. They got a board and drew a picture of a small man. Well, to make a long story short, the ARVN's were making our boys look real bad. So I picked out the best of the ARVN's (you remember how I used to practice) well, I told him to hit the little man between the eyes. Everyone watched us two. I let him go first. He hit the man 1 out of 3. It was just above the left eye. All the ARVN's said "Number 1" which means the best. (The Vietnamese judge things by numbers. 1 is best, then two and on down). So I figured I'd really have to concentrate to beat him. I got at a distance, threw, and the knife bounced off, it was half a turn too much. All the ARVN's called out "Number 10" and the fellas wished me luck, but had their doubts. So I moved up a little and threw. I got him right on the inside of the left eye. Then I took another knife and hit him in the heart. It looks like now I'm the official knife thrower of the platoon. We had to quit though, mainly because the ARVN's hate to [lose], they kind of [lose] face, so we broke it up. But it was fun while it lasted. …

Had we forgotten about those who had died just a few weeks before? Where was our callous attitude? How had I gotten cocky all of a sudden? The answers lie in the nature of things. We couldn't justify the deaths we had experienced and we didn't have time, or a way, to grieve, so we buried everything and acted like all that had happened before was water under the bridge. Yea, water that would surface much later in our dreams and nightmares. I didn't talk in any great detail to my folks about the war after the incident with my squad leader and tried to keep things light in my letters home so no one would worry. Letters to my dad were the only exception, and even then, my letters weren't too graphic. Still, my dad was the only one I could confide in and occasionally I did. We were slowly developing the old attitudes, like:

"Fuck it, what are they going to do, send us to Vietnam?"

"Take care of today, because tomorrow we may be dead."

In that same letter home, I also wrote:

I'm running out of candle, so I'll finish this tomorrow after patrol. You see, I have work to do to, believe it or not.

Well, here I am again. Now let's see, where was I. Oh, you asked about this war over here and how people think about it. Well, to begin with, I can say that this is [definitely] a dirty war, but what war isn't. What is bad though is that we, the American Fighting Men, are not allowed to fight this war with the knowledge we have as a fighting unit. We are hampered by all the politics back home, and because of that, our men are being killed without a just reprisal. What makes it so hard is that you can't tell a friend from an enemy. You can't trust any of these people, because if nothing else, they will [steal] you blind. None of the men here like this war at all, yet, if the United States were to back down and give up this war, there would be more ill feeling than there is now. What we want over here is escalation of the war. Let us fight it like we want, and the war would be over in less than a year. You know how men in war are, all they really think about is getting home. All the [bloodshed] is like water off a ducks back, except when your buddies get it. Yet, we all hope and fight for progress. We want to see something done or accomplished for the 13 months we serve over here. We have a job to do over here, and all we ask is a chance to do it.

You mentioned "hate". That you hoped we would not come home embittered. Well, first of all, there is not near as much hate over here as there is confusion. It is mighty hard to hate someone or something you don't even know or understand. Everyone here mistrusts the Vietnamese, but as far as hate goes, we just put up with them. This is their country and they are welcome to it. I would say that there is more hate for the Americans than the other way around. How would you feel if a soldier from another country came up to Cathy [my sister] winked and said "Ah so, Number 1 Boom Boom," like so many of our men do. I can well understand how the Vietnamese feel, yet they are caught. Without us, they are at the mercy of the VC, with us they have to put up with all kinds of abuse. Therefore, some work with us and the others work against us. The only solution I see is either for the U.S. to pull out all together, or take over completely and carry this thing all the way to the Chinese border. As for the people in the north; well, I can't speak for them, mainly because I don't know a damn thing about them.

I don't know if I have helped you any or not, mainly because I'm not really in a position to talk yet. You ask a man in a fire what it is like, and he will naturally say "hot." I will be able to tell you more when I get home, and can sit down and think it over, without having to worry about getting shot. I know how you feel, but there is so much to this war, so many different sides, that I don't think anyone will ever figure it out. Naturally, I wouldn't mind it one bit if we got pulled out right now, but I can see both sides and will just do my job and bide my time till I get home, if there is much of a home to go to. …

I heard about Martin Luther King getting shot and all the riots. The U.S. is sure going to pot isn't it! Yet, all that seems too far away to wor-

ry about right now. ... But remember this, if the U.S. ever has to call back its troops from Viet Nam, to take care of problems in the country, then war will be real for Americans too, because we don't fool [around]. Speaking for myself, and most of the Marines [around] here, we want peace all over the world, but we [aren't] beyond killing to get it.

This is sure a crazy, mixed-up world isn't it, but like I said before, all I want to do right now is relax and not worry about everything, only Viet Nam; and only that part of Viet Nam where I am. ...

With all my love, Your son, Chuck

Amazing what my mind remembers and what it doesn't. As I have said before, I am relying heavily on my letters home because much of what happened is lost in my memory. I have no memory at all of the events listed in this letter home, although it was all pretty benign and even fun. I have a picture provide by Dan Nordmann that shows that camp where we did the knife throwing and in it our boys are playing stretch. Where you have to put your feet out where the knife sticks, tossing it back and forth until one man falls down. I have one picture showing Dennis Freer playing stretch as the ARVN's looked on and laughed. Life and death! Live while you can because tomorrow you die!

By now, we had been in Vietnam only six weeks but we had learned much and buried much. Lt. Jones had been our Platoon Commander now for about two weeks and he had already made up for the lack of leadership we experienced before under our old Platoon Commander. He led by example and never asked more of us than he was willing to do himself. SSgt. Staggs did the same. They took their turns running patrols and of course leading the Platoon on combat patrols and sweeps. They donned grease paint and did night ambushes as well. Grease paint was small tubes of a greasy paint - black at one end and green on the other - that was used to camouflage our outline when going on patrols and ambushes at night. Otherwise, we would glow in the dark. Lt. Jones and SSgt. Staggs also let us be more independent. They directed and advised and generally kept to Marine Corps discipline, but they also let us do our jobs without micro-management. We still had lessons to learn, but we did it as a team. Knowledge learned was passed around from squad to squad, not just Officer to Enlisted. We cared about each other and we all thought more for our buddies than for ourselves. The memories from the bridge, where my squad leader was tortured and killed, were buried deep. That reaction became a necessity for survival. Death became a part of life.

I was still gunner when we first went to that ARVN camp and on April 7th I wrote:

Dear Chrisie Boy,

Hello there old tennis and golf pro. It sounds like you are really doing good in sports …

Say, it sounds like you and Dad are really getting to do a lot of things together, along with golf, fixing up the yard, and driving. I never will forget the first time Dad let me drive. It sure gives you a good feeling doesn't it. And those mornings when just you and Dad get up together to do things; well, you will always treasure those moments, believe you me. …

Of course, I guess you know by now that my plt. moved out again. (That's the 2nd Plt. of F Co., the one I am attached [to].) We are on highway #1 between the 2-27 area and Da Nang. Darn it, they moved us so quick that I didn't get a chance to make a money order, so now I'm walking [around] with over $300.00 in cash, $200 of which I won in poker. Pretty good, egh! …

Oh, back to this camp I'm at. It looks like I won't be going on patrols for a while (thank goodness). They have our machine gun set up at this bridge just north of the village. So I will have to stay there with my gun. That's a hell of a lot better [than] tromping through rice paddies for sure. But we sure have to watch the Vietnamese so they don't steal us blind. Other than that, there isn't much news to tell you.

Oh, I almost forgot. Be sure and pass this on to the folks. I am now Lance Corporal Van Bibber. It isn't real official yet, because they haven't issued the [warrants] yet; so don't put LCpl on your letters yet. My section leader told me about it today. I'm real happy too. I just might make Corporal before I leave here, I hope. …

With all my love, Chuck

Then on April 8th I wrote:

Dear Mom,

I guess you've been wondering when I was going to get [around] to writing you. Well, I do my best, and I hope it's good enough. …

Say Mom, I didn't mean to make you feel that you were being too much a mother or [anything] like that, you are doing fine as it is. I just don't want you to worry too much. I know you worry, so there's no use telling you not to. I guess it is hardest for a man to say what's closest to his heart, first when it comes to his woman, and second when it comes to his mother, so I guess I flubbed up.

It's the 9th now, and I am still trying to finish this letter. I've been building bunkers since Sunday, so when I do have a chance to sit down and write, I write a little and then give up and rest. It is real hot over here, at least in the 90's; so a [day's] work really saps the juice from you. I hate to see what it will be like when it really gets hot. I got your letter from the 4th of April; it is so good to hear from you. The Hill Country really sounds pretty. I can just picture the [valleys] back home, all full of color from all the wild flowers, and the trees [coming] into bloom. It will sure be nice to get back to it all. …

As far as the war over here, I don't put anything past the North Vietnamese Communists. They will either use this truce time to make peace like in Korea or to build up enough strength to make a big push. They are learning fast that the old guerrilla tactics don't work so good any more. I guess we will just have to wait and see.

You asked if I was on "Operation Pegasus" up by Khe Sanh. Well the answer is no. I am still south of Da Nang. However, we never know when or where we will move to, so just keep an ear open for the 2nd Battalion 27th Marines. …

Say, don't forget to address your next letter to Lance Corporal Van Bibber. Yep, I got the promotion. Maybe now I have a chance to make Corporal before I leave here.

I guess there's only one thing left to say, and that is Happy Easter. May the good Lord shine his grace upon all my family, and depart to all of you His gifts of faith, hope, charity, and above all love. I pray that you all will never have to experience the side of life that I'm on, and I pray that someday, all men will be at peace with one another. …

Oh, I wrote Betty Klein and told her to get one of those pictures of me with my machine gun. … [Betty Klein was a good friend and we had been corresponding]

With all my love, Chuck

I wanted so much to feel "normal" and enjoy things again, like the countryside in Texas in the spring and my friends like Betty Klein. My faith was strong, but deep down I could feel things slipping. I wanted to write the war away but always had to face reality. The "truce" that I referred to was the temporary halt to bombing in North Vietnam by President Johnson. Needless to say, the "truce" didn't mean much to us on the ground, as hostilities continued unabated. I had mentioned the heat in several of my letters and in April, the Southern Monsoon was already in play. Over the summer, the heat would rise to over 100 degrees, with rain picking up every month. It was like living in a sauna bath with no escape except when it was raining. So you could die from heat exhaustion, heat stroke or drowning, not counting bullets and bombs. Choose your poison.

The "easy" duty at the bridge didn't last long. In a letter home dated April 15, I wrote:

> *Dear Dad,*
>
> *Well, how did your Easter turn out[?] Did everyone get all decked out in their Sunday best and meet all their friends at church and have a gay time? I hope everyone is well. Over here, Easter Sunday was just like Holy Saturday and Easter Monday. Every day is the same over here, so Easter doesn't mean that much. Actually, when I stopped and thought about it, not being able to go to Mass and have a priest think for me, there is only one lesson to be learned from Easter. And that is, that no matter what happens, a man can always pick himself up and make a new life. Not even death can stop us from gaining a new life, if we want it. And with this in mind, things are a lot easier to take. I've got the shits again, worse this time, we are going on patrols again, and we have a 24hr sweep [Wednesday]. So things can tend to get a person down. Yet, I'm not down at all. With the Lord's help, I am able to accept all this over here and do a good job, and trust that my best is good enough.*
>
> *You may be wondering why I haven't been telling you all the wonderful tales of blood and guts like I did once before. Well, it doesn't bother me [anymore]. It's just a part of life, and it is something that I think not even you would like to relive. I relive the things at night as it is, so to relive them in a letter is just [too] much. I'm sure you understand. It looks like we will be moving to even more dangerous territory at the end of this week. I'll write you all and let you know when and where I move. …*
>
> *With all my love, Chuck*

The crack in the armor had appeared. I finally told my dad that the war was getting to me. When I said, "Well, it doesn't bother me anymore," I also said, "to relive them in a letter is just too much." It provides an insight to my mixed up feelings. Yes, my faith was strong then. It was that faith that allowed me to do the things I did without worrying over my own death. Still, as time went by and more stuff was heaped on the pile, my emotions and everyday communication with God suffered. One of my greatest feelings of loss and abandonment came from the lack of the spiritual comfort I was used to from priests and pastors. All the chaplains I ever saw were in the Battalion Area, and I didn't get back there very often. Unlike the images I had seen as a boy, of WWII chaplains out in the battle giving aid and comfort to our troops, the chaplains were conspicuously absent from the jungle. It left a bitter taste in my heart and it would take many years before those ill feelings would abate. I'm sure that there were chaplains that did God's work in the field with the troops; I just never saw them myself. In defense of the chaplains, since we operated in such small groups, it would be nearly impossible for any chaplain to service us all. Still, I thought that some should have come out occasionally to visit us.

In my letters to my mom, I continued to be as positive as possible and vague in my account of any actions. On April 16, I wrote:

Dear Mom,

I'm so sorry to hear about Mrs. Stein. ... with this accident; well, I just hope that Dr. Stein will be able to accept [whatever] happens and raise his children as they should be raised. I guess it will be quite a while before Mrs. Stein is all well again. ... [Dr. Stein and his family were close friends of our family.]

As far as the war over here is concerned, all I can say is that it will be over when it is over. I'm [too] much in the middle to be able to look at this thing impartially. So I will save my comments of this till I get home. I'm sure you understand what I mean. ...

Oh, tell Granny thanks so much for the Easter card she sent. Those prayers mean more to me than anything in the world, because I know they come from a real angel. ...

It's just too hot to write any more today. Besides that, I'm just getting over the [screaming] shits again and have to get some rest. ...

With all my love, Chuck

P.S. Tell Dad that if I had a dream like the one he had, that I would be sure and wear an [athletic] supporter just in case it turned out not to be a dream after all.

Quite a bit different than the letter I had written to my dad the day before. Filled mostly with talk about family and friends and Easter, and very little about the war. The bantering back and forth between my dad and I helped to bring some much needed humor into an otherwise dreary existence. He was very wise. In those days, war was a man's business and women were to be "protected." The old chivalry was still present in society in most of the country in 1968. I did talk briefly about the war to my younger brother Chris, but even then, because he was only 15, I left out most of the bloody details. By the middle of the month, things had started to change again and we became more involved in confrontations with the enemy.

On April 22, I wrote:

Dear Tennis Pro Chris,

Say, it looks like you are really doing good in the world of sports. I'm sure proud of you. Tennis is sure a fine sport isn't it? …

I guess you are wondering how things are with me, so I will fill you in on the past few days. We left that ARVN compound Friday the 19th and came back to Battalion Headquarters. Then Saturday morning early, we left again for a sweep. Well, we got the old Marine Corps screw, and they kept us out there till Morning. We got two North Vietnamese Soldiers and a lot of maps and important papers. It wasn't much, but it showed that my Plt. is on the ball. Luckily we didn't take any casualties.

I'm at Battalion again, and will probably go on another sweep [Wednesday]. Then on Friday we will relieve the first Plt. in the area we made the sweep in. It is about a mile and a half down the HWY #1 from the last ARVN camp we were at. Other than that, there isn't much news. You already know I am a Lance Corporal, and you saw the pictures. I'm glad you like them. …

I hate to make this so short, but I have to clean my gun (it gets rusty real fast over here) and try to get some sleep. …

With love, Chuck

April was coming to a close. We had been running patrols, day and night, and been on some major sweeps. On April 26, I wrote:

Dear Dad,

Well, here I am and there you are. It looks like I'm back to normal doesn't it, well am not. At least not like I was before. Of course you know I am a Lance Corporal now, and I guess Cathy has told you about me and Mary Ann. So there is part of my problem. The responsibility of being a Lance Corporal & the difficulty in explaining [myself] to Mary Ann. But that is only half my problems. Guess what! I'm now squad leader. That may not sound like too much, but I'll explain it and then maybe you will see what I'm up against. First of all, our old [last] squad leader was no good, so they sent him to Okinawa. Then they grabbed me as squad leader. First of all, I have 9 men who I am responsible for.

One man's life is enough responsibility, so just picture what it is for 9 men. Not only do I have to take care of their needs, but I also have to lead them on patrols, and that is some job. There is an awful lot to do and remember. Besides having to read a map and compass like a book, I also have to know how to call in [artillery], mortars, air strikes, etc. Not only that, but when we run into the shit and old VC Charlie is after us, I have to direct the fight. Let me tell you, I have never been so scared and [nervous] in my life. Right now we are out in the jungle again and will be here for about a month. I have one day patrol and 2 night patrols every day, so you can see I'm really hopping. Don't expect too many letters for a while, because I have an [awful] lot to keep on my mind. I'm heading out in about an hour, so I have to get the men ready. By the way, the area I'm covering tonight is loaded with VC, in case you are interested.

I'm sorry this isn't very long, but that's life in Viet Nam. You take it easy and write soon. …

With all my love, Chuck

Yes, I had acquired a mail order girlfriend, Mary Ann. We had met briefly in December, 1967 while I was home on leave. The first letter I got from her, I immediately made her my girl. Not fair to her, but she didn't seem to mind, so we started corresponding. In reality, she was someone to cling to in those crazy days. It was just the circumstances of a quick romance before going off to war. That letter speaks for itself. I took my responsibility seriously.

On April 30, I first wrote:

Dear Mom,

I got [your] tale of woe, the one about your bunged up knee. Boy, it looks like knees are the favorite target of Mr. Bad Luck. …

I guess Dad told you already that I am squad leader now? Yep, I've really got the responsibility now. But I guess I've known all along that it would come sooner or later. Since I have been over here in Viet Nam, I have changed a lot in that aspect. In fact, I lead pretty good now, and I am more sure of myself too.

As far as life on the front, well, there's no use going into it. Life is hard all over I guess, and in Viet Nam it's hell.

I got Chris' letter too. He did all right there at Ft. Hood. It's a good thing he didn't let those Army fella's bamboozle him.

Tell Cathy and everyone that I'm thinking of them and love you all. Please forgive me for making this so short, but I am real tired and can't think of much to say. …

With all my love, Chuck

That same day, I wrote my dad:

Dear Dad,

Here's a short note to let you know that I'm doing fine as a squad leader. Last night we got 2 VC in an ambush, I had to call in mortars and set up a defensive perimeter and a lot of other things. Both VC were killed and I had no casualties. We took several grenades and ammo from the dead VC as well as a Russian AK-47 rifle and an M-1 carbine. So we did real good. My C.O. was sure proud of me.

There is no way I can tell you how it was, because it's war, and war isn't fought to be told but to be won. I just thought that I'd let you know that I'm doing fine. I didn't get any sleep for 24 hrs now and last night took 10 years off my life, so I'll close and say may God bless you all and keep you well, especially mom & you & yep that's right Mary Ann.

Love Chuck

Chapter 5

I felt that I could tell my dad more about being in combat, since he was in the Army Combat Engineers at the battles of Leyte Gulf and Northern Luzon in the Philippines in WWII. Little did I know the effect my letters would have on him until much later, after the war. I still feel I owe him an apology, God bless his soul, I just didn't know. My mom may not have known the things I said to my dad, but she agonized every day for her first-born son who could easily have come home in a body bag at any moment. My letters became fewer and fewer and less descriptive as time went on. In late April, our platoon started going out in the bush (the jungle) for 30 to 45 days at a time. We had to pack everything we owned on our bodies, as I have described before. We started out with about three days' rations, which usually meant two meals a day for three days. We learned to be frugal about the packing and would load our spare socks with C-Ration cans, tie the ends together and drape them over the top of our pack. As I have said, we usually had about 80 to 100 pounds of gear including our weapons and ammo and extra ammo for the machine guns, 60mm mortar rounds for the mortarmen and LAWs (Light Antitank Weapons) for the assaultmen. Since I now carried the M-16, I carried as much 5.52mm ammo as I could, most of it already loaded into magazines. We learned quickly, that it was much easier to carry loaded magazines in the green cloth pouches that the ammo came in rather than the loose ammo, which would have to be loaded into the magazines in the bush, or worse, in a fire-fight. So we stocked up on M-16 magazines every chance we could. Some still thought they were John Wayne and carried their machine gun ammo across their chests, but after much complaining by us, the machine gunners, that the ammo was getting dirty and not seating right in the belt, causing miss feeds in the gun, the riflemen caught on.

All this said, I carried about 200 rounds of 5.52 in magazines and an extra 200 rounds of 7.62 belted ammo for the machine gun. Every other rifleman would also carry at least 100 rounds of machine gun ammo. The extra ammo we carried for the M-60 was carried in the cardboard boxes and cloth pouches that they came in. There were two of these pouches in an ammo can and often we would just carry the boxes, leaving the heavy cans behind. In a fire-fight, the riflemen would drop off the boxes of ammo at the machine gun position and go on from there. We never could have too much ammo, for rifles or machine guns. One thing I can say for the Marine Corps, they always got plenty of ammo to us. All we had to do was carry it and use it.

Among the other munitions carried by the platoon were Claymore mines with detonators, C-4 plastic explosive for blowing up caves and caches of enemy supplies, as well as extra M-79 rounds for the bloopermen. Usually one rifleman in each rifle squad carried the M-79 (Blooper). The M-79 was a hand-held grenade launcher which could provide close in support for the squad. It could be fired up in the air like a mortar, or straight out like a rifle. Most of the rounds were point detonating with a slight delay to arm the round. M-79 flechette rounds were also available for direct fire against a charging enemy. Those rounds were like very large shotgun shells containing many flechettes, which are small dart-shaped pieces of steel. Having witnessed the impact of hundreds of flechettes on a human body, I can only say that the result is instant hamburger. Not a pleasant sight, even on the enemy. Both C-4 and M-79 rounds were carried in large pouches with a wide shoulder strap, providing for easy carry and accessibility. Those bags were highly coveted by us grunts and after a while, we all had one. I brought a blood-stained C-4 bag back from Vietnam but my first wife couldn't tolerate it, so it went out with the trash like so much of the Vietnam experience.

Claymore mines were flat curved mines loaded with small metal flechettes. Behind the projectiles was a sheet of C-4. The outer curve of the Claymore was to face the enemy and it was so marked on the mine. It had legs which, when extended, were used to stick the mine in the ground. A blasting cap in the Claymore was attached by wire to the jack-box, a scissor-like mechanism that produced an electric charge when squeezed, similar to those used with dynamite, only much smaller. Like dynamite, it took an explosion provided by the blasting cap to set off the C-4 in the mine. They were very dangerous and were often turned around by the enemy so that when they were detonated, they would kill the men they were designed to save. That was why we always ducked down in our foxholes before setting off a Claymore. Accidental discharges were common. In fact, I remember once when we had set out a Claymore and one man had gone out with the blasting cap, wire attached, to put it in the mine. On the way, his buddy got to playing with the jack-box which was also connected and accidently set off the blasting cap, blowing off most of the man's fingers and seriously injuring his hand.

As a reinforced Combat Platoon we had additional personnel with us. These Marines consisted mostly of the radio operators with spare radios and batteries; the assaultmen with their LAW's and 3.5 rocket launchers; the 60mm mortar team; Combat Engineers for blowing up stuff, especially old ordnance and caves and sometimes a Sniper. The Snipers didn't stay with us long, they just came in, went out and did their thing and left again at the next resupply chopper. Johnnie Cata – who looked like he was of American Indian decent – was usually assigned to operate with Fox Company. He did a great job and we always looked forward to having him with us. In boot camp, I had qualified for an Officer Program since I had had two years of college, but I was turned down because of my vision. I also shot a 237 out of 250 for qualification with the M-14 in boot camp and could have been picked up for sniper school in Vietnam but machine gunners were badly needed and that never happened either. Largely unheralded, we also had two Navy Corpsmen with our Platoon. One would go on large patrols, and the other would stay at the PPB (Platoon Patrol Base) and treat the wounded. We loved our Corpsmen - they were like our pastor, doctor and mom all wrapped up in one neat package. They cared, too. Any Marine worth his salt would die to protect the Corpsman, and any Corpsman would risk life and limb to save a Marine. This symbiotic relationship has existed between the Navy and Marine Corps since the early days of the Navy, and it endures today. God bless Navy Corpsmen.

An army may run on its belly, but without communications our effectiveness would be greatly diminished. Without the ability to call in for supplies or fire support or to maintain contact with patrols and OP's (Observation Posts) and LP's (Listening Posts), we would have been like ducks without a pond. Radiomen and their diligent service were indispensable. The greatest numbers of casualties in any platoon were usually among the primary targets, which were Officers, Patrol Leaders, Machine Gunners and Radiomen. The mortar team was also an important spoke in the wheel. Often, it was the 60mm mortars that would provide the close in cover we needed. When patrols were in danger or a nest of snipers had us pinpointed or enemy mortars had us zeroed in and larger support units were not available for immediate action, the 60mm mortar teams would be called to save the day. The assaultmen usually went with the patrols, as did the machine guns. Considering this mass of humanity and all their equipment, plus the rifle and machine gun squads, there was really no way to be "unnoticed" by VC

Charlie or civilians. Therefore, our main defense was in offense. We made it so uncomfortable for Charlie that he would rather leave than confront us, and we had a great offense. One thing the Viet Cong and the NVA learned early on in the war was to respect U.S. Marines. We didn't get the name "Devil Dogs" for nothing.

Back to our equipment, there was the "extra" gear we carried. Each Marine was required to carry a gas mask, which always got in the way. It served its best use as a pillow. In defense of the lowly gas mask, the Corps needed its troops, and a gas attack could wipe out a whole Battalion if the wind was right. Lessons from WWI were not forgotten, and in modern warfare no one knew the integrity of our enemies. So we wore the gas mask slung around our shoulders and carried it like a woman's purse. Woman's purse? Can you imagine a Combat Marine carrying a purse? But we did, and also found other uses for it. You could carry extra battle dressings (large bandages used for bullet wounds), needle and thread, or bug juice (insect repellent), and whatever you could think of that was small and could fit within the mask. Some men cheated and carried the cases without the mask, leaving more room for comfort items. That didn't last though because if SSgt. Staggs or Lt. Jones caught you, you would have shit details *forever*. Later, the rules would be changed, requiring only two gas masks per squad.

Last but not least of the "must have equipment" was the "Rubber Lady." An olive-drab (green) blow-up mattress like you would use at the beach or at the pool. Just like those beach items, the "mattresses" would inevitably go flat. Marines love their comforts and we were no exception. We carried those stupid rubber mattresses wherever we went. We dutifully blew them up, covered them with our poncho liner/blanket and went to sleep. After an hour or so, depending on how many patches you had on your very own "Rubber Lady," you would be flat on the ground with the rocks and sticks poking your back and ribs and every other part that touched the ground. If you weren't dead to the world, you woke up, blew the thing back up and tried again. After a couple of times, you just left it flat and tried to get some zzz's. It did offer a water barrier from the wet ground, so there was some benefit. Call it a love affair, but we carried those things and cussed them out and blew them up and felt the air go out night after night, and still kept them with us. Who can explain the mind or "Love" of a Combat Marine for his very own "Rubber Lady?"

Most of the time, when we went out on these platoon-sized operations, we either walked there, were driven there in trucks, or were flown into an

LZ (landing zone) that had been preselected and prepped with artillery. Of course, in the latter case, this just let the gooks know where we were, and if things weren't hot, with bullets flying, when we landed, they got hot later. I don't remember how many times we'd move at night after setting up at dusk, but Lt. Jones ensured that he had at least two alternative sites to move to after dark. This was the only way to provide relative security. The best bases, PPBs (Platoon Patrol Base), would be in a small copse of trees on a finger extending out into rice paddies. We could stay there for a few days to rest up because we could easily see any one approaching, but soon we'd have to move. So, along with day and night patrols, we had to saddle up and move and move and move. No rest for the weary - but it kept us as safe as possible and alive to fight the next day.

Once in our "home for the day," we formed a circular perimeter and "dug in" as best we could. The digging in was readily accepted, especially after we got our first taste of a mortar or rocket attack. Nothing like Mother Earth to keep you safe! No sanitary slit trenches here, it was cat holes all the way. An area would be designated for our use inside the perimeter and it was each man's responsibility to dig his hole, do his business and cover it up. Still, at night, when any movement could get you shot, we just moved directly behind our fighting holes and did our business there. Have you ever tried to take a crap lying down? No joke! You either squatted with a very small profile or sometimes you just tried to crap lying down. Since dysentery was common, crapping on yourself became common and everyone just accepted it, cleaning up whenever possible. We all stunk so bad that no one really noticed except the gooks, who did their crapping in the rice paddies.

Since we couldn't have any light at night, we ate one meal in the morning and one in the late afternoon. That meant eating our morning meal, packing up, moving and making "camp" by late afternoon, in time to dig in and eat our evening meal. We would save the cans of peanut butter and crackers to keep the stomach rumbles down at night. We had tried the heat tabs, but the moisture in the jungle got the best of them, so we all carried as much C-4 plastic explosive as possible. High heat and smokeless, C-4 was perfect for chow, hot coffee or blowing up hooches (those straw huts used by the natives) as the case arose. As I have said before, I made coffee whenever I could. It was just that little touch of something "normal." Not only that, but it made the water drinkable when the only thing available was water from local wells or irrigation ditches. The latter was usually filled with mosquito larva and leeches. Boiling was absolutely necessary, nothing like boiled larva and leeches with your water to add some needed protein. With luck and proper planning, we got resupplied about every four or five days by helicopter. Sometimes they landed and sometimes they just dropped off the supplies and took off (usually this happened when they were receiving sniper fire). We would load up everything we could, eat a quick meal and take off to another spot to set up our base. If we were lucky, we got almost everything we needed this way, C-Rations, potable water in heavy plastic five gallon jugs, ammo, salt tabs, bug juice, cleaning supplies for our weapons and whatever else SSgt. Staggs had called in for, like extra clothes if available – for some reason, new uniforms were extremely hard to come by. In our final move for the night, we formed another perimeter, but didn't dig holes. We set out Claymore mines and had watch with one on and one off, two man, fighting positions. Much credit has to go to Lt. Jones and SSgt. Staggs for successfully managing these maneuvers. It took superior planning and execution to have it work and not get everyone killed in the process. With my concerns over the responsibility for nine men, I can't imagine the responsibility they must have felt for over fifty of us.

What is almost impossible to describe so that one could "feel it," was the jungle. There are places few and far between in the continental U.S. that are in anyway close to what the jungle was like in Vietnam. Most films about Vietnam have been made in the Philippines, but that is just an imitation of the real thing. First of all, it stank. All the rotted vegetation, the animal and human waste, the closeness, the humidity and body odor from both humans and animals just made it awful - so bad that sometimes it would be hard to breathe. Then there were the bugs. There was a bug for every part of your body. Leeches loved to attack those warm moist areas where the blood was sweetest, like under your arms, your belly, behind your knees, your ankles and feet and yummy yummy, your groin. Nothing like a tasty meal of testicles or penis! Yes, there were even cases of men having leeches crawl up their penises causing severe problems. Then there were the ants, large and small. They got into everything by the millions, or so it seemed. They bit, stung, laid eggs and just plain drove you nuts. Still, nothing was as bad as the mosquitoes. Even slathered with bug juice, the noise, the constant droning of little wings alone would cause feelings of anger and helplessness. Sleeping in these conditions was particularly troublesome, as the mosquitoes hovered around your head just waiting for a chance to storm in. They got into every pore where there was good skin or moisture to attack. They got in your eyes and ears and in your hair where you couldn't put bug juice. The mosquito repellant was almost as bad. It closed the pores on your skin which made you sweat profusely, causing the bug juice to run off and let the mosquitoes in. It was a never-ending battle, especially at night. About the only relief we got was when we got so dirty and stinky that not even the mosquitoes wanted you, but then the VC could smell you a mile away. That was Vietnam. No winning for losing!

Aside from the nasty vegetation and the bugs, there were the critters, the rats, snakes, water buffalos and tigers, just to mention a few. It has been said that there are a hundred species of snakes in Vietnam ninety-nine are poisonous, and one can crush you. Whether this is true or not, we didn't care. We had heard about the bamboo viper, the two-step snake, where you would die from the bite after taking two steps, and a variety of others that could kill you just as fast. There was open season on snakes as well as VC. Get a snake in your hole and if you jumped out, you could get shot. Shoot the snake and you would give away your position. The only true way to deal with snakes was the trusty E-tool. Ah, the entrenching tool, that little fold-up shovel that saved your life in so many ways, from making a home in Mother Earth, digging a cat hole for your waste, a club for hand to hand combat and a snake basher. We loved our E-tool. Our bayonet and Ka-Bar knife were also useful snake killers.

Other problems existed for us that stretched our tolerance. Those of us who smoked were greatly hindered in our habit. Actually, almost all of us smoked, and if you didn't smoke before you came to Vietnam, you would soon enough. Smoking was the only thing that actually seemed to work to calm the nerves. Smoking during the day wasn't much of a problem. Even if we gave ourselves away by the smell, all Charlie could tell is where we had been, not necessarily where we were and Charlie didn't like messing with Marines during the day. Most of those instances where we did get hit during the day were by long range sniper fire that was more harassing then accurate, or mortars and rockets. Small day patrols, sent out from the main body of the platoon, were not challenged either because even a small patrol could carry a wallop. Being able to call in all types of ordnance, in a moment's notice, was very effective and saved the day many times. The SOP (Standard Operating Procedures) for an attack was to hunker down and call in air strikes, artillery or mortars, whatever was available. For this reason, all squad leaders were required to be well-versed in the call signs and procedures for calling in fire support. Smoking at night was forbidden. However, many a Marine, feeling relatively safe in the PPB (Platoon Patrol Base) would light up a cigarette under his helmet, cup the end in his hands and enjoy. Unfortunately, at times, the smoke would be detected and we would get hit. Not knowing our exact location at night, Charlie's fire was mostly harassment to keep us awake, but occasionally the smoking would bring on mortar fire, which didn't have to be that accurate to be effective. What was a poor weary hungry Marine to do? Can't even smoke? Crap, this shit is for the birds!

Patrols were the worst. They all had a purpose and a procedure. First there was the patrol route marked out in grease pencil on a map. A map of a totally different country, with names of places we couldn't even pronounce. We had to learn to read the contour lines and coordinates or get lost and die. Then there was the compass, which went way beyond Boy Scout day trips. It was necessary to be able to read a compass and shoot a bearing or azimuth from your position to a target. Understand what the map is saying or die. There were so many ways to die in Vietnam. Day patrols of maybe 14 to 17 men were mainly to scout the area, check villages and find ideal locations for the coming night base. These were full combat patrols consisting of at least a rifle squad (the squad leader was also the patrol leader), a radioman, a Corpsman and a full M-60 machine gun team. "Guns Up" was the standard call in any given incident where we took enemy fire. It was also the call to set up a firing point to protect a rifle team which was going to check something out. "Guns Up" became the most hated phrase ever devised for machine gunners. It wore you out, running full bore up to the front of the patrol, not an easy task with a heavy load on your back and exposing yourself to enemy fire, then plop down and be ready to fire at anything that moved or looked suspicious. Usually the patrol leader would direct the machine gun fire because the gunners down in the mud couldn't see the whole picture. However, if targets of opportunity arose, then the gunner would take them on. I went on my share of these patrols, both as the machine gunner and the patrol leader. If you had night patrol, you were allowed to get a couple hours rest at the PPB (Platoon Patrol Base), before everyone moved out. Unless I was leading a night patrol, I would remain with the gun team covering the PPB. On days where I hadn't run night patrols the night before, I would run the day patrol and give the rifle squad leaders a break. You could memorize the route (which was my practice) and locate prominent terrain features from the map. The patrol would move along the general directions on the map, and stop at checkpoints, calling in to the CP (Command Post) or PPB. If you didn't call in then it was assumed you might be in trouble. If the lack of communication went on long enough then someone would come looking for you. It was important to stick as close as possible to the given patrol route so you wouldn't be mistaken as an enemy patrol.

Many of the friendly fire problems in Vietnam were because of misidentification or being in the wrong place at the wrong time.

Night patrols and ambushes were the worst of the worst. Consisting of six to nine men, an ambush was made up of a rifle fire team and occasionally a machine gun team with patrol leader and radioman. A recon patrol would be four to six men who were to report on enemy activity and avoid contact with the enemy. We went out in the dark, following a route on the map, to check points that might or might not be there, with an enemy ambush possible all along the way. If the moon was out it helped greatly, but it also made you more visible, which was very uncomfortable. If it was just starlight, you might be able to see enough to make your way and read the map, depending on your position and thickness of the jungle. A dark cloudy night was one to put a pucker on your asshole and tighten your stomach into knots. All you could do was feel your way along the trail under your feet and sense open/closed areas that you mostly felt or vaguely saw. Reading the map would be near impossible unless you used a flashlight with a red lens. Often, when I had no flashlight or the batteries were dead, I would risk lighting a cigarette under a helmet or poncho and use the glow from the end to read my map and compass. Dark nights were just scary, no matter what you did. That's why I tried to memorize the patrol route and get a feel for where the rice paddies, villages and dense jungle were along the route. Call it a sixth sense or the hand of God. I did it, but to this day I can't really figure out how.

Then there were the LP's (Listening Posts), usually consisting of two or three men with a radio, positioned just outside the perimeter of the patrol base at night to give early warning of an approaching enemy. There was no talking on the radio unless you could see the whites of their eyes. Squeezing the handset of the PRC-25 was the only communication. The OP's (Observation Posts), consisting of two or three men were used to watch for enemy movement during daylight. Two or three men out by themselves in enemy territory was pretty scary, and another cause for tightened guts and assholes. Even men with the shits didn't have any trouble holding it on LP's. LP's were expendable and we knew it. I remember being on an LP once, when the VC walked right by us. All we could do was lay *absolutely still,* breathing in small breaths and only looking out of the corner of our eyes. My dad had taught me that trick while hunting. To look directly at your target often would alert them to your presence, so you looked out of the corner of your eye. Our communication was by squeezing the handset which made a "psst" sound on the receiving radio. The sequence would be something like this: one squeeze for "yes or ok," two squeezes for "no" and three or more for "here they are." Those would be our responses to questions from the base. Anyway, as the gooks walked past, I started squeezing the handset like crazy. This alerted the base and then we all waited. Once they had passed, I waited a while and gave the "all clear" signal. That VC patrol never went toward the base and all was quiet for the rest of the night, but I was one tensed up puppy, all night long. When I got back in the morning and ate something, I got the shits and lost everything. It was a battle of nerves all the time, until you lost those feelings and just became one of the "walking dead."

Now you have a picture - maybe not *the* picture, but close enough for government work. It was April 29th and I was scheduled to take out a night ambush. As usual, I studied the patrol route and the terrain features, compass headings, call signs and the daily radio codes. I went over the route with Lt. Jones so he would know where I was going. The actual ambush site I would determine later while on patrol. I had a sense for these things and would try to look at the area from the VC point of view. I had learned that the VC weren't the "supermen" that others made them out to be. They couldn't see in the dark any better than we could and often worse, because of poor nutrition. They might know the area better, but if we were skillful, they wouldn't detect us until it was too late.

I painted my face, arms and all exposed skin with grease paint, instructing my men do the same. I required everyone to wear long-sleeve camouflage shirts as protection against the mosquitoes, and to break up our outline in the dark. Our trousers were bloused around the tops of our boots and there was nothing loose to rattle and make noise. It didn't take long to discover that long-sleeve shirts were good. With the relatively cool nights and awful mosquitoes, they were a blessing. In addition, they had large pockets for carrying stuff (usually bug juice and toilet paper) and were even handy in the daytime to keep the sun from drying us up. We taped up some special magazines for our M-16's loaded with 20 rounds each. Firepower was a crucial factor in a firefight. Running out of ammo and having to fumble around in the dark and find another loaded magazine at the wrong time could cost you your life. The answer came from those who had gone before us. We learned to tape two magazines together back to back, overlapping about three inches, using black electrical tape we got from the engineers. All we had to do to bring the second magazine in to play was to release the top magazine from the weapon, make a quick turn to bring the second magazine up, insert it, bring the bolt to the rear and release it to pick up the first round, and continue firing.

There were eight of us on the patrol: myself, a radioman, a rifle squad fire team and two of my own men. My machine guns did not go out on recon patrols, but I did occasionally take a gun team on ambush patrols when we were with the Company on Company Sweeps. At these times, other machine guns could cover the Command Post. When operating with just the Second Platoon, I kept the guns with the PPB (Platoon Patrol Base) and placed the guns in the paths of the most likely approaches to our position, as well as providing interlocking fire wherever possible. Lt. Jones rarely told me where to place the guns. He had learned to trust my judgment, and I had learned what he expected. Nevertheless, it was always a joint decision and I would check with him once I had the guns set in.

It was always comfortable to have some of my men with me, but it put an extra knot in my stomach. Having already lost men I knew, I wasn't looking forward to that again. I tried to rotate the men I took from my squad like the rifle squad leaders did with the fire teams. As a result, sometimes David Lopez or Dan Nordmann would go with me, which always gave me a warm fuzzy because I knew, without a shadow of a doubt, that they would have my back.

It was star light dark! With no electric lights within view, on a clear night we could see well enough to get around. My night vision had also improved. We had already moved the PPB for the night and everyone was set in. I guess it was about 10p.m.. I lined up my men with a point man from the rifle fire team, me taking the second spot so I could better direct the patrol, the radioman following me, and the rest of the patrol bringing up the rear. We carried only what was needed for the night - weapons, ammo and grenades - heavy on the grenades! Grenades were my first choice in a night attack, because they wouldn't give away a man's position. Of course, we had helmets or utility covers, flak jackets and one or two canteens of water. The canteens had to be full so as not to have the water slosh around in the canteen. Even though the canteen was plastic the sloshing water could make just enough noise to be detected - thank goodness we got rid of those old metal WWII canteens. This was a silent stalk! Anything less could mean our demise. The grease paint would break up our profile and helped to keep the mosquitoes down. The bug juice smelled too much and I avoided it as much as possible. Another trick to keep the mosquitoes down was to put dirt over the grease paint and help cover the exposed skin. I didn't like Claymores on night ambushes because they were too easy to turn around and do harm to us, or to be forgotten in the excitement. We didn't have bush hats then so we wore our soft covers - the same ones we were issued in the States. The good old Mean Green Marine utility cover! Most men wore the soft covers on night patrols, but some felt safer with the old steel pot. I didn't care, as long as there was nothing to make noise. I carried a flashlight with a red lens for reading the map that held the patrol route and a compass to keep me on track. I also carried a small note pad which listed the radio call signs and fire support frequencies for the radio. Radio silence was paramount once we set in on the ambush, and we only called in at the checkpoints. While on the ambush sight itself, it was handset signals only, no talking unless absolutely necessary.

We stepped out into the unknown. Quietly, one careful step after another, using trails where we could, sometimes moving to the edge of a rice paddy or around the edge of a village. We stalked, we were on the hunt! By this time, most of the men had gone on ambushes with me before and knew what I expected. They trusted me (another knot in my stomach) and I trusted them. We made our first checkpoint and called in to the PPB. Our call sign was Wild Dog. A short quiet call to say:

"Mama Dog, Wild Dog, over."

"Wild Dog, Mama Dog, sitrep (situation report), over." was the reply.

"Mama Dog, Wild Dog at check point Wall out."

Call signs were often names of things using a base name like Mama Dog or Goose 1 and patrols using associated names like Wild Dog or Gosling 2 for patrol names. (The names used here are fictitious). Checkpoints were usually the names of places or things, like "Wall." All call signs were pre-assigned at Battalion and transmitted each day to the platoon by radio. What a puppet show it was, and if strings got tangled, people got hurt. Each checkpoint was pinpointed on a map with a name and grid coordinates. This not only pinpointed the patrol, as long as they were on track, but allowed coordinate references for fire support missions. This was no game. Men's lives were at stake and we could get killed by friendly fire just as easily as a hail of bullets from the enemy. If you didn't know where you were on the map, you could easily wind up calling in artillery or mortars on your own position. Heavy stuff!

We proceeded to the next checkpoint and then the third, calling in each time and keeping things quiet - but nothing ever goes as planned. Later, around midnight, as we were passing by a village on a main trail (we used the main trail because it was so dark at that time), a dog started barking and

I knew the jig was up. As quietly as possible we passed the village and came to a point in the trail where it was even darker and close to a rice paddy. I stopped the patrol and checked my map. Yep, I found the spot and just hoped I had it right on the map. It wasn't too far from a check point, which I used as a reference. I wrote down the coordinates in my note book (thank goodness for that red light) and proceeded to set in the ambush. I figured that the villagers had noticed our passing and maybe passed on that information to the VC or there were already VC in the village and they might follow us, thinking they could sneak up on us from behind. Having experienced the old "get 'em from behind" ploy before, I set the ambush well back off the trail in a shallow ditch close to the jungle where there was a mix of total dark and minimum starlight. The point man and I, with the radioman in tow, set up at the far end of the ambush line which I set along the trail leading back toward the village. My hope was that if they came, it would be from the direction of the village, and not a circle around and cut them off at the pass move. I told the men:

"If the gooks come from the village, let them get down the trail toward me and the point man before opening up on them. Stay quiet and don't look directly at them if they come. Watch out of the corner of your eyes! No moving! No smoking! Stay as still as possible and only take small sips of water if necessary. The point man will set off the ambush and when it goes off, start throwing grenades and firing across the trail. Just put up a wall of lead and let them walk into it."

Then, thinking ahead, I said:

"If they come from the direction of the point man, just hold your fire until I open up, or we are discovered."

We waited and waited.

It was a good ambush and I trusted everyone to do as I had instructed. We had good cover behind us where it was dense jungle, and we would have heard anyone approaching from that direction. Across from the trail was a small line of trees with big spaces between them, and a very shallow irrigation ditch next to a large rice paddy. The area we were in was the "Rocket and Mortar Belt" south of Da Nang and Marble Mountain. The limits of the Belt were the maximum distances from Da Nang from which mortars or rockets could be launched against the bases there. It was a mix of jungle and rice paddies with villages dotted here and there. The trail had curved slightly toward the jungle and back out toward the rice paddy. The point man and I were set in at the curve so we could fire up or down the trail as needed. If the VC approached from my end, I would wait until I thought that they were well into the ambush and then start things off.

We waited.

The reason I told the men to look out of the corner of their eyes was an old trick I learned from my dad while hunting. He told me that animals could sense if they were being watched and to only look with your peripheral vision, out of the corner of your eyes, until it's time to shoot. Well, I figured that if that was true for animals, it would be true for anything being hunted, even men. So I practiced that religiously.

We waited.

I had called in one last time when I set up the ambush and gave our coordinates to the platoon radioman. The PPB knew not to call, or even use hand set signals unless initiated by me first. This wasn't a special ambush, as I had set ambush after ambush before using the same procedures. Yet, each one had to be handled like this was *the* one, even if it was no different than others before. So why should this one be different? Still, Lt. Jones and his radioman stayed by the radio just in case. They were probably doing a one on one off radio watch between Lt. Jones and SSgt. Staggs while trying to get some sleep.

We waited.

The mosquitoes buzzed but the only thing exposed was our hands and faces, which were covered with a mix of black and green grease paint and dirt. With the soft covers on our heads, our scalp was protected too. Our long-sleeved jackets were buttoned from the neck down and at the sleeves. We had done all we could to keep from looking like a bunch of Marines in the grass. The old steel pot was always a certain giveaway unless you could break up the silhouette with sticks or leaves in the canvas that covered the steel pot. At times like this, the mind never stops. It works overtime, keeping all of us in a constant state of alert until boredom sets in. That's the most dangerous time, when men start to relax and lose the edge they once had. I had one small trick that worked well on those closest to me. If I noticed someone nodding off or too relaxed, I would toss a small pebble in their direction to get their attention. That always did the trick. Others in the squad knew the same trick and it served to keep us all reasonably alert. During times of almost complete darkness, I would toss a pebble randomly.

We waited.

It was hot and humid. The sweat started pouring from our clogged pores under the grease paint and dirt. The dirt started to run off and we itched like crazy. Our mouths became like paste and we were thirsty as hell. My thoughts began to wander. Just how long was this going to last? Oh well, it will be over soon and we can go back to the PPB. I tried to ignore the itching and the mosquitoes who were working to get at some now-exposed skin, especially in the mouth, nose and ears. I wanted a smoke. I fought that and was often close to giving in, but I held off. Can't give a bad example to the men. If they couldn't see it, they would smell it and so would the gooks. Thirst had gotten the better of me and I took a small pull from my canteen. It was about 0100 hours. A long way to go till dawn.

We waited.

Suddenly, there they were!

Like ghosts, they appeared just at the edge of the rice paddy and close to the trees, keeping themselves from being silhouetted and spotted by anyone looking their way from the direction of the rice paddies. They were real quiet. It was like being in a blind on a deer hunt - one minute there was nothing and the next, they were there. Bare feet or rubber sandals don't make much noise and these people were used to living here and fighting here. The Vietnamese had been fighting someone seemingly forever. Vietnam had been occupied by other nations in the past, except for a brief period between the 11th and 13th Centuries. Fighting against the Chinese, Mongols, French, Japanese, French again, and now the Americans, there was nothing new here for them, except that they had walked into my ambush.

Whoomp! Whoomp! Burrrrp! Burrrrp! The point man and I threw grenades and opened up on them with our M-16's on full automatic, firing three to five round bursts. When a magazine was empty, we simply removed it and turned it over to insert the second magazine of 20 rounds. The rest of the patrol followed suit. The VC dropped and returned fire with weapons on automatic. A swarm of bullets came at us. We would have been goners if it hadn't been for that ditch we were in, giving us a low profile. Most of the rounds went over our heads. We could hear them hitting the banana leaves and elephant ear leaves, tearing up the jungle over us. After the initial bursts of fire we continued to throw grenades and fire our rifles toward the enemy position. This was a close-up fight with no more than sixty feet between us. The noise was deafening with grenades, M-16s and AK-47s going off all at once. When the return fire seemed to dwindle, I gave the command:

"Cease fire."

My command to stop firing couldn't be heard. I couldn't see a thing. My night vision was shot. The night had exploded in a flash and racket that shook your soul. There was the strong smell of cordite (smokeless gunpowder) and C-4 from the grenades, along with the coppery smell of blood. We all stunk to high heaven with the strong pulse of adrenaline through our systems and the usual odor of unwashed bodies. When I couldn't detect any return fire and the noise had subsided some, I hollered again:

"Cease fire, cease fire."

I called for Tail End Charlie to watch the trail that led from the village and quickly got everyone up and out on the trail. As soon as I counted heads, I moved the whole patrol farther down the trail and into the jungle. I set up a small egg-shaped perimeter with emphasis on the trail. No time to look for bodies now, if there were any. I had touched off ambushes before and knew that the first priority was to move.

It must have been about two in the morning when I finally got around to contacting the PPB. I called in and quietly reported what had happened. Lt. Jones was as calm as usual and he quieted me down - I was all worked up. Worried that there would be more gooks in the area who would have time to regroup, Lt. Jones and I agreed for us to stay where we were until dawn. I gave Lt. Jones my map coordinates and he called in for harassing fire from some 81mm mortars stationed not far away. The rounds came in, three or four at a time, moving randomly around my position at hundred yard intervals, starting at the village we had passed. The mortars started with a Willie Peter round (white phosphorous) to mark their fire, and from which I could adjust as necessary. I adjusted the fire and all went quiet except for the mortar fire around us. Fire support from artillery and mortars was relative easy to call in, since Lt. Jones had preregistered fire on specific points in the area. He would pick points on the map close to our PPB and call them in to register the firing points. Knowing where my patrol was allowed him to make an initial call for fire very close to the desired target of the village. After that, all I had to do was to adjust the fire from my point of view, giving the adjustments in up-down-left-right directions relative to my line of sight. When everyone knew what they were doing, it worked like clockwork. The importance of reading a map and knowing where you are and where the enemy is cannot be emphasized too much. Make a wrong call and it could be deadly. Even if you got the initial enemy location right, if you were wrong on your own location, the "line of sight adjustments" could wind up bringing fire on yourself.

In order to understand the importance of accurate map reading and how fire missions worked, I offer the following example. Take a football field with your position at one goal post and the enemy at the other goal post.

Further, picture a mortar or artillery battery in the grandstands just opposite of the enemy goal post. Now first, you have to identify your position on a map, which is the only way that the fire support team can identify where you are. Secondly, you can tell the battery where the enemy is by either giving map coordinates for their position or by giving a range and azimuth to the target. An azimuth is the compass bearing in degrees from your position to the target.

Now let us say that the football field is situated in a north south location. Your azimuth to the target would be 000 degrees, range 100 yards. Relaying this to the battery, through a FO (forward observer) in a third, off site, location, the guns prepare to fire. They know where you are and they have a relative (relative to your position) range and bearing to the target. They fire a WP as a spotting round and it hits 25 yards short of the enemy goal post. Short from your line of sight, and in line with the other goal post, falling on the 75 yard line.

Time to adjust fire. You call in to add 25 yards and fire for effect. That isn't as simple as it sounds. The battery has to convert your relative "add" to the necessary gun adjustments. In this case, with the gun at a relative 90 degree position from the enemy, your add means that the gun has to aim 25 yards to their right in order to hit the target. Your add is their right, your left is their add. Given any number of different angles and positions, the simple fire mission becomes very complicated, but all officers and artillerymen are schooled in the "Fire Control Problem" and with sufficient training our batteries of mortars and artillery are very accurate on the battlefield. Still, everything is predicated upon that accurate map position.

Air strikes are of a different nature. They rely on two things, your position and the enemy position, or the range and bearing to the target. They can operate like artillery and fly in on a bearing which has been determined by the flight control unit, and drop their ordnance on a specified target, or they can just come in on a bearing and look for the enemy. Once the enemy is detected, they come around for a fire mission. This works very well when the Marines on the ground cannot clearly identify where the enemy is by map coordinates or accurate range and direction. Receiving mortar fire from somewhere over a hill would be an example of this type of air support.

With deadly ordnance flying all over the place in Vietnam, the batteries/ air support also had to know the positions of other units in your area so as not to hit them by mistake, which does happen despite every effort to keep fire on target. That means that even a lowly 8 man patrol/ambush had to be registered on the big map of things.

Now that you are sufficiently confused, maybe you have an understanding of how important the map coordinates for ALL friendly units is. There were patrol leaders who would cheat on patrols by just going out a short distance from their lines and stop, staying there and faking the patrol by calling in the check points until time to return to the base. That practice was extremely dangerous. Not only from the enemy, but also from our own fire support. If no one knows your real position, then anything could happen. I never did that. The only way to conduct this war was to play the game according to the rules.

Understanding how to conduct fire support missions was not generally taught to the average rifleman. Usually the officers and platoon sergeants had a good grasp of these important evolutions, with the squad leaders obtaining a rudimentary education in the process. Having never been to NCO (non-commissioned officer) school or other training for patrol leaders, I had to learn all this by OJT. Thankfully, I was a fast learner, picking up what I learned from the actions of other knowledgeable Marine leaders. Radio procedures were another OJT learning curve, necessary for all operations in the war.

Back to the ambush.

It was a long, long time to dawn. We sweated and sipped some water and sweated. Our mouths felt like the Sahara Desert - a dry gritty thirst that just couldn't be quenched. That always happened at times like this and we all knew how important it was to bring water. The first time we got in a firefight and the water ran out, we understood how important it was to control our thirst and our water as much as possible. Hard to fight while gagging from dry mouth. As I have said before, one of my tricks was one I learned from my dad. It was an old Indian trick he learned from the Ute Indians in Colorado as a boy. Pick up some pebbles about the size of a kernel of corn, clean them off and suck on one or two (just don't swallow!) It causes the saliva to flow and ward off dry mouth.

We jerked at every little sound. Our guts and bowels started to tighten up again. We were turning into nervous wrecks. Remember, we had only been in Vietnam about 2 ½ months. We hadn't hit the devil may care, "fuck it" attitude yet, but we were working on it, or rather, it was working on us. Eventually that attitude was an absolute necessity. We couldn't live as nervous wrecks forever.

Dawn finally came. I asked for the mortars to continue the harassing fire around our original patrol route just in case, and we cautiously checked out the site of the ambush. There, just at the edge of the rice paddies, we saw the bodies of two VC who had been caught in our fire. We also found some hand grenades, ammo and an AK-47 and M-1 Carbine. I reported all this to Lt. Jones and he called off the mortars. I then took the patrol, along with the rifles and ammo, back to the PPB by the safest way possible. We left the dead VC where they lay, knowing that the villagers would take care of them. We really had no good way to haul two bodies with us under the circumstances. Although we stood a chance of getting hit by going back the way we had come, that way was just as safe as any other and it was shorter. We got back to the PPB safely. We had been lucky, no Marine casualties. I like to think that it wasn't all luck, since good preparation and planning went a long way toward safety when the lead is flying. As I had written to my dad, "My C.O. was sure proud of me." I was referring to Lt. Jones. He was my immediate commanding officer and I often referred to him that way. We had done well. We had accomplished the mission we were sent out to do. Tomorrow would be another day. Finally we got some sleep and resupply when the choppers came in.

It was a good move to have the 81mm Mortars keeping heads down around us. On May 1st, I wrote a short note to my Dad and said:

"We ran into 10 VC again last night."

Short note indeed, it looked like we had stirred up a hornets' nest and the VC were everywhere looking to get even for the night before.

The official declassified 27th Marine Regimental Monthly report states simply:

290706H A. "F" Co
B. 290120H
C. 04255645 – 041643
D. Rec 150 rds AW fire.
E. Ret fire, 2 VC kia.
F. H. neg I. 2 M. AK, 1 M-1 carbine.
DTG Div 290705 #18

Translated, it reads:

Reported at 07:06 a.m., on the 29th of April, local time (day time group 290706H, H - denoting local time), it was reported from Fox Company that a patrol made contact with the enemy at 1:20 a.m. around map coordinates 04255645 – 041643. The Patrol received about 150 rounds of automatic rifle fire. The Patrol returned fire, killing two VC. No friendly casualties. Items recovered were two grenades an AK-47 and M-1 carbine rifle.

Close enough for government work. Funny how all that sweat and strain was just narrowed down to a cryptic message like that.

From that report and the "F" denoting the Company, I believe that our platoon was with the Company CP (Command Post) at the time of my ambush. It was common for the Company headquarters consisting of the Company Commander, Executive Officer, Gunnery Sergeant, Senior radio personnel, and the remaining Weapons Platoon personnel, just to mention a few, to take to the field with a given platoon. Otherwise, they remained in the Battalion area coordinating things from there. The Company headquarters didn't have enough troops to defend itself on its own and required a platoon to provide that protection. Even the Weapons Platoon was laid bare, having all the machine guns, mortars and assaultmen distributed out to the Rifle Platoons. One of the good things about being with the Company CP, was that we usually got more chow and a restocking of what uniforms there were. The platoons maintained their PPBs with the Company CP and would rotate being security for the Company and thereby having their share of the "goodies."

The way we fought from the way the Vietnamese fought were very different. More often than not we would stand and fight, or even charge if necessary, it was what we were trained to do. The Vietnamese, VC, NVA and even the ARVN would rather hit and run, with emphasis on *run*. Being hit by a Marine ambush, the enemy would fire just enough to escape, carrying their dead with them if they could. Marines being hit by an enemy ambush would first lay down a volume of fire toward the ambush and then charge the ambush if possible. We didn't run; we fought our way out, often causing the enemy to do the fleeing.

At the end of April, the 2nd Battalion, 27th Marines records show the following casualties for the month:

5 KIA 38 WIA for a running total after 2.5 months of 18 KIA 148 WIA 2 MIA

Chapter 6

A Marine Corps report for the 1st of May states:

010130 F-2-E at coord 039646 spotted 10 VC 25 meters to the N.W. Fired 30 RD's with negative results.

Translated it reads:

Reported at 1:30 a.m. May 1st, patrol E from Fox Co. 2nd Platoon at map coordinates 039646 spotted 10 VC 25 meters (27.5 yards) to the North West of their position. The patrol fired about 30 rounds at the VC with no evident hits.

This was one of my night patrols. There is nothing scarier than running into the enemy unexpectedly, at night. All of a sudden, just about 25 yards away, there they were. They must have felt the same way, like "holy shit, where did they come from?" We were a little quicker on the draw and got out some rounds before they disappeared. Talk about making everything suck up and get in knots, the dark alone caused extreme anxiety, which had to be controlled as much as possible. All senses had to be at their peak. Since we couldn't see much, sound or smells were the primary means to alert us. By the time we came in visual contact, it usually meant real trouble with someone getting hurt, either them or us. True to form, the best visual ability was usually our peripheral vision, so we watched out of the corner of our eyes often. To have made contact so close and so suddenly, with no casualties, was not uncommon. Mainly in those situations it was just - fire in the general area and pray. Although it was reported that there were negative results, who can say? I don't think we stuck around to see and neither did they.

The records also show that the enemy in the area was the 1st VC Regiment of the 2nd NVA Division and unattached VC passing through the area. Plenty of Charlies to contend with. Our platoon had moved back to the ARVN camp south of Da Nang on Highway 1, with the Battalion Area due west of us. Our job was still one of constant patrolling of the "Rocket and Mortar Belt," keeping us hopping day and night.

The A,B,C,D and E designators in the reports indicate a patrol, not the whole platoon. A glimpse into the past is provided by my bloodstained wheel book. A wheel book is a Navy term for a small note book, about 3" by 5", that a Marine or sailor would carry at all times and used to make notes about the various missions.

One page written for a Duc Ky patrol reveals the following facts:

> Revelry 0530, Be on road 0730, Leave 0800, Take ammo and spare barrels etc. to Sgt Horigan.
>
> Take pack, sleep gear, shaving gear
>
> Carry 2 Days Ammo and Grenades and 1500 machine gun rounds per team
>
> Will use halazones in water
>
> Patrols: 2 per day and 2 at night. ARVNs will be on patrol at night.
>
> Day: A B C D – 7 men E – 5 men 1 man stay back
>
> Night backwards F2D & F2E
>
> Guns will be at Bravo – 1 team (Lopez); Charlie – 1 team (Freer) + rockets
>
> Order of March: Gordon – Guns – half squad – Guns & me & rockets – 1 squad – (unknown) and 9 men.
>
> Policy – Day Helmet, Flack etc., Night same, Will use camouflage at night, Wear combat gear at all times outside of PPB.

Halazone tablets were used for water purification. They made water drinkable but left it tasting like watered-down iodine. The answers for the question about the patrol designators is revealed as well. It even makes realize that the D and E patrols were my patrol designators for this operation and I would take a four-man gun team plus a radioman. This would be a full account of my 6-man squad. However, I was not limited to my machine gun teams for patrols, and often I would take out rifle teams for larger patrols. It also shows the typical orders for the jaunts into the Duc Ky area. I don't know about other machine gun squad leaders in other platoons or other companies, but I don't think it was common for machine gun squad leaders to take out patrols. In our case, it worked and I lead many other successful patrols during my time in Vietnam.

On May 8, I wrote:

Dear Mom,

Well, I guess you [thought] I had forgotten all about you didn't you, and maybe I wasn't too interested in your [predicament]. Well actually I'm not. (Ha, Ha). The thing is we have been working ourselves silly. My feet are so sore that every chance I get I take my boots off to let my feet know that there is still a world outside of my boots. Right now, I am still at that ARVN camp running night and day patrols. In fact last night I called in [Artillery] on about a Company of VC. Oh say, I've got a military map, and can give you the name of the vill I'm in. It's Viem Tay, about 8 miles south of Da Nang on Hwy #1. The Battalion Area is about 1400 meters due west of the village. This Friday, we are moving into Duc Ky (pronounced Duck Key). It is about 3300 meters to the South West of the Battalion area. I don't know if you can find where I am on the map you have, but you can give it a go. Don't forget to tell Dad that now that he knows where I am and I know where he is, we ought to start every letter with here I am and there you are. I mean you should have me pinpointed on the map by now, right?

I want to mention here, about my writing. Things are getting real rough. My company, F Co., is the only one left in the 2nd Battalion, 27th Marines that is anywhere up to proper strength. All the other Companies have gotten there asses kicked at Duc Ky. So bear with me if I don't write too much. Oh, and don't get jealous if I write Mary Ann more than I do you all. You see, I have so much to say to her, and one never knows when the time may come that he can't write. So it is real important for me to write her. Of course I haven't forgotten you all in the least. In fact I'm chomping at the bit right now waiting for mail. It's not that I don't get enough, [it's] just that we live from mail call to mail call around here, except when we're fighting. Then we live from one minute to the next.

Say, how's this for a patrol prayer.
Now I take me out to creep
I pray the Lord my soul to keep

If I should die before morning breaks
I pray the Lord my soul to take.

I say this every night before I go out. It's funny how things like that get to be important. ...

Sending my love as always, Chuck alias Hamlet

P. S. Mary Ann put alias [Ophelia] on her letter so I put alias Hamlet on mine to her. We're a crazy pair [aren't] we. Oh, you ought to have read the poem I sent her. I don't know what got into me; I bet she thinks I'm crazy or something.

I ran all the "E" and my share of the "D" patrols, with an occasional "A" patrol thrown in. The records for that incident where I called in artillery states:

071955 F-2-E USMC/ARVN at 038642 received approx 15 s/a fire. ARVN broke and ran back to the PPB. Enemy were on line covering 30 meters. Called in 81mm fire mission.

Translated it reads:

Reported at 7:55 p.m. on May 7th, the E patrol from 2nd Platoon, Fox Company joined with ARVN personnel at map location 038642, received approximately 15 rounds of small arms fire. The ARVN's broke and ran back to the base. The VC had formed a skirmish line of about 30 meters. The remaining Marines called in 81mm Mortars to disperse the enemy.

The next report was on the 8th of May, another of my patrols. The official report states the incident like this:

082145 F-2-E at 038644, broke up enemy ambush. Rec'd sm/a and one grenade. Returned fire. Pursued enemy, lost contact.

Translated:

Reported at 9:45 p.m., on May 8th, the E patrol from 2nd Platoon, Fox Company broke up an enemy ambush. The patrol received small arms fire and one grenade. The patrol returned fire, pursued the enemy but lost contact.

On May 9th I wrote:

Dear Dad,

Well, here I am and there you. This may be nothing new, but at least I'm [consistent], egh! I was just sitting here waiting to take my patrol out at 9:00 [pm] so might as well make the most of my time. Now let's see, what would you like to know.

Oh, first of all, give Mom all my love and give her a big birthday hug and kiss for me. I forgot to do that in the letter I wrote her.

As far as the war is concerned, it's the same. Hell with a capital H. Oh, I sprung a VC ambush last night. We had seen them go into this [graveyard] which was full of shrubs, so I thought of a good ambush place there and went behind it. We hit them before they knew what happened. Yet, they still managed to get away. It's pretty hard for them to stand up against 8 M-16 [blaring] on full automatic. My platoon [Sergeant] and C.O. were real pleased, and even said to some of the fellas that they wished they had a whole platoon of Van Bibbers. Maybe if I get home [okay], and everything works out between Mary Ann and I, then I might be able to oblige them. What do you think of that. (Ha, Ha) All in all though, I've got a real good [chance] of making [Corporal] and could even make [Sergeant] before I leave Nam. …

For now, take care, may God bless, and write soon.

With all my love, Chuck

Boy oh Boy! My writing was so bad and my spelling was even worse. I hope you understand the circumstances and give me a pass on that. I don't know if we hit anyone on that ambush, most of the time we didn't know, but my guess is that we inflected some wounds on them that night.

As I had said before, the ARVN's weren't ones to stand and fight. We had been trained to override our normal impulses to flee and instead to develop the fight response. Then too, we were Americans and the fight response was part of our culture. The Vietnamese may have nice uniforms and pretty weapons, but they weren't Americans. In their camps, they still lived like civilians. They squatted a lot, sitting on their heels. They ate fish heads and rice and anything else they could get their hands on, especially dogs! About the only difference between an ARVN camp and a village was the fact that the men wore uniforms and carried rifles, and the women and children lived in more secure areas than the villagers out in the bush.

Now, that brings to mind a vivid memory that will probably be with me forever. Funny the things we remember and those we forget. I believe it was here at this ARVN compound that the following incident occurred.

It was late afternoon, going on toward dusk, when some of us were roaming around the outskirts of the compound. I believe Dan Nordmann was with me as well as other members of my squad and a couple of riflemen. There was an old concrete pillbox outside of the base/village that was a throwback from the war with the French. It was a fairly large round building with walls about two feet thick and a humped up roof of similar construction, like a very large igloo. The front faced the road, with firing ports positioned so that the entire area around the bunker could be covered by rifle and automatic weapons fire. In the back, which was facing the ARVN compound, was an iron door. It had rusty hinges and made an awful noise when it was disturbed, not necessarily a bad thing because it acted like an early warning system for the inhabitants.

Some higher ranking ARVN's and their families had taken over the pillbox and made it their home. Not a bad place really, for Vietnam. It was strong, cool in the summer and could be warmed with little trouble in the winter. Furnishings were nothing different than the villagers had in bamboo hooches. Bamboo mats on the floor, wooden woks large and small, bamboo sleeping mats, some of which were on low platforms, some salvaged metal pots and things made out of discarded military equipment and artillery shells. The standard cooking fire was positioned in the middle of the floor. Since the building had about a 15-foot ceiling with a hole at the top, the smoke rose like in an Indian teepee, right up to the top. What smoke there was, that is. The Vietnamese were magnificent fire builders. A woman could cook a whole meal over a small smokeless fire that wouldn't even keep your feet warm. They did this by only using very dry thin sticks, what we would call "twigs" back in the States. The twigs faced outward from the fire in the center like the spokes of a wheel. When the fire needed more fuel, they just pushed the sticks in toward the center a bit. There were a couple of these fires built on the floor, one with a tripod, from which hung a pot for boiling rice or other things. Warming dishes were used on the edges of the fires to keep cooked food warm. There was also a very large metal wok on a stand with coals underneath used to cook the main meal. All the ingredients for the meal would be placed around this fire and the meal would commence. The meal would be eaten using chop sticks or just eating with the fingers, which was more common.

I had made some coffee for them once and maybe shared some C-Rations, so their invitation was a way of returning the favor and showing off their favorite foods and home. It really was an honor for us. We went there with high expectations of a real home-cooked meal, maybe of rice, and fresh fish - not fish heads. We were very respectful, not wanting to create ill feelings. As we were escorted inside the bunker, we showed our appreciation of their home by saying:

"Number 1, Number 1," while the host showed off the arrangements inside.

Then we stepped outside as the women went to work in the "kitchen."

Outside, they had built a good-sized fire with a metal rod placed on tripods at each end. It was getting a little cool now that the sun was going down and we stood by the fire, like a good old camping trip. Suddenly, out of nowhere, one of the ARVN's came up with a dog in tow. The dog didn't look like he was any too interested in these proceedings and fought as best he could to get away. Finally, one of the men took a machete, and with a swift blow to the back of the head using the blunt end of the machete, he killed the dog, stone dead. They then took the rod and shoved it from the butt to the throat, after which the dog was placed over the fire. As the hair caught fire, we could see the grins on their faces, supper on the spit. We moved to a position upwind from the dog - way upwind! It didn't take long for the hair to burn off and when it had, the dog resembled a very large rat. They tended the fire to cook the dog/rat, but not burn it. What a sight! One to be burned into the memory banks forever. We remained outside with the men, exchanging familiar words like:

"Number 1, Number 1" and "chop-chop" and "mama-san."

The dog/rat cooked over the coals for a very long time. While it was cooking, the belly on the dog got bigger and bigger. The dog had not been gutted or cleaned in any way. It was like watching someone blow up a large balloon. Breath by breath by breath the balloon would grow until it would pop if blown up for too long a time. The skin on a dog being much thicker than a balloon, it took a while to blow up to the desired proportions as judged by years and years of experience. Just about the time we were sure the belly would burst and splatter all of us with hot dog guts, one of the men went in and brought out a large family wok. Before we could budge an inch, the man placed the wok under the belly of the dog while another man split the belly.

"Plussssssh," the guts came out into the wok in a rush of steaming intestines and other organs. Not a bit was lost. The bladder had already burst, so the fluid was poured out right there on the fire, causing us to move even farther away. Then the men beckoned us to come with them and they went in the bunker and rinsed the guts before placing them on the warming fire where the women had already placed some rice on green banana leaves. They wanted us to eat with them, but figuring this was just the appetizer, we declined and indicated that we had just eaten but might eat again later. Oh yea, I bet they really bought that one! Luckily, no one got sick to their stomach, probably because we didn't have anything in our stomachs to be sick with. We bowed out as the families chowed down, grabbing pieces of hot guts with their fingers and slurping piece after piece. Then one of the men went out, came back with some strips of meat from unknown regions, and placed them on the big wok as well. They offered to feed us again and, not to hurt their feelings completely, I picked up a piece of stringy dog meat and popped it in my mouth. After chewing for a week, I finally got it down and chased it with a fist full of rice. They offered some water in a jug, but we had brought our own, we went nowhere without our weapons and our own water. Those of us who braved the event quickly washed it down before our stomachs knew what was coming. After a few pleasantries like, "Number 1, Number 1," we made our leave and headed back to some C-Rats to appease our stomachs after that dog. Some made it back ok and made their stomachs happy, others weren't so lucky, and dropped their lunch along the way. Did I ever eat dog again? No! Once was enough. It wasn't that the actual meat was bad, it kind of tasted like bear meat back home, red with a greasy taste. But who could ever eat dog again with that "burnt rat" image stuck in the mind, not counting the steaming hot guts?

On May 16th, I wrote:

Dear Folks,

This is a real short note, just to say hello and send these pictures. As you can see I'm still up and kicking. What do you think of that one of me and my squad? Of course I'm missing 3 men, but at least you have a picture of the men I have now. I've become real good friends with them all, unfortunately, and have had some swell times with them. [They're] a real good lot. Being squad leader is really rough, but I guess I'm learning. Well, I've really got to run now. You all take care and write and I'll do the same.

Love, Chuck

I had changed. Besides simply stating that I was missing three men, with no explanation of why, I also expressed my concerns for my men, recognizing how their loss could affect me. Not good when I refer to my friends with term like "unfortunately." It was as if I had already started to disassociate myself from those around me, especially the men closest to me.

We moved into Duc Ky around May 10th. At some point before the 16th, I lost three men, which put my squad down to six men counting myself. David Lopez as team leader, Al Decker as gunner and James Richee as A-Gunner made up the first gun team. Dennis Freer as team leader/gunner and Dan Nordmann as A-Gunner made up the second gun team. My core squad going all the way back to February 14. That picture of my squad showed some pretty beat up men. Ragged T-shirts, torn and faded trousers, dark tans, dirty bodies - a big difference from three months ago, when we first arrived in Vietnam.

The Marine Corps records help fill in the gaps. On May 10th, the report was:

101145 F-2-D at coord 021647 was leaving PPB and had gone approx 50 meters when the Patrol leader tripped an M26 booby trap frag fragmentation grenade. Patrol leader received shrapnel in his legs, back and back of the head. Man was carried back to PPB and emer MedEvac was called for one USMC WIA. MedEvac completed at 101215. Upon returning to PPB one other man received minor shrapnel wounds in one leg. Non-MedEvac.

Thank goodness that wasn't me running that patrol. Then, on May 14, the report reads:

141445 F-2-A at coord 019619 received approx 50 rnds sm/a fire from est 4 VC at coord 017607. Radio malfunctioned from movement of initial contact. Fired back with approx 100 rnds sm/a fire. Enemy broke contact. Unable to check area as was outside of TAOR. Sustained 1 USMC KIA. Brought KIA to Bn CP for further transfer.

Translated:

Reported at 2:45 p.m., May 14th, the A patrol from Fox Company, 2nd Platoon at map coordinates 019619, received approximately 50 rounds of small arms fire from an estimated 4 VC at coordinates 017607. The radio malfunctioned from movement of initial contact. The patrol fired back with approximately 100 rounds of small arms and automatic weapons fire. The enemy broke contact. The patrol was unable to check the area because it was outside of the Tactical Area Of Responsibility. The patrol sustained one USMC KIA. The patrol brought the KIA to the Battalion Command Post for further transfer.

Not much of an epitaph for a dead Marine. However, you don't have that in this war. In WWII, after the Marines buried their dead on Iwo Jima, the survivors would pass among the graves and mourn their fallen comrades. Not in Vietnam! One minute a man was alive and the next he was dead and shipped off to "who knew where?" Only many years later could we mourn the dead, each in our own way. The Marine killed that day was:

PFC Michael Francis Dalton 0311, rifleman. He was 18 years old.

From the coordinates given in the records, it may have been a chance shot that killed Dalton since an accurate shot of over 1200 meters by the VC was almost unheard of. Then again, the estimate of the enemy position could easily have been in error. Either way, Mike Dalton paid the price for our freedom.

Jim Seabolt, a member of 3rd Squad, remembers when Dalton was hit:

"Once the patrol came under fire, we hunkered down behind a dike. Dalton rose up to see where the fire was coming from and that was when he got shot in the neck."

Dalton fell down next to Seabolt, dead where he lay. Tom Montie, another member of 3rd Squad was also there and he remembers that Dalton was carrying the radio for this patrol:

"When Dalton stood up behind the dirt dike that the patrol had taken cover behind, he caught a bullet in the front at the base of his neck, killing him instantly," he stated.

Montie further stated:

"Mike didn't just look over the dike, he stood up to shake off the PRC-25 radio, and that was when he was hit."

That may have been when the radio "malfunctioned" as stated in the reports. We all lost buddies in that damn war, Jim Seabolt and Tom Montie had seen their share and then some. Dalton was fun to be around. He had a roundish face and when he smiled, it just made you smile too. Mike Dalton was also the Marine injured by shrapnel on May 10th. From his letters home, his brother Tim remembers that Dalton said he had been wounded by shrapnel in a letter posted just a few days before Mike lost his life. Like most Marines, Mike just sucked up the wounds, let the Corpman patch him up and continued fighting. Now that's "guts." Semper Fi. Mike. We all missed him a lot.

A few weeks earlier, Mike had written a letter home, expressing his feelings in a poem. Much thanks to his brother Tim for providing this moving insight.

Take a man. Put him alone
Put him 12,000 miles from home
Empty his heart of all but blood
make him live in sweat and mud.
This is my life I have to live
and why my soul to the Devil I give
You Peace boys rot in your easy chairs, Because you don't know it –
Like over here.
You have a ball without even trying
While over here boys are dying
Plant you signs on the white house lawn.
All you want is to ban the bomb
You burn your draft cards march at dawn
tell us all, get out of Nam!
There is nothing else for you to do.
And I'm supposed to die for you.
MFD

They will hate you till the day they die
You make them hear their buddies cry
I saw his arm a bloody shread, then
I heard them say this one's dead.
Isn't it a large price to pay,
so that you will live another day.
We had the guts to fight and die
He paid the price but what did he buy?
Not a thing except to die.
But who cares about a marine
His wife, his parents and his sons.
But their about the only ones.
MFD

On May 18, 1st Platoon in Fox Company lost another man. His name was:

Byrl Gaertner, LCPL. He was 20 years old.

From information on the Marines.togetherweserved.com web site, Gaertner's death was reported in the "Pacific Stars and Stripes," Tuesday, May 28, 1968, Tokyo, Japan. Since the three Platoons in Fox Company were usually operating independently from each other, we in 2nd Platoon were not aware of his death at the time.

The Marine records give a better picture:

180835 F-1 at coord 020610 observed 4 VC (at coord 023607) moving south. Opened fire to see if enemy would return fire. Enemy returned fire – called in Arty fire mission. Sustained 2 friendly WIA's, one needs emer medevac.

The 4 armed VC had rifles and belts, & wearing only shorts. Later spotted approx 20 men in full Khakis and full gear. Returned fire with probable hits. Estimate rein forced Plt of enemy. Also called airstrikes but could not observe. Results total including WIA's in initial report. 7 WIA's. 1 KIA. 5 WIA's medevaced by helo 1 KIA and 2 WIA's medevaced by amtracs to BAS 2/27.

Translated:

Reported on May 18 at 08:35 a.m., the first platoon of Fox Company at coordinates 020610, observed four Viet Cong at map coordinates 023607. The enemy was moving south. The platoon opened fire to see if the enemy would return fire. The enemy returned fire and the platoon called in an artillery fire mission. The platoon sustained two friendly WIA's, one needed an emergency medevac. The four armed VC had rifles and cartridge belts, and were wearing only shorts. Later, the platoon spotted approximately 20 enemies in full khakis and a full load of equipment. The platoon returned fire and recorded probable hits on the enemy. The enemy force was estimated to be a reinforced platoon of VC. Airstrikes were called but the platoon was unable to observe any damage to the enemy. The total Marine casualties from this action, including the WIA's mentioned in an initial report, were seven WIA's and one KIA. Five WIA's were medevaced by helicopter. The one KIA and two WIA's were medevaced by Amtrak vehicles to the Battalion Aid Station of 2/27.

An Amtrak is an armored tracked vehicle used to transport troops and/or supplies overland in relative safety because of the armor. They were mainly used in large operations like Operation Allen Brook, which was in full swing at this time. The main area of interest in this operation was the area called Go Noi Island. It was so designated because it was a land mass bound on four sides by the Ky Lam, Thu Bon, Ba Ren and Chiem Son rivers. The operation was mainly a search and destroy mission on a large scale. Elements of 2/7, 3/7, 1/26, 3/5, 3/27 and our own 2/27 would be the main forces involved from early May to the middle of July. Operation Mameluke Thrust was also conducted in the area adjacent to Go Noi Island. This was all part of the 2nd Tet Offensive attempted by the VC and NVA in 1968. The rocket belt around Da Nang was full of enemy rocket and mortar teams and this was my Platoon's area of operation until June 23, when we were the mop-up troops for Allen Brook. The first night in Go Noi, we were hit by enemy mortars and later we swept the area with the engineers, clearing the forested areas with explosives and defoliants. The heat was a major problem, getting up to 110 to 120 degrees. Water was a real problem too, since the enemy had contaminated the wells with oil and dead animals. Water from the rivers was out of the question. Even our water purification tablets could not make the water drinkable. I remember scooping water out of a well covered with green scum, dead frogs and dead birds. I boiled it to make coffee. Boy, that coffee was a real life saver, even if it did taste nasty. However, I get ahead of myself.

So, why did I lose three men by the 16th of May? I believe that those three men were the riflemen I had gained in April, used to fill the positions of ammo humpers in my squad. I believe that they were given to me to fill in for those who had been killed or wounded in my squad. The 1st and 3rd Platoons who had been dwindled down by the operations we were on also saw an increase in replacements in April. It still amazes me how our platoon, 2nd Platoon, managed to stay as strong as we were. I'm sure that God was with us, as He was with everyone, but the main temporal reasons for our success were Lt. Jones and SSgt. Staggs. They were smart, dedicated and savvy to the ways of our enemies. We got dwindled down too, but not easily. I believed our Company Commander, Captain Collins, recognized this as well and as a result we were often the security platoon for the Company Command Post, and when in a pinch, we were the first called to, "Take care of business." The actions of 18 May are a perfect example of the expertise in our Platoon, and confirmation that Lt. Jones' methods worked.

The records report:

181915 F-2 at 988612 reported 6 enemy 60mm rnds on PPB just vacated at coord 993611. Enemy coord were 992602 outside TAOR. Called in fire mission on enemy position.

Translated:

Reported on May 18 at 07:15 p.m., 2nd Platoon, Fox Company, at map coordinates 988612 reported six enemy 60mm mortar rounds landing on the Platoon Patrol Base (PPB) which had just been vacated at coordinates 993611. The enemy coordinates were 992602 which is outside the Tactical Area Of Responsibility. The Platoon called in fire missions on the enemy position.

The old trick of moving the PPB every night from the initial position to a "secret" one sure paid off that night.

It was May 22, and I wrote:

Dear Dad,

Well, here I am and there you are. Yep, it looks like I'll be here and you there for about 9 or 10 more months. But these past few days I have [been] wondering whether I was going to be here today or not. First of all, we got back from Duc Ky Monday morning. While we were out there, my machine gun team got separated from the rest of the platoon and we walked over 3000 meters through enemy territory to a bridge where Golf Company is stationed. The same bridge we were at about a month and a half ago. The one where we lost those 3 men. Well, needless to say, we were all scared stiff, and I had to lead us out. One good thing though, the men followed me and did what they were told. Of course, I had one loud mouth, but I didn't even pay any attention to him. We made it [okay], without anything happening. I sure got ribbed afterwards by the rest of the platoon. Well, that was Number 1. Number 2 was last night. We were all sleeping soundly on our cots here in Battalion. Then about 3:00 all hell broke loose. Old "Charlie" rocketed us. The first rocket hit about 20 yards from my tent and threw me out of the rack [cot] onto the floor with the concussion. When I woke up everyone else was in the bunker and when I started to get up and go the rest of the rockets came in. There were about 6 more that came in, and here I was flat on my face hoping and praying that I wouldn't get hit. Well, I didn't, but I was sure shook. I made light of it with the men, but inside all I could do was thank the Lord that I was alive and not even wounded. So as you can see, I am still here and I [reckon] you are still there, so let's hope it [stays] that way. …

With all my love, Chuck

Yep, those were some crazy things, but my letter didn't say it all. To start with, with the "Mini Tet" going on, all the bases in the vicinity of Da Nang were getting rocketed and mortared regularly. That was the reason for the small ops (operations) we were on. Duc Ky was full of VC and it was a primary area for them to hold up and get supplies. The skirmishes and casualties out of that area resulted in the bulk of the KIA's and WIA's suffered by our Battalion in May. One of the things we did to take away Charlie's ability to live and resupply in the Duc Ky area, was to burn down huts where we found things like rice caches, tunnels, weapons, ammo etc.

On the day when I was separated from the platoon, I had three men with me, burning some hooches, while the rest of the platoon did the same. The smoke was thick as pea soup and when we were done and started to hook back up with the platoon, they were nowhere to be seen. We were in an open area with a copse of dense jungle close by, and we didn't have a radio to call them. I moved us up close to the edge of this tree line and told one of the men to go in and see if the platoon was in there. In case they weren't there, I didn't want to risk everyone by taking all of us in there. It was a pretty spooky place. Well, a little while later, he came out and said that no one was there. I looked around and could see no good place for us to take cover so I looked at my map and saw that the Golf Company CP was the closest safe haven for us. I told the men what I wanted to do and we took off for the Golf CP, about three clicks (a click is 1,000 meters) away. I got some guff, but the last thing I wanted was for us to be caught out there all alone. I figured that if we looked like a patrol then maybe Charlie would let us go, thinking the rest of the Marines would be behind us. We started out, and then it happened. I went to switch my M-16 off safe to semi-automatic and the damned thing wouldn't budge. It was rusted in place. I didn't let on to my men that I had a weapon that wouldn't work and I never told anyone about that. As we walked along, I acted as if we were on patrol and didn't make it obvious that my M-16 was a piece of junk. I would fiddle with the selector switch from time to time, but it stayed stubbornly frozen on safe. I still had my .45 but that's not very useful at anything over fifty yards, and we were walking out in the open hundreds of yards from the nearest tree lines. I kept it that way, because to get too close to a jungle area was to invite an ambush. The VC weren't all that good at long range shots, unless they were a regular sniper or had a scoped rifle. Even then, they weren't a match for any of our Marines carrying an M-16 or M-14. Yes, we still had some men carrying the M-14, which fired the same ammo as the M-60 machine gun. Tom Montie from third squad was one of those M-14 men.

Continuing on my trek, I sweated bullets, bullets with no rifle to shoot them from. It took us about an hour and a half to hook up with Golf Company. They contacted our Platoon by radio and the rest of 2nd Platoon came and got us. I was asked how we got separated and I related what had happened, only to find out that the platoon had been in that first patch of jungle all along. I quietly confronted the man who had gone into that area with the facts, and he reluctantly admitted that he hadn't gone in at all, that he had just gone in enough to be out of sight, waited a while and came out saying that the platoon wasn't there. I didn't make a fuss over that and I don't think anyone else ever knew. Fear can grip us all and is nothing to be beat up over. That man would exhibit extreme bravery later on, giving his life for his friends.

While with Golf Company, I got some oil, took my M-16 apart, and got that selector switch to working again. The switch was indeed rusted. It seems that although the M-16 was primarily aluminum, the selector switch and the parts around it were steel. It was amazing how quickly that rust and corrosion could happen. Even daily cleaning often wouldn't be enough. Eventually the Corps changed from oil to a compound call L.S.A. (Lysergic Acid Amide) which is still in use today. It was supposed to stick to the metal better than oil, acting as both a lubricant and a preservative. The M-60 machine guns were even harder to keep clean and functioning. They were steel weapons and required constant cleaning and heavy doses of L.S.A. to keep them working, but too heavy a dose attracted sand and dirt which clogged the mechanisms. We also had problems with some of the ammo. Some people believe that there were saboteurs in some of the ammo plants in the U.S., but whatever the case, some specific brands of machine gun ammo were more subject to problems than others. The problems we had with that brand of bad ammo was mainly weak cases, causing the round to swell in the chamber of the breach of the M-60, preventing the casing from being extracted by the bolt of the weapon after it was fired. When that happened, the next round would get picked up and jam up the feed mechanism. Usually the solution was to flip up the feed tray, remove the ammo and take a cleaning rod and push from the front of the barrel to drive out the bad casing. Now try doing that in the middle of a firefight. Good luck! That was one reason for carrying a spare barrel, which we did religiously. We hated carrying that heavy bag with the barrel in it, but we loved it when it was needed. If the spare barrel wasn't handy then there was no choice but to take the plugged-up barrel out of the gun, pull out the cleaning rod and do it that way. There were times when we had to do just that during a firefight and it was "hairy" to say the least. To accomplish this, we let the bipod legs down and holding the legs, removed the barrel to correct the problem.

Another bad condition we faced in a firefight was the carbon that built up in the breech of the gun, causing the bolt to move slower and slower until it couldn't move fast enough to set off a round. When that happened, all you could do was pull your .45 Colt Automatic, replace the barrel if you can and try and clean up the gun without being killed first. Being a machine gunner was deadly enough, but the mechanical problems of the M-60 in adverse conditions made it even harder to stay alive when everyone is trying to kill you.

Also on May 22, while in the Battalion Area, we were told that some "Home Town" releases were going to be sent to our home towns and we needed to fill out a form for those news releases. Here is what my parents received from the Fleet Home Town News Centers:

> News Release News Director
>
> Radio Station KNAF 41-F-60
>
> (J0364) VIETNAM (FHTNC) May 22—Marine Lance Corporal Charles A. Van Bibber, 21, son of Mr. and Mrs. Richard J. Van Bibber of 907 W. Schubert, Fredericksburg, Tex., is serving with the Second Battalion, Twenty-Seventh Marine Regiment in Vietnam. As a member of the battalion he helps capture or destroy enemy forces. He accomplishes this through weapons fire, tactical maneuvering, and both large and small scale operations.
> His unit is also engaged in a civic action program designated to assist the Vietnamese people in completing self-help projects, such as the building of wells, culverts, small bridges and schools. Equipment and materials are made available through the Marine Corps Reserve Civic Action Fund.

So, while I was getting rocketed in the Battalion Area, my folks got this news. Form letter for sure, aimed at calming the public back home. Funny that it would say that we were helping to build up Vietnam while in reality, we were out in Duc Ky blowing up the villages, wells, bridges and rice caches. We blew up everything that the letter said we were building. Ah, the irony of war.

On May 30, I managed to get another letter out:

Dear Mom,

Well, here I am again in all my glory. Like I told you before, I just don't have the time to write as often as I'd like. Besides, it is so hot over here that even old VC Charlie doesn't work during the day. Of course, that doesn't mean that we Marines don't work, oh no! We go on just as many patrols and dig almost as many holes as before. I just got back from Duc Ky yesterday, and will start night patrols tomorrow. Then, on [June 4th] we go back to Duc Ky for another 3 days. Therefore, by now you ought to see the pattern. 3 Days in Duc Ky, 6 days here in battalion, 3 days in Duc Ky etc. Of the 6 days here in Battalion, 3 days we run patrols, so that gives me 3 free days every 9 days. Now, do you understand why I'm not writing so much. …

Oh, besides the heat, it rains every day at 4:00 and gets everything soaking wet. Most of the time it quits around 5:30, but once or twice a week, it keeps on raining into the night. This weather over here is real miserable to say the least, and it tends to make me miserable and mean. But that's good, because then I can get more VC and do my job better. …

With all my love, Chuck

I had also received a care package from home with lots of goodies. The best ones were the powdered ice tea, more baggies and best of all, Sunday funny papers, with Dick Tracy and The Phantom. Those packages from home were always such a great thing. Besides lifting the morale, they lifted the belly too. One of the things of note in all these letters was how I always referred to "my job" and "work." Made a difference then to look at things that way and I don't ever remember talking about how I "killed" someone, I just say that they "got hit" or "were killed." Another thing was when I began using the term "men" rather than "boys." It didn't take long for all of us to grow up and become men.

My letters home became fewer and fewer. In March, I had written about 14 letters. In April, that number was down to ten and in May, it was down to six. Some of this was because of the constant movement and patrols. Also I was beginning to get worn down, and it was increasingly hard to write home about combat.

It was around this time that I had a wild time on a night patrol around the Battalion area. Dan Nordmann remembers that patrol as well, as it was a larger than normal patrol of 10 - 12 men. This was an all-nighter. We left the base around 2200 hours and wouldn't be due in until dawn. This wasn't an ambush as such, since the route was so long, but whenever we stopped for a rest, I always set us in like it was an ambush just in case. As I've said before, the Battalion Area was a large base with chow hall, canteen for drinking beer, offices, tents, water point, supply office etc. Immediately outside of the base was a maze of concertina wire that was booby-trapped and mined. In order to get into or out of the base, except by the main road, you had to know the route. It wasn't hard to follow once you knew it and besides, the ground had been worn down to a hard packed surface by the constant patrols going in and out of the base. There were a pair of bunkers on each side of the trailhead in the compound that were manned by M-60 teams with a sergeant of the guard in charge. They also had radios with direct communication to mortar teams in the compound as well as one to contact the operations people. It was from this point that we went out on the patrol.

As was my custom, I stayed pretty close to the point man so I could more easily direct him on the route I wanted to take. I usually stuck close to the route given me but I would improvise some to avoid close encounters with civilians or possible enemy ambush sites. I had no doubt that we were watched as we left the compound, and it was my duty to minimize detection as the patrol proceeded. Although the patrol was to be a long one, time-wise, the actual path was not that long, so there was plenty of time to stop and rest and/or set up ambushes. The patrol went smoothly enough. We had to skirt around a village and take some little-traveled paths in order to avoid booby traps and ambushes on the main trails. Vietnam had just a few roads, as we know them, and all of those were dirt. The main means of travel for the Vietnamese people was on foot, resulting in wide hard-packed dirt trails that were used as the main means of travel with some more narrow trails going off to other locations. I called in at the checkpoints and occasionally stopped for a smoke break. Smoking at night was not the norm, but the moon was up and we were all dying for a smoke. We would light our cigarettes under our helmets and cup the end in our hands, especially in the moon light. I didn't figure it would make matters worse and the men always appreciated this since almost all of us smoked. I sure did enjoy my Camel cigarettes. They were non-filter in those days, so I got plenty of the calming nicotine. Bad for the lungs, but at that time who cares when you could be dead at any moment. Knowing that the smell could also bring on some VC, I set up in good ambush sites with good fields of vision. I guess in a way I was trying to lure the VC into my ambush. I was a hunter, using every trick in the books.

We had walked for quite a while, resting when we could, and wound up at our last checkpoint earlier than expected. I called in and told them that we would wait there until dawn. At dawn we were expected to fire off a series of pop flares as a recognition signal prior to entering the wire. Pop flares were hand-held tubes firing a colored flare which were used to give signals in the "code of the day," like green-white-green or red-white-green in one minute intervals. We waited in the grass at the edge of the tree line for dawn to come. Dan Nordmann was at my side and we were waiting patiently. Just before dawn, we saw a series of pop flares go up from the edge of the tree line about 200 yards from where we were. Although the sequence was right, the colors weren't. Then we noticed in the predawn light what looked like one of our patrols coming in through the maze. At least that was what we thought, because they were wearing clothes and helmets like ours. I turned to Dan and said:

"That's not us!"

"Your right," he said. "Where did they come from?"

He was just as puzzled as I was, since we didn't think that there were any other patrols out in our assigned sector. I got on the radio and called in to report what we were seeing and confirming where we were. I was told to stay put until notified. As we watched, the "other patrol" got closer and closer to the guard gate. All of a sudden, all hell broke loose. Illumination rounds blossomed in the air over that part of the wire, the machine guns in the bunkers opened up and mortars came in on the wire there. From our viewpoint, it was a magnificent show. However, from the viewpoint of the "other patrol" it was certain death. Once all the firing was over, the "other patrol" lay dead in the wire. We saw Marines come out from the compound with weapons at the ready; they checked things out and returned. Then another group of Marines came out and brought all the bodies and gear into the compound. Finally, we got the call to come in, and to give the code of the day with our pop flares. We did that and walked through the maze, which had pools of blood all over the place. We came in the gate and were debriefed by the Officer of the Day. It seems like the VC had gotten hold of some of our clothes and helmets and had watched as our patrols had come and gone from that gate through the wire. They had no way of knowing the proper sequence of the pop flares for that day. They took potluck and did their best to penetrate our defenses. It was pretty disconcerting to think that they were out there all that time and could have attacked us just as easily as they had attempted the penetration of the wire.

I have said before how important it was to stick to a given patrol route, well here in May was a perfect example. The Marine Corps records report the following:

270100 F-2-A and F-2-B at 983613 engaged each other in a firefight. One patrol apparently F-2-B was off its designated patrol

> route. 2 Non battle casualties resulted. One emer 1 prior.
> Investigation by F-2 actual will occur at first light.
> Medevac requested and completed at 0254.

Translated it reads:

Reported on May 27 at 01:00 a.m., the A and B patrols from Fox Company 2nd Platoon at map coordinates 983613 engaged each other in a fire fight. One patrol, apparently the B patrol, was off its designated patrol route. Two non-battle casualties resulted. One required an emergency medevac and the other a priority medevac. An investigation by the platoon commander (F-2 actual) will occur at first light. The medevac was requested and then completed at 02:54 am.

Looking into this report, I remember that I was leading the F-2-A patrol. It was a large night ambush. I had a gun team with me, probably Freer and Nordmann, as well as rifle teams from 3rd squad. I believe that Freer was with me, since Nordmann remembers the incident well. I know that the rifle teams were from 3rd Squad because Tom Montie from 3rd Squad also remembers the incident. This was a Company sized operation, and we had been walking for three days or more on a Company sweep. As I have said, I had gained a reputation as a patrol leader, especially on night ambush patrols. Captain Collins, the Company Commander used me often this way whenever 2nd Platoon was with the Command Post. I don't remember who was leading the other patrol, but Dan Nordmann remembers that while we were in the ambush position, the other patrol appeared and naturally, we opened up on them not realizing that they were our own people. No one should have been there but the enemy and us. Someone in my ambush opened up and as luck would have it, one man in the other patrol was hit, while the others took cover. We discovered that we were all friendly and we banded together to take care of the wounded. I remember it like it was yesterday. I was performing first aid on one of the wounded men. There was blood on his left thigh area so I dropped his trousers and got out a battle dressing to care for the wounded area. To my surprise, his thigh was fine - the blood had come from his left testicle. Yep, he got his balls shot off, or rather, one of them. I put the battle dressing on with the pad between his legs and tied over his left hip. He grabbed my arm and said, "Where am I hit? Am I hit in the balls?" He had wild eyes and was starting to go into shock so I told him no, that he was just hit in the thigh. I could see the look of relief on his face as I called in the medevac helicopter. Then I called in to the CP and notified them of the situation. There was another man wounded as well, but not that seriously. Dan Nordmann remembers that the man hit in the balls was a mortar man, from Weapons Platoon. This pretty much says it. Stay on your patrol route or you could get killed by your own men!

The next day, the B patrol had more trouble. The report for May 28 says the following:

281315 F-2-B at 985610 tripped booby trapped 105mm rd. Sustained one WIA Emer MedEvac. Completed at 281418.

Translated:

Reported on May 28 at 1:15 p.m., the B patrol from Fox Company 2nd Platoon at map coordinates 985610 tripped a booby trapped 105mm artillery round. The patrol sustained one WIA emergency medevac. The medevac was completed at 02:18 p.m..

Fox Co. 2nd Platoon was busy in May, besides the incidents mentioned, we had found several dud 81mm mortar and 105 artillery rounds and blew them in place. There were tunnels blown and we discovered a wrecked U.S. aircraft and blew that as well. Patrols had spotted several VC and called in artillery.

The casualty count at the end of May for 2/27 was:

KIA 11 WIA 161 for a running total after 3.5 Months of KIA 29 WIA 309 MIA 2

Statistics from "The Wall", state that the month of May, 1968, had the most monthly casualties listed from the whole of the Vietnam War. 2,415 casualties were recorded that month.

Chapter 7

Duc Ky, Duc Ky, Duc Ky! That seemed to be all we heard and we dreaded the call. Duc Ky had been evacuated early in May and was declared a "free fire zone," where anything that moved was fair game. We had been performing saturation patrolling of that area since the beginning of May and it looked like we would be on patrol there forever. We were constantly on edge, with little time to relax and regroup. Sleep was just a memory from the past. My letter writing became as rare as sleep was - I was tired almost to the point of exhaustion all the time. We ran patrols day and night, no matter where we were, even when back in the Battalion Area. Although not yet involved in what people would call "Major Operations," we saw our share of action to be sure.

June would also bring on the highly successful "Killer Teams" consisting of a FO (Forward Observer) for calling in artillery and mortars, an SS (Scout/Sniper) team, patrol leader, radioman and rifle fire team. Killer Teams would go out for one to three days on their own, with the single mission to seek out the enemy and eliminate them. I participated in these Killer Teams as the patrol leader. I remember that running a "Killer Team" patrol was an extra heavy responsibility. We went out at night and returned at night. We took three days' rations, which would have been 6 C-ration meals, three canteens of water, poncho and poncho liner and various items like C-4, toilet paper, and a spare battery for the radio. There was also the normal equipment of helmet, flak jacket, weapons and ammo. We did not take machine guns because this was basically a sniper patrol and we were just there to provide security for the snipers. All our personal gear was left behind.

I remember one killer team patrol that I took out which included a Marine Dog and his handler. We all loved the dogs and worried over them just as we did our own buddies. After taking the patrol out to the base area as pinpointed on the map, we hunkered down and waited for dawn. In the predawn light, the snipers moved away from us a short distance and set up their ambush. I set up the rear guard to watch their back.

Shortly after dawn, we heard a shot from the direction of the sniper team. Then, the team called in asking for the FO. We all went and we could see a bunch of what looked like NVA hiding around some blown up buildings. The FO called in some 105mm artillery and many enemy casualties were observed. Later that day, the dog handler said he was going out by himself with his dog to see if he could detect any more enemies in the area. Time slipped by and soon it was dusk. The snipers, who had set up a new hide earlier, came in to our base area, but no dog. Dusk turned to dark, and still no dog.

I always used Lt. Jones' trick of moving after dark, to avoid being mortared or ambushed, and just as we were ready to move, the dog and his handler slipped through the jungle to join us. That Marine/Dog team was amazing. They snuck up on us like Indians, never making a sound. Good thing too, because if they had been detected, someone would have surely shot them. The handler apologized for coming in late, but he had been pinned down for a while by many NVA moving around his hide. We were all grateful for their return. It was a good thing for us that the Vietnamese didn't use dogs to hunt us down. To them, a dog was just a meal. They couldn't see past their bellies. Good for us, bad for the dogs.

That morning the FO called in for air strikes on the area the dog handler had scoped out the day before. We observed the area of the air strikes and later moved to a new sniper hide.

The next two days were uneventful. The dog went out to recon the area and the snipers set up sniper hides. I timed the return trip so that we would arrive back at the base around midnight. As time went on, I got better at the killer team patrols and I was called on often to run these patrols.

The sniper teams did an excellent job and they did much to take out the enemy and save Marine lives. The sniper I remember most was Johnnie E. Cata. Working mostly as a team with his scout/spotter (not to be confused with the Kit Carson scouts who were Vietnamese), or with small teams, like the Killer Teams, snipers lacked the protection of large units of Marines, making them more vulnerable than the average Marines. They took down the enemy face-to-face, which through the high-powered scope made each kill appear up close and personal. The scout/snipers were never appreciated as they should have been. Their fellow Marines were the only ones to really understand and acknowledge their work. Johnnie Cata made it back from Vietnam. He passed away on April 29, 2010. God bless you Johnnie!

On June 1st I wrote home:

Dear Dad,

Well, here I am and there you are. You know, that heading ought to be written in stone and preserved for all time[,] it is so original and meaningful. …

Say, I explained to Mom why I haven't been writing so much lately, and I hope you get the message. Really, I'd like to write more, but I just can't.

Ho Ho, what a pleasant [surprise]. I got your letter just now. So am answering a sap, oh sorry, I mean A.S.A.P. (Ha Ha got you on that one.) Yep, I got the package and can't tell you how much the knife and sling mean to me. That was real nice of you to put them in envelopes, but those witticisms were kinda sick, ha, ha. Oh, as far as the knife is concerned, well I have been doing a lot of practicing, and can now hit an object up to and anywhere between 20 ft or so with my knife so now I have a real fast weapon at my disposal if the situation ever calls for its use. No really, I'm a real Jim Bowie now, ha, ha. …

About this mess over here. Well, I sure do wish they would turn us loose. There would be a lot of blood all over the place you bet, but I bet that once the ball got rolling, that it wouldn't take more than 6 months to end this thing. It is real shitty the way it is now. This last trip to Duc Ky we took 3 WIA's (wounded in action) 1 Marine got his balls shot off, 1 got hit in the upper leg, and the other hit a booby-trap and damn near got his arm cut off at the elbow plus a lot of scrap-metal in his legs. He is real lucky just to be alive. And guess what! We didn't get one Gook. That's right not one. There are all kinds of people running around Duc Ky but no one is supposed to be there. Yet we can't open fire on anyone unless we get shot at first. It makes me so damn [mad] that I wish I could go in there and just kill all those people or do something, anything. Oh well, I guess I am just blowing off steam. It sure will be nice to get home and forget all this. …

With all my love, Chuck

I was losing it. Today, I can't imagine myself wanting to "just kill all those people."

On June 10th I wrote:

Dear Mom:

Well, believe it or not, it's little old me again. I've been back from Duc Ky now 3 days and will go back out on the 13th unless we go on an operation before that. You know how the Marine Corps is, all kinds of [bum] scoop that always keeps you completely dumb-founded as far as knowing what is coming up next. Boy, these past 3 days have sure flown by. I honestly don't know where the time goes anymore. I just get rested up a bit, and then I have to run patrols. Then as soon as I get used to the patrols, it is time to go back to Duc Ky. Not only that, but I'm running patrols from 1:00 to 6:00 in the afternoon now, and that really shoots the heck out of the day. Well, that's life in Vietnam. …

Say, I heard about Bobby Kennedy's assassination the other day. Boy that sure is bad isn't it? Why can't people learn to settle differences some other way? Don't they realize the violence only breeds more violence? It really worries me, because our country is falling apart from within, and there is no telling what will come of it. Only the good Lord knows what is in store for us in the future, but I can't help but wonder and worry about the type of world my children will have to grow up and live in. I just hope that I am strong enough to uphold the principles I know to be true and right and teach these to my children. Well, that is a while off right now, and I have my own problems over here. …

Well, I guess I've rambled on enough. I've got patrol in a little while so I'll have to sign off. You take care of yourself, and have a good summer. I'll try and write again before I have to go out, but don't count on anything. Give everyone my love, and I'll be thinking of you all.

With all my love, Chuck

Duc Ky dominated my thoughts then, but the condition of my country was also important. With the deaths of Martin Luther King and Bobby Kennedy, it looked like the country was going to hell in a hand-basket. I don't think that the people in the States ever stopped to think of the effect their conduct had on the men fighting in Vietnam. It seems like everyone had their own agenda and that was all that mattered. Men fighting for their country want to know that the country they are fighting for is behind them and that their homes, families, towns, and cities are a place of peace to return to. One thing Vietnam taught us was:

"Good luck with that one; it's all just a fantasy."

The Marine Corps reports from the 1st to the 10th for our platoon indicate the following:

011850 F2B had one NVA following their patrol. NVA moved to coord 001614 and joined 3 others. NVA's wearing gray uniforms and packs and carrying carbine type weapons. Called 81mm mission, checked area with neg result.

Translated:

Reported on June 1st at 6:50 p.m., the B patrol from Fox Company 2nd Platoon had one NVA following their patrol. NVA moved to map coordinates 001614 and joined three others. The NVA's were wearing gray uniforms and packs and carrying carbine type weapons. Patrol called in 81mm mortar fire mission and checked the area with negative results.

021045 F2A at 006618 foune [*sic*] one dud grenade. Blew in place by an engr. One USMC approx 25 mtrs away sustained minor shrapnel wound in leg. WIA walked in with patrol and was treated in Bn BAS.

Translated:

Reported on June 2nd at 10:45 a.m., the A patrol from Fox Company 2nd Platoon found one dud grenade at map coordinates 006618. An engineer blew the grenade in place. One Marine approximately 25 meters away sustained minor shrapnel wound in his leg. The WIA walked in with the patrol and was treated in the Battalion Aid Station.

091620 F-2-D at coord 000614 found one 105mm dud WP Rd. Blew in place with C-4

Translated:

Reported on June 9th at 4:30 p.m., the D patrol from Fox Company 2nd Platoon at map coordinates 000614 found one 105mm dud white phosphorus round and blew it in place with C-4 explosive.

The 105mm Artillery piece was a highly mobile rifled cannon that could be towed by truck or lifted by helicopter and set up almost anywhere. The 105 was probably the most used artillery piece in Vietnam, and as such, it was not uncommon to find dud rounds scattered around the countryside. From my marching orders, I was the patrol leader on the ninth. I alternated between the A, D and E patrols at this time.

I was running day patrols from the seventh to the tenth. Whether I blew the dud round or an engineer did, I do not recall. However, I do remember that by this time, I had learned to use C-4 with blasting caps and detonator, so I very well may have done that myself. From my experience and the experience of others, I had learned also to take extra cover when blowing up ordnance and keep a good distance from the blast. It was important to blow dud rounds in place for several reasons. To move them could cause the round to go off. To leave them would mean that the VC would wind up making a booby trap out of them and that usually meant killed or injured Marines. Our patrols were aimed at tracking down the enemy and discovering their supplies. Equally important was to discover unexploded ordnance and make it inactive, which usually meant blowing it up. My limit was 81mm mortar rounds and 105mm artillery rounds. Anything larger was left to the engineers.

You might think that the war in Vietnam was full of fights, battles, and horrible things, and it is true that those things existed. If you see the modern movies and read some of the most popular books about the Vietnam War, you probably would feel that the war was one firefight after another. In fact, if the books and movies didn't do that, most of them would probably be less entertaining and would find a much smaller audience, leading to smaller profits and possibly even extinction. After all, isn't excitement and drama why we watch movies and read novels? Up until this time, the war just wasn't that way. Month after month, the combat reports mention just a few incidences of engagements with the enemy or the finding and disposing of war material. How many patrols did I go on until finally a report was made of a 105mm dud being blown up? They don't list anything when there is nothing to list, and rightly so, because who is interested in a constant string of reports that simply say, "Patrol went out, Patrol came back, nothing to report." However, to the Grunt Marine that was all wrong. Why don't they report the pit falls encountered, like running into a mama-san and getting the waddin's scared out of you, or following betel nut trails thinking it was blood? Why don't they report the constant fight against the bugs and the jungle that's encountered *all the time*? Why don't they talk about the knots in your stomach and your bowels and your muscles from constant tension? Why don't they talk about what it's like to go on a patrol with just a few men, traveling far from your base and having only the radio (as long as it works) to keep you in touch with those who could help you? Why don't they talk about the night ambushes that really tear you up, playing on a natural fear of the dark and the unknown, knowing that one false move could get you and everyone else stone cold dead? Or, maybe even worse, blown to bits and lying there while your legs or arms are over there five feet away, or your guts are hanging out and you can't get them back in, or you can't breathe because you have a hole in your lungs, or you can't see because you are blind. I could go on and on. I don't want to discourage the reader, but I do want you to try to understand that for every "action" that's noted, there were hundreds of patrols that bore no fruit at all and still carried the same effects on the men in combat. Then there was the lack of sleep. You couldn't go into a deep sleep, because if you did and you had nightmares and you hollered out, you could get killed. The constant knowledge that everything you would normally do could get you killed finally set in and it left you scared to be scared. You *had* to shut down. You had to ignore all thoughts that didn't fit with the moment. You became the walking dead. It didn't happen at once, it took months and the more exposed you were to the "kill or be killed" mindset, the closer you got to that inevitable attitude, "Fuck it, what are they going to do, send me to Vietnam?"

Duc Ky had become a "no-man's land." We were on search and destroy missions every time we went there. On one patrol, we were checking out a village which had been prepped by artillery fire. It appeared to be deserted. We were only a small squad sized patrol and we had split up to check the hooches for rice and weapons and such. I came upon this hooch and went up the stairs to check it out. The hooches there were elevated several feet to keep things dry in the monsoon season. I didn't find anything but as I came down the stairs I noticed what looked like a body sprawled out under the hooch. It was dark under there and all I could really see were the legs sticking out a little.

I've relived this so many times in my mind, but you need to feel the feelings too. I had none. I was operating on automatic, except that all my senses were on edge. I had learned to carry my M-16 at the ready, locked and loaded, with the pistol grip in my right hand, the barrel pointing forward, the selector switch on automatic and my finger on the trigger. I kept my arm locked in to my side so that the barrel moved with my body. I had learned to shoot by sight this way, never moving the rifle from my side unless I needed to take aim, and then it was a simple maneuver to bring the weapon up to my cheek and fire. Kinda like shooting a shotgun in a way, having developed a real sense of coordination between my eye and my rifle barrel. This left my left arm free to do other things. I first developed this maneuver when I carried the M-60 machine gun and had to operate it by myself. The M-60 was well balanced and could easily be fired from the hip one-handed, as the recoil would help keep the barrel up. The left hand was needed to help feed the belted ammo. The main drawback of the M-60 was that you had to maintain a loop of ammo at the feed point. If you didn't do this, the weight of the belt pulling down from the feed tray would be sufficient to stop the gun from firing. Usually the A-Gunner (assistant gunner) would maintain this loop for the gunner. However, when you're on your own, you had to improvise. This method, for machine gun or rifle, saved my life many times and became automatic for me.

So here I was, senses screaming at me. Nerves instantly on edge and ready to act. Immediate action was right there at my fingertip on the trigger. I looked under the hooch and what did I see, *a dead body*??? Holy sheep shit!!! I reached down with my left hand and grabbed the bare ankle, my right hand holding the M-16 pointed at the body, finger on the trigger. The skin felt cold and clammy so I tightened my grip and started to drag the body out from under the hooch. I thought I felt the body move. It was the body of a woman. I felt the M-16 bucking in my arm, releasing bursts of hot lead. I never even knew that I pulled the trigger. As it turned out, the woman was already dead before I got there. I left the body and continued on patrol. Nerve wracking!

And so, the first part of June was no different for me than April, May, or even March, if you discount the events that took the life of my squad leader and his friends. Just long periods of uneventful patrols broken up by a few serious fights. Another incident involving a Vietnamese woman occurred on the 10th when I was back in the Battalion Area:

Back in the Battalion Area on the 10th of June, the patrols continued, and the reports went out:

100825 F-2-A at coord 988621 observed one VN running as patrol proceeded through treeline. Searched family bunker and found one VN woman without ID card brought suspect to 2/27 CP for questioning.

Translated:

Reported on June 10 at 8:25 a.m., the A patrol from Fox Company 2nd Platoon at mapcoordinates 988621 observed one Vietnamese running as the patrol proceeded through the tree-line. The patrol searched the family bunker and found one Vietnamese woman without an ID card. The patrol brought the suspect to the 2/27 Command Post for questioning.

101115 F-2-A at coord 007619 found one M-72 believed to fire mortars. Blew in place with C-4.

Translated:

Reported on June 10 at 11:15 a.m. at coordinates 007619, found one M-72 believed to fire mortars. The M-72 was blown in place with C-4 explosive.

The M-72 was the designator for the LAW, Light Antitank Weapon that fired a rocket projectile. It was our version of the RPG that the enemy carried. I believe that I was on this patrol for two reasons, one is the capture of the Vietnamese woman and the other is the blowing of the LAW with C-4. I had learned to blow up things with dynamite as a teenager building fences and that translated easily to C-4. Since everyone carried C-4 for heating our chow, it was readily available. I carried my C-4 in a green canvas bag, the same one I brought back with me from Vietnam. I often did this on patrols when there were no engineers available.

I had expected to be in the Battalion Area until the 13th, but on the 10th, we were "Thrust" into operation Mameluke Thrust. The report reads:

10-11 June Elements of Company F, Company H and a provisional platoon from H&S Company participated as a blocking force in Operation Mameluke Thrust.

That would keep us out in the Duc Ky area for an additional six days.

On the 16th I wrote home:

Dear Mom,

Well, here it is Sunday the 16th, and we have just come back from Duc Ky. That makes 6 straight days in the boonies, with plenty of VC to keep us busy. Actually, the medevac copters were catching most of the hell. But the [Huey] Gunships (helicopters) made the difference as usual. All in all it was plain old hell. ...

It's been about 3 weeks since she [girlfriend Mary Ann] has written too. Needless to say, that is kinda [disheartening] since the only means of communication I have with her is mail. I don't know, maybe I ought to wait and start over with her when I get home. But who knows when I'll get home. It might be tomorrow, and then again it might be in 8 months. You know, it sure is hard to explain to someone how you feel when you are 12,000 miles away. Well, that's my problem I guess, so no use bothering you with it.

Oh, yes that was terrible about Bobby Kennedy's death, but with death all around me, I just can't get real shook up about it. He went a lot easier than some of my buddies over here. I think you understand what I mean.

Well, it looks like I'm just about out of things to say. I'm real tired, since I just got in about 3 hours ago, and it is 8:00 at night now. ...
With all my love, Chuck

Still counting on the girlfriend, someone to hang on to, someone to look forward too. I wanted so badly to think that someone, other than my family, cared. I was getting a little cynical too. The patrols went on and on, sometimes bringing results. It is helpful to remember that I often ran the A patrols as well as the D and E patrols.

The records from the 11th to the 20th report the following:

121530 F-2-B at 993607 observed 2 VC at 995602 running. Fox snipers spotted 2 VC. Fired at VC, 1 cont running. One KIA. VC was hit in the stomach. Sniper observed the VC grab his middle as he fell. Body fell behind weeds so it cannot be observed.

Translated:

Reported on June 12th at 3:30 p.m., the B patrol from Fox Company 2nd Platoon at map coordinates 993607 observed two VC running at map coordinates 995602. Fox Company snipers spotted the two VC and fired at one. The other VC continued running. The first one was killed. The VC was hit in the stomach and the sniper observed that the VC grabbed his middle as he fell. The body fell behind some weeds so that it was no longer observable.

151415 F-2 at 984610 spotted 2 VC across blue at coord 984609. Fired on VC. Observed 2 VC KIA for 30 minutes.

Translated:

Reported on June 15 at 2:15 p.m., at map coordinates 984610 Fox Company 2nd Platoon spotted two VC across the river at coordinates 984609. The VC were fired upon and two VC were observed to have been killed. The bodies were watched for 30 minutes.

"Across blue" meant across a river. TAOR's, tactical areas of responsibility, were routinely laid out along river lines. Most Vietnamese rivers were deep and strong flowing and only crossable by boat or bridge. When a patrol would observe some VC on the other side of a river, they would take them on but would not be able to go there and search the area.

151745 F-2 @ 984610 spotted 1 VC @ 984609 fired 1 rd. Res unk. Unable to check as area is across blue.

Translated:

Reported on June 15th at 5:45 p.m., at map coordinates 984610 Fox Company 2nd Platoon spotted one VC at map coordinates 984609. One round was fired. The results were unknown and the Platoon is unable to check the area as it is across the river.

151801 F-2-A at coord 979648 found one 60mm dud. Blew in place with ½ lb of C-4.

Translated:

Reported on June 15 at 6:01 p.m., the A patrol from Fox Company 2nd Platoon at coordinates 979648 found one 60mm mortar dud round. The mortar round was blown in place with ½ lb of C-4.

161015 F-2 @ 985613 – 2 USMC per WIA. Tripped M-26 grenade booby trap – 1 wounded in leg & 1 wounded in chest & arm. Called medevac – F-2 resumed patrol.

Translated:

Reported on June 16th at 10:15 a.m., at map coordinates 985613 Fox Company 2nd Platoon had two USMC wounded when they tripped an M-26 grenade booby trap. Of the two WIA, one was wounded in the leg and the other was wounded in the chest and arm. A medevac mission was called in. The Platoon resumed the patrol.

180915 F-2-Z @ 014607 saw 3 VC @ 012602 walking S. E. 1 dressed in black, 1 in green, 1 in blue. No weapons. F-2-Z shot VC in black in chest. Observed body did not move. For ½ hour. Other VC ran into tree line.

Translated:

Reported on June 18th at 9:15 a.m., patrol Z (sniper patrol) from Fox Company 2nd Platoon at map coordinates 014607 saw three VC at map coordinates 012602 walking south-east. One was dressed in black, one in green and one in blue. No weapons were observed. Sniper shot VC in black in the chest. He observed the body for ½ hour. No movement from the body. The other VC ran into the tree line.

190015 F-2-A @ 012618 1 USMC Per fell on punji stake struck in irrigation ditch. Sustained minor wound. Corpsman treated & patrol continued.

Translated:

Reported on June 19th at 00:15 a.m., the A patrol from Fox Company 2nd Platoon at map coordinates 012618 one Marine fell on a punji stake, which was stuck in an irrigation ditch. He sustained minor wounds. After the corpsman treated him, the patrol continued on its way.

As noted before, there were only two corpsmen assigned to our platoon. One would go on the day patrols and occasionally one went out on night patrols/ambushes.

Another of my patrols. I remember this patrol in particular. The picture is clear in my mind. The punji stakes were pointing up and at a slight angle and very close together so as to better penetrate Marine boots. Luckily, our boots had a metal/plastic insert in the bottom, which helped deflect things like punji stakes. That Marine was fortunate, as the hole was shallow and the stakes didn't penetrate his foot, however, they did puncture the canvas upper of the boot and got him in the ankle.

A punji stake is a sharpened bamboo stick that's usually dipped in some kind of poison or biologic agent, like human shit, and stuck in the ground with the sharp end up. Often, what would seem to be a minor wound would get infected by the stuff on the tip of the punji stake and lead to blood poisoning if not treated early. The Vietnamese would use these stakes everywhere that they thought Marines would walk, and often would dig pits and place these stakes in them, then cover the pit with banana leaves or something. They were highly effective and caused the men on patrol to have to watch where they walked. I tried to stay off the beaten path to avoid booby traps, but punji stakes seemed to show up everywhere.

On June 20th, I wrote:

Dear Chris,

Gee, I'm sorry I haven't written, but I thought I had written and thanked you for the newspaper and letter. It sure was nice, I got a lot of enjoyment out of it.

Say, it sure sounds like you have a busy summer ahead of you. That is a mighty full [schedule] you have, with working, driving, baseball, etc. You know I can still hardly believe that you are getting $1.60 [an] hour. The most I have ever made was $1.35 [an] hour at Steins, and that *was full time work when I was 19 years old. You are doing real good for yourself. ...*

Let me let you in on something Chris, this war is really rough. I can't really explain it, because there is so much that happens. Sometimes I feel like saying to hell with it and I don't really care if the Gooks get me or not, but that doesn't last long. I'm always on my toes out in the bush, I can't afford to let my guard down. But sometimes you have to do certain things , or certain other things just happen, and you wonder what this is all about; and why you do things you would never have thought of doing before. It kinda gets you down sometimes too. ...

I am going on an operation in a day or two, and won't be able to write for 3 weeks to a month. But bear with me. If there is any way of getting a letter off I will. We are supposed to get mail every 2 or 3 days. ...

Oh, grab Dad by the ass and tell him to drop me a line. And tell him that I am up for Corporal. My Plt. Commander put me up for meritorious promotion. I'll let you know if I get it. ...

With all my love, Chuck

Although seemingly inconsequential, this letter was pretty significant as I look back. I never talked directly about when "...you have to do certain things, or certain other things that just happen...," but the killing, burning, and tearing down the lives of these people was getting to me. As a reasonably normal American young man, all the things I had been experiencing were way beyond my sense of morality. As I've said before, I had to view the enemy as "targets" and not as people in order to keep up the fighting. I had no problem with this at the time, but the effects of all this was working inside of me, and it was concern for my men and other Marines that overrode all this in my spirit. However, it would eventually catch up with me.

On the 21st I wrote:

Dear Dad,

Well, here I am and there you are [finally]. It's been quite a spell since I've gotten a letter from you, so I decided to just wait till you wrote.

First of all, let me say that it is so hot over here that even the sun is sweating. No lie, I can hardly believe that any place could be this hot, besides the fact that we live in canvas tents, whew! It's worse than Houston or San Antonio put together. I understand your not writing, but believe it or not, I worry when I don't [hear] anything from anyone for 3 weeks. Just think how it would be if you didn't [hear] from me for a month or two, which reminds me. We are going on operation Allen-

brook Sunday, and will probably be gone for 3 weeks to a month. I'll write [whenever] I can, so don't worry about me. Operation Allenbrook is just about over now, and we are going in for the cleanup. So as you well know, anything can happen. The area of the operation is a mass of enemy bunkers and fortified positions, so it looks like we will have a little bit of World War II fighting ahead. But don't worry, old "Machine Gun Chuck" will be all right.

Say, do me a favor will you, and see if you can find out from Mom or Cathy what the scoop is on Mary Ann. It has been nearly a month now since I've gotten a letter from her. Maybe I don't know how to take a hint, because I'm still writing her [whenever] I can. Oh well, so much for my problems. …

That fishing hole up at Ingram sure sounds like a swell place. Be sure you let me know how many fish you catch with that black moss. As to your question about [whether] I go fishing or not, well, all I can say is that over here the fish bite back. No I don't get a chance to go fishing. In fact, it is hard enough just to find water good enough to put iodine in and drink. Boy what I wouldn't give for a glass of cold water from home.

Let's see, oh, about Kennedy's death, well, I don't really blame the country as a whole, it is just that with killing going on over here every day, it is sometimes hard to understand why the people back home, many of which don't know the first thing about what it means to kill or be killed. It just seems that some place in the world there shouldn't be killing, and that place for me is the U.S.A. …

Well, I'm all packed up, and will be leaving early tomorrow morning for 1 day down in Duc Ky, and then Sunday morning we get on [choppers] and head for the operation. …

With all my love, Your #1 Son, Chuck

The records for the 21st report the following:

211000 F-2-A at coord 015629 saw a light at 012630 and suspected VC activity. Fired hand illum and saw 3 VC on Anderson west. Suspect they were mining the road or waiting in on ambush. Also spotted 1 VC running west on Anderson Trail. Called in Fire mission. Checked area with Neg results.

Translated:

Reported on June 21st at 10:00 a.m., the A patrol from Fox Company 2nd Platoon at map coordinates 015629 saw a light at map coordinates 012630 and suspected VC activity. A hand illumination was fired and three VC were seen on the Anderson Trail west. Suspects were either mining the road or waiting in ambush. One other VC was seen running west on the Anderson Trail. A fire mission was called in and the area was checked with negative results.

We were back from Duc Ky on the 22nd and ready to board the Ch-47 Chinook Helicopters for the move to Go Noi Island where operation Allen Brook was in progress. Before I get into the operation, I have to tell what happened on the helo (helicopter) pad before we took off. There we were, with all our gear, all 100 pounds or so, ready to make a major insertion into the operation. The helo pad was hot and crowded, with the heat making little mirages over the tarmac. Then out of that mirage came a figure with no pack or weapon, waving his arms in front of his body and over his head, back and forth, trying to get our attention. We looked, shook our heads and looked again. Not only was he waving his arms, he was also running (if you could call it that) toward us with his legs spread out in a posture like he was extremely bow-legged. As he came nearer in that straddle legged hop, it was really more a hop than a run, waving his arms, and a big smile on his face, we began to recognize him. He was one of us that had been medevaced a week or so ago, one of the casualties from the 16th, when our patrol hit a booby trap.

We all called out to him and I said, "Hey, I thought you were dead." He laughed and said, "No, not me, look at this," and he proceeded to drop his trousers. He wasn't wearing any underwear, like most of us - we stopped that practice long ago because of the sweat and chaffing that underwear caused. There in all its glory was a huge black/blue/purple bruise right where his private parts were and on the inside of both thighs. It was so dark, that you couldn't tell one part from another. It was as if he had been hit by a very large basketball right in the groin. We all laughed and hollered, "Wow, what happened to you?" He said he was hit by a large mud clod right in the middle of his groin. He said that everything worked ok, but he was real sore and the bruise hurt just to look at it. He was smiling because he wasn't going on this operation with us and would have some rest here at the base while he recuperated. We didn't have long to talk with him because he had to get off the helo pad before the Chinooks (helicopters for troop transport) came in. Man, what a sight. One you just never forget. We were ready to go to Go Noi at 0700 on June 23rd.

Chapter 8

While we were running in and out of Duc Ky in the "Rocket and Mortar Belt", Operation Allen Brook had been going on since the 4th of May. The enemy had concentrated NVA troops and supplies on Go Noi Island about 15 miles south of Da Nang and was ready to head north on May 5th, the same day the mortar and rocket attack started against the bases in and around Da Nang, but the start of Allen Brook on the 4th put a hamper on their plans. This was the start of what was later called the "Mini Tet," the second phase of the original Tet offensive, which began the end of January 1968. A good account of everything that was going on can be found in *U. S. Marines in Vietnam: The Defining Year 1968*, by Jack Shulimson et. al. It details all the activities of Operation Allen Brook, which stopped the enemy offensive. Go Noi Island was so named because it was a mass of land surrounded by the Chiem Son, Ba Ren, Thu Bon and Ky Lam rivers.

My participation in Allen Brook didn't start until June 23rd, however a brief account of what had occurred on Go Noi prior to the 23rd is important and will set the stage for our entry into the fray. This is not an attempt to cover any one unit's participation in the action, or to exclude anyone either. There have been many books written about the battles on Go Noi and I will leave it to them to provide those details.

As described in *The Defining Year: 1968*, the communists had controlled Go Noi for years, establishing a military command post complete with political propaganda teams and acting as a safe haven for both VC and NVA units. There were major stations with a training center, hospital, barracks, supply depot and all the normal parts that would make up a major military base; however, these were primarily below ground. There were at least three VC units, and NVA groups such as the R-20 Battalion, V-25 Battalion and 7-3 Sapper Battalion on the island all controlled by the 44th Headquarters group for operations in Quang Nam Province. Units from the 2nd NVA Division also used Go Noi for a base of operations.

On May 4th, units from the 2nd Battalion 7th Marines (2/7) crossed into Go Noi and started the attack. They were up against fortified hamlets connected by trenches and tunnels. The enemy was dug in with bunkers and cave complexes similar to the defenses the Japanese used in WWII. It was noted after the fighting that some bunkers had survived with little damage even after a 2,000 lb. bomb hit 50 meters away. 2/7 was reinforced by Kilo Company 3/7 on May 7th and the combined companies continued the assault. By May 8th, the Marines had accounted for 88 enemies killed and 9 KIA and 57 WIA Marine casualties. On the 13th of May, India Company 3/27 was flown from the Liberty Bridge area into the Que Son Mountains to act as a blocking force for the other 3 Companies which were already engaged in the fight. A large sweep began, hoping to trap the 2nd NVA Division against the Chiem Son River as the Marine units moved back toward Liberty Bridge.

Liberty Bridge was the only way to cross the Ky Lam River on Highway 1 between Da Nang and An Hoa (pronounced "An Wa"). It was easily recognizable by a blown-up bridge that lay next to it. All the bridges that had originally spanned the rivers enclosing Go Noi had been blown and dropped into the rivers, leaving Liberty Bridge - a U.S. constructed bridge - as the best jumping off point onto the island.

On May 15, the Marine Command ordered all units to withdraw to Liberty Bridge, allowing the enemy to assume that the Marines had completed their operation. It was a ploy. On May 16, Marine Companies from 1/7, 2/7, and 3/7 reentered Go Noi, 2,500 meters northeast of Liberty Bridge, just after midnight. They ran into a hornets' nest. An NVA Battalion in Phu Dong (2) faced them and the heaviest fighting of the Operation ensued. The result was 130 enemy dead with Marine losses at 25 KIA & 38 WIA. When the fighting was over an NVA Installation with regimental headquarters, security and a major supply staging area was discovered. Even stronger resistance was encountered the next morning (May 17th). India Co. 3/27 was in the lead of the attack and they ran into an ambush with strong defenses in place. As a result, I Co. became trapped in a desperate situation. Attempts to relieve I Co. were made by Alpha Co. 1/7 and Golf Co. 2/7 but due to the very high thick grass and severe enemy resistance, the relief effort failed. A helicopter assault was arranged and later in the morning of the 17th, Kilo and Lima Companies of 3/27 were trucked across Liberty Bridge for the air lift east into Go Noi. Later that afternoon, the relief assault started with the companies landing in a "hot" LZ (Landing Zone) under mortar and long range weapons fire. K 3/27 finally linked up with I Co. and the enemy withdrew. The results of this action were 81 North Vietnamese dead and

Marine casualties at 39 KIA & 105 WIA. I Co. alone had suffered 15 KIA and 50 WIA.

The casualties of I Co. could have been worse if not for PFC Robert C. Burke. According to *U. S. Marines In Vietnam: The Defining Year 1968*, "Chapter 17":

> The casualties of the company may have been even higher if it had not been for the heroics of Private First Class Robert C. Burke. A machine gunner with the company, he quickly took his weapon "and launched a series of one-man assaults" against the enemy emplacements. Providing covering fire, he permitted other members of Company I to come up and remove the wounded from exposed positions. He continued to advance upon the enemy and to suppress enemy fire until he fell mortally wounded. He was awarded the Medal of Honor posthumously.

On May 18th, 3/7 was replaced by 3/5 and the 27th Marines assumed responsibility for the operation. I Co. and K Co. 3/27 were sent in to handle some snipers and ran into a formidable NVA unit, which brought the advance to a halt. Artillery and Air Support were called in but were limited by the closeness of the Marines to the enemy. K Co. suffered many casualties, many of whom were from the excessive heat of 110 degrees and above. Mike Co. 3/27 was then called in and together with I and K companies, continued the fighting until the NVA withdrew. 3/27 sustained 15 KIA, 35 WIA and 94 NBC (Non-Battle Casualties). The NBC casualties were mostly from the heat. Twenty enemy dead lay around the area.

After May 16, the 7th and 27th Marines fought a more or less conventional battle against well-fortified enemy positions. One tactic of the NVA was to let Marine units pass through a close-in ambush and then cut loose. This prevented the use of Air or Artillery Support and in response; the Marines took to preparing an area first with support units before sending in the ground troops.

3/5 experienced heavy fighting as well. At the end of May, the Battalion overran what appeared to be an NVA regimental command post, and the battle resulted in heavy casualties on both sides. By the end of May, the Marines reported that for all Marine units involved, there were 138 KIA, 686 WIA and 283 NBC.

Earlier in May, Operation Mameluke Thrust was initiated by units of the 7th Marines and 26th Marines in an effort to eliminate the rocket and mortar attacks that were occurring at the start of the Mini-Tet and to prevent the buildup of enemy forces west of Da Nang. The Song Lo Dong Valley (Happy Valley as we called it) southwest of Da Nang and the area north of the Arizona Territory were the main areas of concern. The Arizona Territory was a large area full of villages, rice paddies and VC just west of the An Hoa Base, and running north to the Song Vu Gia river. It was called that because of all the hostile Indians in the Arizona Territory in the United States during the Indian Wars of the late 1800's. Happy Valley, north-west of Go Noi Island, was a particularly difficult place to operate in because of the terrain. It was covered with a triple canopy consisting of dense kunai grass and elephant grass 8 to 10 feet high, thick vines, and larger trees like teak and mahogany 110 feet high. Fighting in Happy Valley was not happy at all.

Back on Go Noi at the beginning of June, 1/26 and 1/27 continued on with Operation Allen Brook, following orders to "search and clear" the Island. An attempt to clear the foliage using more than 31,000 gallons of fuel in 55-gallon drums rigged with igniters and dropped by air failed due to heavy dispersion of the fuel and a heavy rain. The Marines were then limited to "search and destroy" missions by units on the ground. After light contact on Go Noi, it was determined that 1/26 and 1/27 would end the operation and move west; however, on June 5th everything changed when Delta 1/26 and Bravo 1/26 were caught by entrenched North Vietnamese and came under heavy fire. These companies lost 7 KIA and 55 WIA while accounting for 30 enemy dead.

On June 6th, the 1st Engineer Battalion replaced 1/26 and was tasked with razing Go Noi Island, turning the whole Island into a parking lot. The 27th Marines would provide security. Everything was going well until June 15 when B and D Companies 1/27 were attacked by B-40 rockets and heavy automatic weapons fire. The Marines returned fire and finally drove the enemy from their positions. Then on June 19, B & D again faced a dug in force of Vietnamese. The fight raged for 9 hours before A & C Companies 1/27 came in and enveloped the enemy. Marine casualties were 6 KIA, 19 WIA, 12 NBC (from the heat) and enemy casualties of 17 NVA dead.

Later on June 23rd, 2/27 relieved 1/27 and the clearing of Go Noi continued. This was when my platoon entered the Go Noi and our fight began. I will get into that later. The clearing and fighting continued into July and on July 16th - 2/27 was replaced by 3/27. The 2/27 reports tell of a loss of 4 KIA and 147 WIA while on the island. Enemy losses were 144 killed. Clearing the island would continue until August 23rd when the enemy launched phase three of the Mini-Tet.

Meanwhile, Operation Mameluke Thrust also continued into June, and on June 14th, 3/5 moved out from An Hoa into the Arizona Territory leaving Kilo Company to guard the An Hoa artillery firebase. Soon after entering the Arizona, I Company came under heavy fire killing the Company Commander, a platoon sergeant and the Company Gunnery Sergeant while seriously wounding the Company Executive Officer, First Lieutenant Joseph T. Campbell. Lt. Cambell, even though severely wounded, directed the movements of his company and the evacuation of the wounded, refusing evacuation until all his men were flown out. Before he could be evacuated, he died of his wounds. For his action, he received the Navy Cross, posthumously.

The next day, K 3/26 received mortar fire while providing security for a convoy. Corporal David M. Sivak's actions on that day are notable and are given here in recognition of his fighting spirit, and an example of the fighting spirit of the Marines involved in Operation Allen Brook and Operation Mameluke Thrust.

As stated in *U. S. Marines in Vietnam: The Defining Year 1968,* by Jack Shulimson the following exploits are described in Chapter 17:

> Corporal David M. Sivak during the mortar attack volunteered to recover a machine gun abandoned during the initial contact. He crept uphill toward the weapon until a North Vietnamese soldier in a nearby fighting hole spotted him and began throwing hand grenades. Although wounded in the chest by a fragment, Sivak emptied 12 full magazines from his M16 at his tormentor.
>
> Sivak finally reached the machine gun and continued advancing into the enemy position. The NVA soldier suddenly stuck his head out from a hidden tunnel. Deciding against running toward his comrades for fear of being shot in the back, Corporal Sivak threw the machine gun at the North Vietnamese, who then ducked back into the tunnel.
>
> The enemy soldier looked out from the tunnel a second time and Sivak attacked with his bare hands. The Communist fired his rifle, creasing Sivak's leg, and Sivak knocked the weapon from the man's hands. As the two grappled in the confines of the hole, the North Vietnamese bit the Marine savagely on the arm. Angered, Sivak bit him back, then drew his Kabar (the Marine Corps issue fighting knife) and stabbed his opponent. The enemy soldier produced his

own knife and stabbed Sivak in the back, but it was too late. The Marine had gained the upper hand. Sivak continued stabbing until he realized that the man had died.

Corporal Sivak remained in the hole until his comrades overran the hill. From captured documents, the Marines learned that the dead man was part of a nine-man North Vietnamese mortar forward observer team. Only when Sivak lost consciousness did his fellow Marines realize that he was wounded.

Corporal Sivak's adventure was not yet over. The story of his experience at the 1st Hospital Company is best told in his own words, recorded only three weeks after the incident:

"I went to 1st Hospital and the doctor started checking me out for malaria and I told him that wasn't wrong and he said, "What's wrong?" .... I said, "Well, I got stabbed in the back, I got bit in the arm, I got shrapnel in the chest, and I got shot in the leg." He couldn't believe it until he looked at it. He thought it was kinda funny. I wasn't in a mood to laugh at it. They thought I might have to get rabies shots from where I got bit in the arm, but I made out. All I had to do was get a tetanus shot. I was scared because rabies shots, you get 16 of them, they said, in the stomach. I got a weak stomach."

Corporal Sivak's platoon sergeant, reflecting on Sivak's harrowing experience, said only, "I think the bite was worser than the stab."

I guess the moral of that story is:

"Don't Bite a Marine, He Will Bite Back."

They don't call us Devil Dogs for nothing. The 5th Marines, 7th Marines and 26th Marines would continue Operation Mameluke Thrust until the latter part of August when the North Vietnamese 3rd Offensive was initiated.

As stated before, 2/27 entered Go Noi Island for Operation Allen Brook on June 23rd. We loaded up on Sea Knight helicopters and once we landed on Go Noi, a perimeter was established and the Company CP (Command Post) was set up. I was given a sector of the perimeter to cover and I set the machine guns up to provide coverage of likely avenues of approach. As a reinforced company, we had three 60mm mortars, plenty of LAW's, M-79 grenade launchers, and of course, six M-60 machine guns. The CP also sported the Battalion Command Group, Engineers and Forward Observers for fire support as well as a sniper team. In addition, we had an M-48A3

Patton Tank which carried the M-41 90mm cannon. (90mm equals about 3.5 inches)

The records indicate the following:

Company F On or about 220700 June 68 embark one Sqd on one truck in the Bn CP to be transported to the Ha Dong bridge, where they will provide security for that installation until relieved by units of 1/27

Foxtrot Company will stage on the East side of LZ 412 at 0700 and standby to be helilifted to Go Noi Island on 23 June 1968.

Uniform. Jungle utilities, light marching pack, 3 canteens per man, cartridge belt, jungle kits, entrenching tools, and normal arms and helmets. Two extra pair socks; two gas masks per Sqd.

Leaving the base in Sea Knight helicopters was an experience in itself. We knew that we would probably be landing in a hot LZ, and that we would probably take enemy fire on the helicopter as we approached the landing zone. The Sea Knight was loud and noisy and filled with odors from sweating bodies, oil leaks, gas, exhaust fumes, and urine, as some of the new guys lost control of their bladders. Some of the men were resigned to their fate and others were scared to death.

As we landed in an area that had already been prepped with Artillery and Air Strikes, the dreaded incoming never happened. We formed a wide perimeter to further secure the landing zone. The choppers came in like clockwork, disgorging their Marines and taking off, all in a matter of minutes. Soon, the whole Company was in place, Marines filling in the gaps that existed in the lines from the initial landing. Once the LZ was secured, the Battalion Command Group and other support units along with a tank, arrived to complete the temporary base.

After getting set in, the tank spotted 8 VC and called in mortars. The Marine reports states:

232030H F-2 Tiger at 978532 saw 8 vc at 978531. Fired 3 M-79 rds. Called in 60mm mortar fire mission on target.

Translated:

Reported on June 23rd at 8:30 p.m. local time (the H indicates local time), a tank with Fox Company 2nd Platoon at map coordinates 978532 saw eight

VC at map coordinates 978531. Three M-79 rounds were fired and 60mm mortars were fired on the target. ("Tiger" was the Marine code name for tank.)

As mentioned before, the military maps from the web site www.rjsmith.com are very useful to those interested in tracking our movement in Vietnam. The Go Noi was in an area marked by north-south grid lines 950 to zero to 048, and east-west grid lines 520 to 565. Note that the last number in the set of three designates 100-meter increments. This mapping system allowed us the ability to pinpoint a location within 100 meters and an additional number could be added for 10-meter increments. All of this was very important, especially on large Operations like Go Noi, where thousands of Marines were fighting thousands of the enemy.

Later that night we received mortar fire as reported:

232245 F co at 979533 rec'd 9 rds 60mm mortar fire in cp area from coord 973536. Fired 15 60mm mortar rds on target. Observed 2 secondary explosions. Sustained 5 USMC & 1 KCS minor wia's.

The report was then corrected:

Bn J # 9 232245H – line G should read 8 USMC (All Minor) (7 USMC and 1 Kit Carson)

Translated with corrections:

Reported on June 23rd at 10:45 p.m. at map coordinates 979533, Fox Company received nine rounds of 60mm mortar fire in the Command Post area. Rounds were fired from map coordinates 973536. Marines fired fifteen 60mm mortar rounds on the target. Two secondary explosions were seen. Sustained 8 USMC casualties (All Minor) (7 USMC and 1 Kit Carson Scout).

The Kit Carson Scouts (KCS) were a group of former Viet Cong used as intelligence scouts.

It was no fun eating dirt as the mortars rained in. It was a good thing we always dug fighting holes. The good part was that we weren't facing artillery fire. Hats off to those brave souls that had to suffer under enemy artillery fire. We had been lucky so far, with very few mortar attacks, mainly due to Lt. Jones's style of platoon maneuvers. As a result, when we got hit on the night of the 23rd by nine rounds, it got our attention right away and confirmed that we would be up against a formidable force.

Further reports state:

> On 24 June 1968, Companies E and H 2/27 conducted recon patrols and displaced to vic map coordinates BT007532 where they established a joint combat base and conducted normal night time security and combat/ambush patrolling. The Command Group and Companies F and G 2/27 along with the First Engineer Clearing Team, displaced to vic map coordinates AT974528 to conduct clearing operations. While at this site the concept and techniques of total destruction of all enemy installations and favorable terrain was perfected.

And the daily reports detail the actions:

241715 F-2 at coord 979529 rec'd 25 rds auto fire from two VC at 978527. Called in Arty which fired 20 rds. Contacted Cow Poke - air strike – 1,000 20mm rds. Neg results.

Translated, the report reads:

Reported on June 24th at 5:15 p.m., Fox Company 2nd Platoon at map coordinates 979529, received 25 rounds of automatic fire from two VC at map location 978527. Artillery was called in and twenty rounds were fired. Cowpoke was contacted and it fired one thousand 20mm rounds. No positive results were seen.

Cowpoke was the code name for an Air Observer aircraft in communications with a ground unit. It was a Bronco/OV 10A twin boom, propeller driven aircraft that could maneuver where the jets couldn't because of their speed. Cowpoke could drop flares and smoke bombs for spotting the enemy. It had four M-60 machine guns in the twin booms. Early versions carried a 20mm cannon in the booms and it was this prototype that was used at Go Noi. It could also carry air-to-surface rockets, air-to-air missiles and conventional bombs. The slow flying (top speed 281 mph) Cowpoke was always subject to small arms fire and the men who flew them were the brave beyond brave. Many times, caught in a difficult situation, we would look up and there would be Cowpoke tearing things up and bringing in A-4 Phantom airstrikes upon the heads of the enemy.

The reports continue:

On 25 June Companies F and G along with the engineers conducted a sweep from the CP to vic map coordinates AT970540. One platoon of F Co conducted a long range combat patrol from the CP to vic map coordinates AT995530 and back. Companies E and H conduct extensive day and night combat/ambush patrolling.

Also on the 25th:

250700 F-2 received 15 rds auto fire from right flank. Called fire mission – Battery 1. Air strike SD – 2.

Translated:

Reported on June 25th at 7:00 a.m., Fox Company 2nd Platoon received fifteen rounds of automatic fire from their right side. Two fire missions were called in, one was Artillery and the other was Air Support.

250710 F-2 exploded SFO sic. Sustained 2 WIA. Medevac requested – medevac completed at 250840H.

Translated:

Reported on June 25th at 7:10 a.m., Fox Company 2nd Platoon exploded a Surprise Firing Device (SFD). Two Marines were wounded. A medevac was requested and completed by 8:40 a.m.

250845 F 2/27 Plt Swp ALLEN BROOK; 250710H, 978530; While on Plt swp two Marines det unk type SFD; Med evac called & comp 250810H; 2 WIA (1 emer, 1 pri)

Translated:

Reported on June 25th at 8:45 a.m., Fox Company, 2/27 on a Platoon sweep for Operation Allen Brook at 7:10 a.m., map coordinates 978530, had two Marines detonate an unknown Surprise Firing Device. Two Marines were medevaced at 8:10 a.m., one emergency and one priority. (This was another report for the same incident which occurred at 7:10 a.m., elaborating on the incident and giving the medevac conditions for the two Marines that were wounded.)

250945H F 2/27 Plt swp ALLEN BROOK; 250845H, 978530; Med evac chopper rec'd sniper fire in LZ; Plt Ret'd M-79 fire, huey fired 15 rockets, plt moving toward sniper poss.

Translated:

Reported on June 25th at 9:45 a.m., Fox Company, 2/27 on a Platoon sweep forOperation Allen Brook at 8:45 a.m., map coordinates 978530, medevac chopper received sniper fire in the landing zone. The Platoon returned fire, firing the M-79 Grenade Launcher. A Huey helicopter fired 15 rockets toward the sniper as the Platoon moved toward the sniper's position. (This is more information about the incident that started at 7:10 a.m., detailing further contact with the enemy.)

A lot happened that day. Our platoon had been sent out alone on a long-range patrol and VC Charlie had us pegged. It was nerve wracking. Naturally, the Company Commander picked 2nd Platoon again for this dangerous mission. We had already proved ourselves in the Duc Ky area, constantly patrolling and maneuvering as a single platoon. The other platoons got their share of the pie as well. No one went unscathed in Go Noi, be it physical wounds or the constant nerve wracking patrols in heavily infested enemy territory.

Further reports continue the story:

260020H F 2/27 CP Allen Brook, 251830H, 976531/972533, 982538, Co F Sqd Ptl vic 976531 obs 5 En in green uniform vic 972533, took En under fire w/SA & M-79 called air strike on position. Following air strike, began to swp through area and rec AW fire fm several wpns vic 982538. Adjusted 81mm mortars I arty F/M. on suspected en positions. Then swp area w/neg res.

Translated:

Reported on June 26th at 00:20 a.m., Fox Company 2/27 on Operation Allen Brook, June 25th at 6:30 p.m., was at map coordinates 976531 and 982538. A squad patrol from F Company in the vicinity of map coordinates 976531 observed five enemies in green uniforms in the vicinity of map coordinates 972533. The squad took the enemy under fire with small arms and M-79 Grenade Launchers. Air strikes were called on the enemy position. Following the air strike, the squad began to sweep through the area and received automatic weapons fire from several weapons in the vicinity of map coordinates 982538. The squad called in 81mm mortars and one artillery fire mission on the suspected enemy positions. The squad then swept the area with negative results.

260900 F-2 at coord 975528 found 1 60mm booby trap with trip wire and 1 500 lb bomb. Also found 2 Chi-Com grenades on belt with first aid pouch. Blew 60mm & grenade with M-26 hand grenades. Engineers blew 500 lb bomb.

Translated:

Reported on June 26 at 9:00 a.m., Fox Company 2nd Platoon at map coordinates 975528 found one 60mm booby trap with a trip wire and one 500 lb bomb. Also found two Chi-Com grenades on a belt with a first aid pouch.

The Platoon blew the 60mm booby trap and the Chi-Com grenades with M-26 hand grenades. The engineers blew the 500 lb bomb.

A report of the Killer Teams in action:

> Approximately 1830 on 26 June a killer team from Company F vic 978534 spotted 2 VC walking along a treeline. The team opened fire and called 60mm and 81mm mortar fire. A sweep of the treeline revealed one wounded VC. He was returned to the CP but died before he could be evacuated.

Another report states:

262105 F 2/27 Sqd Cbt Ptl Allen Brook; 261830H; 978534/975533; Spotted 2 VC walking along treeline, 1 wearing shorts & kakie *sic* shirt, the other wearing black PH, Fired SA & M-79, called 81 & 60mm F/M. AO came on station and directed arty. Searched area found 1 VC KIA.

Translated:

Reported on June 26th at 9:05 p.m., a squad combat patrol from Fox Company 2/27 on Operation Allen Brook at 6:30 p.m. and map coordinates 978534 and 975533 spotted two VC walking along a tree line. One VC was wearing shorts and a khaki shirt and the other was wearing black pajamas. The patrol fired small arms and M-79 rounds at the enemy and called in 81mm mortar and 60mm mortar fire missions. The Arial Observer came online and directed the artillery mission. The patrol searched the area and found one VC KIA.

Also on the 26th:

> On 26 June Companies E and F (-) conducted extensive day and night combat/ambush patrolling. One platoon from Company F conducted a recon patrol to vic AT984535.

The platoon that did the recon patrol was likely to be 2nd Platoon. Our Platoon was often used for difficult tasks. Captain Collins, the Fox Company Command Officer, had great faith and confidence in Lt. Jones and 2nd Platoon and repeatedly called on us to lead the way. Recon patrols were nothing new to 2nd Platoon.

On June 26, I wrote to my family:

Dear Folks,

Well, here I am in Viet Nam's [hellhole], and this operation, well you wouldn't believe me if I told you. What we are doing is providing security for the Engineers while they level all the villages in this area, and the area is about 14 square miles in area. This is hard enough with all kinds of NVA running around [mortaring] us at night and sniping and trying to trap us during the day. But the really hard part is the heat. It gets at least 100 every day, and there is absolutely no shade. Practically all the trees and houses anything that would provide shelter is either blown up or dozed under. This place looks so bad that not even ghosts would want to live here. But so far we've been lucky, we have only had about 6 casualties in 3 days, and [surprisingly] enough no heat casualties yet. But if they keep us going the way we are now, well there may not be many left in the [platoon]. But that's neither here nor there. I have no idea how long this [operation] is going to last, so you will just have to bear with me as far as mail goes.

Oh, I am down to 5 men in my squad now, counting myself. That makes 2 men in a gun team, a gunner and assistant gunner, and I have to be with both guns as much as possible, so I'm really on the go. Oh, and maybe, just maybe, come the 1st of July I might make Corporal. Right now my Plt. Commander, Lt. Jones, relies a lot on me, and has put me up for [meritorious] promotion, so wish me luck.

Oh, one more thing about this operation you might be interested in. We are getting resupplied every day by helicopter, [that's] how the mail comes in (even though I haven't gotten any yet) and goes out. We get 2 meals a day and fresh water every day, so things could be worse. Those helicopters are really life savers in more ways than one. I could go on and on about this operation, but most of it isn't pleasant and can't be put in a nice way so let's just forget it.

Say mom, do me a favor will you. Find out from Cathy what the story is on Mary Ann. I had been writing her as much as possible before I came on this operation, but still, it's been well over a month since I've heard from her. … so far I've gotten the impression that maybe she would like to maybe call things off, since she hasn't written. …

Well, take care of yourself, write soon, and don't worry about me, I'll be all right. Oh, say some prayers for a couple of my men will you, [they're] going to need 'em.

Hey, [someone] just reminded me, HAPPY 4TH of July. I bet I've got a lot more [fireworks] around here than you all do, like [napalm] bombs,

> *250 & 500 lb bombs, 105 and 155 illumination and of course tracer bullets. The only thing is [around] here we have 4th of July every day and night. Give everyone my love, and until next time, with all my love.*
> *Your Son, Chuck*

I had to talk about fireworks to blot out the reality. Nothing about this operation was pleasant. The heat was almost unbearable. There are few places, if any, in the continental United States that have the heat and humidity that we experienced on Go Noi. Add to that the suffocating vegetation that held the heat and humidity like a sauna bath. Day and night, it just didn't let up. The night was worse when you were in your fighting hole, covered with mosquito repellant and dirt and grime, and grease paint, sweating and sweating and sweating with no relief. The constant tension added to the sweat parade and as a result, your clothes were drenched and chaffed against your skin at every move. Thirst was a constant haunt, hanging over you like a torment straight out of hell. You couldn't dare waste good water to try and cool off a little, and you certainly didn't want to use local water that was poisoned by dead creatures. The rivers were undrinkable, but given the chance, you could wash off and get some relief there if you were brave enough to bare it all with the VC and Mister Charles just waiting to kill you.

I remember the patrols through the elephant grass and boy, was that scary. You couldn't see or hear a thing. The grass was as thick as fleas on a dog's hind leg. The constant swish of the grass against your legs as you and your patrol walked along prevented you from hearing those telltale sounds of an ambush ahead, like the loading of a rifle or the safety being moved and the little clinks of metal against metal. Things I had learned to pick up on were now out of reach. These patrols were like walking in a Halloween corn maze - only there were no trails to follow. Evil beings could appear at every turn, and boy, could they hurt you. Trying to follow landmarks was even harder. There was a map and a compass and a line on a map that you were to follow. Soldiers of all types were everywhere and you could be killed by your own men just as well as by the enemy. The only solution was to proceed in small increments, following azimuth readings on your compass and trying to keep long-range terrain features in sight, which was even more difficult given the flat terrain and the tall elephant grass. Slow going, but better slow than dead. I found myself transferring any fear to a resignation of my circumstances and a real emotional deadness that would leave me devoid of emotions for a long time. We didn't carry our packs on patrol, just weapons, ammo, grenades and two or three canteens of water along with the must-have toilet paper. The jungle utilities we wore had large pockets on the sides and we crammed them full of the little things we needed. My hips were constantly sore from the weight of my cartridge belt loaded down with two canteens of water, Ka-Bar knife, Colt .45 automatic and ammo. In addition, the heavy flak jacket, with an additional canteen and bayonet attached, increased the misery. Along with the weight was the sweat, which was also constant and permeated every inch of clothing. My jungle utilities rotted on my body from the constant sweat. I specifically remember how the upper part of my trousers would be soaked through from the sweat of my thighs. I was lucky that I carried an M-16 at this time. My gunners suffered even more under the added weight of the 23 lb. machine gun and at least 200 rounds of ammo. The riflemen were loaded too. We carried our rifle ammo in bandoleers draped over our neck and across our shoulders. These bandoleers were loaded with seven M-16 magazines carrying twenty rounds each. And I carried at least three of these bandoleers fully loaded. In addition, the riflemen carried extra machine gun ammo and LAW's and sticks of C-4 for the Engineers to use. There was just no way around it. When they said to "saddle up," they weren't kidding. As I've said before, we wore the machine gun ammo in the cardboard boxes and cloth bandoleers that they came in. That kept the ammo clean and you could tie the straps of the bandoleers together and drape it around your back, which made it easier to carry. Some units in Vietnam did carry the machinegun ammo exposed, crossed over the chest, but that wasn't too smart, since X marked the spot, and brass is shiny. However, one thing everyone learned quickly was that if you did carry your machine gun ammo that way, be sure that the pointy end of the bullets didn't point toward your neck. It's a shame that the sculptor of the Three Soldiers Statue in Washington DC didn't learn this lesson before he did his work. Oh, well, you had to have been there to know all these things, I guess.

Now try to carry all this stuff (you really needed it too if you got in a fight) and be quiet walking through the elephant grass. I bet we sounded like a herd of elephants. No matter how much we tried to cut down on the clink clank of our gear rubbing against each other, or the water sloshing around in our canteens, the noise of our progress through this awful area was deafening in the quiet of this sea of grass. All we could hope for was that when we got hit, not if, that we'd be spared those first rounds and could put out overwhelming firepower, which would kill the enemy and chase away those who survived. It was our training and our dedication to each other, to the platoon and to a larger extent to the Corps, that kept us going, day in and day out, night in and night out; but mostly, it was just us and our buddies watching each others back. You had to have been there to get the whole effect, but hopefully by now, you get the picture. I have repeated myself several times about the gear we carried, but that is just a reminder of what we put up with each and every day.

In my letter from the 26th, I mentioned that I was down to two two-man gun teams. I don't remember who it was that was gone, or why, but asking my mom to pray for them indicates that they were probably wounded. I know that there were six of us going into Go Noi, my core squad. I don't remember anyone getting wounded in the mortar attack we received on the 23rd and as I reported, we hadn't had any heat casualties yet. My best guess is that one of my men got sick and had to stay at the Company CP for a while or maybe even wind up being medevaced on one of the supply helicopters. Dysentery was common, and if it got severe enough it could put you out of action. There were any number of other diseases that could also put you out for a while. One good thing came of all this - my squad received two riflemen as ammo humpers, which were sorely needed. Not a pleasant task for them, since the machine gun team always attracted more fire than other positions. It was these two men who were gone from my squad by the 26th.

The fight continued. The reports state:

272140 F at 992533 rec'd sm/a rds, auto fire & 10 M-79 rds from est sqd size enemy from coord 984529. Ret'd sm/a, 60mm, 81mm & arty. Enemy broke contact.

Translated:

Reported at 9:40 p.m. on the 27th of June, F Company, at map coordinates 992533, received small arms fire, automatic fire and ten rounds from an M-79 from an estimated squad sized enemy force at map coordinates 984529. The Company returned fire with small arms, 60mm and 81mm mortars, and artillery. The enemy broke contact.

Continuing the reports:

272215H F 2/27 plt cbt ptl ALLEN BROOK; 272215H; ptl fired on by M-79 fm treeline; Ret'd SA, req med evac emer 3 USMC emer.

Translated:

Reported on June 27th at 10:15 p.m., a Platoon from Fox Company 2/27 on a platoon combat patrol in Operation Allen Brook, at 10:15 p.m., was fired on by an M-79 from a tree line. The patrol returned small arms fire and called in an emergency medevac for three wounded Marines.

272245H F 2/27 CP Allen Brook; 272140H; 992533/984529; Rec'd sqd size probe, SA, AW & 10 M-79 rds; Ret'd M-79, SA, 60mm, 81mm & arty F/M. En broke contact. Div DTG 272255H

Translated:

Reported at 10:45 p.m. on June 27th, the Fox Company 2nd Platoon Command Post on Operation Allen Brook, at 9:40 p.m. on June 27th, received a squad sized probe from the vicinity of map coordinates 992533/984529. The probe was made by small arms, automatic weapons and 10 M-79 rounds. The Command Post returned fire with M-79 and small arms, as well as 60mm and 81mm mortars. An artillery fire mission was also called in. The enemy broke contact. Division report Day Time Group 272255H.

Also on June 27th:

> On 27 June, Companies E, F, and G, the engineers and the command group displaced to vic AT 993532 and commenced the destruction of the largest forested area on the island. 18 days were required to completely level the area. Company H conducted a combat sweep to vic BT006540 and established a combat base.

By now, you may have noticed the reported enemy use of our M-79 (Blooper) in the reports. I am sure that those reports are true, since the enemy scoured the countryside looking for lost munitions that could be used against us. There may even have been some supply of M-79's through other sources. However, I think that at times, the incoming explosive rounds were actually from rifle grenade launchers instead of an M-79. There were many rifles found among the VC from previous wars, including WWII. M-1 and M-1 carbine rifles were plentiful. The M-1 had an attachment whereby a hand grenade could be fired in an arc much like a mortar round. This was the same principle employed in the use of the M-79, therefore, it was easier to just call all incoming explosive rounds that were not mortars or artillery, as M-79 rounds.

Be it M-79 or M-1 grenade launcher, our own weapons were often used against us. The ARVN army also had access to our weapons, carrying the M-16 and the M-79 as well. We never trusted the ARVN's, as they had proved to be "less enthusiastic" about conducting the war than was expected, and we also believed that there were VC imbedded in the ARVN forces. Even the Kit Carson Scouts were suspect.

On the 28th reports state the following:

> On 28 June, Company F conducted a combat sweep to vic AT997544 and established a combat base.

Also from a different report:

> Foxtrot Company conduct a combat sweep from present position to vic coord BT007541. Seize village at that location by 281430H and establish a combat base. Conduct extensive daylight and night combat ambush activities in AO.

Translated:

Foxtrot Company to conduct a combat sweep from their present position to the vicinity of map coordinates BT007541. Seize the village at that location by 2:30 p.m. on June 28th and establish a combat base there. Conduct extensive daylight and night combat ambush activities in the Area of Operations.

A letter on June 28 had more to say about Go Noi:

> *Dear Dad,*
>
> *Well, here I am and there you are. I'm sitting here in my birthday suit in about 110 degree heat under a lean to I managed to throw up against the sun. There is a slight breeze blowing, but I'm still sweating like hell. We are at a river right now, and had our first bath in a week, after we secured the village, which was no minor affair. These North Vietnamese Army troops are pretty smart. We hit them with artillery and air strikes, but they don't give away their position. Then when we start across an open area they hit us hard with automatic fire. You have to hit the deck and roll about 3 times before you fire back. If you don't [they] concentrate fire on you and you're a dead duck. I've lost 2 men that way. That puts me with only 5 men in my squad counting myself, and for a machine gun squad that's not near enough. … If you think you know how war is, you should be a machine-gunner for a day, which reminds me, if I lose another man I'm going to have to hump the gun again, oh boy, you know what that means.*
>
> *Hey, guess what, I get to go on R&R on the 21st of July if I make it till then. I'm going to [Penang]. It's in Malaysia some place. It's a new R&R center, so it should be real nice. Not as commercialized and exploited as the old R&R centers like Hong [Kong] and [Tokyo]. I'll let you*

know how it is, and will try to get a few things for you all. But mainly I'm just going to relax and not duck every time I hear a crack or crunch of the bushes. Boy, it sure will be nice to get back to the States.

I'm still a little worried about Mary Ann, but not as much anymore. I have too many things to worry about over here. ...

Well, I guess I better sign off and get dressed before old "Charlie" decides to hit us. Tonight ought to really be a dilly. We are out in front of the Engineers about 2000 meters all by ourselves, so anything can go tonight. Take it easy and write soon.

With all my love, Your Son, Chuck

It is strange to me that some things that I write about in my letters are missing from the Marine Corps records. I know that I just wrote what happened and I also know that all that happened didn't get into the records. This was probably due to the magnitude of the war and this operation in particular. I have found evidence of men who were listed as KIA on the Wall on a certain date, only to find out that they were only wounded on that date and died months later in a hospital in Japan. I lost two men, probably in a fire fight that wasn't listed in the reports I have access to. These were the two ammo humpers that were recently assigned to my squad and I didn't have the time to adequately train them in the tactics of a machine gun team. My core squad was still intact, with one man out for reasons unknown. I was just one bullet or mortar or heat stroke away from having to carry the machine gun again, and like I told my dad;

"You know what that means."

To support my findings, Tom Montie, a rifleman from 3rd Squad, 2nd Platoon, Fox Company, one of our good buddies, was wounded at 07:00 a.m. on June 28 by a booby-trapped M-26 grenade while on patrol. This information was given by Tom Montie from the medical tag that he wore when he was medevaced to the Battalion Aid Station (BAS). There are no reports in the records that I have access to that record that event. I'm sure it is recorded somewhere in the maze of military documents that were kept from the Vietnam War. It happened, of that I am sure.

Again, the reports tell the story:

292020H F Co Allen Brook, 290730H, 017546/017548, Viet Civ reported VC at above coord. Ptl linked up w/F-3A sqd cbt ptl checked area.

Translated:

Reported on June 29th at 8:20 a.m., F Company on Operation Allen Brook, at 7:30 a.m. on June 29th, received a report from a Vietnamese Civilian that some VC were located between map coordinates 017546 and 017548. The patrol linked up with the F-3A patrol. A squad combat patrol checked the area.

Still on the 29, the reports state:

292206H F Co Allen Brook, 290830H, 006544, Marine spranged [*sic*] ankle, evac on resupply helo, 1 NBC

Translated:

Reported on June 29th at 10:06 p.m., F Company on Operation Allen Brook, at 8:30 a.m., June 29th, at map coordinates 006544, a Marine sprained his ankle. He was medevaced by helicopter on the resupply mission for that day. One Non-Battle Casualty.

The reports for June 30th state:

Company F swept to vic BT018536 from where a blocking force was set in from BT019533 to BT020530 to BT017528.

301930 Co F at 006544 found 9 82mm rds, 3 B40 rockets, 2 B40 boosters, 500 30 cal rds, 600 7.62mm rds, one 57 recoilless rd, 3 fin assm for B40 rockets. Sent to Bn S-2.

Translated:

Reported at 7:30 p.m., on June 30th, Company F at map coordinates 006544, found nine 82mm rounds, three B-40 rockets, two B-40 rockets boosters, five hundred rounds of .30 cal ammunition, six hundred rounds of 7.62mm ammunition, one 57 recoilless round and three fin assemblies for the B-40 rockets. All munitions were sent to the Battalion Intelligence S-2 section.

From the time in March when my squad leader was killed until this point, four and a half months later, I see where I had become reckless and almost tempting fate to shoot me or wound me in some way so I could get out of this hell. I even got to smoking when it clearly wasn't prudent to do so. This often brought on an attack, but I never put two and two together to understand that. I would think, "Wow, just when I wanted a smoke. What a strange thing." I was changing and not for the good. I did get real good at my job, patrolling, tracking and killing, but I lost perspective and all care for life, including my own. Death was all around me and I was death to those who opposed me. What an awful way to live, if live is what you could call it. Even the loss of my men didn't really faze me when they came and went so often and I only got to know them for a short time. As long as my core squad, the men who were with me at the bridge where my squad leader got tortured and killed, were okay, then I was okay enough. Or so I felt at the time. My anger at the Corps had subsided as well. I had finally understood that anger would get me nowhere, so I buried it.

By the end of June, the casualty count from Go Noi Island for the 27th and 7th Marines was 159 KIA, 2 USN KIA, 770 WIA and 1 USN WIA, 142 USMC WIA (minor), 329 USMC NBC and an enemy count of 277 killed and 583 wounded.

The casualty count for 2nd Battalion, 27th Marines at the end of June was:

KIA 3 WIA 79 for a running total after 4.5 Months of KIA 32 WIA 388 MIA 2

Chapter 9

In the predawn light I awoke instantly, as if I had never even been asleep. A few precious hours of sleep was all we ever got, if we got that much. Our nerves were on edge 24/7, and not even sleep would truly give us any relaxation. Our anger at the Corps was redirected toward the enemy. We could only accept our circumstances and do the best with what we had. Getting two C-ration meals a day and some drinkable water had become something to be happy about, no griping there, unless the two meals happened to be "ham and mothers (lima beans) and even then, we'd just stoically eat our meals to appease our growling empty stomachs.

The routine was to get up, shave if possible – to shave we had to either dry shave or use regular body soap - heat a can of chow over a C-ration stove, which was made by cutting slits in the bottom of an empty C-ration can, popping in a chunk of C-4 to heat the meal, light it with my Zippo cigarette lighter, and make a canteen cup of instant coffee. Then check my gear, clean my weapon and standby for orders. We had learned the hard way about keeping our weapons cleaned and oiled in this unbelievably hot, wet, humid environment. Day in and day out, this was our life since leaving the Ha Dong Bridge in March, broken only by brief sojourns in the Battalion Area.

The Battalion report for the start of July is as follows:

> The primary effort of the entire Battalion was directed towards Operation Allen Brook for the first half of the month. (For details of all aspects of the operation, see Supporting Documents – Combat After Action Report) The effectiveness of a tactical innovation of significant consequence was highlighted by the killing of 13 VC by Killer Teams in a single day, (1 July). A team consisting of an artillery forward observer, scout/snipers and fire team size security, was sent to an area of likely enemy movement and left there for an entire day. It is felt the success of this technique far exceeded

the kills made by keeping the enemy off balance and detecting his movement before he was able to position his forces for an attack.

And:

Counter Sniper/Harassing Fires. Enemy contacts were harassing in nature and established a pattern. The Battalion Command Post and base of operations was fired upon with regularity, usually in the evening. Small squad sized units were employed in concealed positions about 500 meters out from the perimeter. When the enemy moved into fire on the Battalion position the concealed (Killer) teams would attack from the rear while the perimeter held fire. This Killer Team technique inflicted numerous casualties on the enemy and almost completely eliminated harassing attacks on the Battalion Base of Operations.

Scout Observer/Arty FO/sniper Teams. Small teams consisting of an Arty FO Forward Observer and/or scout observer, a sniper team and a fire team for security were used extensively to bring long range small arms and artillery fire to bear on enemy units moving out of range of infantry units. These teams were especially effective in engaging enemy units outside the AO or across natural barriers. These teams accounted for 23 kills.

It was July 1st, and I had a little time before we went out again, so I wrote to my younger brother Chris:

Dear Chris,

Well, I got your letter and present (the funny papers) Saturday, but it was too late to read them when I got them, so guess what, yesterday Sunday afternoon, I fixed myself a cup of C-Ration coffee and sat in my wet fox hole and read the Sunday funnies. Yep, needless to say I enjoyed that more than anything I've done over here so far. I just can't tell you how much it meant to me, especially coming from you. Thanks so much.

Hey, I'm glad to see you on the ball. That job hauling hay will do a lot to build you up, and that money will always come in handy. Just don't blow it foolishly, especially since you know how hard it is to make at times. Look at me, I work 24 hrs. a day 7 days a week and make 26 cents an hour. How's that for getting money the hard way. …

This is the 9th day for us on this operation, and believe you me I'm sure looking forward to the end whenever that may be. It rains almost every day now, and about the only way to keep halfway dry is to [make] a [lean-to] and hope like hell that the wind doesn't change, which it usually does. I've been wet and muddy now for 9 days, so you can imagine how I smell, plus the fact that I haven't shaved, and cut and scratched all over and sweat like a [demon] when the sun is out. So in conclusion, now maybe you can see how much the funny papers meant to me. I sure hope the Phantom lives. He didn't get a Med-Evac did he, ha, ha. …

With all my love, Chuck

Also on July 1st, I wrote:

Dear Mom,

Well, you think you got problems. 2 days ago we stopped and set in in a Company sized perimeter. I was set up with one of my machine guns in the north-east corner of the perimeter in a ditch about 3 feet deep and 2 feet wide. I built a lean-to to keep out the sun and lay down to rest a bit. It wasn't but about an hour later when it started to rain like hell, and it kept raining hard for about 2 hours. So what you may ask, I had a shelter and couldn't get too wet! But what I didn't tell you was that within 15 minutes that ditch had a good foot of water in it, and if you got out of the ditch you got soaked anyway, so there I was in about 6 inches of mud and a foot of water hoping that Charlie wouldn't hit us, because my rifle had fallen in the mud and the barrel was clogged plus the fact that my ammo was all dirty and wet and, the only position you could get in and stay half way dry was a semi-squat and my legs got sore as a bone, and you say. "So You Think You've Got Problems?" And something like this happens almost every day out here! But at least I don't have a 'living bra' and don't know what to feed it. Thanks so much for the card, it gave me a good laugh, which I sure needed yesterday when I got your postcard. …

Oh, I [finally] got the letter from Mary Ann. I never figured she was so serious about Mike. Well, that's life I guess. I just wish I was home so I could really make a play. But maybe everything is better in the long run. …

Well, I've got to go on patrol tonight, the first one we've run since this operation began for us, so it ought to be fun, oh yea! Take care, and be good as you always are and don't worry about me, [I'm] just fine. A little older maybe but that's all.

With all my love, Chuck

Yep, it was an "official" Dear John letter from my girlfriend, or in my case, Dear Chuck. However, not her fault, I had just made too much of a brief encounter. And who would they pick on that day to run the first patrol in "Indian Country?" Yep little old me. I sure got tired of being "wanted" all the time. A "little older?" More like a *lot* older, in body, mind and spirit. Up until this time, we had operated mostly as a company or as a platoon, with very few squad patrols. July 1st finally caught up with me.

In the records for July 1st:

012115H F 2/27 CP ALLEN BROOK; 011800H; @021536; Evac 1 NBC, second degree burns on both arms; Med evac 1 NBC on resupply helo; 1 NBC/1NBC.

Translated:

Reported at 09:15 p.m. local time, July 1st, F Company 2/27 on Operation Allen Brook, at 6:00 p.m. local time and map coordinates 021536, had one Non Battle Casualty with second degree burns on both arms. The NBC casualty was medevaced on the regular resupply helicopter.

012155H F 2/27 CP ALLEN BROOK; 011945H; @021536/020534; Rec'd 15 M-79 rds, 500-600 SA rds fm north & south & east of perimeter.; Ret'd SA, M-79, 60mm, 81mm & arty F/M; En broke contact & retreated. Div DTG 012230H.

Translated:

Reported at 09:55 p.m. local time, July 1st, F Co. 2/27 on Operation Allen Brook, at 07:45 p.m. local time and between map coordinates 021536 & 020534, the Company Command Post received 15 M-79 rounds and 500 to 600 small arms rounds from the north, south and east of the perimeter. The Company returned small arms fire, M-79 rounds, 60mm and 81mm mortar fire and called in an artillery fire mission. The enemy broke contact and retreated.

012216H F 2/27 CP ALLEN BROOK; 011800H; @021536; NBC rec'd 2nd degree sunburns on arm; NBC evac. Div DTG 012232H.

Translated:

Reported at 10:16 p.m. local time, July 1st, F Co 2/27 on Operation Allen Brook, at 6:00 p.m. local time and map coordinates 021536, had a non-battle casualty with second degree sunburn on his arm. The NBC was medevaced.

That night, the records show:

020245 011945 F6 Co PPB at 021536 rec'd heavy sm/a & 15 M-79 rds. Ret'd heavy sm/a & auto wpns fire, M-79 fire, 45 60mm mortar rds, 82 81mm mortar rds and called in arty fire mission. Sustained 2 minor wia's.

Translated:

Reported at 2:45 a.m. on July 2nd, the Fox Company Commander (F6) in a Platoon Patrol Base received heavy small arms fire and 15 M-79 rounds from map coordinates 021536. The base returned fire with small arms and automatic weapons, as well as M-79 fire, 45 60mm mortar rounds, 82 81mm mortar rounds and called in an artillery fire mission. Two minor WIA's occurred.

Looks like I was better off out on night patrol that night than in the PPB. Here on the Go Noi, it was harder to move a whole company than it was to move a platoon, as we did when we were out in Duc Ky. As a result, the CP and PPB's were more likely to get hit, which required more night patrols. As stated in the Marine Corps reports, Killer Teams accounted for 13 enemies killed on July 1st. I believe that my night patrol on July 1st was a Killer Team and that we contributed to the total enemy KIA list for July 1st. As I've said, I had gained a reputation as a night ambush patrol leader and as a result, that also included Killer Team operations.

Further reports state:

021320 021300 Fox-2-A found a 250 lb bomb. Fox-2-A and engineers blew 250 bomb with C-4.

Translated:

Reported at 1:20 p.m. on July 2nd, the A patrol from Fox Company, 2nd Platoon found a 250 lb bomb. The patrol and engineers blew the 250 lb bomb with C-4.

Also on the 2nd, the Battalion report states:

> On 2 July, Company F conducted a combat sweep to the blocking position of Company G, linked up with G Company and established a combat base in the vicinity of BT010530.

Reports from July 3rd state:

031315 031215 F-2-A @ 003524 sniper Team saw 2 VC with mortar rds. Fired at VC – 1 VC WIA.

Translated:

Reported on July 3rd at 1:15 p.m., the A patrol from Fox Co. 2nd Platoon with a sniper team saw two VC with mortar rounds at map coordinates 003524. The sniper team fired at the VC accounting for one VC WIA.

031515 Co F CP; 031030H; 998533; Man trip M-26 SFD w/trip wire; Called med evac comp 031345H; One USMC WIA pri. DTG 031525.

Translated:

Reported on July 3rd at 03:15 p.m. local time, the Fox Company Command Post at 10:30 a.m. local time and map coordinates 998533, had a man trip a special firing device with a trip wire attached. A medevac mission was called in and completed at 01:45 p.m. One Marine WIA was medevaced on a priority mission.

032000H F Co ALLEN BROOK; 031300H; 983529; Det 60mm SFD; Emer evac compl 031344H. Div DTG 031940H.

Translated:

Reported on July 3rd at 8:00 p.m. local time, Fox Company on Operation Allen Brook, at 1:00 p.m. local time and map coordinates 983529, had a man detonate a 60mm mortar special firing device. An emergency medevac was called in and completed at 1:44 p.m..

The reports from the 4th of July state:

041410H Co F sqd cbt; 041300H; 994516; Spotted 5-10 VC one w/ wpn; Called in F/M VC tried to cross river Obs one VC in impact area, obs people trying to get wpn fm KIA, Called another fire for effect rds on target one more VC KIA.

Translated:

Reported at 2:10 p.m. local time on July 4th, a squad combat patrol from Fox Company 2/27 at 1:00 p.m. local time and map coordinates 994516, spotted five to ten VC, one of whom had a weapon. Called in an artillery fire mission as the VC tried to cross the river. One VC was seen in the impact area and people were seen trying to get the weapon from the dead VC. Another fire mission was called in with fire for effect directions. The rounds were on target and one more VC was accounted for as a KIA.

041415H Co F sqd cbt; 041200H; 003534; F one (1) 60mm SFD w/ pressure det; Destroyed.

Translated:

Reported on July 4th at 2:15 p.m. local time, a squad combat patrol from Fox Company 2/27 at 12:00 p.m., July 4th and map coordinates 003534, found one 60mm mortar special firing device with a pressure detonater. The SFD was destroyed.

042000 041815 Seg Fwrd @ 923538 had convoy pass thru – Came under fire – rec'd 20 rds sm/a and 4 rds M-79. Surpressed [*sic*] sniper fire w/approx 2000 rds 50 cal; 1000 rds 30 cal. 2/27 ret'd fire with 200 rds 105mm. 2 USMC KIA: 1 VC KIA.

Translated:

Reported at 10:00 p.m. on July 4th, a convoy passed through the position of 2nd Battalion 27th Marines at 6:15 p.m. on July 4th. The convoy came under enemy fire and received twenty small arms and four M-79 rounds. The convoy suppressed sniper fire with approximately 2000 rounds of 50 caliber machine gun fire and 1000 rounds of 30 caliber machine gun fire. 2/27 returned fire with 200 rounds of 105mm artillery fire. Results were two USMC KIA and one VC KIA.

It was July 5th and I had written my family:

Dear Mom, Dad, & Kids,

Happy 4th of July a day late. Yep, and what a 4th it was. We had patrol yesterday from 1:00 to 5:00 what fun! And while we were out, one of my gunners and I got the bright idea of killing a chicken and having a real 4th of July supper. Well, that's just what we did. I shot a chicken, got him in the neck just above the breast too, plucked him right away and gutted him. Then when we got back off patrol we started a fire and got some ½ gallon juice cans to boil it in. I cut the chicken into pieces, the legs, breast, [thigh], tail, and wings. Then we found some hot peppers and put them in the water with the chicken plus a lot of salt. Well, we boiled the chicken for about 40 minutes; I used the bent stick trick to keep the water from boiling over. Anyway, it was real good, and just a little stringy. I guess because these chickens run wild and scared. I think we could have boiled it about 25 minutes longer, but it was still real good. And the broth we had left over, well I think that was almost the best part. It was real hot from the peppers, but it sure was good. Let me tell you, this was one 4th I'll never forget. Oh, I almost forgot , we also went around and scrounged up some Kool-aid and made 2 gallons of Kool-aid to go with the chicken. It's a shame I didn't have a camera or something, we were really a sight to see. We looked like a bunch of hobos who hadn't eaten for a month. Then with the beards and all, well you can just imagine what we looked like.

Everything is going as well as can be expected, there's no telling yet when this operation will be over. About the only thing I know for sure is that I'll be going on R & R the 21st to the 26th. I'll write you when I get back and tell you all about it. …

Say, that letter from Jeannie was sure nice. Jean, I love you very much too; and can't wait till I get home to see you. You be good and have a lot of fun this summer, and next year in school. …

With all my love, Chuck

My little sister Jeannie was only 7 when I wrote that. My sister Cathy and brother Chris were older and would write me from time to time. My little brother Billy and little sister Jeannie would send little notes in with a letter from Mom from time to time. It was always so warming to hear from them and feel the love that only little children can give. On one occasion, my little brother Billy (he was 9 at the time) wrote me and said:

Dear Chuck,

How are you doing. Who saids the Marines are better then the Army. Have you got shot any yet. If you do bring back the wound so I can see it.

Love, Billy

Doesn't get any better than that.

A morning patrol from our Platoon, with a sniper team, saw some action on the 5th:

051130H 051115 F-2-A spotted 2 VC moving in westernly [*sic*] direction. VC wearing khaki uniforms with pack and cartridge belt. One VC carrying M-1; other weapons unknown. F-2-A sniper team fired two sniper rds. VC made run for gully. F-2-A called Arty mission. 24 rds VT. Excellent coverage. Couldn't observe VC anymore. Cannot check it as across Blue. Friendly @ 994523; Enemy @ 99255180.

Translated:

Reported on July 5th at 11:30 a.m. local time, the A patrol from Fox Company 2nd Platoon, at 11:15 a.m. July 5th, spotted two VC moving in a westerly direction. The VC were wearing khaki uniforms with pack and cartridge belt NVA uniforms. One VC was carrying an M-1 rifle. The other weapons were unknown. The patrol sniper team fired two sniper rounds. The VC made a run for a gully. The patrol called in an artillery fire mission of twenty four rounds of Variable Time fused (VT) ammunition. Excellent coverage was observed. The patrol couldn't observe the VC anymore. A check of the area could not be made due to the fact that the area was across the river. The friendly position was at map coordinates 994523 while the enemy position was at map coordinates 992518.

The mention of the M-1 rifle, the one that won WWII, makes it clear that the enemy had such weapons. In fact, in some VC units there were many M-1's and M-1 carbines available, mostly either captured from the French, pilfered from ARVN units or obtained through the black market. In the initial arming of the South Vietnamese Army by the U. S., the M-1 Garand and M-1 Carbine were standard issue.

Also on the 5th:

> On 5 July Companies E & G swept to vic 020550 and established a joint combat base. From this base they conducted extensive reconnaissance patrolling. Companies F and H conducted daytime patrolling and security for the Engineers and the Battalion CP.

051320 Co F sqd cbt w/sniper personnel; 051115H; @994523/992518; Ptl obs 10 VC moving in a Westerly direction wearing Khakie [*sic*] uniforms w/packs, cartridge belts & 2 wpns.; Sniper tm fired two rds VC ran call Marine Arty good coverage could not check area due to river barrier. Div DTG 051355H.

Translated:

Reported at 01:20 p.m. on 5 July, a squad sized combat patrol with sniper personnel from Company F, at 11:15 a.m. local time on 5 July, at map coordinates 994523/99218 observed ten VC moving in a Westerly direction wearing Kaki uniforms with packs, cartridge belts and two weapons. Sniper team fired two rounds. The VC ran and the patrol called in Marine Artillery. Good coverage was observed. The area could not be checked due to a river barrier. Division report Day Time Group 051355H.

On the 6th we were exposed to herbicides like Agent Orange, the reports state:

> Air delivered herbicide operations were conducted on two occasions and found to be quite effective.

060825 060715 Seg @014545; 2 F-4's conducting cover for herbicide mission. Dropped 12 500lb bombs after C-123 marked an enemy position w/smoke 100 meters from friendly position, Location of air strike @ 014546 – Callsign of airstrike was LOPEZ 54 & LOPEZ 55. At time of incident there was no ground contact. No friendly casualties.

Translated:

Reported at 8:25 a.m. on 6 July, two F-4 fighter jets conducted cover for a herbicide mission at 7:15 a.m., 6 July at map location 014545. Twelve 500lb bombs were dropped after a C-123 aircraft marked an enemy position with smoke 100 meters from the friendly position. The location of the air strike was map coordinates 014546. The call sign of the airstrike was LOPEZ 54 and LOPEZ 55. At the time of the incident, there was no ground contact. There were no friendly casualties.

This was a danger close mission for the aircraft, since the strikes were so close to friendly positions. All efforts were made to avoid hitting our own troops, hence the report of no friendly casualties. Nevertheless, shit happens, and later on, I would personally witness just such a catastrophe where our own men were hit by airstrikes.

The military attitude toward the herbicides is amply described by this segment from the reports:

> For the 27th Marines:
>
> Insure persons are instructed that herbicide is not, repeat, not harmful. Take the following action:
>
> (1) Wash herbicide from exposed skin.
>
> (2) Do not eat food exposed to herbicide.

Need I say more?

Another report on the 6th:

062000 061945 F-2-C @ 998533 Heard movement in front position @997535 – Called 60mm and Movement stopped.

Translated:

Reported on July 6 at 8:00 p.m., the C patrol from Fox Company 2nd Platoon at map coordinates 998533, heard movement in front of their position at map coordinates 997535. The patrol called in 60mm mortars and the movement stopped.

The 7th was one to remember. The records say the following:

> Company F moved the Bn Cp to Liberty Bridge to escort five tractors back to the Bn Cp.
> Foxtrot Company be prepared by 0700 to provide on order security escort for special Engineer operation. Upon completion of operation resume assigned mission. Coordinate night activities with Golf who will provide one platoon for patrolling purposes. Be prepared to conduct normal activities of if Engineer operations is not conducted.

070900 070900 Fox @ 975545 found 2 box mines 40-50 lbs each. 1 live and 1 decoy. Blew in place with C-4.

Translated:

Reported at 9:00 a.m. on 7 July, Fox Company reported on 9:00 a.m., 7 July at map coordinates 975545, that they had found two box mines weighing forty to fifty pounds each. One mine was active and one was a decoy. The patrol blew the mines in place with C-4.

071100 071005 Fox @ 958546 found 40-50 lb box mine. Blown in place.

Translated:

Reported at 11:00 a.m. on 7 July, Fox Company reported at 10:05 a.m. on 7 July, at map coordinates 958546, that they had found a forty to fifty pound box mine. The mine was blown in place.

071115 071020 Fox @ 953543 tank hit mine approx 250 lbs – pressure detonated. Tank aflame and rounds cooking off. Damage assessment to follow. Leaving security for tank. Continuing mission. Called medevac. 5 WIA medevacs – 2 emer, 3 prior

Translated:

Reported at 11:15 a.m. on 7 July, Fox Company reported at 10:20 a.m. on 7 July that a tank hit a mine at map coordinates 953543. The mine was approximately a 250 pound bomb detonated by a pressure device. The Tank caught fire and had rounds cooking off. A damage assessment will follow. The patrol left the tank and continued the mission. A medevac was called for. Two emergency and three priority WIA's were medevaced.

Further reports tell of the personal actions by myself and the other Marines who were providing security for the convoy:

> Approximately 1020 on 7 July, Company F was moving to the Liberty Bridge as security for an armored column. In route they discovered four 40 to 50 pound box mines. Later a 250 to 300 pound mine exploded under a tank. The tank immediately caught fire. Members of Company F attempted to bring the fire under control but were driven back by exploding small arms and 90mm ammunition. Quick action by several Marines prevented several casualties as they pulled stunned men away from the burning tank. Five Marines were medevaced.

From the records of the 1st Tank Battalion:

> On Operation Allen Brook, Company B (Rein), 5th Tank Battalion supported the 27th Marines with three tanks.
> At 071015H, one tank from Company B, 5th Tank Battalion, hit a mine at (AT952544) while in support of 2/27. The mine caused the fuel cells to rupture and the tank caught fire. The fire extinquishers aboard the vehicle were all fired but were not adequate to extinguish the fire. The fire caused the ammunition aboard the vehicle to detonate. The vehicle was destroyed. There was one friendly WIA (med-evac). [One tank crew member]

Then on the 8th, the reports continue:

> On 8 July Company F conducted extensive day and night combat/ambush patrolling.
> Foxtrot Company continue assigned mission. Conduct extensive combat operations to seek out and destroy his enemy forces, his installations and supplies.

Also on July 8, I wrote the following:

Dear Dad,

Well, here I am still in the boonies, in my third week of this two-bit operation, and your guess is as good as mine when it will be over. Yes-

terday we went on the *Death March as it is called. It is about a 3 mile hump from the railroad tracks to Liberty bridge. I know you don't know what I mean yet, but now let me explain. There is only one road that you can take, and it is all through Gook Land, of course all Viet Nam is gook Land. But this road is always heavily mined, and so quite [dangerous] plus the fact that there are no Marines [operating] in that area at the moment. Well, we had a LVT (Light Vehicle Tracked) and 2 tanks going with us and we were to pick up 4 bulldozers at Liberty Bridge and come back with all of the dozers and tanks. On the way we lost 1 tank and 4 men. One of them died in my arms with a broken back. You know Dad, now I know what you meant when you said "Why cry, Chuck, you don't even know what pain is." Yep, that really hit me hard, besides the fact that that one Marine with the broken back was a close friend of mine. Anyway, it took us about 7 hours to get to the Bridge. We got there took a little swim and headed back. We made it back in about 4 hours. Oh, all this time [it] was between 95 and 110 [degrees], so you can imagine what that walk was like. I sure know why they call it the Death March now. I just hope we never have to make that trip again. Well, I'm still alive and kicking so I really don't have anything to gripe about. …*

Oh, another thing that happened on the March. We received some automatic fire, so we called in air strikes. Well, the air strikes were about 300 meters in front of us so we didn't get down and under cover. Anyway, one of the 250 lb. bombs went astray and landed about a 100 meters short, and all of a sudden I heard a piece of scrap-metal come, z-z-z-z-z-z zap and hit one of my men sitting right next to me. I hollered for the "Doc" and bent over him to see how bad he was hurt, and you'd never guess what I saw. He wasn't hurt at all, only bruised. He was wearing his [magazines] [M-16 in cloth bandoleers] across his chest like "Poncho [Villa]", and the piece of scrap-metal hit one of his [magazines]. It sure knocked hell out of the magazine, let me tell you. Boy, I've never been so shook up, well almost never. I thought sure he had had it. So, how do you like that for a quirk of fate[?] …

With all my love, Your Son, Chuck

First of all, you notice my awful spelling again. However, did you notice how easily I talked about our own men getting killed or injured, even friends of mine. I can truly say that after five months of combat, I had lost almost all of my ability to feel emotion. I've searched widely to determine who it was that I said, "Died in my arms with a broken back." I am sure he was one of the emergency medevacs, but have been unable to come up with a name. It is entirely possible that the Marine I talked about with the "broken back" had only passed out from his injury, but in reality, I think it just wasn't reported on the July 7th. I've found many discrepancies between the dates of when men got hit and when they died. I hold my letter to be true, especially since I had seen enough death to know it when I saw it.

Whichever the case may be, it was a traumatic event to have a tank blow up and catch fire with rounds cooking off and men suffering from the explosion and the fire. At least we were able to pull the tank men and others away from the damaged tank. Of the five men listed as WIA on that patrol, one was from the tank and the other four were from those of us on the security patrol.

It was at this time that I found the bullet which came close to killing me. One of the 50 cal. rounds that cooked off from the tank landed at my feet and buried itself in the sand. It was still hot when I dug it up. It had no rifling marks on it, so I knew it was from a cook-off.

After it cooled, I put it in my pocket saying, "I'm safe now, I have the one with my name on it." I still have that bullet and I am still alive, so I guess it's working.

The 9th was more of the same:

"Foxtrot Company continue assigned mission."

The records report on the 10th of July:

101005 F Co ALLEN BROOK; 100815H; @982538; Tank hit box mine 1 WIA minor; Set up sect security waiting for escort fm Bn CP. Div DTG 101000H.

Translated:

Reported at 10:05 a.m. on 10 July, Fox Company reported while on Operation Allen Brook that at 8:15 a.m. local time and at map coordinates 982538 that a tank hit a box mine. There was one minor WIA. A sector security was set up while waiting for an escort from the Battalion Command Post. Divisional report, Day Time Group 101000H.

101330H F Sniper tm; 101200H; @ 974549/982554; spotted one VC in green uniform w/pack & bag of rice; Sniper fired & killed VC; (1) VC KIA, DTG 101310H

Translated:

Reported at 1:30 p.m. on 10 July, Fox Company Sniper team reported at 1200 p.m. local time, 10 July and map coordinates 974549 to 982554 that they spotted one VC in a green uniform with a pack and bag of rice. The sniper fired and killed the VC. DTG 101310H.

101535H Co F scout sniper; 101430H; @ 974549/982559; Obs four (4) VC one (1) in treeline three (3) on river bank; Called Marine arty fire cracker ...; Good coverage on target two (2) VC KIA, Two (2) VC KIA. Div DTG 101635.

Translated:

Reported at 3:35 p.m. local time on 10 July, a Fox Company scout sniper reported at 2:30 p.m. local time and map coordinates 974549 to 982559 that he observed four VC, one in a tree line and three on the river bank. He called in Marine artillery with fire-cracker rounds. He observed good coverage on the target, with two VC KIA. Division DTG 101635.

101706H F Co SS scout sniper tm 2/27 ALLEN BROOK; 101655H; @ 974549/98285590; Obs (1) VC under tree wearing green uniform & pack; Sniper tm fired (1) rd.; 1 VC KIA. Div DTG 101743.

Translated:

Reported at 5:06 p.m. local time on 10 July, a Fox Company, 2/27 scout sniper team on Operation Allen Brook reported at 4:55 p.m. local time and map coordinates 974549 to 98285590 that they observed one VC under a tree wearing a green uniform with a pack. The sniper team fired one round. One VC KIA. Division DTG 101743.

> Foxtrot Company establish blocking force in accordance with Regt regimental Frag Order 1-68. Be prepared to move rapidly to engage and destroy any enemy forces coming near or within our blocking area. Clear fire missions with 26th Mar Coordinate right flank element with Hotel.

> 101915 Fox-2 @ 974549; Spotted 9 VC wearing black uni forms carrying automatic and bolt action rifles. VC were accompanied by 6 female. Called in arty on 970549 No sm/a as it was 400 meter range and did not want to comprise position for the night.

No search for same reason. VC moved into the treeline [*sic*]. 9 possible WIA.

Continuing on the 11th:

Fox-2 consolidate into a 360 degree defensive position at block site and maintain position at block site till relieved by Seg Golf unit at 110800. Then displace to Seg CP.

Foxtrot Company displace Foxtrot 1 and 3 to Bn CP about 101730. Conduct extensive all night patrolling …

Company F provided security for the Engineer Clearing operation and the Bn CP.

Approximately 1715 on 11 July, a platoon combat patrol from F Company spotted 15 VC vic BT998510 carrying a mortar tube and satchel charge. They were moving east to west along the river. E Btry, 2/13 fired for F Company with good coverage on target. Seven bodies were observed for 35 minutes. Enemy losses were 7 KIA's.

111851 F Co; 111400H; @ 995524-996581; Obser 17 VC; Call Mar arty F/M fire mission checked area 5 VC KIA; 5 VC KIA. Div DTG 111842.

Translated:

Reported at 6:51 p.m. on 11 July, Fox Company reported at 2:00 p.m., 11 July at map coordinates 995524 to 996581 that they had observed seventeen VC and called in a Marine artillery fire mission. The area was checked and there were five VC KIA. Division DTG 111842.

111852 F Co; 111510H; @ 995524-99835191; Obser 4 VC; called Mar arty F/M checked area – neg results. Div DTG 111842.

Translated:

Reported at 6:52 p.m. on 11 July, Fox Company reported at 3:10 p.m. local time and map coordinates 995524 to 99835191 that they observed four VC and called in a Marine artillery fire mission. The area was checked with negative results. Division DTG 111842.

111853 F Co; 111715H; @ 995527-99835191; Obser 15 VC; called Mar arty F/M. Obser 7 VC KIA; 7. Div DTG 111846B.

Translated:

Reported at 6:53 p.m. on 11 July, Fox Company reported at 5:15 p.m. local time and map coordinates 995527 to 99835191 that they observed fifteen VC. A Marine artillery fire mission was called in. Seven VC were observed as KIA. Division DTG 111846B.

112222 F Co; 111600H; @ 993531; Old viet woman approached CP. Considered VCS VC sympathizer; Woman was taken to 27th Mar CP. Div DTG 112036H.

Translated:

Reported at 10:22 p.m. on 11 July, Fox Company reported at 4:00 p.m. local time, 11 July and map coordinates 993531 that an old Vietnamese woman approached the Command Post. She was considered a VC sympathizer. The woman was taken to the 27th Marines Command Post. Division DTG 112036H.

In two days, Fox Company had accounted for 16 VC KIA and 9 VC WIA. Along with the constant patrols and sniper missions, we were still heavily involved in providing security for the "Total Clearing Operation", turning Go Noi Island into a parking lot.

The clearing operations had two phases as described below from the records:

> Several audacious maneuvers were planned to take maximum use of the fire power and terrifying shock effect of the tanks. In one instance a tank infantry assault was launched by Company F. A deep envelopment was made against a fortified hamlet to drive the enemy into a friendly blocking firce [*sic*]. The momentum of the attack was broken when the lead tank hit a mine destroying the track and shearing two road wheels and arms. Later in the evening the blocking force came under heavy enemy attack, resulting in two confirmed enemy KIA's.
>
> On another occasion a light section of tanks and a platoon of Company E went deep into enemy territory to destroy a suspected enemy base. The enemy had made frequent forays from this area to harrass [*sic*] clearing efforts. The maneuver was successful until a tank threw a track while negotiating a berm wall.

LVTE's were used to clear densely forested areas, heavily mined areas, and to carry fuels for burning. The reports continue:

> Terrain. Throughout the Go Noi Island there is a heavy vegetation, that in all cases impaired movement and ground observation. ... thick underbrush was prevelent [*sic*] in the area and was excellent for concealment, boobytraps and mines. Avenues of approch [*sic*] were limited to existing trails in most instances, allowing excellent use of boobytraps by the enemy. Units were confronted with a succession of treelines which concealed snipers and small harassing elements.
>
> Analysis of the "Selective Clearing" concept quickly revealed that even though the most advantageous installations and natural terrain features were being denied the enemy, many areas of almost equal tactical advantage were left untouched. In some cases it appeared that the process of selective destruction had the effect of clearing fields of fire for the remaining positions. Also it is believed many caches of ammunition, supplies and food were being passed over by partial clearing techniques.
>
> To eleminate the inherent disadvantages of "Selective Clearing" a concept of "Total Clearing" was executed. It is felt that this was the approach that would most effectively alter the terrain and eliminate Go Noi Island as a suitable base of operations for the enemy. This reasoning was borne out by subsequent experience as the enemy immediately reoccupied area in which partial clearing had been conducted. But where total clearing had been accomplished the area was entirely unsuitable for enemy occupation. Also a preponderance of enemy weapons, caches and ammunition stocks were uncovered in final stages of clearing. The innovation of burning bunker material was added.

And thus the decision to turn Go Noi Island into a "parking lot" was born. I remember those manuevers in a tank/infantry assault. It was classic WWII fighting that the Marines had used in the Pacific campaign against the Japaneese. One such occasion stands out in my memory and I think it was the assault by Fox Company that was talked about in the reports.

The tanks had moved up to the treeline which acted as a boundary between the jungle and a large open area. Our Company was distributed along a line between the tanks forming a frontal assault line which was aimed at an area in the jungle at the far side of our position. We were told to watch out for booby traps and spider traps as we made our assault.

Spider traps were holes in the ground covered with a bamboo mat, dirt and anything else that would make the hole "disappear." Inside the hole, an enemy would lay in wait until we had passed by his hole so he could pop up and shoot us in the back.

Soon we were moving, firing our weapons into the treeline in front of us as the tanks did the same with their 90mm cannons and machine guns. The open ground we crossed was littered with debris and even if there were spider traps, we could't see them.

Everything seemed to be going well as we crossed that "no man's land." All of a sudden, one of the tanks that were out in front of us exploded. The explosion was totally unexpected and I crouched down to get my bearings and to figure out what had just happened before I jumped from the frying pan into the fire. This was a habit I had developed which proved to be my salvation many times. It stemed from my hunting experiences in Texas where there were a lot of open areas. Even the slightest noise could be a deer and the best move was to squat down and be quiet, and try to determine where the noise had come from and what had made it.

Once that tank exploded, we started to get some small arms fire from the treeline ahead and a village just behind it. Our assault had stopped and we were like sitting ducks. Soon we started up again, heading for the village.

Time to move. The assault had started again. I got up, facing the village ahead and started to walk toward it. Then it happened, the hairs on the back of my neck stood up and I felt spooked. I turned around to see what it was that had made my senses jump. I was carrying my M-16 at the hip, which was my usual assault position, and as I turned, I could see the barrel of a rifle coming out of the ground at about a 45 degree angle and moving down. The son of a bitch was trying to shoot me in the back! Not even thinking, I cut loose with an automatic burst from my M-16. The position of the barrel was perfect, aimed slightly down from my hip. As the bullets raked the area, the rifle I saw flew up and out and the cover of the spider trap slammed down. Call it a sixth sense, or the hand of God, but I had it. More times than I can remember, that little voice or touch or tingle at the back of my neck alerted me to danger. I never questioned it, I just reacted. Even to this day, although my senses have dulled over time, I still react the same way when I feel immediate danger. It just never goes away completely.

Shook up that there was just a split second between me and eternity, I went over to the hole and stuck the barrel of my M-16 in it and cut loose. After that I opened the cover and there was a VC, looking like a piece of swiss cheese, all slumped down at the bottom of his homemade grave. I just dropped the lid and turned to catch up with the rest of the guys.

The rest of the Company had moved up ahead of me and were searching the village. As I approached them, I could hear them call out that they had found some rice or weapons or tunnel holes which had to be checked out. What we found there was a whole complex of tunnels and rooms that were used as a hospital and supply dump, with sleeping quarters and mess hall. I didn't go down into those tunnels - my size prohibited it. Besides, I had to set up my machine guns to cover the Company from an attack. The enemy had fled, leaving everything just as it was.

I didn't think much about what had happened. I was tired and hungry and thirsty. We made our position for the night around that village, heated some C-Rats and I made some coffee with water I found in the village well. I had to save the water in my canteens because I needed it when there was no water anywhere to drink. Water was such a constant ache for us, especially in a firefight. With all the dust and the heat and the adrenalin, my mouth would get bone dry to the point where I would gag. The pebble trick worked well enough on patrols and such, but the dry mouth that happened during and after a fight could only be soothed by small sips of real water. I always had water. Even if I had to boil it from a local well or a ditch, let it cool and pour it into my canteen, I had water whenever possible. Still, water was not always available, and during those times, I just gagged and tried to control my awful thirst until an opportunity came to get water.

I set the watch for my guns and tried to get a little sleep. I awoke about every hour or so and would get up and check my gun positions. The men were real savvy by this time and had set up their own watch schedule according to how many men would be in a position. All I really had to do was make sure that the guys on watch were alert. I had some new guys in the squad while in Go Noi and I watched them like a hawk to make sure they were standing up to what was happening, but by this time, all my new guys were gone. That may have been unnecessary since they were Marines, but I couldn't take the chance. I planned on surviving this hell hole and helping my men survive as well.

Back to the process of "Total Clearing," the primary tool used in clearing the jungle on Go Noi Island, besides the spraying of herbicides was the LVTE (Light Vehicle Tracked Engineer), with a MK 154 Mine Clearance Launcher. As described in the Marine Corps Weapons guide:

> The system has the capability to house and fire three LDCs (linear demolition charges) using three MK22 Rockets. The over-pressure

> created by each of the LDCs will clear a path 16 meters wide and 100 meters long through a minefield consisting of single impulse, non-blast resistant, pressure-fused mines. The width of the lane and the ability to neutralize mines is dependent upon the mine type and fusing. The MK154 LMC (Launcher, Mine Clearing), mounted in an AAVP7A1 (Assault Amphibious Vehicle P7A1), can deploy three linear demolition chargers from the water or land. Each linear demolition charge is 100 meters long and will be the initial minefield-breaching asset used. Because the LDC is only effective against single impulse, non-blast resistant, pressure-fused mines, a mechanical proofing device must also be used in a lane that has been explosively breached.

So, there you have it. Instant road! It worked fine for the LVTE, but for foot troops providing security, it was a real quagmire. Everywhere you stepped, there was a wooden trap waiting to break your ankle or leg. Tripping and falling, we provided what security we could for the LVTE. Luckily, I don't remember us getting hit by the VC during these occasions. Lucky, because they could have picked us off one at a time with no problems. They probably saw this beast of an LVTE spitting hell fire and brimstone and didied most scosh (meaning that they ran away "didied" very quickly "scosh").

From this point, the constant translations are probably a little much, so I will forgo them and only translate information that has not been introduced before.

Again in the reports:

On 12 July, Company F conducted security for Engineers and Bn Cp.

120050	F-2-A at coord 998534 spotted 3 VC wearing pack uniform cartridge belt with weapon @ 988537. Too far away to engage in small arms. F-2-A fired 60mm. Good coverage on target. Will check at first light.
121420	Co F Sqd cmbt; 121345H; 000525-002519; Observed four (4) VC in open carring wpns and equip of unk type; Called Marine arty F/M at above coord VC split into two groups. Called another arty F/M on coord 994517 rds on target dis no more movement. Div DTG 121430H.

122318 F Co; 120945H; 993522-993518; Spotted two VC; Fired SA wounding one (1) apprehended VC WIA; 1 VC WIA. Div DTG 122300H.

On July 13th, the reports state simply:

Seg Fox Continue assigned mission of clearing land operation. Be prepared to deploy F (-) in support of Seg G on 30 minutes alert.

F (-) meant Fox Company minus some elements (usually a platoon), and that the Company was to proceed without them. From later reports, it is evident that our platoon, 2nd Platoon, was the missing element in the Company. Once again, we were operating on our own.

Further reports from the 13th:

> Approximately 0600 on 13 July a killer team from Company F vic AT997522 observed 3 VC on a raft in the river. The sniper team took the raft under fire, killing all three. About 15 minutes later 2 more VC were observed across the river and killed by sniper fire.

130600 F-2-C spotted 3 VC with weapons on raft in river going west to east wearing black. Fired 1 rd sniper fire, 1 M-79 rd, 5 rds M-16. Overturned raft; can not salvage gear. 3 VC KIA.

130615 F-2-C spotted 2 VC with weapons and pack going east to west wearing black PJ's/. SST (scout sniper team) opened up and dropped both VC can ob serve bodies with packs and weapons.

131415 Fox-2 @002532; 2 Marines tripped pressure detonated device. Both double amputation of lower limbs. Called medevac completed for 2 USMC. Completed at 131720.

Jim Seabolt remembers the 131415 incident. He remembers that it was by some railroad tracks. My memory is that we were going across some rice paddies, bordered on the left by railroad tracks. Everyone had been told to stay off the dikes because they were usually booby trapped. Two men got tired of sloshing through the mud and went up on the dikes and triggered a booby trap that consisted of a flare canister filled with explosive. When the explosion was triggered, it sent two halves of the canister whizzing across the ground at about knee height, cutting their legs off like two hot knives. A flare canister is usually about six inches in diameter and two feet long. I remember trying to tie off the stumps right after it happened, since they were just a few yards away from me. Very quickly, Doc Mac, the Corpsman, came up, as well as Lt. Jones and SSGT. Staggs and the Radioman. Since I was the machine gun squad leader, I automatically left the area and got a perimeter formed, got my machine guns set in and waited for the medevac that would be coming.

Medevacing the wounded was always a tricky thing. The gooks would race for the area where a medevac was headed and try to shoot it down or engage the Marines involved. Most of my attention was focused on the perimeter, keeping my men ready for whatever might come our way. My most vivid memory was when they popped the smoke grenade to show the helicopter where to land. As I looked over across the rice paddy, I saw them load what was left of the two men who lost their legs. The chopper got off okay and that was that. We soon formed up again to continue our sweep, making as much distance between us and where the medevac had been as possible. I believe that they bled to death by the time they were lifted onto the medevac chopper, since it took the medevac chopper just over three hours to get to us, and that's a long time to survive with both legs blown off.

I cannot confirm the names or final condition of these two Marines, but listed on the Wall, there are three Marines who died on July 13, 1968 from "Explosive Device," listed as dying in Quang Nam Provence, Vietnam, which is the area we were in. One was a machine gunner from E Co. 2/26, so I know it wasn't him. I do not know what the units were of the other two men, but they might be the men I am talking about. If I am right, and even if I'm wrong; these two Marines made the ultimate sacrifice and I praise them for their valor. Once again, the moral of the story is:

"Don't walk on the dikes, it can get you killed."

How did I determine that it was a flare canister? I saw the pieces in the rice paddy. In an effort to confirm this, I did find the following information in the records:

131415H BT002533 Tripped unknown type booby trap

Most booby traps were readily identified, but a flare canister would not be on the list as shown below from the Marine Corps manual on Mines and Boobytraps - FMFRP - 43:

> MINE AND BOOBYTRAP INCIDENTS
>
> The major contact with the enemy was mines and boobytraps. All mine incidents envolved [*sic*] box type mines. Boobytraps in-

cluded M-26 grenades, 60mm mortar rounds, M-33 grenades and 105mm (artillery) rounds.

During 1968, 37.7 percent of all Marine casualties were caused by the accidental detonation of a mine or boobytrap. In other words, more that one of every three Marines killed or wounded in SVN (South Vietnam) becomes a casualty as the result of a mine or boobytrap. Although a Great many detection means, ranging from intricate electronic devices to specially trained dogs, have been developed, experience has shown that an alert Marine, aware of what to look for and where to look, is the most effective detection device.

A report from the 14th states:

142235 F Co plt perimeter 2/27; 142115H; 993532-996532; Obs enemy movement; Called 60mm illum and HE high explosive F/M. Will check area. Div DTG 142243H.

The patrol records continue:

Approximately 1125 on 15 July vic of AT993528 a platoon of F Company on a combat sweep discovered a cache of weapons including 1 sub-machine gun, three sniper rifles (1 with scope), medical supplies, poncho with liner, and assorted clothing.

Foxtrot Company at 0615 provide engineer security for destruction of western portion of Battalion CP. Continue to provide security until old CP is destroyed. Upon completion of destruction effort displace to new Battalion CP. Conduct local night activities and ambushes.

On 15 July Company F provided march security. All units establish new combatbase/CP.

On the 15th I wrote:

Dear Mom,

Well, I have to hand it to you, you're really getting on the ball here lately, and I want you to know that I really appreciate your letters.

I'm back at Battalion now, getting my shots and everything ready to go on R & R. I sure am anxious to go. Like we say around here, I'm going to visit "the World", and I'll probably have to go back out in the bush to recuperate. But for now it sure is nice to be off that operation. ...

Well, there really isn't much else to say right now. You'll get a nice long letter after R&R. There's not much happening [anymore], so I'm having a fairly good rest already. I can't get enough sleep, though. Well,

if anything comes up I'll let you know. I'm still waiting on word about my promotion. The rest of the company will be in tomorrow, so there's no telling where we will be going next. Take care & keep up the writing.
With all my love, Chuck

July 16th would see the end of Operation Allen Brook for 2nd Battalion, 27th Marines. My Company was back at the original Battalion Headquarters off the Anderson Trail and the patrolling continued. I had been prepped for R & R, but not released yet. My flight by helicopter to Da Nang to catch the plane to Malaysia wouldn't happen until the 19th. My R & R was scheduled for the 21st to the 26th, in Penang, Malaysia. As was common for me, they used me all they could, and I remember being the patrol leader on the patrol listed below:

181930 F-2-C @ 985678; Spotted 20 VC in black PJ's with rifles. Called fire mission, 3 rds WP white phosphorous and ad just, 4 rds Firecracker.

A "Firecracker" round was a special round fired from a 105mm Howitzer. It contained many smaller explosives which were released when the "Firecracker" exploded in the air. The explosives would then fall to earth and explode. They were very effective against large groups of VC.

On the 19th, I caught a flight to Da Nang. Once I landed, I was back in the regimented life of the Marine Corps, a huge difference from the life I had been living in the jungle. At first I was very disoriented and had some anxiety about being away from my men. I had to turn in my weapons (M-16 and .45 Auto) to the armory, which only added to my anxiety, and I was given a locker to stow the rest of my combat gear. I just felt so naked and helpless, with no means to defend myself if necessary. Just because it was Da Nang was no assurance that we wouldn't be attacked. I went to the Navy Exchange, a retail store for military personnel, and purchased some civilian clothes, bought a ready-made cup of coffee and ate all I could. The clothes I bought were very important, since I could not wear my uniform in Malaysia.

Malaysia had just recently been opened up as an R & R center due to an agreement with the Malaysian government. The Australians maintained a treaty with Malaysia and as such, had garrisons there with a modest number of troops. The Americans were considered guests, and could be booted out of the country at any time if things got out of control. Hence, no uniforms.

I flew out of Da Nang in a civilian plane either the night of the 20th or the morning of the 21st. It was a reasonably short flight to Malaysia and I believe we landed at the Bayan Lepas airport in Penang, which had been constructed in the early 60's. We then boarded busses and went to George Town. Penang is a state in Malaysia with George Town as the capital. Part of Penang is an island separated by the Strait of Malacca, which is crossed by a bridge today, but we had to take a ferry in 1968. Once we got to George Town, we were briefed by the local U.S. commanding officer and turned loose to enjoy our stay and told to return to the command on the 26th for our return flight to Vietnam.

This remembrance is not to glorify or detract from my R & R. It was what it was, and given a different time and place, it probably would have been completely different. I'm not trying to condone my behavior, just to report it and maybe try to understand it. Would that it had been different, because it was not right in the sight of God. In a way, looking back, it's like we were treated to a conjugal visit like Spartacus at the gladiator school - give the beast what he wants for a moment before turning him loose in the arena again. That was what it was like. Not a visit home to family and friends, rather an effort to appease the beasts that had been created. I'm sure that the "powers that be" didn't look at things that way, and that given a different state of mind on my part, it would have been different. But looking back, was it wise or helpful for myself and other young men, many of whom were experiencing their first time away from home, fresh out of jungle combat, to be turned loose to fend for themselves without sufficient supervision? With few exceptions, after battles in the Pacific during WWII, the G.I.'s were given a respite from the fighting, but not just released into society with almost no supervision. Actually, it was just a preview of what was to come when we went home. Out of jungle combat and into society with no gradual transition. In so many ways, we received the worst treatment as American fighting men that had ever been perpetrated upon veterans in the history of the United States.

There I was on the streets of George Town with no idea what to do. How do you go from combat to "civilization" overnight and not be confused? As I was walking the streets, a young man pedaling a bicycle-driven two seater jingshaw came up along side of me and started fast talking me into letting him be my guide, transportation and constant companion while I was in George Town. At first I rejected him, but he was so persistant that I couldn't resist. He offered me a good price (money could buy anything) and I accepted. His name, or rather the name he gave me, was Chico and he did look a little like the Mexican friends that I had grown up with in Texas. He turned out to be a faithful companion, sticking with me when no one else would. I think he genuinely liked me and I returned the feelings as best as I could. His jingshaw was a bicycle driven two-wheeled cart, usually decked out with all the bells and whistles available to make it an atractive ride.

I hopped into the jingshaw and away we went. Chico seemed to know my every need before I did. First he took me to a nice hotel and helped me get a room on one of the upper floors. Since the only luggage I had was a carry-on bag with my shaving gear and such and the clothes on my back, it didn't take long before we left and headed down the street. The main streets were actually paved so it was a pretty easy ride. Not long after we left the hotel, Chico pulled over and asked me what I would like. Not understanding him right away, I just indicated that I would like to get a bottle of Bourbon and relax at the beach which wasn't that far away. He spoke broken English, but it was enough to get by and we communicated pretty well.

His suggestion was to go get a girl. Now prostitution was legal and well regulated by the state. This was a main means of income for families with young women and the others involved. It was not the sleazy thing that's practiced in other parts of the world. It was much like the brothels in Nevada, with a madam and emphasis on cleanliness, without the kinky stuff. It was more of a place to have a real companion for a few days. The girls seemed happy enough and treated the men well in the Oriental tradition. I was lonely for any companionship and the thought of a warm "girlfriend" was hard to resist, especially after my "Dear John". Chico coached me on how to act and we went in the house he had stopped at. I believe he had personal connections with this house as well.

I walked in the house and was led to a small room, looking much like a turn of the century living room. Not overly done, but full of heavy drapes and plush couches. The ceiling height wasn't much over six feet, and I found myself ducking a lot. I must have looked a mess because the madam looked me over and talked to Chico several times. Their conversation went back and forth a while and finally the Madam relented. Chico told me that she had doubts about letting one of her girls go with a U. S. Marine fresh out of combat, but finally setteled on a price. I had to pay up first before she would bring the girls in. The terms were fifty dollars for five days. Everything seemed on the up and up, so I paid up and waited for the girls to come in.

The girls lined up at one end of the room and waited for me to choose. I felt embarassed and tongue-tied. Chico said something to me, and I believe he pointed to one girl in particular, whom I believed he had some ties to, family or otherwise. Anyway, she was a Malaysian girl, probably around twenty or so, with a shy smile and a what seemed a warm heart. Her name to me was Peggy. Good name for a GI girlfriend. She was modest in her dress, wearing silken pajamas in some kind of print. She looked and acted like just what I needed, a warm companion to help me relax and put the war behind me for a few days. It was good at the time; I don't think I would have been able to handle being completely alone with my nightmares.

We hopped into Chico's jingshaw and hit the town. All I really remember about the first two days is that Peggy and I spent as much time alone as I could muster. She was so soft and giving and tender that I felt like my soul was being soothed. She tolerated the nightmares and woke me whenever she saw them coming on. She and Chico took me to local eateries and treated me like one of the family. I know it started with the money, but it quickly evolved to a personal relationship, and for a while, it worked.

The third day of my R & R, I started drinking heavily. Somehow, all the attention I had wasn't enough and I tried to drown out my nightmares. That day, I remember riding with Peggy in Chico's jingshaw, buying fresh fruit in the roadside markets. Then I spotted a booth selling American whiskey. I bought a 5th of Jim Beam Bourbon and we continued on our way. Early that evening, bourbon in hand, drinking it neat, it wasn't long before we stopped at a local bar to see some of the local color. That was where it started.

We got a table, the three of us, and Peggy noticed a girlfriend of hers. She went over to see the other girl and I went to the bar to order some drinks. While I was at the bar, I overheard some guys talking to their girls, telling them how hard they had it in Vietnam and all the battles they had been in. Naturally, I got interested and being not quite sober, I butted in and asked them what outfit they were in. They replied that they were in the Army stationed at some headquarters company in Da Nang. I lost it! It seemed like all the dead and wounded came flooding back to me, calling out for respect from two wannabe's. Without thinking, I cold cocked the both of them, and anyone else that came into my field of fire. I was back in Nam and couldn't stop. Everyone fled! I walked out of the bar and made it back to my hotel. It was dark and as I passed the front desk of the hotel, I noticed someone pointing at me, with what appeared to be police close at hand. I scurried up the stairs, determined not to be captured. I had seen what getting captured could get you.

I'm not sure exactly how it all came about, but I found myself trapped on a landing between floors, police above and below me. As one of the men approached from below, I told everyone to stop, that I would kill anyone who tried to take me. In my warped state of mind, I was convinced that the gooks were trying to capture and torture me. No one moved. They all knew I meant business and no one wanted to get hurt. They knew what I had done at the bar.

Trapped on the landing, ready to kill before capture, I heard a voice call out, "Hey mate," in an unmistakable Australian accent. It caught my attention and as I turned I saw an Aussie. I knew them by sight from the interactions I had had with them in Nam. He wore the standard uniform and instantly made me feel at home. I started to talk to him and he assured me that nothing bad would happen to me if I turned myself over to him for the night. The adrenaline subsided and I went peacefully with him and his mates. They didn't handcuff me or anything, just escorted me across the channel to their base to sleep it off in their cell. Once we got there, they gave me some coffee and we exchanged war stories. Quite a few of them had already done a tour in Vietnam and were very understanding - some real mates.

It was Wednesday, July 24, 1968. I was being escorted from the Austrailian brig on the mainland to the military headquarters in George Town. I got there around mid-morning, standing tall before the commanding officer of the R & R center. As I stood at attention, the Captain looked over my "file."

He looked directly at me and said:

"Marine, do you know what you did?"

"Yes sir," I answered.

"I ought to put you in chains and send you back to Vietnam today. Can you give me one reason why I shouldn't do just that?"

"Yes sir, I will behave and I just want to finish my R & R." I replied, as I stared straight ahead, still at attention.

He thought a while and said:

"Marine, I'm going to let you finish your R & R. But if you so much as spit on the sidewalk, I'll have you in chains and on a plane back to Vietnam before you can blink a eye."

"Yes SIR," I replied and was released to finish my R & R.

As I exited the building, there was my faithful friend Chico. He stuck with me all the way. I asked him about Peggy, and he told me he had talked to Peggy and that she was afraid and didn't want to come back, but after talking to her she had agreed to come back if I was good. I said okay, and we finished the day sightseeing and eating the local food, especially the fruit which was in season. No more booze for me. One of the fruits was rambutan, my favorite. It was a red egg-shaped fruit with soft spines sticking out of it. You peal the skin off and inside is this uniquely sweet whitish fruit with a single seed inside. You don't eat the raw seed as it is poisonous.

The next day, our last day in Panang, was a group trip to the far side of the island, sponsored by the R & R center. The area we were taken to was a park by the sea, complete with castle ruins and a Buddhist temple. We swam in the ocean, watched snake charmers and toured the ruins and monastery. I even got blessed by a Buddhist Monk, figuring I could use all the help I could get when I got back to Vietnam. After returning to my hotel, I gathered my belongings, said goodbye to Peggy and Chico and boarded the bus for the trip to the airport and back to my job - Combat Marine, Machine Gunner, Vietnam, 1968.

I arrived back in Vietnam on Friday, July 26th, 1968. After landing in Da Nang, I went to retrieve my combat gear and weapons. I "saddled up," caught a helo to the Battalion area, and back to the old routine of patrols, ambushes, missions and basic survival. Once I got to my squad in the Battalion Area, I wrote home about my R & R:

> *Dear Folks,*
>
> *Well, I'm back I Viet Nam now and oh how I wish I wasn't. You know, a person can really fall in love with the Orient. I can't explain how beautiful the East can be, because you have to see it to believe it. I'm sending you a couple of pictures that I had taken. I'll have to wait till I can get my film developed before I send you any more. If I can't get it developed here I'll send the film to you. The girl in the picture is Malaysian, and is real sweet. She showed me all over the island, helped me order from all the different foods the Malyasians cook, and just pampered me like a baby. I really lived like a king for 5 days, except for the night I spent in jail. I'll explain about that later. Right now, I just want to drop you this line and let you know that I'm fine. They don't have an A.P.O. [Army Post Office] or F.P.O. [Fleet Post Office], Mail System in Penang so I had to wait till I got back here.*
>
> *Say, it sure was wonderful talking to you all, that really started my R & R off right. It won't be long now, just about 6 more months and I'll be home. ...*
>
> *The pictures were taken at the Sleeping [Buddha] Temple in Penang. I've numbered the pictures and will explain them to you. In #1 the Buddhist Monk is blessing me and asking [Buddha] to watch over me. In #2 he's telling me not to worry about Viet Nam because [Buddha] will protect me. #3 is Peggy and I in our Jingschaw or cyclo in front of the temple. The cyclo is one of the main means of transportation in Penang.*

The cyclo boy's name is Chico, he stayed with me all 5 days, taking me all over the City any time of the day or night. He was a real fine fella. I'll have some more pictures pretty soon I hope. ...
With all my love, Chuck

The rest of the month for my Company, is listed in the records:

262040 F2A at 970686 spotted 3 VC with wpns at 970688. Fired 60 mort. Checked area with negative results.

262120 F2A at 971686 spotted movement on patrol route. Fired 60mm, sm/a, grenades, Checked area with neg results. 1 man rec'd minor wound from friendly grenade.

Lacking from the reports is the incident where Tom Montie was wounded. The medevac tag he wore that day, July 26th, states that on 262320H July, 11:30 p.m., his patrol was hit by an enemy grenade. Tom had a shrapnel wound in the left shoulder and he was medevaced as soon as possible.

Obviously, his wounding was at least 2 hours later than the report of the wounding by friendly grenade, but somehow it did not make it into the daily reports. Not uncommon for the system at that time and place.

More reports from the 27th:

270310 F/2/27 Sqd CP; 262342H, @971697-974683; Suspected VC posit.; Called mar arty f/m.; Checked area neg res recheck at first light. Div DTG 270233H.

270946 Co F plt bridge sec; 270730H; @997687; Reported explosion at bridge at above coord, one 8′ x 8′ cross beam dst. Engr report bridge will be repaired today. Div DTG 270945.

Translated:

Reported on July 27th at 9:46 a.m., a Platoon from Company F (2/27), which was providing bridge security, reported an explosion at the bridge at map coordinates 997687. One 8′X 8′ cross beam on the bridge was destroyed. The engineers reported that the bridge would be repaired today.

Back in combat. One week, from start to finish, but no shock on returning. It was as if the R&R had never happened. Once again I had to dodge bullets and dance around booby traps.

Further reports tell the following. I believe that these patrols were my welcome back parties:

280015 F2D @ 993667 called in Arty & 81mm"s. Searching area – Neg results at this time. F2D saw one VC @ 985668. Fired at him but he got away. Checked area out and found nothing.

280638 F/2/27 Sqd Bridge security; 280115H; @993684/000688; ARVN cmdr informed f co that one VC Co had over ran ARVN ambush at 000688. Req 60mm f/m from f co; Alerted all bridges and fired 60mm f/m.

280705 F/2/27 Sqd Bridge sec; 280115H; @ 993684-000688; Follow up report; Checked area spotted vc in vic 996654 fired 60mm & M-60. VC moved into treeline and disappeared.

280707 F/2/27 PPB; 280015H; @993667/985668; Follow up rep; While leaving area obs 1 VC by treeline vic 985688. Took VC under fire. He ran into treeline & disappeared.

281640 F2A @ 984640 found 1 dud 105 rd. Blew in place with C-4.

282215 From: Seg 6

To: All Seg Stations

In recent nights all neighboring command posts and contonments [*sic*] have been subject to enemy mortar attacks. So far we have been sparred these attacks. But certainly not as an oversite on the enemies part.

All unit Commanders:

Alert their supervisors that we are probably a priority target for mortar attacks.

Take precautionary steps to minimize casualties if an attack occurs.

Steps take [*sic*] will be.

Establish an early warning system at least one man awake in each billeting space.

Have helmets and flack jackets close by.

Be ready to rapidly take shelter.

Alert all sentries to immediately sound the alarm upon detecting in-coming.

301350 F2B @ 993689 found 1 60mm dud. Blew in place with M-26.

310717 F/2/27 PPB; 310550H; 977693; Man tripped what may be M-26 SFD; Priority medevac; Comp 0813. Div DTG 310821.

310550 F2B @ 977693 man tripped sfd. Called medevac (3 prior) Completed at 0813.

The constant reports given in this period covering Operation Allen Brook may seem a little overkill in the description of our participation in that operation. If you get tired of reading these reports, remember, that those feelings are minimal compared to the constant stress on the men involved. If you feel the anxiety implied by the constant reports of casualties, you may understand in part the pressure on our fighting men in Vietnam. Booby traps were the great equalizer for the enemy. We could bomb them from the air, shell them with artillery and mortars, cut them down with machine gun fire and rifle fire, but we could not stop the booby traps. It was like walking on an ocean of thin ice, not knowing if or when a crack might form and send you to the bottom. This stress would be carried by combat Soldiers and Marines long after their return home. That same stress is seen today in the troops returning from Iraq and Afganistan. Whether called an SFD (Special Firing Device) or an IED (Improvised Explosive Device), they are just different names for the same fearsome terror practiced by guerrilla forces everywhere.

On the 31st, I wrote:

Dear Mom,

Well, I sent you the film from my R & R. I hope you get it [okay] and hope the pictures come out [all right]. Some of them ought to be real pretty. I really had a great time. In fact, I even thought and forgot about staying in [Penang]. I was up at 8:00 every morning and went strong until 3 or 4 in the morning[.] I really made it last. There was only one break in it, and that was the night I spent in the brig. The Third night there I got real drunk and kinda went a little crazy. I thought I was back in Viet Nam. I nailed about 3 G. I.'s before they got me down. The R & R officer was real understanding and at 12:00 noon the next day, I was on R & R again. So I only lost about 8 hours and got a good [night's] sleep. But I know one thing. It will be a while before I get drunk after I get home. There's just too much in my memory. But that's over and forgotten. All I can say is that I had the time of my life and I will never forget Penang.

But, I'm back here now, so I'll have to forget it for a while. Just think, in less than 7 months and I'll be home. That sure will be nice won't it?

Right now we are back at Battalion waiting for word about what we are to do now. We will all probably be transferred out of 2/27 this month, so I'll expect a delay in mail when I get transferred but that's neither here nor there. …

Tell Chris that I got his papers and Magazines and Iced Tea. Thanks a whole lot. It was the best package I've gotten in a long time, with a little of everything in it. …

With all my love, Chuck

A milder version of the truth. I didn't want Mom to worry more than she already did.

An interesting comparison between Vietnam and other wars fought by U. S. Forces: In WWII, American, British and even German troops were given periods of rest, sometimes up to several months, between battles, and the Marines in the Pacific were given rest periods between island campaigns. Time to really relax and get back in shape. Even when the rear areas were much less than desired, the troops had the ability to rest, eat, play and be removed from the dangers they had been facing. Not so in Vietnam. Even at the In-Country R & R centers, there was always the threat of mortar or rocket attacks. In this war, Marines who lasted long enough saw over 380 days of constant danger. With almost constant patrols, VC snipers and booby traps, the constant exposure to combat had devastating effects on those who managed to survive, even if they had not received any physical wounds. A five-day R & R didn't really help much to let the men rest or relax. However, just the thought of R & R could keep a man going longer than what seemed possible, which I believe was the true purpose of R & R.

By the end of July, the casualty count for 2/27 in July was:

KIA 6 WIA 119 for a running total after 5.5 Months of KIA 38 WIA 507 MIA 2

Chapter 10

August had arrived. I was back from R & R and settled in to the old routine. We were stationed at the Battalion area, running patrols in the Rocket and Mortar Belt outside of Da Nang. Way outside! The Battalion was preparing for the move back to the States and we would soon be transferred to other units. We had to get through August first.

The Battalion records tell the tale:

> During the month of August, the Battalion continued its saturation patrolling of the rocket belt and normal maintenance and improvement of the combat base. The major portion of the month was devoted to preparing for the departure of the Battalion. Gear was packed and staged and personnel readied for reassignment or redeployment to CONUS [Continental United States]. Training continued at a normal rate despite departure plans. During the last eight days of the month enemy contact increased through-out the TAOR resulting in four major engagements and one important rescue operation.

On August 2nd, I wrote:

Dear Dad,

Well, I'm off for the bush again. I've got to take a patrol out for 3 days, so I don't have much time. ...

I'm doing fine, everything is just like it has always been, except for one small detail. I'm really homesick now after my R & R, but am getting over it slow but sure. But time seems to be going slower. I guess that is because we have been in Battalion now for 2 days. This month will go slow anyway, because most of the Company will be transferred on the 1st Div. Mix-Up. This is where they switch everyone around so there won't be a whole lot of people going home at the same time out of the same unit.

So I'll be sweating it out, hoping I don't get sent up North on the DMZ. But if I do I do and I'll still get home [okay].

Dad, I've really got to run now so I can get everything ready for patrol. …

With all my love, Chuck

Then on the 3rd I wrote:

Dear Folks,

Well here's a short note to let you know that I'm on the run again. We are headed for An Hoa to provide security for some Army artillery. Phewy! …

I'm real busy trying to get everything together to leave in a few hours. So I guess I'll just sign off. …

With all my love, Chuck

The letter from August 2nd indicates that I was taking out what looked to be another "Killer Team" patrol. However, things changed the next day when the Company was sent to the 5th Marines.

The records indicate the following:

3 Aug – Company F to OPCON 5th Marines.

The records from the 27th Marines do not reveal any action on our part after being sent OPCON (Operational Control) to the 5th Marines on August 3rd; neither do the records from the 5th Marines for that same period. Only my memories and letters give any clue to what occurred. The 5th Marines were involved in two operations at that time, Operation Allen Brook in the Go Noi and Operation Mameluke Thrust in the Happy Valley area. Fox Company 2/27 was sent to an artillery firebase in the Happy Valley area, supporting Operation Mameluke Thrust. David Lopez remembers when we landed on the mountaintop, "We came out of the helicopters with guns up, at the ready, like it was a hot LZ. The Army guys laughed at us because the area was already secure, but they didn't laugh long when they realized it was only one Marine company there to relieve maybe a Battalion of Army people."

On August 7th, I wrote:

Dear Chris,

Well, it's me at last. I bet you have been wondering [whether] I was ever going to write you or not and believe it or not, I've been wondering when I was going to get to write. So far, [practically] all my [daytime] has been spent trying to keep dry, and that itself is quite a job.

Right now I am on top of a Mountain about 20 miles [southwest] of Danang. We took over from the Army (they couldn't take it) and have brought in 6, 105 Arty Pieces [105mm artillery]. Boy have we been giving the Gooks hell. Of course we have had our share of hell too. Mainly from the weather. It rains here at least once a day and it is all we can do to try and keep a little dry. Right now I've got our bunker pretty dry. I've got a wood floor in it made out of ammo boxes and a drain trench all around, so when it rains all we have to worry about are the thousand and one drips from the roof. Oh well things could be worse. Then there is the wind. It blows like crazy up here all the time, especially when it rains, so when we are wet we're also cold. This mountain is about 800ft high and there are absolutely no trees up here. So we made beautiful targets for snipers on the other side of the valley. It's only about 1000 meters across the valley, so we are well within sniper range from one ridge to the next, and especially from the tree line below our position. Hopefully, we will only be here about 4 or 5 more days, but nothing is certain around here, so I'll just have to wait and see. …

With all my love, Your big brother, Chuck

We called it a mountain because 800 feet rising steeply to the top was really high when you're at sea level. The firebase we were on had bunkers from the previous Army occupation, so all we had to do was fix things up. We were resupplied regularly and had plenty of chow, even if it was only C-Rations - our steady diet the whole time I was in Vietnam.

On August 9th, I wrote:

Dear Mom,

Well, It's little old me again. I know it's been a while since I written you, about a week now, but I've been pretty busy. You know from Chris' letter that I'm up on this mountain. Well, it's really not as bad as I expected it to be, except for the patrols. I run one patrol every 6 days up here. Each Plt. Takes a turn and each squad in the Plt., so it works out to 1 patrol every 6 days, and we are supposed to leave here either the 11th or 12th, so I hope I don't have another patrol. The area all around this mountain is extremely hilly, and everything is covered in rain forests, which is the same thing as jungles. The brush and grass is so thick that you have to cut your way through with a [machete], and the trees are so high that you never see daylight. It is really hell. I guess Dad knows *what I am talking about. Boy, give me those beautiful muddy, flat rice paddies. We left on patrol yesterday morning at 7:00 and were supposed to be back at 12:00. We didn't get back till 5:30. So you can see that it wasn't exactly an easy patrol. Right now my arms and hands look like hamburger they are so cut up, that elephant grass and all the thorn bushes are really bad. But nevertheless I'm fine and will probably be back in Battalion in a day or 2.*

I haven't gotten any mail since we've been out here, so I can't comment on things at home. We get our resupply from the 5th Marines and our mail just hasn't been making it. ...

With all my love, Chuck

Once again, the leadership and camaraderie in our platoon proved itself. Our platoon was assigned a sector to patrol and with Lt. Jones, SSgt. Staggs, the three regular squad leaders and I, we had one in six rotation. Lt. Jones and SSgt. Staggs were never above the rest of us in taking their part in our patrolling whenever they could. They were true leaders, leading from the *front*, not the rear, as is advertised in today's world.

The patrol I talked about in my letter was a very watered down version. I remember that patrol clearly. First, it must be understood that those who mapped out patrol routes had nothing to go by other than a military contour map. They draw a line and say, "Do it.," but the reality is often very treacherous and hazardous. On a map, that patrol started on the top of our mountain, went down for a while, turned right, ran more or less parallel to the top, and then turned right again to end back on top. Sounds pretty simple and easy, right? Oh no! The mountaintop was actually a ridge with very steep sides. I remember starting out with my patrol of about nine Marines heading down at an extreme angle. This was starting out as Mountain Climbing 101, not patrolling. I didn't take a machine gun with me, but Lopez and Nordmann were with me (one man from each gun team) with the rest made up of other weapons platoon personnel and of course, the essential radioman.

As we descended from the top of the mountain the vegetation got thicker and thicker. With no trail to follow, we had to bull our way through where we could and finally turned to machetes when we got into the bamboo. After a reasonable time, I turned the patrol to the right and proceeded across the slope, still in bad terrain. Around 1100 hours, we came upon a small stream bed coming down the mountain. It was strewn with large rocks and boulders and a rivulet of water. We were tuckered out and stopped to eat a bite. Most of us had tins of peanut butter and crackers with us, carried in the side pockets of our jungle utilities. Our patrol gear consisted of a web belt with canteens, Ka-Bar knife if you had one, rifle, loaded magazines in cloth bandoleers, flak jacket, helmet and personal items. I also carried my .45 and magazines. There were two machetes carried as well, one by the point man and another in reserve. By the time we reached the stream bed, just about everyone had taken a turn as point man, including myself. Swinging a machete is not child's play and in the heat, humidity, extra thick elephant grass and bamboo, it's pure hard labor. About twenty minutes of constant whacking would be enough to wear out all but the newbies who hadn't been worn down yet. Unfortunately, there were no newbies to help us this time.

We hadn't crossed a trail yet, and I knew that we probably wouldn't on this route. The only "trail" was the one we were making. It was getting late, past the time we were supposed to return. The one thing I kept strong in my mind was the possibility of an ambush by the gooks. Yet, every time I thought of that, I had to also remember that they weren't supermen. I didn't consider the VC to be any better in the bush than experienced Marines. Not that we weren't vulnerable, but as long as I stayed alert and used what I knew about the jungle, I felt safe.

Since we were going to be late I tried to call in, but all we got was static. We just weren't in a good position for radio communication. I had to make a decision - continue on the patrol route on the map, or just head for home. One thing for sure, we *had* to be back by dark or risk getting hit by the VC, or our own troops on the perimeter. I opted for the latter. The stream bed was the only clear path and I took it. It was steep and climbing over those boulders was difficult at best, but climb we did.

Like every good plan, there is always something that can get in the way. For us, it was the jungle. The stream bed didn't last as long as I hoped, and petered out at a spring only 50 yards or so up hill. I didn't need a map or compass; all I needed to do was go up hill. Still, it was possible that we could drift farther around the mountain and still come up beyond our perimeter. To avoid this, I angled the route up and to the right, which should bring us back to the center of our perimeter, or so I hoped. It was back into the jungle again, always moving up and slightly to the right. Back to hacking with the machete through the bamboo. The elephant grass had given way to bamboo and was almost as thick as the elephant grass. I changed point men often and took my turn in the rotation. It was now a matter of "get back or die" - that was the urgency I felt. It's no easy task to be responsible for the lives of eight other men, all relying on your judgment for their safety. I wasn't worried so much about the VC, I figured they would have to be crazy to try to do what we were doing, and I bet that they would die laughing anyway if they could see our struggles.

It wasn't just the bamboo either. The patrol route started off at the end of the ridge which, although steep, made a more gradual descent than what we were faced with now. Now it was very steep, and at times the dreaded bamboo became our savior as our feet flew out from under us and all we could do was grab a bamboo stalk to keep from tumbling down the mountain. Normally, we always patrolled with a good twenty to thirty feet between each other to keep from bunching up. I can hear in my mind SSgt. Staggs hollering at us after we first got to Vietnam:

"Spread it out, one grenade can get you all."

And he was right, in most cases. In this instance though, it was one man on top of another, helping each other to climb the steep slope. This went on seemingly forever. As we progressed upward, we didn't need a watch to tell us that time was running out. As the sun started to descend, the jungle got darker and darker. It could still be bright sunlight on top of the mountain, and near dark on the slopes. Dan Nordmann remembers it was one of the worst patrols he had ever been on, hacking away with the machete and seemingly not making any real progress.

Just as things were looking bad, with all of us plumb worn out, we popped out into sunlight just about where I wanted, at the middle of the perimeter. As we came dragging ass into the relative safety of our lines, the artillerymen stared open-mouthed at the apparition that was approaching them. Of course I was bawled out for being so late, but after everyone understood what we had been up against, all was forgiven, but not forgotten. I like to think that subsequent patrols learned something from our experience and avoided similar hazards at the hands of map-readers laying out patrol routes. Dan Nordmann remembers having similar problems when he was on a patrol with Lt. Jones. There just weren't any good routes around that mountain.

Despite the thick jungle, the VC did eventually make it close enough to snipe at us and keep us on our toes. I remember one night in particular. We had set out some early detection devises on the concertina wire (barbed wire configured in a circular formation forming a barrier several feet wide) that surrounded our perimeter. The wire was about twenty yards in front of our fighting holes with another twenty or thirty yards of clear ground beyond that. The early detection devices we had on the wire were empty C-ration cans with a few rocks inside. Any motion on the wire would set the rocks to rattling around in the cans and alert those nearby that something was going on there.

It was well into the night and I was on watch in my bunker. It was normally quiet with just the faint sounds of water dripping off the jungle leaves and animals moving around down below us. Then it happened! At first, it was just a rattle here and a rattle there as the wire was disturbed and the rocks in the cans let out their distinct sounds. As the sound increased, more men were aroused by it, or were awakened by their buddies. Cans really started to rattle and the whole line of men on that side of the perimeter were alert and ready for action. The sounds increased to a steady crescendo, and we started to get what we thought were incoming grenades. Before any of the grenades had a chance to explode, the line opened up with rifle and machine gun fire. The sounds continued for a short while and then stopped as quickly as they had started. We remained alert the rest of the night, waiting until dawn to see all the dead VC that must be out there.

Early dawn arrived, and no matter how hard we looked, we couldn't see any bodies in front of us. The wire seemed to be intact, so that was a relief. As the day got brighter, a patrol was formed to go down to the wire and check it out. Since the wire lay down slope from us, with an even greater grade downward after the wire, it was decided that any VC on the ground may well be below our line of sight from the top of the mountain. We covered the patrol and waited for them to return.

Before long, we heard the patrol call out that we ought to come down and look. We kept our lines manned with a few men while the rest of us went down to see what all the ruckus was about. As we approached the wire, all became evident. There before us lay the bodies of what we thought at first were large monkeys. After closer examination, we discovered that they were rock apes. They were like apes, only larger, with no tail and ugly faces. They stunk like hell. We took the bodies and swung them over the edge of the steepest part of the hill, good food for the tigers. I have come to understand that these "rock apes" are considered the "Bigfoot" of Vietnam. It was a shame that we destroyed some very unique creatures.

Finally, we put the "crime scene" in order. The rock apes must have smelled our trash pit, which was pretty close to where all the action was, and tried to cross the wire. As the noise in the cans started, they reacted by throwing rocks which we misconstrued as grenades and the rest was history. Excitement over, we went back to our normal daily routine.

It was August 11th, and I wrote:

Dear Dad,

Well, it looks like the V.A. is trying to give you the shaft, and boy does that burn me up. There isn't much I can do, but I will do what I can. Just don't give in. …

Guess what, I'm half way clean for a chance. Yep, it rained last night, the first time in about 4 days, so I got out the soap and really scrubbed down. You should have seen the top of this mountain. It looked like a nudist colony, with about a hundred Marines jumping up and down, in the raw, daring Charlie to shoot us. How crazy can you get, egh! Oh well, at least we are clean for a change.

I still don't know when we are going to leave this place, so I can't give you any news about that. So I guess I might as well fill you in on all the [bum] scoop about the 27th Marines. First of all, we started hearing that the 27th was going home as far back as May. Yep, May 15 we were supposed to go home. Then it changed to June 15, then September 1, and now they are saying we were supposed to go home Sept 1, but that we were extended till Sept 15. So as you can see, your guess is as good as mine [whether] the 27th will get home or not. Then there are the transfers. Most probably those of us who are in Nam for the first time will be transferred and complete our 13 month tour. However if we do go home with the 27th, we will have completed 1 tour, since when a unit comes over and then goes back, that length of time whatever it may be, is [considered] 1 tour. So don't get your hopes up, and in fact, it would be better to just forget the whole thing till I call you from Calif. Or maybe even San Antonio and tell you I'm back. I don't expect any favors from the Marine Corps, and if I do luck out and leave next month, I'll probably pay for it some way, you know the service. You never get anything for nothing. …

After I get back from Viet Nam I will start taking some correspondence courses to add toward my college degree. I hope to complete a year of college while still in the service, then when I get out I will take my last year at Texas U. or some similar well known University and go on and get my Masters Degree. …

Well, I guess it's about time I close, there's a war going on over here, believe it or not. … I sure hope everything works out all right with the V.A. Write again soon,

With all my love, Chuck

The Veterans Association was not very veteran friendly in those days, and my dad always had problems with them where his service connected disability was concerned. On the 17th, I wrote:

Dear Mom,

Well, here it is a beautiful rainy Saturday, which will [inevitably] lead to a beautiful rainy Sunday, which will etc. Yep, it looks like the Monsoon Season is close at hand. It has rained up here every day except 1 during this past week. I have just fixed myself a cup of C Ration coffee and lit myself a Kent (without the filter) [Kent was a brand of filtered cigarette] and so being in a sufficiently happy frame of mind I decided to write again. By the way, we only get mail up here every three days so there's another reason for my joy.

Let's see, first of all, if you haven't already guessed, I'm still on top of that mountain, and the way it looks, I'll be here till around the 1st of Sept. or until I get transferred, [whichever] comes first. Actually it isn't too bad up here, I've got a semi-dry bunker and 1 patrol every 6 days, so actually I've got it pretty easy [compared] to what I was doing before we came here. But as you know, man is never satisfied and so naturally, I'm a little bored. Tell Chris that his Monthly package would sure be nice to have up here. (hint, hint) I'll write him today or tomorrow. …

I wrote to Congressman O.C. Fisher as an angry Marine in Viet Nam asking him to help Dad with the V.A. I don't know if it'll do any good, but at least I put [my] two cents worth in. I just wonder how I'll be treated if I get disabled. I'd like to see the V.A. try and put me out like they are trying to do with Dad. I'm not a machine-gunner for nothing, ha, ha. …

With all my love, Chuck

On August 19th, I wrote:

Dear Chris,

Well, little buddy, it looks like you came through in the pinch again. Yep, I was about to go nuts with boredom, when boom, I got your package. You'll never know how much that little monthly package with the funnies and [Kool-Aid] and all really perks me up. …

Now tell me, who needs an ex-machine-gunner back in the States, except for "The Organization," and Al Capone is dead anyway. Seriously, if I were you I'd think about joining the Air Force after High School. Then you could go to college on the Veterans plan after you got out. But don't let anyone knock the Marines unless they have been in the Corps. It's hell while you are in, but it's something to be proud of when you get out. ...

Your big brother, Chuck

The time at that firebase was a welcome reprieve from the grind we had been in since arriving in Vietnam. It was a good time to relax, get some sun, when it came out, write letters and have three meals a day - C-Rations of course. We were living the life of Reilly up on that mountaintop, except for the patrols, and we never saw what was coming. On August 23, we were lifted out by helicopter and put down at our base on the Anderson Trail. We were then trucked to the vicinity of the Cam Le Bridge. The Cam Le Bridge was located just south of the village of Cam Le, which was southeast of Da Nang, about 2 km from the Da Nang airfield. Although I have memories of our involvement in the battle for the Cam Le Bridge, I lack the overview of that action. Therefore, I am including excerpts of other works which can give that "Big Picture."

Cầu Cẩm Lệ
ĐÀ NẴNG
1968

United States marines and South Vietnamese rangers moved on foot and in armored personnel carriers across a bridge on the southern edge of Da Nang while searching for Viet-Cong infiltrators. Enemy units have tried to gain control of the bridge in recent attacks.—A. P. wirephoto AUG 3 1 1968

A detailed description of the Battle for the Cam Le Bridge from the viewpoint of the 1st Battalion, 27th Marines is provided below, taken from *Youngblood: A History of the 1st Battalion 27th Marines, 1968* by Gary E. Jarvis PhD. A heartfelt thank you to Dr. Jarvis for his permission to present these pages.

"Battle for Cam Le Bridge"

Young blood: A History of the 1st Battalion, 27th Marines 1968 by Gary E. Jarvis PhD, Pages 225 to 234 of Dr. Jarvis' book are shown below.

August 22, 1968

At 2115 hours, a squad patrol from Charlie Company was engaged in a firefight with five (5) VC at coordinates 965650. Two (2) of the VC were killed and two (2) enemy weapons were captured. One (1) Marine was also wounded.

August 23, 1968

Under the cover of the early morning darkness, the NVA assumed an offensive posture and launched their long awaited Third Offensive. The first attacks against the Marines of the 1st Battalion, 27th Marines occurred at 0300 hours when the Communist forces attacked a Bravo Company platoon perimeter base while another NVA force simultaneously attacked a Charlie Company platoon perimeter base. The Bravo Company platoon perimeter base (coordinates 970697) was attacked by a NVA/VC force, which fired rockets and small arms. Military records indicated that the size of the NVA force was an estimated squad, which was contrary to the general attack plans of the NVA. It was a common practice for the NVA not to attack unless they outnumbered their foes by a ratio of 2:1 or more. Nevertheless, the Marines successfully repulsed the enemy attack but not without losses. Shrapnel from the enemy's fatal rocket barrage killed three (3) Marines: PFC Ricky G. Harrison, PFC Robert J. Miller, PFC Gregory Woods and five (5) other Marines from Bravo Company were also wounded. When the enemy retreated, the Marines found (1) Viet Cong soldier left on the battlefield. The rest had escaped into the darkness with their dead and wounded.

While Bravo Company was engaged in a battle with the enemy at 0300 hours, a platoon perimeter base from Charlie Company (coordinates 973642) located less than 500 meters away simultaneously received incoming mortar rounds that were followed by a ground assault by the VC/NVA, killing corpsman Charles R. Golling. Fourteen (14) Marines were wounded. Three (3) Viet Cong were killed and three (3) weapons were captured. The communist attacks on the two (2) platoon perimeter bases were part of the enemy's strategy for diverting attention away from their true objectives.

Captain Ron Gruenberg, the CO of Company C, recalled the following regarding August 23,1968: *"the intelligence reports concerning another NVA push on Danang were coming hourly. To secure our platoon patrol base the Engineers created a berm for the platoon. After repeated requests, I was finally granted permission to move my HQ group out to the platoon position and reinforce it with what little men we had left. The coordination to get through several different ARVN units was a nightmare but we finally got there just in time for the attack. Intelligence later verified that an entire NVA Regiment lay in waiting for the attack on Danang had let us slip by... Fortunes of War. Lt Crane Davis' platoon base became affectionally [sic] known as Fort Apache. It was during the assault on Fort Apache that we received a call from Battalion to send out a patrol and determine the situation at a similar ARVN position up the road from us. I gave them a firm negative. At the time, we were endangered of being overrun. The next day we did send the patrol and found them all dead."*

Two and one-half hours (0530 hours) after the two platoon perimeter bases were first attacked, regimental headquarters informed the battalion that the Cam Le Bridge (coordinates 016715) had fallen into the hands of the enemy. Company D 1st Military Police Battalion was responsible for security of the bridge and during fierce fighting, they lost control of the southern end. The Communists had also captured a 50 caliber machine gun mounted in an old French Bunker on the southern end of the bridge and were firing it at the Marines.

Regimental headquarters ordered the 1st Battalion, 27th Marines to exert maximum effort to retake the bridge. By then, there was little doubt that the NVA had launched their planned third offensive. While the Marines in 1/27 made preparations to retake the bridge, Marines from the 1st MP Battalion held their ground and fiercely repelled the enemy's efforts to take control of the north end of the bridge. They were determined not to give another inch to the enemy.

Since the command post of the 1st Battalion, 27th Marines was only four (4) kilometers southwest of the captured bridge, the battalion commander, Major Kenneth J. Skipper, ordered Company A and Company D located at the battalion command post, to waste no time proceeding to the Cam Le Bridge and launch a counterattack immediately. Battalion's plan was to initiate a convergence of forces scheme of attack. First Lieutenant Robert Baribeau, the CO of Delta

Company, left the battalion compound with three platoons of Marines to attack to bridge from west to east. Within five minutes of receiving the battalion commander's order, at 0645 hours, Captain William 0. Moore, the company commander of Alpha Company, rushed out of the compound with only two reinforced squads led by First Sergeant Ronald L. Burtsell. The Alpha Company Marines were ordered to attack the bridge from the south to north. Burtsell and Moore left with anyone available in their company, even clerks. The company commander had limited Marines at his disposal since two of the company's three platoons were already detached and one squad from the remaining platoon was out on a patrol. One of his platoons was on Christmas Island, 1,000 meters northeast of the bridge, and the other was supporting a combined action platoon, CAP, in the hamlet of Lo Giang (1), 1,000 meters southeast of the bridge.

While on his way to the Cam Le Bridge, Captain Moore's troops passed through an ARVN compound where Moore stopped to talk with U.S. Army advisors. The advisors pinpointed the suspected positions of the Communist who held positions on both sides of Highway 1. As the Marines proceeded north near the outskirts of Cam Nam, which was only two kilometers from the NVA's positions on the south end of the bridge, Captain Moore received orders from Major Skipper to send one of his two squads to assist the platoon in Lo Giang (1). Lo Giang (1) was suspected to be surrounded and under attack. Sixteen (16) Marines left to reinforce the Marines at Lo Giang (1). Captain Moore requested permission to proceed toward the bridge but was ordered by Major Skipper to stay in position until a platoon of tanks could arrive to support the attack. Shortly thereafter, the Marines sent to Lo Giang (1) radioed back that they had found the hamlet quiet. Since they were not needed by the combined action platoon Marines, Captain Moore asked Major Skipper for the Marines to be returned for the inevitable counterattack on the bridge. The Major denied his request.

At 0915 hours, the original combat patrol from Alpha Company was at coordinates 018717 when enemy small arms fire and automatic weapons fire pinned them down. The enemy fired at the Marines from a bunker and entrenched defensive positions at the southern end of the Cam Le Bridge, which was located at coordinates 016715.

For almost six hours, the platoon was pinned down and unable to move. Two Marines were wounded during this incident.

At 0920 hours, Delta Company, under the command of 1stLt Robert Baribeau, a mustang Marine officer known for his tactical acumen, was conducting a sweep in the vicinity of coordinates 007704. While sweeping east toward the direction of the Cam Le bridge, which was approximately 900 meters away, Delta Company received small arms and automatic weapons fire from an entrenched enemy in a tree line, halting the advancing Marines. Air strikes were called before the Marines continued their advance toward the Cam Le Bridge. During a hostile exchange of weapons fire, three (3) Delta Company Marines were wounded. After the air strike ceased, the enemy retreated to the east with Delta Company right on their heels. In a futile attempt to stop the advancing Marines, the NVA left behind snipers who fired at the Marines from well-concealed positions. The enemy small arms fire did little to deter the tenacious Marines from moving forward. The enemy frequently used one sniper or a team of snipers to cover their retreat in an effort to slow down advancing Marines.

At 1145 hours, four 90mm gun tanks and a flame tank from Company B, 5th Tank Battalion arrived and the two ad-hoc Alpha Company squads that constituted the original Company A platoon, supported by the tanks, moved toward their objective, the Cam Le Bridge. The road near the hamlet of Cam Nam was raised above the surrounding rice paddies with sharp drops on both shoulders of the road. Consequently, the two squads were forced to march single file on both sides of the road. As the two squads made their way toward Cam Nam, Delta Company, 1st Battalion, 27th Marines swept toward the east and attacked Cam Nam from the west.

In less than three (3) hours, the Delta Company Marines along with an attached platoon from Bravo Company had swept through five hundred (500) meters of enemy occupied territory and advanced to the vicinity of coordinates 012705 by 1215 hours. As the Delta Company force moved closer toward the bridge, which was approximately 400 meters away, small arms and automatic weapons fire from the vicinity of coordinates 013705 halted their advance. The attached platoon from Bravo Company was also on the receiving end of the enemy's devastating initial small arms and automatic weapons fire. The enemy had held back their fire until the Marines were within 100 meters from their concealed positions before they opened fire from entrenched positions.

The vigilant Marines saw many Marines near them hit the dirt, falling to the ground wounded from the enemy gunfire. Doc Grimshaw, a combat weary corpsman in Delta Company, had taken cover behind a rice paddy dike alongside an M-60 machine gunner and LCpl John Sloatman III. Doc spotted two wounded Marines trapped in the enemy's hail of fire. Sloatman said "don't do it Doc. Wait until the fire dies down." Doc Grimshaw refused to wait. He left the relative safety of the dike and under a hail of heavy enemy fire, the corpsman miraculously reached the exposed site of the wounded Marines. But his premonition from months before came true when a enemy machine gun round struck him right between the eyes, piercing his skull and exposing gray brain matter. Another bullet severed one of his fingers. Doc Danny Grimshaw, a truly brave Navy corpsman, died instantly. Subsequently, the Marines laid down their own devastating field of fire and angrily assaulted the enemy positions. Again, the Communists fled as the Marines overtook their defensive positions, leaving three (3) VC/NVA behind. Remnants of the enemy force fled with their dead and wounded, escaping to the northeast. Besides Doc Grimshaw, there were other casualties. Thirteen (13) Marines were wounded and the courageous Sgt Luther J. Thedford from Bravo Company died from bullet wounds in his abdomen. Both Sgt Thedford and Lt. Charles Collins, who sustained a severe wound from a 50-caliber bullet which shattered his upper arm, had adamantly refused to be evacuated until their mission had been accomplished and the other wounded were evacuated, Sgt Thedford's unselfish refusal to be evacuated inevitably resulted in his death.

Before the day was over, the dead and wounded were carried out. Doc Danny Grimshaw, a corpsman who was killed by the NVA with a 50 caliber machine gun round to his head, was hand-carried in a olive-green poncho by LCpl Billy Frye, LCpl Gary Jarvis, LCpl Michael Magaw and one (1) other Marine in Delta Company from the battlefield back to Camp Duong Son. On the way back to the battalion rear area, LCPL Jarvis, while carrying the left front corner of the poncho, wrapped Doc Grimshaw's head in a shirt to prevent the other Marines from seeing Doc's exposed brain. Carrying the lifeless body of their heroic corpsman off the battlefield through rice paddies all the way back to the battalion rear area, which was over 2000 meters, was a very painful unforgettable experience for all the Marines. Out of profound respect, Lt. Baribeau personally turned over Grimshaw's body to the battalion corpsman as the Marines entered the battalion compound. Doc Grimshaw had volunteered for a dangerous mission and paid the supreme price. Senior Corpsman Grimshaw was posthumously awarded the Bronze Star Medal with Combat V for his heroic actions on August 23, 1968.

First Lieutenant Robert "Bob" Baribeau, the commanding officer of Company D, 1st Battalion, 27th Marines, succinctly recalled Company D's role in the retaking of the Cam Le Bridge on August 23, 1968:

"At approximately 0530-0545, I was called into the COC (Combat Operations Center) Bunker where Major Skipper informed me that the Cam Le Bridge had been taken by NVA. I was given orders to take Delta Company and proceed as quickly as possible and attack from West to East. Alpha Company was to attack from South to North. Our mission was to retake the southern end of the Cam Le Bridge. I moved D Company down the road from the battalion command post, as it was the most direct and fastest route. We then moved off the road and went due east toward the Cam Le Bridge. We arrived at an open rice paddy. On the other side of the rice paddy was a small village. I sent 1st platoon B Co to the right to cross the rice paddy and enter the tree line. I had 3rd Platoon cover the left flank. They also moved toward the tree line in the village. I kept 2nd Platoon (-) in reserve along with my command group. First Platoon received fire and became pinned down. As 3rd Platoon moved forward, they too received fire. Two of the Marines from 3rd Platoon moved by fire and maneuvered to approximately 100 yards of the tree line and became pinned down and unable to advance.

I received a call from Air overhead, asking if they could help. I replied in the affirmative. Ordinance (bombs) could not be used as the South end of the Cam Le Bridge was on the other side of the village and they feared severely damaging the bridge. However, they informed me that they could use their guns. I instructed Lt. Charles Collins, B Company's 1st platoon commander, to have the most forward Marines place an air panel directly in front of him. I subsequently, informed a pilot that he could strafe forward of the air panel. The pilot made a pass, firing rounds right in the area in front of the air panel. I then ordered a platoon to move forward approximately 25-40 yards and place the air panel to the front of their most forward Marines. I again notified the pilot that he could strafe the more forward area in front of the air panel. I repeated the forward advance move one more time so that we could reach the tree line at the village. After 1st Platoon reached the tree line, 1st Platoon swept to the left and 3rd Platoon moved to the tree line. Second Platoon and the command group followed.

Once in the village, we moved toward the Cam Le Bridge. We managed to evacuate our wounded. As we battled forward, Delta Company flushed out several NVA who ran into a Pagoda. A tank that was attached to Alpha Company moved forward and torched the building with the NVA inside. Subsequently, I received a radio call from battalion, informing me that they were going to TOT (artillery time on target) the area and that I was to evacuate the area immediately. I radioed battalion and informed them that I could not execute their order because Doc Grimshaw had been killed and his body was still lying out in the battlefield where we were to pull back from. I informed battalion that I still had one of my men to bring back. We were always taught and strongly believed that we always bring back our dead and our wounded. Once Doc Grimshaw's body was recovered, I then informed the battalion CP that all dead and wounded were retrieved and I was moving my men from the area so as to TOT the target.

After Delta Company moved from the area, the artillery performed their time on target, using the artillery battalion in its full sense. Subsequently, we received our orders to return to the battalion CP. "

While Delta Company (2d and 3d platoon D Co and 1st platoon B Co) was in a fierce battle with the communist forces west of Cam Nam, Captain Moore's Marines moved forward along the eastside of National Route 1. As the under strength Company A platoon advanced to less than 400 meters from Cam Nam, the large well-entrenched enemy force opened fire with mortars, RPGs and small arms. The enemy's devastating heavy volume of fire killed two (2) Marines and wounded four (4). Realizing the seriousness of the situation, the First Sergeant of Company A, First Sergeant Burtsell, unhesitatingly deployed his men to advantageous positions and with bullets penetrating the dirt at his feet, he moved throughout the fire-swept area, aiding the wounded as he simultaneously directed his men's fire. Soon after, First Sergeant Burtsell led his men on a determined assault against the enemy emplacements. The Marines inched forward with only low-lying rice paddy dikes for cover as they fired their weapons and maneuvered toward the enemy. As the attacking force got to within two hundred meters from the hamlet, an RPG round hit one of the lead tanks but it caused only minor damage. Captain Moore pointed out the source of the RPG round to the tankers. With the enemy rocketman in their sights, the tankers fired three (3) rounds of white phosphorous, four (4) rounds of "Beehive," and forty (40) rounds of high explosive. The fire was a bit too much for the Communist troops. The enemy soldiers hastily ran from one building to another within the hamlet, trying desperately to evade the tank's deadly firepower, which was intensified by the fire delivered by the ground troops. There was no escape for the enemy. The tanks cut them down with machine gun fire and fired 90mm rounds at any structure used as cover. But the enemy did not surrender. In one instance, several enemy soldiers tried to flee by jumping into a jeep and driving off. Their attempted departure was halted by tank fire, causing the vehicle to burst into flames. Enemy machine gun fire from a straw hut was also squelched when a flame tank saturated the hut with burning fuel. In a short time, all the structures in the entire hamlet were on fire. Virtually every structure was leveled. Capt Moore aptly summed up the situation in the hamlet with his statement "This about ended our problem."

But the bridge still remained in the hands of the Communists who had blocked the highway with vehicles for cover in an attempt to slow down the Marines' attack. The motor vehicle obstacles were virtually eliminated with five rounds of 90mm fire from the tanks as the Marines moved forward toward the Cam Le Bridge. As they maneuvered through the burning hamlet, Alpha Company received word that a platoon from Company E, 2d Battalion, 27th Marines would arrive to assist them in the bridge counterattack. More troops became available for the counterattack when Captain Moore ordered his platoon on Christmas Island to join the counterattack from the east. The platoon on Christmas Island had already made one unsuccessful attempt to recapture the bridge.

The .50-caliber machine gun retrieved by the NVA, when they captured the bridge, fired burst after burst of rounds at the Marines who were attempting to recapture the Cam Le Bridge. At 1405 hours at coordinates 012705, the original platoon that was dispatched by Alpha Company encountered B-40 rockets, automatic weapons and small arms fire from the enemy held French bunker and defensive position at the southern end of the Cam Le bridge (coordinates 016715). Marine tanks fired at enemy positions as First Sergeant Ronald Burtsell directed accurate suppressive fire and led the Company A Marines forward through the fire-swept terrain. The Marines overran and secured the enemy positions, causing the enemy to abandon their entrenched positions. As the enemy retreated, Burtsell directed supporting arms fire, which aided the Marines who were advancing through the village of Cam Nam. First Sergeant Burtsell received the Silver Star Medal for his heroic actions on 23 August 1968. At 1545 hours, Captain Moore radioed battalion command and notified them that the bridge was secured. It had taken the Marines nine long hours to take the bridge back from the Communists.

At the conclusion of the battle for the bridge, twenty-two (22) VC lay dead on the battleground. Days later, there were ten (10) additional dead VC discovered after the bodies surfaced in the river, bringing the total enemy dead up to thirty-two (32). The fight for the bridge was a victory for the Marines but not without Marine casualties. Alpha Company had two Marines killed in action: PFC Henry H. Ballew and LCpl Leo Miller Jennette. Four (4) other Company A Marines were wounded.

While searching the bridge area, the Marines discovered several South Vietnamese Popular Force soldiers hiding beneath the bridge. They had been there since the battle began and had hid there during the entire battle.

Another noteworthy enemy engagement was reported on August 23,1968. At 1405 hours when a platoon from H&S Company was on a recon patrol in the vicinity of 003668, the Marine platoon came in contact with an unknown size enemy force. At the conclusion of the firefight, there were five (5) VC killed and one (1) Marine was wounded.

At 1700 hours on 23 August 1968, the 2d ARVN Ranger Battalion assumed the tactical area of responsibility for the area east to the main supply route, MSR, north of Grid 69, west of Grid 04 and south of grid 71. The Marines continued to conduct their assigned operations.

After Company D had returned to Camp Duong Son following the Cam Le Bridge battle, Lt Baribeau was called to the Battalion COC Bunker and given orders to a rescue a combat patrol from another unit (not a 1/27 unit) that had been ambushed. Lt Baribeau along with his Company Gunny and his Delta Company reactionary force saddled up and as they approached the ambush site, the D Company Marines received fire from a village. Lt. Baribeau prepped the hostile area with artillery fire as he moved his company toward the village and discontinued the artillery fire as the Marines entered the targeted area. The Company D Marines swept the area and found dead NVA everywhere. According to Lt. Baribeau, one of the NVA was alive but playing dead. When the NVA twitched, he was shot and killed. When he was flipped over, it was confirmed that he had his finger on the trigger of a fully loaded AK-47 that was ready to fire. Lt. Baribeau, later, personally carried this AK-47 back to the battalion rear area. In the meantime, the trapped and pinned down Marines were taken out. Subsequently, Major Skipper ordered Lt. Baribeau and his Marines to return in the darkness to Camp Duong Son for hot chow. Though Lt. Baribeau knew that such an order was tactically flawed and his company gunny had told him to "tell Major Skipper that you can't move at night" especially since moving in the dark through enemy infested territory at that time was foolish, he reluctantly and against his own personal judgment, complied with the battalion commander's orders. Lt. Baribeau cautiously moved his Marines through the enemy infested territory. When Lt. Baribeau reached the Bn. CP, he turned the still loaded AK-47 over to Lt. John Bouldin.

LCpl Richard Hunt, one of 1/27's S2 Scouts, also provided his recollection of other actions on August 23, 1968. It is as follows:

"About midday on 23 August 1968, Pfc. Otto J. Ostenfeld, another S-2 Scout, and I were in the Battalion Command Post, having returned from an earlier patrol. An aerial spotter known as a 'bird dog' working with Marines attacking the Cam Le Bridge had observed an enemy group of unknown size proceeding toward the Battalion Command Post. Orders were given assembling a patrol of approximately three squad sized units comprised of any able bodied Marine available. As all Marines are trained as riflemen, cooks, mechanics, clerks and others were given their first op-

portunity to serve in this capacity. Three separate prongs left the command post in the direction of the enemy unit. The group Ostenfeld and I were with was the center prong. Coming through a tree line, the Scouts observed enemy troops taking up positions to ambush the left prong. These enemy were immediately engaged with devastating results. One of the enemy KIA was found with a RPG off safe that was intended for the left patrol. Another Viet Cong was wounded; he shot one of the Marines with an AK47 in the neck and head. The enemy soldier died in this exchange. The Marine was emergency evacuated. Protocol required that any chopper not already on an emergency mission assume the pickup. I recall that this evacuation was handled by the helicopter, flying the Commanding General 1st Marine Division. After loading the wounded Marine aboard, the patrol swept a nearby village and returned to the Battalion Command Post. I noticed that blood on my hand and rifle was not drying as it would normally after working with the wounded. It was then that I realized I had been hit sometime during the exchange. I recall that the results of this H&S Company patrol were approximately six enemy KIA and two Marines WIA. Ostenfeld was later WIA after he was reassigned when 1/27 departed Viet Nam. While on a second tour with a Combined Action Unit, he was KIA."

August 24-25, 1968:

In the vicinity of coordinates 000662, a squad size combat patrol from Charlie Company made contact with a large enemy force. The 1st Battalion, 51st ARVN Regiment reacted to the contact. There was heavy continuous action for two days. An initial report showed that there were 200 VC killed. The remainder of the battalion's units continued to patrol their areas and provided security for perimeters. On August 25, ten (10) enemy bodies surfaced in the Cam Le area. The bodies were uncounted enemy from the 1st Bn., 27th Marines battle with the NVA on 23 August.

August 26, 1968:

The NVA were engaged in combat at coordinates 969656 by security patrols. Sporadic contact with the enemy resulted in three (3) NVA killed, two (2) Marines killed and one (1) wounded Marine. Lance Corporal William J. Bilboa, Jr. and PFC Gary Lyn Clapp, Marines from Charlie Company, were the two Marines killed. One (1) AK-50 and six (6) 60mm mortar rounds were captured. Delta Company's 1st Platoon returned from Rough Rider Duty.

Fox Company's action in the Battle for the Cam Le Bridge is not documented in Dr. Jarvis' account, since his focus was on 1/27. He does account for E 2/27's assistance to A 1/27, but somehow F 2/27 is left out of the picture. With limited documentation for 2/27, it's no wonder that Fox Company was not identified in this battle by other sources. Only the records from the 2nd Battalion, 27th Marines provide corroboration for our involvement at the Cam Le Bridge. Dr. Jarvis' account gives an excellent idea of the scope of the battle, which is largely forgotten in the annals of the War in Vietnam. Recognition of Fox Company 2/27's participation is almost nonexistent. Another account of the Battle for Cam Le Bridge can be found in *U. S. Marines in Vietnam: The Defining Year 1968;* however, even in this account, Fox Co., 2/27 is not mentioned. For our part, it started with our transfer off the firebase and into the area south of the Cam Le Bridge in support of A 1/27, which was counterattacking the south side of the bridge.

The 2/27 Marine Corps records speak for themselves:

23 Aug Company F and 1st Platoon Company E assist A Company 1/27 in recapture of Cam Le Bridge from estimated NVA Company; 22 NVA KIA.

That was a terse account of the actions that almost decimated our platoon. This is what I and others remember:

On the morning of the 23rd we got the word to saddle-up. Whether we knew where we were going or not, we did know that we were heading into a fight. Locked and loaded, we were lifted by helicopter to the Battalion Area.

This was a major event for my platoon. After coming off that mountain, we were assigned Sparrow Hawk duty, which was a quick reaction force staged at the helicopter pad and manned by a rotation of platoons. The word came down that the Da Nang area was being hit by rockets and mortars. Units from the MP Battalion had chased the NVA, who attempted to penetrate the defenses around Da Nang, into a village near Hwy. 1 south of Dog Patch - an area on the outskirts of Da Nang known for its houses of ill repute - and probably not more than 15 miles from the 2/27 Battalion Area. We were loaded onto 2.5 ton trucks, (6 x 6's, Deuce and a Half), and trucked north up Hwy 1. We were fully loaded and ready for a fight. After a while, we were unloaded from the trucks and formed up into two lines, one on each side of the road. Hwy 1 was an elevated roadway, about eight feet above the surrounding rice paddies. We marched for a short distance and were met by Marines from the MP units already there. We sat down on the off-side of the road from a village where the NVA had taken a stand, and waited for orders.

There were only five of us in my gun squad at that time counting myself. The first gun team consisted of Decker and Richee. Dan Nordmann as gunner and David Lopez as A-gunner made up the 2nd gun team. Freer was on R & R which put Nordmann on the gun. I stayed with the number two team since they were the least experienced with the M-60. The platoon was finally called to action. We dropped our packs and carried only weapons, ammo, grenades and water, with some battle dressings thrown in. Battle dressings - large bandages for serious wounds - were often carried on the helmet held in place by a large rubber band or strap of cloth. Wherever they were carried, no one went anywhere without one, because that could be the one that saves your life or one of your buddies. The riflemen dropped off their extra machine gun ammo at the gun positions, and we got on line.

The platoon was placed facing the village, about 200 yards to our front. My gun teams were placed between rifle squads with Lt. Jones and SSgt. Staggs and the radiomen behind us. We were all spaced about 15 to 20 feet apart and formed a line of attack like this:

Third Squad	Gun team #1	Second Squad	Gun team #2
First Squad	Lt. Jones/Radio	Corpsmen	SSgt. Staggs

At a given signal, we started moving out across the rice paddies. The rice paddies here were dry, thank goodness, and there were paddy dikes every so often. We had advanced about 50 yards before the first shots rang out. It's strange, but even at that relatively short distance, the rounds arrived before the sound did, so a puff of dust would rise up as the round hit the ground just before you heard the shot, or so it seemed, probably because the shots were muffled by the jungle area from which they were fired. With all the extra machine gun ammo at our disposal, we had to ask the riflemen near to us to help carry it.

As the enemy rounds started coming in, we dropped and got behind the closest cover we could find. We could see the flashes of the rifles going off at the bottom of the tree line of the village. They were dug in and ready for a fight. We moved in fire team rushes, where one fire team (3 or 4 men) would rush forward to the next area of cover while the rest of the platoon laid down covering fire. Since we were such a small unit, squad rushes would have exposed too many men at once, so wisely, Lt. Jones stuck with fire team rushes. With seemingly random rushes, the enemy never knew who was going to move or when. With only two machine gun teams, we moved as best we could when the time looked good. As squad leader I directed the movement of my guns, but under the circumstances, I was lucky to move myself. The riflemen carrying our extra ammo moved with their fire teams and we had to catch up to get more ammo. The one thing we couldn't allow was to let the riflemen get ahead of us. We had to keep up with the line of fire or risk hitting our own men. Consequently we moved with the front of the line. Exposing ourselves to enemy fire.

Everything seemed to be going well. We were really laying down the lead aimed at the bottom of the tree line - better to aim low than high. Along with our rifle and machine gun fire, mortars were falling on the village as well. Then, as in most fights, anything that could go wrong would go wrong, Murphy's Law. Two critical problems occurred. First, a wild-eyed water buffalo appeared out of nowhere at the edge of the village and started heading toward us. Water buffaloes can get up to 10 feet long, 6.6 feet tall and weigh over 2,500 pounds, with curved horns that could kill in one swipe.

"Yipes!!! That crazy thing is coming this way," was the cry.

M-16's opened up on it, but at a distance, if they hit, they just made it mad. The call went out, "Use the machine gun. Shoot the damned thing with the 60'." Then the second problem happened. Decker's machine gun was the closest to the water buffalo and when he tried to fire, his gun quit after just a few rounds. I watched him lift the ammo feed tray on the gun, reload a belt of ammo and try again, and the same thing happened. I instantly left Dan Nordmann with directions to keep firing at the village, and ran and stumbled and ran and tripped and ran my way over to Decker and Richee. I too went through the drill of trying to fire the gun and realized that there was nothing we could do with it at the time. It was M-16's only for them. Decker got an M-16 from some of the wounded around him, and continued fighting. Without thinking, I got up and repeated the run-fall-trip routine back to Nordmann and Lopez. I told them to get that water buffalo. In the time I had taken to run back and forth from Nordmann, the water buffalo had advanced within about 75 yards of us and by then it was confused and just running back and forth across our lines. I could see the fire from the M-16's hit the water buffalo and see the little puffs of dust spring up off the mud-soaked hide. Still, it wouldn't go down. In the intensity of the moment, Nordmann wasn't able to hit it and I took the gun, got a bead on that creature from Hell, firing several 3 to 5 round bursts at him. It wasn't long before he went down, dead as he fell. I probably shouldn't have taken the gun from Nordmann, but there was no time to help him. That "red eyed, fire snorting water buffalo" had to go down.

All this time the line hadn't moved an inch. No one wanted to go out there and face that water buffalo along with the enemy fire. Even facing Mister Charles (the NVA) would have been better than facing that thing, "Hell fire on four legs." No sir, not me. To make matters worse, the NVA had used this charge as their version of a tank, making matters difficult for the Marines caught out in the open who were doing their best to kill the enemy and stay alive at the same time. To charge at that distance would have been suicide for us and to withdraw would have been worse than a charge.

Ta da - the Cavalry arrived! Behind us on the highway came one of our heavy tanks from the 1st Tank Battalion. We turned and watched it stop directly behind us and turn the turret toward the village. Then it was our turn to send the "buffalo" their way. Kabam! The 90mm gun on the tank cut loose and you could see trees at the edge of the village blow up and head for the clouds. They continued to fire over our heads to pin down the enemy and we continued our assault. It was just before the end of the tank barrage that I looked toward the village and saw what looked like an old man in white pajamas - white pajamas usually designated a villager, and often a village chief. The last I saw of him, he was in the open waving his hands back and forth over his head. He was still wearing the typical conical hat of the Vietnamese peasants. Then the 90mm off the tank fired and in an instant, the old man disappeared. After the blast, the conical hat was floating in the air and a fog of white and pink appeared where the old man once stood. All the firing stopped from both sides and a deathly quiet settled over the area. As one unit, the men started to sweep the village for any VC or NVA. The fight was over. That hit on the old man was the last shot fired. No place for sympathy. "Hell, he probably was a VC and it was just a trap," was the consensus of all that had even noticed the incident. I just accepted it as a matter of bad luck and his ticket got punched, big time. Besides, it could just as well have been me or one of my men.

As we advanced on the village we found that the enemy had fled. We picked up enemy weapons and ammo, helped put the emergency WIA's on medevac helicopters and loaded the lightly wounded and KIA's on trucks. Eventually we retrieved our packs, were loaded up and taken back to the Battalion Area. During this whole time, I don't think anyone had had any water. It was still in our canteens. Too much excitement to even think of drinking anything. On the way back, we guzzled our canteens like we would never get another drop of water for the rest of our lives. As we departed, we could see air strikes in the distance behind the village and assumed that the enemy was being "pursued by fire."

That evening Decker came to me and said that he needed a new machine gun or at least I needed to send his gun back to be repaired because his was broken. He was convinced that the problems he had on that firefight were from a faulty gun. I told him to first go clean his gun like it was for an inspection and come back. He did so and when he came back, I took him and the rest of the squad to the test range where everyone went to test fire their weapons before going out on patrol. Of course I had to carry a radio, get permission to fire and call back when we were ready, so there would be no concerns that we were under attack. Decker put down the bipods that were attached to the end of the barrel, got in the prone position and put the butt of the gun into his shoulder. He pulled back the cocking handle, which pulled the bolt to the rear, locking it against the sear of the trigger housing, and made sure the weapon safety was on. Richee lifted the feed tray and loaded a belt of 7.62mm into the gun, closed the feed tray and tapped Decker on the head, letting him know that the weapon was ready to fire.

The M-60 fires from the open bolt position. When carried on patrol, the gunner usually carried a short belt in the gun with the round at the end of the belt positioned just right in the feed tray so that when the bolt was brought to the rear, it automatically moved into the path of the bolt that was now locked to the rear. When needed for action, all he had to do was pull the bolt to the rear, take the safety off and fire while the A-gunner clipped another belt onto the one he was firing. When on the assault, most machine gunners would have the gun loaded with the bolt to the rear, so that all he had to do was take the safety off and fire.

Well, the gun fired like it was brand new. Didn't miss a lick, no matter how many bursts were fired, or how long the bursts were. I didn't want to embarrass Decker, so all I said was, "Keep your guns clean." and walked away. To their credit, no one razzed Decker about the incident and that was the end of that - almost. Al Decker was devastated! Maybe it would have been better if he had had some kidding, but dying is nothing to kid about. At any rate, he was totally upset. I talked to him and found out what he was upset about. It wasn't about the gun being dirty, it was about his feelings of letting down the guys around him who depended on him. He blamed himself for the wounded, even if they weren't near him. It was a moral battle between himself and himself. After that event, he became one of the best machine gunners there ever was. He fought not for himself, but for his fellow Marines, often taking chances way beyond the call of duty. He did it as a matter of course and never looked back. He pulled himself up from the depths of the hell that he was in and rose above fear and self-loathing to put himself in the hands of God. He never got a medal or any other special recognition, so I hope this small note will make amends for that. God bless you Al Decker! Richee too felt the same pain as Al and like his Gunner, Richee rose above the norm to always do his best and fight for the men he was pledged to defend. God bless you James Richee!

My memory goes blank until sometime after we had taken the bridge and had the dead and wounded laid out on the bank of the road waiting for a medevac. LCpl. David Lopez, LCpl. Jim Seabolt, and LCPL. Tom Montie remember the happenings well. Jim Seabolt was one of the Marines that had been wounded and he, along with Tom Montie, were the closest to LCpl. George Kyricos, the "Greek," who also had been wounded. As we were resting with the wounded, we started to receive some incoming small arms and mortar fire. It was close. Then the worst happened. An incoming mortar round came in and hit the "Greek" square in the chest and blew him up. As his body caught the mortar round, it blew apart in little pieces. He had saved the rest of us by absorbing most of the shock and shrapnel. Everyone there remembers picking pieces of George off themselves and shuddering in the process because it could just have well been any one of us. Both Jim Seabolt and Tom Montie received concussions from that explosion.

I have had a vague memory all these years, of having a mortar round come in and hitting a Marine. He took all the shrapnel and I caught the blast and passed out for a minute or so. I could never put that memory in any context until I had talked to other men who were at Hwy. 1 with George Kyricos. It was that incident on August 23rd that accounts for my memory loss. It also accounts for my initial confusion in trying to place my memories of our involvement in the Battle for Cam Le Bridge in time and space. In confirmation, I recently talked to Dan Nordmann and he said that I was indeed there by George when he got hit. Dan recalls that he came up to where the wounded were along Hwy. 1 after the "Greek" got blown up. Tom Montie, Ralph Gibson, Jim Seabolt and I were there among the wounded. He noticed that I had blood and pieces of George all over me and asked what happened. I told him about George, and he then proceeded to help load what was left of George's body and the wounded on trucks for the return to our base. Dan also said that he picked up as much of George's 782 gear as possible, especially the M-16 magazines. Dan said:

"There were other Marines, from a different unit, that were trying to take George's gear. I told them to back off. That gear belongs to our buddy and it is going with him to the base."

Slowly but surely, memories return and once that happens, I can put them to rest. Well, as much as possible anyway. The war is never very far from my thoughts and dreams.

Jim Seabolt (from 3rd Squad) wrote me, recalling the action and his experience when the "Greek" was blown up:

> Ralph [Gibson] [another member of 3rd Squad] told me, that just prior to getting a shot in my right knee, I had run out, under fire to drag someone back. I do not recall that. However, when I got hit, that I do recall! Mac our Corpsman cared for me, and all the guys carried me to the other side of Highway 1. I was then placed an arms distance from the Greek, and after we shook hands, my left to his right, it was then that he caught a large shell right through his heart area, and because he was up on his right elbow, he absorb [*sic*] all of the force of that horrible blast. I got none, but Tom [Montie] was thrown up in the air, I believe! One of the men that carried me across that open field, was George King, a precious brother of color, with a "broken ankle", and I've never gotten to thank him. There were a lot of heroes on that field that day, but I was not one of them. Ralph [Gibson] went on to serve three tours of duty, and I wished I could've been there with him, so he could keep me out of trouble. I ended up in Philadelphia naval Hospital, where I met Dave Lopez, also an amputee, like myself. I did, however, have the honor to shake hands with the one and only, CHESTY PULLER! He was there to visit his son, who, as we all know, later took his own life. So, how do I feel about all that? I hold no grudge against the country of Viet-nam, nor it's people, and I do hope that someday, I will be able to afford to go there for a visit. Thanks for your service, and all that it took to write a book. I hope it's a best seller. Blessings to you, in Jesus name, James R. Seabolt USMC, ret.

The reports state the action simply:

231700H (late entry) Co F Co/Swp vic (BT014702) While sweeping into CAM NAM got within 75 meters of treeline vic (BT012703) Rec'd heavy SA, rifle grenades and 60mm

> mortars. Called Marine Arty F/M. Moved all wounded east of Hwy #1. Gun ships fired on en position. Fired 60mm. Rec'd more En 60MM. Med Evac completed. Res: 19 USMC WIA. SEVEN (MED EVAC), 12 (Minor), One (1) USMC KIA.

A listing of our platoon, with those listed as dead and wounded on the 23rd of August, 1968 at the Battle for the Cam Le Bridge is as follows:

Platoon CP.	1st Lt. Jones – Platoon Commander	WIA – Aug, 23
	SSgt. Staggs – Platoon Sergeant	
	Sgt. Houregan – Right Guide	
	LCpl. Howard - Radioman	WIA - Aug, 23
1st Squad	Cpl. Slade - Squad Leader - Replacement	
	LCpl. Miller	
	LCpl. Harris	
	Pfc. Kile	
	Pfc. Thomas	
	Pfc. Mitchell	
	Pfc. Smith	
	Pfc. Kinney – Listed as VD, Not sure if he was with us	
	Pfc. Shelley – Listed as UA, Not sure if he was with us	
	Pfc. Bellazin - Replacement	
2nd Squad	Cpl. Shields – Squad Leader - Replacement	
	LCpl. Purden	
	LCpl. Richardson	WIA - Aug, 23
	Pfc. Gregory	
	Pfc. Washington	WIA – Aug, 23
	Pfc. Whitley	WIA – Aug, 23
	LCpl. Kyricos	KIA – Aug, 23
	LCpl. McDowell	
	LCpl. Tecklenburg – Replacement	
3rd Squad	Sgt. Farmer – Squad Leader	
	LCpl. Montie	WIA – Aug, 23
	LCpl. Gibson	
	LCpl. Seabolt	WIA – Aug, 23

	LCpl. Williams	WIA – Aug, 23
	Pfc. Brooks – Replacement	
	Cpl. Combest	
	Pfc. King	
	Pfc. Conner	
	Pfc. Miles	
Rockets	Sgt. Ledesma – Weapons Platoon Section Leader	WIA – Aug, 23
	LCpl. Carbough	
	LCpl. Heyna	
Machine Guns	LCpl. Van Bibber – Squad Leader	
	LCpl. Freer – Gone on R&R	
	LCpl. Lopez	
	LCpl. Nordmann	
	LCpl. Decker	
	LCpl. Richee	
60 mm Mortars	Cpl. Gorden – former squad leader from 2nd Squad	
	LCpl. Cano	WIA – Aug, 23
	LCpl. Freeman	
	LCpl. Erskine	WIA – Aug,23
	Pfc. Melton	
Corpsman	Hn. Mac Laughin	
	Hn. York	
Sick, Lame & Lazy	Sgt. Lillard	WIA – Aug, 23
	Cpl. Cohtern – Not sure if he was with us	
	LCpl. Karaser – Not sure if he was with us	

On August 23rd, 2nd Platoon, Fox Company had suffered 1 KIA and 12 WIA out of 48 Marines from our platoon who participated in that action. Sgt Lillard, even though he was sick, couldn't let his men down and fought anyway. The casualty rate in our Platoon for the 23rd was 27%, leaving 35 men, including Lt. Jones, even though he was wounded, to continue the fight. From the reports, with 1 KIA and 19 WIA, 2nd Platoon, Fox Company suffered 65% of the casualties during that action.

With the medevacs completed on Friday evening, August 23rd, we returned to the Battalion Area with the rest of the Company. We had an uneventful night and the next morning we got the word that an NVA Battalion had taken cover around the hamlet of Qua Giang (2) southwest of the Cam Le Bridge. Taking most of the day, on the 24th, we moved on line to assume blocking positions around the hamlet while 1st and 3rd Platoons of our company did the same. This was to block any escape by the enemy. After arriving in our position, Lt. Jones spread us out to cover a wide area on the west side of the hamlet. As a result, we were spread pretty thin which is very uncomfortable for fighting men in foxholes. We all dug in good, making our fighting holes as deep as we could to provide cover with two men per hole. I placed my two gun teams between the rifle squads to provide the best coverage with over lapping fields of fire. After we were dug in, we ate cold C-Rations, no fires tonight, and waited for whatever might come our way. The area we were covering was a large rice paddy on the western edge of the village. Visibility was good and we were sure that no one could come onto that rice paddy without us knowing about it. We had a quiet night, but believe you me, no one slept on watch that night!

The action on the 25th is described in the Marine reports as follows:

> 5th Tanks. On 24 August Company F was deployed to conduct a joint operation on the 25th with the 1st Battalion, 51st ARVN Regiment. Again tanks from the 3rd platoon, Company B, 5th Tanks supported. On the 25th all units advanced toward the village on Qua Giang (2) and were taken under heavy automatic weapons and small arms fire. Fire from the tanks, 81mm mortar, artillery and nine flights of fixed wing air were employed against the enemy position. The village was cleared and seven members of Company F and the Tank platoon were recommended for the Vietnamese Cross of Galentry by the 1st Battalion, 51st ARVN Regiment.

Sunday morning, the 25th of August, broke clear and hot with no disturbances from the village area. We did our morning constitutional and even heated our chow in our now deep foxholes. We continued to try and rest some so we continued the one-on one-off watch during the rest of the day. Ready at any moment to let loose with a hailstorm of lead should anyone try to cross the rice paddy in front of us. We had what was left of our Mortar

Squad (three men) behind us to provide more firepower to the fray, as well as what was left of our Rocket Squad (two men) with their LAW's and 3.5 Rocket Launchers. Thirty-five men in all.

While we were on the blocking force, we could hear the rat-tat-tat of a .50 caliber machine gun as well as cannon fire from tanks and small arms fire from the units assaulting the village. We didn't know exactly what was happening other than that the 51st ARVN's were assaulting the village with tanks and APC's. We sat back, listened to the cacophony of death being fired in the village, and were sure that we would have little to do other than sweep the area after the battle was over.

It was past noon, maybe around 1400 hours, that we got the word that the ARVN's hadn't done a thing other than fire into the village from the outskirts of the tree line. We all looked at each other with knowing expressions on our faces; this wasn't the first time we had to deal with ARVN forces and their reluctance to engage in combat. Then the word came down over the radio. Lt. Jones was ordered to take his platoon to the area where the ARVN's were and sweep the village and also maintain the blocking force. What? Was somebody crazy? We didn't balk at the orders, but it was with trepidation that we proceeded. Lt. Jones left Sgt. Houregan in charge of the blocking force along with the 1st squad, rockets, and mortars and one Corpsman (Doc Puckett). Then he took SSgt. Staggs, 2nd Squad, 3rd Squad, my Machine Gun Squad (both guns) and a Corpsman (Doc Mac) toward the ARVN position. After the battle at Cam Le, 2nd Squad had 6 men, 3rd Squad had 7 men, and my machine gun squad was 5 men including myself. A total of 21 men counting Lt. Jones, SSgt Staggs and the Corpsman, Doc Mac. When we arrived at the ARVN positions, we found them still firing into the village from the safety of the tank and an APC (Armored Personnel Carrier) with a .30 machine gun, well outside the tree line at the edge of the hamlet. The ARVN's withdrew with their APC, leaving the tank for our support. Lt. Jones formed us up on line with himself and the 2nd Squad and the machine gun team of Decker and Richee on the left of the line, SSgt Staggs, 3rd Squad and my other gun team of Lopez and Nordmann on the right. I stayed with Lopez and Nordmann.

I chose to stay with Lopez and Nordmann because the regular gunner, LCpl. Freer, was out on R & R and I had put Dan Nordmann on the gun. He didn't have much experience being the gunner, so I figured that along with David Lopez who was an experienced team leader, and myself, that things would be ok. Al Decker and James Richee were a solid team who had been together for many months and I felt confident that they would be ok.

In front of us, at least on my side of the line, was an open area with a large bomb crater. It looked to be from a 500 lb bomb or larger. It was about 25 yards across and maybe 15 ft deep in the soft soil. As we approached it, we had to split around it and as we started to do that, an arm came out of the side of the crater and threw a grenade at us. Holy Sheep Shit, Batman! We hit the deck and luckily the grenade went over our heads to explode in some trees behind us. We were on the very lip of the crater and the VC that was inside couldn't judge our exact location. We received a few more grenades and then "Superman" showed up in the person of David Lopez. He was one tough little Mexican. Maybe 5 ft 5 in or less, and slim and trim, Lopez had declined the job of carrying the 23 lb. M-60 machine gun. Instead, he took the position of number 1 team leader, tunnel rat, ammo humper and any other number of jobs that came along. I respected him to no end and always trusted him with my back. I knew that he would protect Dan Nordmann with his life.

The VC in the bomb crater had created a hole in the side of the crater and covered it up to the point where only a small slit was left open from which he reached out and threw his grenades. He was well protected since it was a small hole on the side of the crater, with his only danger point being from the opposite side of the crater, or so he thought. Lopez, Nordmann and I were the closest to the "Arm of Death" and were pinned down by those grenades. Then Lopez pulled the pin on a grenade, got up and ran over to the lip of the crater just above the hole. On the way, I could see him let the spoon fly off the grenade, leaving him only 5 to 7 seconds before it exploded. He plopped down on the rim, rolled over, tossed the grenade in the hole, and rolled back to the top of the rim. Classic Marine Corps maneuver. The ground lifted with the explosion and smoke came out of the hole. The arm was never to be seen again. Thank God for my little buddy Lopez. He saved us all.

Lopez's actions were doubly dangerous because he had let the spoon fly before tossing the grenade. Remember that the grenade wasn't armed until the spoon was released. One false move and Lopez would have blown himself up and any others near him. However, he was just following lessons learned. Early on in our combat experience, we had thrown grenades by simply pulling the pin and throwing the grenade. That maneuver meant that it took 5 to 7 seconds to explode once it was armed in midair. The time it took to hit the ground and then explode allowed a quick-acting enemy to pick up the grenade and throw it back. The solution was to pull the pin, let the spoon fly, wait a second or two and then toss the grenade. Problem of returning grenades solved.

We didn't have any time to rest or regroup after that, because Lt. Jones with 2nd Squad was already getting ahead of us on the sweep. The tank that was with us was on my side of the line and slightly ahead of us. It hit real soft sand, lost steerage and broke down, making it impossible to proceed any further. We still had open ground to cover on the opposite side of the tank, so we split around it to try to hold the on-line sweep. We hadn't received much in the way of enemy fire yet so we continued on to a place just short of the tree line at the edge of the hamlet thirty yards away. We started to receive some fire from our right front which forced us closer to 2nd Squad on the left, and we got bunched up a bit. We were almost to the tree line, with only a small field about 20 yards across and 75 yards long running parallel in front of the trees when all Hell broke loose. I was with Lopez and Nordmann on the right side of the line, which would provide good machine gun fire across the face of the line if needed. Then a hail of bullets came at us from two directions. We were caught in an L-shaped ambush, a classic ambush that was well executed by well-trained NVA troops. All we could do was to get down and take cover, because to go out into that field was certain death. We were pinned down good. And the worst of it was SSgt. Staggs had passed out earlier from the heat and wasn't there to direct the right side of the line. Lt. Jones with 2nd Squad was receiving heavy fire from their front and left. We were closest to the right side of the ambush and all we could do was get down and stay unseen for a while.

Not long after the ambush started, I heard two things. In the noise of battle, I could hear the steady bursts coming from Decker's machine gun and then the deafening silence of that gun when it stopped. Soon, the dreaded call "gun down" came from the area of the 2nd Squad, echoing in my ears. "Gun Down" meant Decker and Richee's position. Not thinking of anything else, I jumped up and ran the length of that field to where Decker and Richee were, tripping on mud clods along the way as I traversed the field. Somehow, I didn't get shot or wounded in any way. Looking back, I'm sure that my Guardian Angel deflected the bullets, because they were thick as flies on a pile of gook poop.

I got to Decker and Richee's position and there they lay, machine gun lying still in front of them. As I came to a halt and went to ground, I came face to face with Al Decker. He was a mess, shot up in the chest and face, eyes still open and mouth askew. He was dead before he knew what happened. I turned to Richee and saw that he was still alive. They had taken on the enemy headfirst, in true Marine Corps fashion. Never a thought about their own safety, just the safety of the riflemen they were determined to protect.

Suddenly SSgt. Staggs came roaring back from the area near the tank where Doc Mac had set up his aid station, hollering:

"Charge, charge!"

Staggs was a very big Irishman with a red handlebar mustache and the body of a heavy-weight wrestler. No one messed with SSgt. Staggs. When he said, "Charge!", we charged. We had charged before in other encounters so once we heard his call, we just got up and charged. Gotta love that Staggs! Dan Nordmann, on the right side of the line broke the ambush on his end. Like the seasoned veteran he was, he started firing the M-60 from the hip, really putting out the lead, advancing into the tree line on his end, Lopez feeding ammo to him as fast as possible. At the same time, the rest of the line got up and assaulted the tree line in front of us and to the left. In a matter of minutes, the ambush was broken and we advanced into the village.

At some point, I remember holding Richee in my arms as he died. I sat him up and held his head in my lap as he bled to death from several bullet wounds to the gut. He looked up at me with his black eyes, pools of horror that had seen too much, and said:

"Decker's dead, Decker's dead."

It was the last words he spoke and his last thought was for his buddy Al Decker. There is no racism in combat, just Marines, and Decker and Richee proved that over and over. Al Decker was a big strapping white man. James Richee was a skinny, mixed blood, black man whose life had been the streets of Los Angles before he entered the Marine Corps. Not a likely match, but brothers to the end. Our machine gun squad was tight and most of the time we hung together. When in the rear, Richee would visit the "Brothers" in a courtesy call, but always preferred the company of his real brothers in our squad. We all loved each other so much it hurt.

Instantly, I turned cold and calculated. I went berserk and my lack of specific memories after that attest to my rage.

I took the machine gun, readied it for combat and threw extra belts of ammo over my left shoulder. Leaving Decker and Richee, I assaulted with what I thought was 2nd Platoon. I moved into the village, firing on anything and everything that moved. We went through the village and secured it, and returned to the aid station to bring in the dead and wounded. Doc Mac had already called in a medevac for the seriously wounded, and the rest got ferried out by an APC. Our dead were also loaded on the APC. There was no other transportation and the rest of us had to walk out. The fight had started about 1500 hours and we walked out about 2100 hours. The six-hour fight was intense and we were all dog tired. I remember carrying the M-60, spare barrel, belts of ammo and my own rifle and equipment as we humped out of there. I was so tired I just wanted to lie down and pass out, but that wasn't to be. I remember saying to myself:

"Put one foot in front of the other. Put one foot in front of the other." - over and over as I progressed down the path that we were on.

Lopez and Nordmann dragged along with me, all of us struggling to keep going. Our uniforms were rags and I'm sure that an outsider would see us as "death warmed over." Somehow, we made it back to our Battalion Area. How long it took or how we got there is lost to time. Tom Thomas remembers that he went back to the Battalion in APC's with the dead and wounded that had not been medevaced out of there, but all I remember is walking forever.

Tom Thomas was with the 1st Platoon and he remembers the action as well. At the Cam Le Bridge on the 23rd, he remembers being ordered to set up his gun across a rice paddy where some important VC Officers were expected to emerge. Tom remembers setting his sights up to about 900 meters and pre-firing a burst to get his range. He figured that if they (the VC) came out of the trees around that area, all he had to do was wait for them to walk into his fire. Sure enough, here they came and he opened up and down they went. That night was spent back at the Battalion Area and the next day, Fox Company was ordered to move to the Qua Giang (2) village. Thomas with 1st Platoon, formed part of the blocking force on the east side of the village beginning close to where the ARVN's were firing into the village. As Bob Tecklenburg remembers:

"We passed 1st Platoon on the way into the village."

As reported in the records of the 1st Tank Battalion:

251700H Aug 1968 Three tanks from Company B, 5th Tk. Bn., supported 2/27 at (BT004672) in an assault on two or more companies of NVA at (BT004672). The tanks fired the 90mm guns during the assault. One tank sustained an RPG rocket hit but was only slightly damaged. The action oeased [*sic*] after dark with no sweep being made of the area. There were two friendly WIA (one med-evac, one non-evac).

Also in the reports:

SUMMARY OF SIGNIFICANT EVENTS

At 251030, while in support of Segment F, SB-31 and 34 spotted 15 V.C. in treeline at (BT004671). Tanks fired on the target with 90mm. No sweep made.

At 251032H, while in position at (AT968084), S B Co. tanks received small arms fire from (AT967580). Tanks returned fire with 90mm and MG. Enemy position silenced.

At 251130H, while in support of Segment F, SB-31 spotted 2 snipers in a house at (AT004671). Tank fired 90mm. No sweep made.

At 251245H, while in support of Segment F, SB-34 spotted 2 snipers in a house at (AT004671). Tank fired 90mm. No sweep made.

At 251700H, while in support of Segment F, 3rd Plt. engaged an enemy force of unknown size. Tanks fired 90mm and MG with unknown results. Action resulted in two USMC WIA (1 med-evac)

There must have been one tank supporting each Platoon of Fox Company, and the one we had with us broke down early on in the fight. From the memories of Tom Thomas, his 1st Platoon assaulted the village after dark, which match the records from Bravo Company, 5th Tank Battalion that was attached to the 1st Tank Battalion at the time. It also confirms that 1st Platoon went in after 2nd Platoon had made the initial push into the village. Captain Collins, the Fox Company Commander, realizing that 2nd Platoon had lost their Platoon Leader and a significant number of platoon members, decided to finish the assault with the 1st Platoon. Thomas said that in the assault he remembered body parts in the bottom of a large bomb crater, which I believe were from Lopez's heroic action to take out the grenade thrower. He said that the tank with them got hit by an RPG (rocket-propelled grenade) and that two tankers were wounded. He helped remove the tankers from their smoking tank, then hoisting his M-60 machine gun and carrying plenty of extra ammo, he continued the assault of the village. At one point, everyone was pinned down in front of him and he started to fire over their heads at the unseen enemy. His platoon sergeant then ran over and chewed him out for firing so close to the other men. Realizing his error, Thomas corrected his fire by standing up and continuing the assault firing from the hip. One man from his Platoon was killed, and that was LCpl Calvin Bob Pierce, with many others wounded. Thomas remembers seeing Pierce shot in the chest and slumped over an M-60.

I had thought that my memory was lost after Decker and Richee were killed, but after talking to Thomas, I realized that I too remember a tank getting hit by an RPG and that the tankers were wounded as confirmed by the records of the Tank Battalion. Tom said he also remembered loading the dead on an APC, which means he was there at the end, about 2100 hours that night. With all that in mind, I think I got mixed up. I must have stayed with Decker and Richee a short time, and when I assaulted I got mixed in with 1st Platoon on the other side from where Tom was. Easy to get mixed up at times like that. That would account for my memories of the tank being hit by an RPG. It would also account for the difference between my memories of the tanks and those of others in my platoon. Lopez remembers Richee crying out that he didn't want to die and later seeing someone holding Richee as he died. After that we loaded their bodies on the APC and Lopez remembers walking back in the dark to a place where we could catch trucks to take us back to the Company area. From Lopez's memories, I believe that Richee dying in my arms is clear but it must have been after I returned from 1st Platoon.

After we got back in the Battalion Area and had a night's rest, I was told to saddle up and catch a chopper to Da Nang and report to Graves Registration. I was confused, but no matter, I was so numb that I just did whatever I was told. The regimentation kept me going. No time to grieve. No thought of grieving. Just empty compliance. I could still function, but I was dead inside. Dan Nordmann remembers going with me and Sgt. LeDesma (the machine gun section leader) who had been wounded on the 23rd and needed further medical care.

Arriving in Da Nang, I found Graves Registration which was responsible for cataloging each KIA that came in throughout I Corps. I Corps was responsible for the northern area of South Vietnam and encompassed most of the Marine units in Vietnam. Sergeant LeDesma took Dan Nordmann into Da Nang, telling Dan that he didn't need to see our dead buddies. It was my duty anyway. I managed to find my way to the Graves Registration Office. Once there, I was questioned about the battle at the Qua Giang (2) hamlet. I was then taken to the "meat locker." The dead Marines that came in were laid out in metal trailers like the ones the big rigs haul. The trailers were loaded with ice beds, with straw scattered along the walls and over the blocks of ice stacked two tiers high. Each trailer was also air conditioned. I was told that they needed me for identification purposes and without further ado, they uncovered two bodies. There they were, Al Decker and James Richee looking at me just as they had the day earlier. Looking at them, I was taken aback because the Graves people hadn't even taken the time to close their eyes. As Decker stared up at me, his face still all shot up with his lips peeled back. I fell into another funk. I identified them and signed an affidavit verifying that they were the men labeled on the tags that were tied to their toes. Then, without a word, I turned and walked away from two of my men, two of my brothers, two friends that I had shared my life with.

Somehow, I returned to the Battalion Area and kept on with my job as the Squad Leader/Gunner with Lopez as my A-gunner. Dennis Freer (gunner) and Dan Nordmann (A-gunner) would form the second team. We were now down to four, with no help in sight. I had now lost seven men from my machine gun squad, six from the replacements we had received and one more from the original nine man squad. In total, my squad had lost five original members and six replacements. Eleven men from a nine man unit. A 122% loss, and the losses were far from over.

Of the 21 men who attacked the village of Qua Giang (2) on the evening of Sunday, August 25, 1968, the following were killed or wounded:

Platoon CP Lt. Jones – Platoon Commander WIA (a second time)

2nd Squad	Cpl Shields – Squad Leader	WIA
	LCpl Tecklenburg	WIA
	Pfc Freeman	WIA
3rd Squad	Sgt Farmer – Squad Leader	WIA
	LCpl Gibson	WIA
	Pfc Brooks	WIA
Machine Guns	LCpl Decker – Gunner	KIA
	LCpl Richee – A-Gunner	KIA
Others	LCpl Pierce (1st Platoon)	KIA
	16 WIA from other platoons	

A total for Fox Company on the 25th of: 3 KIA, 23 WIA.

Nine casualties out of 21 men, a 43% casualty rate for the men who participated in that fight on the 25th. Second Squad was down to four men, with Corporal Gordon resuming his position as squad leader. Third Squad was down to four men, with no squad leader. The Machine Gun Squad was down to four men, including LCpl. Freer who was still on R & R. First Squad still had six men but the CP was down to two with SSgt. Staggs now in charge of the Platoon. After two major engagements, the casualty rate for the Platoon CP was 50%. 1st Squad remained intact, no casualties. 2nd Squad, 64% casualties. 3rd Squad, 60% casualties. Rockets, 33% casualties. Machine Guns, 40% casualties. 60mm Mortars, 50% casualties.

From the original 2nd Platoon of about 61 men and estimating a 50% replacement rate based in part on known replacements, (67% for machine guns), the casualty rate from February 15, 1968 to the end of August, 1968 is estimated to be as follows:

2nd Platoon reinforced)	-	70% Casualties
Command Center	-	80%
1st Rifle Squad	-	59%
2nd Rifle Squad	-	80%
3rd Rifle Squad	-	80%
Machine Gun Sqd.	-	122%
60mm Mortar Team	-	56%
Rocket Team	-	56%

The records indicate the following:

251800H	Co F Co/Cbt swp vic (BT002668) Co F combined swp w/1/51 est ARVN encountered elements of V-25 Bn. At vic (BT0033670) Co F moved thru obj area met resistance by VC in spider holes & trenches. Continued swp. Res: Three (3) USMC KIA, Eight (8) USMC WIA (MED EVAC), Four (4) USMC WIA (MINOR), Twenty-five (25) VC KIA, Captured one (1) B-40 rkt, misc gren and 782 gear.
251800H	(FOLLOW UP) Co F Co/Swp vic (BT002668), Make following changes: WIA's fm (12) to (23). Fm (8) med evac to (11). Minor WIA's fm (4) to (12). Captured B-40 rkts fm (1) to (4).

On the 25th all units advanced toward the village of Qua Giang (2) and were taken under heavy automatic weapons and small arms fire. Fire from the tanks, 81mm mortar, artillery and nine flights of fixed wing air were employed against the enemy position. The village was cleared and seven members of Company F and the Tank platoon were recommended for the Vietnamese Cross of Galentry [*sic*] by the 1st Battalion, 51st ARVN Regiment. Company F was credited with 215 enemy KIA's while receiving 19 WIA's and 3 KIA themselves.

It is difficult to get accurate numbers for the casualties in the Battle for Cam Le Bridge. The Company numbers may vary, but I was fortunate to receive the actual Platoon roster from August 23rd through August 25th as well as the rosters for the Platoon casualties from Lt. Jones. Those total numbers remain, over the three-day period of the 23rd through the 25th, as: 3 KIA and 18 WIA out of 48 men who participated in that fight. A 44% loss for the 2nd Platoon. It should also be mentioned again, that Lt. Jones was wounded on both the 23rd and the 25th. He just would not leave his men until his wounds prohibited him from further action. That my friend is "LEADING from the FRONT."

Other accounts of the actions at the Cam Le Bridge and Qua Giang are given below:

From an article written by then LCpl Robert L. Tecklenburg, a writer in his own right, compiled from his memories and others:

"TWENTY-SEVENTH MARINES AT CAM LE BRIDGE: THREE GRUNTS LOOK BACK"

By Barry Jones (First Lieutenant, Platoon Commander, 2nd Platoon, F Co. 2/27)
Chuck Van Bibber (Lance Corporal, Squad Leader, Machine guns, 2nd Platoon)
Robert Tecklenburg (Lance Corporal, Rifleman, 2nd squad, 2nd Platoon)

Fox Company, Second Battalion, 27th Marine Regiment struck a mortal blow to the NVA's 38th Regiment in a fight to the death near the Cam Le River Bridge south of DaNang in the marine regiment's final battle in Vietnam.

From August 23rd to the 27th, 1968, three platoons of Fox supported by 3rd Platoon, 5th Tanks engaged the enemy, forcing them to retreat westward back into the mountains.

August 18th, the 38th NVA Regiment operating with the 402d VC Sapper Battalion launched their third offensive of 1968 against the city of DaNang. Their objective was to reach the airfield and inflict as much death and destruction as possible before melting away into the countryside. Following heavy fighting, the NVA were halted at the outskirts of the city, but the VC force successfully penetrated DaNang's defenses and moved to strike the airfield.

VC Sappers, utilizing a mortar and rocket attack, seized and held the Cam Le River Bridge just south of the city in the initial stage of their thrust. After being forced to withdraw from DaNang city by MP's from Company C, 1st Military Police Battalion, the Viet Cong continued to hold the bridge. Early the morning of August 23rd, Company A, 1st Battalion, 27th Marines, with assistance from two platoons of ARVN Rangers, attacked the VC force.

Chuck Van Bibber, Squad Leader of the machine gun squad remembered: "Company F 2/27 and 1st Platoon Company E 2/27 assisted Company A 1/27 in the recapture of the Cam Le Bridge from an estimated NVA company."

Fox Company had just returned to the 2/27 base camp from Operation Mameluke Thrust with the 5th Marines. The men were loaded up and trucked to about a mile from the Cam Le Bridge where they moved quickly through flooded rice paddies toward the fighting while under an intense mortar barrage. M-48 tanks raced down the road.

"As we neared the river, my platoon formed up and prepared to assault," Tecklenburg, a young rifleman with second squad, second platoon said. "We attacked the enemy from across an open field that lacked even rice stubble to protect us from enemy fire. Second platoon, on line, pushed steadily forward under continuous small arms and mortar fire. About half way across the field, we hit the deck (ground) and began laying down heavy small arms fire on several houses in a tree line about fifty meters in front of us. The order reached us to pull back while artillery and airstrikes were called in."

Second platoon suffered 1 KIA and 6 WIA. Later corrected to 1KIA, 10 WIA "Second Squad—my squad lost George Kyricos, killed by mortar fire while 3 others were wounded," Tecklenburg continued. The combined attack eventually dislodged the NVA from the bridge with 22 KIA. The company returned to the battalion base camp that evening.

The 38th NVA Regiment, having fallen back earlier, was now positioned between the ARVNs 51st Regiment and the 27th Marines. With marine air and artillery support, the ARVN Regiment attacked NVA positions in the village of Qua Giang on August 24th.

But the battle-hardened NVA regiment had reinforced their positions and was waiting. They greeted the ARVNs with automatic weapons and mortars. The 51st ARVN attack failed to dislodge the NVA after a day of heavy fighting. Fox Company, 2d Battalion, 27th Marines were called back that evening. "We set in a 360 degree position near the village, watched and waited, prepared to move in on the 25th," Tecklenburg recalled.

"Marine records show that Fox was ordered on the 24th to join the ARVNs on the 25th for the joint attack. The ARVNs did not engage them in heavy fighting. They just stayed on the outskirts of the Ville and fired into it with the M2 .50 caliber machine guns on their APCs. We went into the fight about 1500 hours. Lt Jones (Platoon Commander) left 1st squad as a blocking force, and took the rest of us in," recalled Van Bibber.

Fox Company had spent all of that day dug in across a barren field from the village acting as the 51st ARVN's blocking force while they attempted to drive the enemy from their redoubt. "I remember watching the fight in the sweltering heat while prop driven Skyhawks repeatedly dropped their payload of one 500 pound bomb each on the village. The ground under us shook each time they released their ordinance. This continued through much of the day," Tecklenburg said.

Platoon commander Barry Jones stated: "I remember calling in air strikes through the afternoon and evening. and some arty… Around late afternoon, I remember hearing a Huey coming in with the Regimental commander, Colonel Schwenk. I went back to the company CP to encourage our Skipper, Captain Bill Collins, to avoid an assault if at all possible. But the Colonel gave the order for a frontal assault with us (second platoon) leading the way…"

Fox Company relieved the 51st ARVNs. Second Platoon—2nd and 3rd squads and the machine gun squad from second platoon--spearheaded the attack. Twenty-two marines began the assault. With an M-48 tank for support, the platoon entered Qua Giang.

"Moving forward, we had to walk around the 51st ARVNs pulling back in their armored personnel carriers. We saw that they had never entered the village, firing their fifty calibers into thick thickets instead. The ARVNs didn't look at us as we passed by. The marines of first platoon backing us up had a look of relief on their weary faces. I passed a friend who joined the unit the same day as me sitting on the ground, smoking. He eyed me with a "you poor bastard" nod of his head," Tecklenburg recalled, but couldn't remember his name.

"My squad moved forward, spreading out on-line to begin an assault. We followed the tank as it rumbled head-long into a bombed out shell of what once was a village. Debris, piles of rubble, twisted barbed wire, collapsed walls and roofs was all that remained. Vietnamese dead lay scattered everywhere" he remembered. "The civilians, if they were lucky, had probably fled several days earlier."

"Second platoon, let's go," Sergeant Farmer yelled.

The enemy was ready. They greeted the marines with sniper fire, automatic weapons and grenades, hitting them from all directions as they steadily moved forward. The platoon continued its assault through the smoking haze of the destroyed village.

Stated Jones: "The NVA were ready for us and must have known that it was a fight to the death. As we went on-line and began assaulting through the ville, the cacophony of gunfire, explosions, etc, was deafening. I can remember yelling out when I saw grenades coming out of bomb craters but not being able to even hear myself." But second platoon continued to move forward under intense small arms fire.

"There was this 500 pound bomb crater and as second squad moved around it on the left, third moved around it on the right. All of a sudden we were taken under fire by grenades coming from a hole in the side of the crater. All we could see was an arm come out and lob a grenade over the rim towards us. That was when Lopez ran up and plopped down on the rim with a grenade. He rolled over after the grenades were thrown and he tossed his grenade into the hole. That was the end of the arm," stated Van Bibber.

"It was virtually instinctive training that carried us forward as coordinated communication was impossible," Jones recalled. "After passing through bomb craters, I remember one of our marines whose name I don't remember running up to me and shaking his

M-16 in my face to indicate that it was destroyed in the breech by an AK hit, and he was without a firearm. I gave him my M-16 and unholstered my .45. I also had pockets full of grenades. I next remember a bunker holding a machine gun firing on our guys. I took it on, getting some grenades into it as I got hit. I didn't realize that I was hit at first, as I thought I'd tripped or fallen, but I couldn't get back on my feet. Then I saw my bloody knee and broken left arm at the wrist. I was losing a lot of blood when I saw the NVA who shot me in a nearby tree firing toward our guys. I shot him with my .45 until he dropped his AK and rolled around the tree limb where he had tied himself. I must have passed out shortly thereafter."

"Moving into what was left of Qua Giang, I heard bullets zinging over my head immediately. Men yelled, ordinance exploded everywhere, the volume of gunfire increased dramatically. I moved up behind the tank, growling and rumbling as it slowly moved forward into a narrow pathway between piles of rubble. I could smell diesel from its exhaust in the sweltering heat," Tecklenburg vividly remembered. "Inside my head, quiet reigned, but my eyes were everywhere searching out the enemy—the ground, behind rubble, in the trees and bushes. I heard the report of their weapons, but I saw no one."

The tank stalled. "Move around it!" someone yelled. "Keep moving!"

"Cautiously but steadily we began to flank it, walking in single file. On both sides of the tank lay rubble from blasted concrete walls. The smell of cordite, smoke and sweat hung heavy in the hot humid air. Small arms fire and explosions continued around me," Tecklenburg said.

Unknown to them, the platoon had walked into an L-shaped ambush. Second squad was on the left while 3rd moved along the right flank. The enemy struck from the left and directly in front with grenades and small arms fire.

"The M-48, at first our protector, had now become another obstacle. We would have to go it alone, infantryman against infantryman. The odds suddenly were much more even," Tecklenburg added.

"I was at the rear corner of the tank, walking forward into the dust and smoke. I passed the corpsman and saw that he was already tending to wounded who were beginning to collect behind the protective cover of the tank," he recalled. "Our company commander stood there talking excitedly on the field radio. I have no recollection of what he was saying, and, for me, it did not much matter. My life, as I look back, was on a different course as we pushed headlong into the gunfire."

"This is where we got pinned down, where Decker and Richee got killed. When I heard 'gun is down' from 2nd squad, I ran across the face of the ambush from where 3rd squad was, over to my gun team. When I got there, Decker was dead, shot in the face and upper chest. Richee was dying. I held his head in my arms and he looked up at me. The last thing he said was, "Decker's dead." Then he died in my arms. Richee was shot in the gut, "Van Bibber remembered, "I think he could have made it but he gave up after he saw that Decker was dead."

"I cleared the gun and joined 2nd squad. Our platoon sergeant, SSGT Staggs came running from the rear where he had been treated for heat exhaustion. He yelled, "Charge!" Van Bibber continued. "We charged the ambush. By that time, we pretty much fought individually, killing anything that got in our way. I believe that was when Lt. Jones got hit."

"'Teck, Freeman, the Lieutenant's hit! Get him out of there!'" Tecklenburg remembered the platoon sergeant suddenly yelling from somewhere to the left.

"We rushed out over the rubble of what had been part of someone's home. We passed the sergeant and another marine firing into trees, buildings, everywhere in front of them. Completely focused on the rescue, I stumbled over rubble, the remains of a house, to reach Lieutenant Jones. He lay in the rubble unconscious, blood oozing from his leg and midsection somewhere. I ran forward of him to provide covering fire. Freeman, behind me, stopped, and kneeled to tend to the wounded officer. Also kneeling, I began firing into an area of rubble and shrubs directly in front of me. Several tall palms hung over us. Suddenly, an explosion, an air burst directly in front. I saw a yellow flash, shrapnel sprayed the area. Then nothing as I was knocked out. Freeman and I were both blown flat to the ground and unconscious. Within minutes, seconds, who knows, I regained consciousness. Looking around me I discovered I was lying prone to the ground with my head in a daze, ears ringing from the blast. The lower half of my body felt numb. I was peppered with small bits of steel. My legs, I fretted. Are they there? I looked to Freeman and at that moment caught his empty stare. I wanted to yell for him to look at my legs, but I saw that he had also been wounded and seemed also in a daze. I reached down to feel them. They were still attached, and the numbness quickly subsided. I moved them, just because I could. I had survived whole. I made an immediate decision, retrieved my rifle, and looked for someone, anything, to shoot at," Tecklenburg said, adding more detail as the memory became more alive.

"Another explosion, similar to the first, rocked me," he continued. "Again, I was blown flat to the ground. Seconds, minutes, the universe passed by me. Regaining consciousness, I again reached for my rifle."

"'Get the hell out of there!' someone barked from behind me. Marines rushed out to us. They grabbed the Lieutenant. I stumbled to my feet and followed them, dazed, peppered with small bits of shrapnel. I was disoriented, dizzy, and feeling somewhat detached from the action around me, but relieved to be alive. My world in some strange way had suddenly changed forever."

Jones added: "A couple more of our guys got both Bob and I back to Doc McLaughlin. I remember coming-to as I was drug from the ville and refusing pain meds from Doc as I did not want my hand to be amputated later at the hospital because I could not feel anything."

"I saw the corpsman and was quickly examined. He tagged me for evacuation along with Freeman and Lieutenant Jones. At first, I hesitated to leave, thinking I wasn't hurt badly enough. We're a tight-knit group bound by our honor, and my honor demanded that I stay. I could not allow anyone to think I was taking the easy way out. But Doc insisted that I go. That was the encouragement I needed. I went," Tecklenburg said.

"Within minutes, we with other wounded were taken by med-evac choppers to the Naval Support Activity hospital in DaNang and the next day I was sent to Cam Ranh Bay by plane to recover from my wounds."

Stated Van Bibber: "Of the 22 later corrected to 21 who entered the village of Qua Giang from Second platoon, only thirteen later corrected to 12 walked out. That's all I remember until we humped out of there about six hours later, after putting the dead and wounded on APCs." Three marines from second platoon were killed in the ville that day.

On August 27th, Fox Company completed their assault, driving the remaining NVA and VC from the area. But here the company also paid a price, suffering additional wounded including the company commander, Captain Collins.

"Thinking back on that horrible day, it often seems like it happened to someone else—another Bob Tecklenburg. Everything seemed like it was act/react, fight or flight. Or as a friend would say, 'Your reptilian brain was in charge,'" Tecklenburg concluded.

A Marine Corps Narrative of the engagement of August 25th summarized the battle this way:

On the 25th all units advanced toward the village of Qua Giang and were taken under heavy automatic weapons and small arms fire. Fire from the tanks, 81mm mortars, artillery and nine flights of fixed wing air were employed against enemy positions. The village was cleared and seven members of Company F and the tank battalion were recommended for the Vietnamese Cross of Gallantry by the 1st Battalion, 51st ARVN Regiment. Company F was credited with 215 enemy KIA's while receiving 19 WIA's and 3 KIA's. Later corrected to 3 KIA's and 23 WIA's (**THE MARINES IN VIETNAM: 1954-1973**)

Differences in some of my memories quoted in Bob Techlenburg's account and my subsequent research are primarily due to injuries I occurred at that time. In fact, it was his article that gave me the impetus to write this book. Things may be confusing at times, but that has been my experience as I review the past. Especially in the account of the Battle for Cam Le Bridge. I truly had no idea how much the blast that killed "The Greek" affected my own memories. Simply stated, it is the "Confusion of Battle."

George Kyricos on August 23rd, Allan Decker, James Richee, and Calvin Pierce on August 25th made the ultimate sacrifice for their country at the Battle for Cam Le Bridge and Qua Giang (2). We will NEVER forget them. Semper Fi Marines.

For his heroic actions on both the 23rd and 25th of August, 1st Lt. Barry T. Jones received the Silver Star with "V" for valor. Everyone who was there agrees that this award was one well deserved. His citation reveals the story:

> The President of the United States of America takes pleasure in presenting the Silver Star to First Lieutenant Barry T. Jones (MCSN: 0-XXXXXX), United States Marine Corps, for conspicuous gallantry and intrepidity in action while serving as a Platoon Commander with Company F, Second Battalion, Twenty-Seventh Marines, FIRST Marine Division (Rein), FMF, in connection with combat operations against the enemy in the Republic of Vietnam. On 23 August 1968, Company F was supporting friendly forces attempting to seize the Cam Le Bridge in Quang Nam Province from a large North Vietnamese Army force. As First Lieutenant Jones' platoon crossed an open area during an assault on a well-fortified enemy position in the nearby village of Cam Nam, the Marines became pinned down by a heavy volume of hostile fire. Skillfully deploying his squads, First Lieutenant Jones repeatedly exposed himself to enemy fire as he moved from one position to another, shouting words of encouragement to his men and directing the evacuation of casualties. When supporting tanks arrived, he unhesitatingly maneuvered across the hazardous terrain to skillfully direct their suppressive fire and, after the enemy had been defeated, moved to the helicopter landing zone, where he was supervising the evacuation of the wounded Marines, when he was injured by hostile mortar fire. Refusing treatment, he continued to assist in removing the casualties and then deployed his men into a previously assigned blocking position before allowing himself to be treated. On the evening of 25 August 1968, First Lieutenant Jones led an aggressive assault against a well entrenched enemy force in Qua Giang Village. With complete disregard for his own safety and armed with only a pistol and hand grenades, he fearlessly attacked an automatic weapons emplacement which had pinned down one of his squads, killing one North Vietnamese soldier and forcing the others to flee. Although seriously wounded during his bold assault and in great pain, he steadfastly continued his determined efforts until gravely weakened by his severe injuries, he consented to be medically evacuated. By his courage, aggressive fighting spirit and unwavering devotion to duty throughout, First

> Lieutenant Jones upheld the highest traditions of the Marine Corps and of the United States Naval Service.

Needless to say, Lt. Jones set the bar for my relationships with officers. It would be a sad statement that I never again enjoyed the leadership of such a gallant officer.

The records indicate the following, not including the correction that was later posted after the action, with 3 KIA and 23 WIA:

24-25 Aug	Company F conducted joint operation with 1st Battalion, 51st ARVN Regiment against estimated NVA Battalion in hamlet of Qua Giang (2). Company F credited with 215 NVA killed. Company F had 19 WIA and 3 KIA.

The fight continued on the August 27th:

27 Aug	Helicopter shot down just south of the Battalion TAOR with Battalion elements taking part in the security and recovery operations. One pilot was medevaced; three crewmen were killed.
27 Aug	Company F engaged an estimated enemy company vic Bo Mung (2). Company G sent to conflict, Company F lost their CO WIA; Company G lost their XO WIA: both medevaced. No estimate of enemy casualties.
27 Aug	At 1600 1/1 arrived to relive 2/27 of operational responsibility of TAOR. Relief in progress.

A more detailed account of the action on the 27th is given from the records:

> On 27 August at 0030 a helicopter on a Firefly mission was hit by .50 caliber fire and fell in flames to the ground just south of our TAOR. A six man volunteer force was picked up from the 2/27 CP and dropped in the area of the downed chopper, an area unprepped by friendly fire support. The small force searched the area and extracted the wounded pilot. At first light a force from Company G that was under constant fire again searched the area. The three bodies of the remaining crewmen were found in the wreckage. The force and the KIA's were safely helolifted out of the area. Also on 27 August an element from Company F came in contact with an es-

> timated NVA Company in the vicinity of Bo Mung (2). Elements of Company G were deployed to the area along with three tanks from B Co, 5th Tanks. A heavy firefight ensued resulting in 25 wounded from the combined units including the CO of Company F and the XO from Company G. Enemy casualties were never estimated but presumed high.

The XO is the Executive Officer of a Company, second in command under the Commanding Officer.

On August 29th, I wrote home to my family:

> *Dear Folks,*
>
> *Well, here I am at last, and I [reckon] you all are still there. I got [off] that mountain on Aug. 23, and have been real hard at it ever since then. You have probably read about the new offensive that North Viet Nam has launched around An Hoa and Da Nang, and are wondering how I am. Well, now that our Company is really whittled down to size they decided to bring us out of the field. I lost two more men out of my squad, so please pray for their souls for me, because I can't ask for favors or [forgiveness] from the Lord yet, not while I am still over here. That's why I believe more and more that it is your prayers that keep me safe. And if I die, well, it is only just. You know what it says in the Bible, "He who lives by the sword will die by the sword". That's why I'm not really worried about [dying]. If I do, then It is only just; and if I don't well then the Lord has something else planned for this poor soul.*
>
> *Say, don't send any packages any more until you get my new address. I'll be getting transferred in about 2 or 3 days and will send you my new address as soon as I can. …*
>
> *With all my love, Chuck*

If I sounded a little despondent or fatalistic, I imagine I had reason to do so. I didn't go into any details about August 23rd and 25th, as I was in the process of internalizing everything and couldn't put it in words if I had wanted to. I had become even more detached from the losses in Vietnam and clung harder to my remaining Vietnam family members, David Lopez, Dennis Freer and Dan Nordmann. With Lt. Jones gone, as well as most of the regular rifle squad leaders, my section leader Sgt. Ledesma, and even our Company Commander, Captain Collins, it really was an empty world.

Looking back again, it's hard to talk about Decker and Richee. Al Decker was built like a bull. Strong and stocky. He smiled easily and loved to joke and kid around. He was also real serious about his job as a machine gunner. Always ready to move when the call for "guns up" went down the length of a patrol. He was also steadfast in his opinions and didn't take shit off anyone. I didn't worry much about him because he was so strong and capable. He was my number one gunner and my friend. I miss him every day I breathe.

James Richee was just the opposite of Decker. He was quiet, even with the "brothers." He was thin, but had that wiry strength and stamina that carried him through all the trials he faced. He was dark-complexioned with mixed features. Although quiet, he was always ready to stand up for himself. He was real scrappy. I miss Richee.

Together, Decker and Richee made a great gun team. They learned to trust each other and put aside any racial prejudice they may have carried with themselves to Vietnam. It didn't take long before they were real brothers - and like brothers, they stood up for each other but would squabble between themselves on occasion as well. Once when we were back at Battalion Headquarters, we went to the beer tent, got some brews, and sat around on the picnic benches that made a kind of pavilion. I never could drink much beer; it just didn't sit right with me. I was more a whisky man. As night fell, everyone else had more beer than they could hold, and we started back to our tents. For some reason, Decker and Richee got into an argument and they continued to squabble as we walked back to our area. I was walking alongside Decker and Richee was bringing up the rear. They continued to argue and then they started to call each other names. As I have said, they were both very strong willed and didn't take any guff. Well, Richee said something that made me and Decker turn around. He said something about shooting the SOB. As I turned around, I heard Richee jack a round into his M-16. Facing Decker, Richee threatened Decker again and Decker started to react in kind, making a move for his .45 automatic. Fearful for them both, I knocked the gun from Decker's hand, pulled my own .45 and stepped between them, facing Richee. As I tried to talk some sense into him, I took a step toward him to disarm him. Richee got scared and fired off a blast of automatic fire from his M-16, which ripped the ground near me. Everything seemed to happen at once, and as the blast came out of Richee's rifle, I took another step forward and knocked the rifle from his hands. Richee was just as surprised by his rifle going off as I was. I believe his pulling the trigger was just a reflex. Mad as hell, I threatened him with my own .45 and told both of them to knock it off and get some sleep. That broke the tension and everyone crashed. Everyone but me. My heart was racing as I realized how close I had come to getting killed. The next day Decker and Richee made their apologies and that was that. Neither one of them remembered the incident clearly enough to understand it, and I didn't pursue it. I needed these men, and I knew that, like blood brothers, they had clashed, and that was all it was. There were never any two men, in my experience in Vietnam, who loved each other more. They lived as a team and they died as a team. Semper Fi, brothers!

Why our Platoon was chosen for that final assault on the village of Qua Giang (2), no one but Colonel Schwenk, the Regimental Commander, knows for sure. But it was known by some at Headquarters, that 2nd Platoon, Fox Company could be counted on in a pinch and was considered to be one of the best Platoons in the Battalion. Colonel Schwenk, the Battalion CO and Captain Collins, Fox Company Commander, had full confidence in our Platoon Commander, 1st Lt. Barry Jones. It wasn't the first time that we were chosen for difficult tasks. Whatever the reason, that battle just about wiped 2nd Platoon off the face of the earth.

Our involvement at the Cam Le Bridge can be summed up best by saying what every officer knows in his heart of hearts, that those in command always use their best units/men to achieve important goals. Although this attitude is not necessarily embraced by the men involved, still, they do the bidding of those appointed over them and ultimately suffer the consequences.

A final article, written by SSgt. Bob Bowen and printed in the *Sea Tiger*, a military paper written and published in Vietnam, dated September 20, 1968 states the following:

> .... August 23, an advance unit of the V-25 VC Ba. [sic] attacked the Cam Le Bridge on the southern outskirts of Da Nang in preparation for an all out assault on the city's major military and civilian installations.
>
> .... Late in the evening of August 24, Fox Co. 2-27 was called on to act as a blocking force for a South Vietnamese Army unit which was in heavy contact with the enemy battalion in the village of Qua Giang, five miles south of Da Nang.
>
> Fighting continued throughout the night and into the next day. At 4pm, on the 25, the Marines launched an assault on the village, breaking the back of enemy resistance in the area. The communists

lost 215 of their number in Qua Giang, reducing the V-25 Bn. To less than 50 percent effectiveness.

Two days later on August 27, what is believed to be remnants of the V-25 Bn. Launched a "do-or-die" attack against the command post of "F" Co., 2-27. The enemy was beaten back with the assistance of two relief platoons from "G" Co., and tanks from the 1st Tank Bn.

The V-25 Battalion has not been heard of since.

On September 17, Twenty-seventh Marines marched in a parade in San Diego, Calif. Their uniforms were neatly pressed, their shoes highly polished. Their step was that of well-drilled troops, and the medals they've won were prominently displayed above their left breast pockets.

Gone were the cautious glances of the seasoned warrior. Gone were the mud-caked boots from countless rice paddies. Gone were the buzzing of malaria-bearing mosquitoes.

The Twenty-seventh Marines are home.

An interesting development occurred over thirty years later when two Florida businessmen went to Vietnam. An article in the *Chicago Sun-Times* by Mike Bransom, dated Thursday, July 5, 2001, says it best:

"Dog Tags Returned to Mother after Three Decades"

Two men find Marine's tags and about 640 others for sale in Vietnam

ORLANDO, Fla ... The mother of a Marine killed in Vietnam received his dog tags in an Independence Day ceremony after two Florida businessmen found them for sale in a back-alley market in Ho Chi Minh City.

Rob Stiff and Jim Gain were so sickened at the discovery of Lance Cpl. Allan George Decker's tags that they returned to Vietnam in May to buy them and hundreds of others. Upon returning to America, they began trying to reunite soldiers and their families with the lost tags.

Wednesday, the men gave Decker's mother the tags at the Orlando cemetery where he was buried after his death in 1968. The moment had added meaning for her because July 4th is her birthday.

"I just hope that other families can find the kind of peace that I have felt today," Ruth Decker said. "The Lord had his hand in this from the beginning."

Servicemen usually wore the tags – silver rectangles that listed a soldier's name, military identification number and blood type – around their necks, but in the field many put them in their boots so they wouldn't jingle.

Stiff and Gain weren't looking for war mementos when they traveled to Vietnam in January. They wanted to check the commercial climate for possible business ventures. In a market not frequented by tourists, they found the dog tags dangling from a string.

"It was really eerie and we were disgusted," said Stiff, 27.

Despite their revulsion, they left the tags there. But back home in America, they couldn't escape the memory. In May, they returned to Vietnam to buy all the American dog tags they could find. They returned home with about 640. The total cost of the tags was $180. They sometimes paid less than 14 cents for each.

Stiff and Gain transcribed what was printed on each the best they could, then compiled a database of names and ID numbers to list on their Web site: *www.founddogtags.com.*

A dozen tags matched names listed on the black granite Vietnam Veterans Memorial in Washington, DC.

One of the first names they uncovered was Decker's. With the help of Rep. Rie Keller, an Orlando Republican, and the Defense Department they tracked Ruth Decker to her home in Punta Gorda and called her June 21.

"She was so full of joy," Stiff said.

On Aug. 25, 1968, Decker, a 19-year-old Marine, was killed in Quang Nam province, one of more than 58,000 Americans to die in Vietnam.

"Allan was killed on a Sunday, and we didn't receive the word until the following Thursday," said Ruth Decker. "My husband and I were just crushed."

"But the next day, we received a letter from his buddy," she said. "He said that Allan believed in God very strongly, and He will take care of him. And that was my consolation right from the beginning."

I pondered this event for years, trying to figure out what happened to cause Decker to lose his dog tags. He always kept his dog tags, both of them, on a chain around his neck. He didn't practice the habit of wearing one on his boot as so many others did, in fact, we all did that. Therefore, it would be real easy in the blood and mud of that dirty hole, for Decker's dog tags to fall off and be lost to time until some Vietnamese person, seeing the shiny metal, dug them out of the dirt in the place of that long-forgotten battle. It also accounts for my having to go to Graves Registration and identify his body. Needless to say, I was real shocked when I first got the news, because I was right there when Decker was killed. But now I understand. God bless Al, and his saintly mother, who keeps his memory alive. Valentine's Day, 1968, was the last day that she would ever talk to her son, Allan. I often receive a Valentine's Day card from Ruth reminding me that Valentine's Day, 1968 was the last time she ever talked to her son. We share a common grief, which makes our bond the stronger.

Well, at least the Regimental Colors were home, along with some of the men who were in Vietnam. The majority of us who remained in Vietnam were transferred to other units. A short history of the 27th Marines sums it up:

> From Wikipedia:
>
> The 27th Marine Regiment was activated on January 10, 1944 as a result of the massive increase in the Marine Corps during World War II. The regiment first saw action during the Battle of Iwo Jima. During the course of the battle they suffered 566 killed, 1,706 wounded and had 4 Marines receive the Medal of Honor. After the surrender of Japan the regiment was deactivated on January 10, 1946.
>
> The 27th Marines was again reactivated during the Vietnam War on January 1, 1966 but was mainly used as a pool for new replacements before they went overseas. After the Tet Offensive in 1968, President Lyndon B. Johnson authorized an increase in U.S. troop strength in Vietnam and the 27th Marines was one of the units sent. They became the first Marine regiment to fly into a combat zone. Their deployment overseas put a severe strain on manpower in the Marine Corps and they were returned to the United States before the close of 1968.
>
> A homecoming parade was presented as a Memorial Ceremony in downtown San Diego to the lives the regiment had given in Viet-

> nam. The unit was then reassigned to MCB [Marine Corps Base] Camp Pendleton within the area of the base called Camp Margarita or the 33 Area. Until June 1969, the 27th Marines was made up of "Short timers", that is Marines having only months remaining of active duty.

An interesting side note: the 27th Marine Regiment took a total of 2272 casualties (566 KIA and 1706 WIA) from February 1945 through April 1945, a total of about three months. When reactivated for Vietnam, the Regiment took 2,222 casualties (287 KIA, 1933 WIA, and 2 MIA) between February 1968 and August 1968, a total of about 6 months. I am very proud to have served with the 27th Marine Regiment, the Regiment of John Basilone and the Battle of Iwo Jima. Oorah!

With a difference of only three months and 50 casualties, the regiment was consistent in its losses. However, in 1945, the 27th Marine Regiment came home in glory and the men were honored as heroes by the citizenry of the country, while in 1968, with only a short parade in San Diego, the men who came home later were treated with disdain and, in some cases, outright hatred by some U.S. citizens. Just the facts. Still, facts can say many things. Is horrific combat over three months in Iwo Jima comparable to prolonged combat over 6 months in Vietnam? Not to me. The battles of WWII far exceed those in Vietnam in casualties and in horror. Helmets off to that Greatest Generation. What about the men who didn't go home with the 27th Marines, who continued to experience combat for another 7 months, if they survived that long? What have we learned today, with increases in PTSD and suicide, reportedly from multiple tours in a war zone? The logical conclusion would be, if you have to go to war, then declare it as such and pursue the war with definite goals, withdrawing once the final objective has been achieved. It's a shame that logic is lost in the politics that dictate war in the first place.

I hold no grudge for those times. The American people have recovered from their shame and now embrace the combatants returning from the wars in Iraq and Afghanistan. If it took Vietnam to cause this change in the public, than I say that Vietnam was worth it. However if the people ever again turn on the men and women in our combat units, then I say:

> We, our country, are lost. Our honor and courage that has kept this country free will be gone. My time in Vietnam will have been wasted, along with the 58,282 killed; 303,644 wounded; 1,655 miss-

ing in action; and between 69 and 119 prisoners of war that died while still incarcerated; as well as the countless numbers of Vietnam Veterans still suffering from bodily injuries, Agent Orange and Post Traumatic Stress Disorder.

Who knows what America will be like, what the world will be like, the next time the 27th Marine Regiment is activated? War will be with us always, but what kind of people will we be? What will the cost be for the 27th Marines, for our nation? Only stout hearts and clear minds and a willingness to fight for freedom down to the last breath will win over the evil that threatens us each and every day. In God we Trust! Semper Fidelis Marines!

By the end of August, the casualty count for 2/27 in August was:

KIA 15 WIA 109 for a running total after 6.5 Months of KIA 53 WIA 616 MIA 2 Total 671

The Average Monthly Battalion strength during the time in Vietnam was 1100 men

The percent killed/missing or wounded in the Battalion was 61%

Chapter 11

The possibility of my death was growing exponentially. I knew it and trusted in the Lord. That was all I could do, other than work to be a better killer than my opponents. Work on it I did. As the time for my transfer to the 5th Marines in An Hoa (pronounced "An Wa") - just a few miles south of Liberty Bridge off Hwy. 1 - neared, I put my sorrows aside and increased my alertness.

On September 1st, I wrote:

Dear Folks,

Well, I am at Battalion now, and have been here for a whole 24 hours. We are packed up waiting for choppers to take us down toward An Hoa again for another operation. Our orders are already made for transfers, and as soon as they decide to let us go we will be transferred. As the 27th goes home and we get transferred. As far as I know I will be going to the 5th Marines. Oh, since there are only 4 of us left in the squad I am humping the gun again.

I got yours and Dad's letter Mom, and sure was happy to get them. Oh, I also got an answer from Congressman O.C. Fisher. He said he would be glad to look into Dad's case, but he needs the case number and all other [pertinent] information. When you write him, say that you are writing in reference to the letter from LCpl Charles Van Bibber concerning Dad Mr. etc. …Bill, you be sure and save that money and put it in the bank. Then pretty soon you will have enough to buy a new bike like I did when I was little. …

So Chris, just keep with the spirit you've got now and don't worry about size. Remember, it is not what a man looks like on the outside, but how solid he is on the inside. …

[Jean] listen to Mom and Dad, don't be afraid to ask questions, and above all else, to be truthful all the time. Never lie Jeannie. And always do what Mommy and Daddy say. …

I give you all my love and prayers Granny, and never forget that your family loves you and wants to give you all we can. If it wasn't for your faith and courage our family would not be as strong as we are, especially with Dad and I being the [heretics] we are, ha, ha.

Dad, well, the way I feel about you and Mom, the way I feel about you; just can't be put down on paper in any better way than to say I LOVE YOU-ALL!I pray and trust that the Lord will see me home safely, and if I should die, I pray that the Lord gives you the strength to understand that, the Lord willing, I would have passed into a better life. ...

With all my love, Chuck

P.S. Give Cathy all my love. I'll write her as soon as I can.

I made a point in this letter to talk directly to each member of my family. Things had changed. I knew before that my chances of being wounded or killed were pretty high, but somehow that knowledge always seemed impossible in a way, like most young people, it just isn't anything you really think about. But after the deaths of Al Decker and James Richee, the chance of my death became all too real. I could go crazy fighting it or I could just accept it and go on. I chose the latter. I was no longer young. I was now an old man, body and soul.

By the end of August, the 27th Marine Regiment had been relieved of it's duties:

Info 301800	2nd Battalion, 27th Marines transferred OPCON of 2/27 TAOR to 1st Battalion, 1st Marines.

On September 4th I wrote:

Dear Folks,

Well, here I am and there you are; I'm all wet and your unforgivably dry. Yep, the monsoon is here to stay. It has rained everyday now for the last 5 days [Typhoon Bess], and it doesn't look like it's going to stop.

I'm back [at] Battalion again, waiting to go someplace else. They are sure getting their 2 [cents'] worth out of us before we get transferred. The way it looks now we should get transferred around the 7th, and word has it that the machine-gunners will be going to the 5th Marines. So meanwhile I'm just biding my time. Like they say, they can fool with us all they want, but they can't stop the clock. ...

With all my love, Chuck

My final letter from the 27th Marines on September 8th reads:

Dear Folks,

Well, I'm caught in Da Nang; waiting to go to An Hoa and check in with the 5th Marines. I'll write you as soon as I get there so you can get some letters off to me. I'm enclosing a picture of myself that you may find quite interesting. You can sure tell I'm back in Nam, can't you. I hardly recognized me, myself.

You all take care, and write as soon as you get my address, [okay]!

With all my love, Chuck

An understanding of the 5th Marines in early September is provided by the records for that time:

> Drafts of incoming personnel during the month of September increased the strength of all battalions. The normal rotation of key officers and NCO's throughout the Regiment was particularily [*sic*] heavy during the same period. To compensate for the loss of key leaders training of relief's by the relieved for 5 to 10 days prior to change-over. Indoctrination of new troops pressed training in enemy mines and explosive devices, terrain familiarization, and enemy capabilities.
>
> The added strength of fresh troops and emphasis on training and indoctrination significantly increased the combat effectiveness of the Fifth Marines.
>
> Enemy
>
> On 9 Sep 68 Operation SUSSEX BAY terminated primarily due to the disruptive and unfavorable weather conditions which prevailed during typhoon "BESS". Enemy activity throughout the Regimental AO decreased slightly in intensity and frequency as compared to the previous month.
>
> Weather
>
> Typhoon "BESS" dominated the period 2-5 September with high winds and heavy rains. During this period Air/Ground operations were reduced to a minimum. The remainder of the month was mostly clear to partly cloudy with occasional afternoon and evening showers.

Welcome to the 5th Marines. It was a soggy mess. Weather plays an important role in wartime operations. Regardless of the best efforts of Man, no one can change the weather. It reminds me of General George Patton's prayer for clear weather during the Battle of the Bulge. Only God can change the weather. And just like Patton, we were stopped in our tracks by weather. Typhoon "Bess" had us in her grip.

During the end of August 1968 and the beginning days of September, Golf Company 2nd Battalion 5th Marines commanded by Captain H. J. Poole, who took over Golf Company on the 15th of July, was busy with ongoing operations. I would report to Weapons Platoon, Golf Company on September 9th, just as Operation Sussex Bay wound to a close.

Again the records report the actions of that time:

> SECOND BN (MINUS) FIFTH MARINES LT COL STEMPLE
> H AND S CO 2/5 Headquarters and Service Company
> CO E 2/5
> CO G 2/5
> SECOND BN (MINUS) FIFTH MARINES: COMMENCING AT FIRST LIGHT SWEEP NORTH TO SIEZE AND SEARCH REGT OBJ'S 21 AND 22. SEEK OUT AND DESTROY OR CAPTURE ENEMY FORCES, WEAPONS, MATERIEL, AND POSITIONS.

From the records:

> During the period 29 August to 9 September 1968, the Second Battalion (-) participated in Operation SUSSEX BAY in coordination and cooperation with ARVN and ROKMC forces. On 11 September the Second Battalion resumed its participation in Operation MAMELUKE THRUST II. The primary mission of the Battalion was to locate and destroy enemy forces, base areas, and caches of materiel and supplies. Secondary missions included providing security for the Liberty Bridge area and protecting the MSR as well as providing security for the local rice harvest. Control of the company assigned to provide security for the Liberty Bridge area and those forces utilized to protect the MSR was normally exercised directly by the Battalion Rear in order that the Battalion (-) was better able to conduct offensive operations.
>
> On 23 September 1968 Company H came under the operational control of First Battalion, Fifth Marines as did Company F on 25 September 1968.

This accounts for the Battalion minus (-), meaning that the Battalion was not complete, consisting only of the H & S Company (Headquarters and Service), Company E and Company G, Company F and H having been transferred to 1/5. ROKMC stands for Republic of Korea Marine Corps. Those ROK Marines were a terror to the VC. They hunted and treated the VC with the same methods that the VC used on us. No one crossed the ROKs.

The road (Hwy. 1), spanned by Liberty Bridge was the Main Supply Route (MSR) for all bases along the coastal plane. An Hoa was supplied via this road and it was essential to keep the route open. I had had many experiences along Hwy. 1, not the least of which was the "Death March" in July. By the time I was inducted into Golf Company and assigned to 2nd Platoon, the 3rd Platoon of Golf Co. was providing security for the Battalion area, primarily along Hwy. 1. They ran road sweeps (R/S) and set up observation posts (OPs) along the immediate area along both sides of Hwy. 1 from An Hoa to Liberty Bridge, providing security for both the Bridge and the road. During this time though, our 2nd Platoon was operating with the Company out in the Arizona Territory (so named because it was full of "hostile Indians", VC).

On September 10th I wrote:

Dear Folks,

Well, here I am and there you are. And where am I you may ask, well my address is Golf Co. 2/5, Weapons Plt.; 1st Marine Division; FPO San Francisco, Calif. 96602. I don't know which plt. I'm going in yet, but I [reckon] I'll be going into Weapons Plt., so put it down. …I don't know what the 5th Marines is going to be like, but so far I don't like it at all. Most of the people have only been in Viet Nam for 3 months or less, so there is still a lot of petty stuff to put up with. I sure miss the old 27th. But I'll be [home] in about 5 1/2 months, so I guess I'll just bide my time till March. …

With all my love, Chuck

I was in An Hoa, just a few miles south of Liberty Bridge, the original home of the 5th Marines. A little background on 2/5 is in order, to provide answers to the type of unit I was assigned to.

As the 27th Marines landed in February, 1968, all Battalions of the 5th Marines were in the process of moving out to the area around the DMZ (Demilitarized Zone). The 2nd Battalion, 5th Marines had already made the move on January 31 with Golf Company in the lead. Operation Hue City then commenced on February 3rd, continuing until the 29th, 1968 was a leap year. Golf 2/5 was a primary component in the forces facing the enemy attack on Hue City.

The 5th Marines were hit hard up at Hue City and the various operations in the northern portion of Vietnam. Their old TAOR was from the village of Cao Hai to the southern slopes of the Hai Van Pass. Those of us transferred from the 27th didn't fit right in with Golf Company at first, and several factors contributed to this.

The core of Golf Company was established in November of 1967 at An Hoa and molded by fire at the Battle of Hue City and other actions in the Hai Van Pass. Their story was much like ours in the 27th and the attrition among their friends had resulted in a closing of the ranks, as had happened to myself and others while we were in the 27th. These were all normal combat experiences and the reason why the Corps had previously tried to keep units together. Vietnam saw a departure from that policy, being a war of replacements. Most Marines went over as replacements and came back as individuals. This mass influx of new but experienced troops into other units created difficult situations.

A poem written by Charles "Mike" Ervin, squad leader 2nd Platoon, Golf Co. 2/5 sets the stage for what was to come:

"CHRISTMAS OF 67"

The Christmas I remember
was at Liberty Bridge.
Yes, in the Arizona
Just beyond Charlie Ridge.

We slept in trenches
Standing watch at night
With Arty whistling overhead
And pop-flares so bright.
Here I was dressed
in a jacket of flak
Wrapped in wet liner
Nestling down for a nap.

When all of a sudden
came this weird sounding noise:
Damn, It's Charlie!
He's serenading us, boys!

Yes, it was Charlie

With propaganda machines
Playing tunes of sugar plums
And white Christmas scenes.

He played them all night
The best I remember
But, it wasn't like home
This Vietnam December.

No, Grunts have dreams
Of fun in the field.
But, this Christmas was no dream, son.
This Christmas was real.

Now as I sit here
All safe and warm
I invoke a blessing
For all far from home:

May our spirits be with you.
Hold your head high!
Merry Christmas to all
And to all, "Semper Fi"!

Mike Ervin
Golf 2/5 67-68

By the end of July, the 5th Marine Regimental Headquarters along with the 2nd Battalion had moved back to An Hoa. August would find Golf Company again in a major fight against NVA forces. On the 18th, seven men from Golf Co. would lose their lives, with an additional 20 WIA.

The records indicated the following:

> From 17 August the Second Battalion, in conjunction with the 2nd Battalion, 7th Marines and the 3rd Battalion, 5th Marines, participated in a regimental-size cordon and search operation in the vicinity of Chau Phong village. Heavy resistance was encountered in the vicinity of La Thap (1). For this operation the company in garrison at An Hoa was released, and for the balance of the month the battalion continued to maneuver with three of its companies in the field. In

addition to inflicting 40 KIA's upon the NVA/VC forces, the Battalion captured 50 individual and crew served weapons, large quantities of equipment and supplies and over 80 tons of bagged rice concealed for ready use in shallow underground caches. The Battalion continued to maneuver northwest to Go Noi Island and on 29 August commenced Operation SUSSEX BAY.

At 181500H, Company G, at AT945517, received S/A and A/W fire from the vicinity of AT 946517. The company returned 150 rounds S/A fire, 23 rounds M-79 and 10 rounds M-60 fire. As the company continued to advance, it received a heavier volume of S/A, A/W fire and handgrenades [*sic*] from an estimated platoon of NVA. Company G fired 250 rounds S/A, 300 rounds A/W, 50 rounds M-79 and 35 handgrenades [*sic*]. A 105mm mission of 60 HE rounds and 6 fixed wing air strikes were called, then Company G swept the enemy position. Results: 7 USMC KIA, 13 USMC WIA Evac., 7 USMC WIA NonEvac, and 27 NVA KIA (Conf).

Along with those from G 2/5, E 2/7 and G 2/7 a total of 9 men would pay the ultimate sacrifice.

The men killed that day from Golf Co. were:

Cpl. Michael "Chubby" D. Hale 0311
Pfc. Douglas S. Scroggins 0311
Cpl. James O. Spaw 0311
Pfc. Wallace O. Travers Jr. 0311
LCpl. Larry W. Walker 0311
SSgt. Freddy R. Williams Platoon Sergeant
LCpl. Michael R. Witt 0311

Five of those killed were from 2nd Platoon, with a significant number wounded. Seems like 2nd Platoon Golf 2/5 would be rode hard and put away wet much like my old platoon in the 27th Marines.

Staff Sergeant Freddy Roosevelt Williams was awarded the Silver Star in the following citation:

The President of the United States of America takes pride in presenting the Silver Star (Posthumously) to Staff Sergeant Freddy R. Williams (MCSN: XXXXXXX), United States Marine Corps, for conspicuous gallantry and intrepidity while serving as Company Gunnery Sergeant of Company G, Second Battalion, Fifth Marines, FIRST Marine Division in connection with operations against the enemy in the Republic of Vietnam. On the afternoon of 18 August 1968, Company G was attacking the hamlet of La Thap (1) in Quang Nam Province when the lead element came under intense mortar, antitank rocket and automatic weapons fire from a well entrenched North Vietnamese Army force, wounding several Marines and pinning down the remainder of the company. Rapidly assessing the situation, Staff Sergeant Williams completely disregarded his own safety as he unhesitatingly moved across the fire-swept terrain and pulled one of the injured men to a position of relative safety. Undaunted by the hostile fire, he fearlessly returned across the hazardous area to the side of a second wounded comrade, and while attempting to carry the casualty to a covered position, Staff Sergeant Williams was mortally wounded. By his courage, bold initiative and selfless devotion to duty, Staff Sergeant Williams saved the life of a fellow Marine and upheld the highest traditions of the Marine Corps and of the United States Naval Service. He gallantly gave his life in the service of his country.

Mike "Chubby" Hale is remembered by Mike Ervin who was wounded that day:

Chubby reported to Golf Co. 2nd Battalion 5th Marines at An Hoa South Vietnam about the same day I did (11Nov67). We shared our lives from that day forward. His closest sidekick was Bob Setlak – it was sort of like a Laurel and Hardy combination. Chubby was killed at An Loc 6 on 18Aug68. I took my last ride with Chubby when they evaced me to DaNang. Believe me when I tell you we have not forgotten.

Another memorial for Chubby by Larry Christensen a boot camp buddy:

Michael was a wonderful person to have known. I remember him from boot camp, like the rest of us, trying to survive. He always could make us laugh or would joke around a little. He was one of few who really stands out in my memory from MCRD. I was saddened to learn of his loss so many years ago. Michael, your [*sic*] not forgotten, you will always be in our hearts.

A remembrance of Larry W. Walker by Jim Lewis also of 2nd Platoon, Golf Company 2/5:

US Marine LCPL Larry Wayne Walker, Vietnam Veteran, Native of Greensboro, NC.

> US Marine Lance Corporal Larry Wayne Walker, casualty of the Vietnam War. As a member of the Marine Corps, LCPL Walker served our country until August 18th, 1968 in Quang Nam, South Vietnam. He was 19 years old and was married. It was reported that Larry died from small arms fire or grenade. His body was recovered. Larry was born on March 9th, 1949 in Greensboro, North Carolina. LCPL Walker is on panel 48W, line 050 of the Vietnam Memorial Wall in Washington D.C. He served our country for one year.
>
> We served together. 37 years ago today, we lost a good Marine, friend and a heck of a radio operator. And most of all, his laugh and humor. Everyday [*sic*], we think of you and miss you. You are missed, respected and loved. Know you are missed and loved and talked about with respect. A good Marine, a better friend and you saved so many with your radio skill.

The action on August 18 would be a part of the "Mini Tet" of August. Five days after Golf's contact with the NVA, Fox 2/27 would be fighting in the Battle for Cam Le Bridge, causing extensive casualties in my platoon. The similarities are uncanny. Golf Company, 2/5 on 18 August lost 27 men, 7 KIA and 20 WIA. Fox Company 2/27 on 23 August lost 20 men, 1 KIA and 19 WIA, and on 25 August Fox Co. lost an additional 26 men, 3 KIA and 23 WIA. Forty-six men in all.

Golf Company was being whittled down. The core group was getting smaller and smaller and those that remained were tired and worn out. And they were getting "short". The next worse thing to being a newbie was being short. "Short" meant there were only a few more months or weeks ahead before transfer back to the "world", the good old U. S. of A. And being short just increased the anxiety and wear and tear on Marines. Not knowing all that had happened before in 2nd Platoon, I clashed with my squad leader Mike Copeland, and he took the steps necessary to put me in my place. I can see where I had obtained an "attitude" and was still shook up by the deaths of Decker, Richee and the "Greek" only a few weeks earlier, which he knew nothing about. Still, we managed to work together and get the job done.

The base at An Hoa was all set up by the time I got there on the 9th of September. I was assigned to 2nd Battalion, Golf Company, along with my good friends and fearless fighters David Lopez and Tom Thomas. All three of us were assigned to 2nd Platoon, Golf Company, 2/5. Thomas would be my gunner in the number one gun team, while Lopez took over the number two gun team. Lopez and I were the only two from my machine gun squad in the 27th Marines to have been transferred together. Dan Nordmann had gone to Lima Company, 3rd Battalion, 5th Marines, and Dennis Freer had gone to Delta Company, 1st Battalion, 5th Marines. But Lopez and I didn't know that at the time. As far as we knew, we were all that was left of the original machine gun squad. Years later, I would find out that Nordmann only lasted a week or so with his new unit when he was shot in the neck. Luckily, he survived. He was treated for his wounds and sent back to his old unit, only to be hit by shrapnel from a mortar round a few weeks later and sent home for good after that. He recovered from his wounds, finished his hitch in the Corps and went on with his life. Happily married with children, he has lived a great life and gives of himself freely to his comrades in arms, helping to organize and run annual reunions for Lima 3/5.

Dennis Freer would survive his time with Delta 1/5 and return to the States, finish his hitch in the Corps, go on to enlist in the Air Force, and make it a career.

Lt. Jones and the rest of the men who were wounded at the Battle for the Cam Le Bridge would heal and return to civilian life. Lt. Jones would become a psychiatrist and retire from a successful practice. After recovering from his wounds, Bob Tecklenburg from 2nd Squad would be transferred to CAP (Combined Action Platoon) 3-2-5 located north of Da Nang. After leaving the Corps he would work as a counselor for the Veterans Administration until his retirement. Since then he has become a well-known author.

Of the others from 2nd Platoon, Fox Co. I know that Tom Montie, Ralph Gibson and Jim Seabolt from 3rd Squad survived. Jim Seabolt works with others, especially veterans, in a Christian Ministry in Alabama. He lost a leg as a result of the Battle for the Cam Le Bridge. Tom Montie enjoys retirement and Ralph Gibson is doing well.

For now though, Lopez, Thomas and I were on our own. After checking in at the Battalion Headquarters and receiving an assignment to Weapons Platoon, Golf Company, we were located in the "tent city" that would be our home whenever we were back at An Hoa. It was located not far from a 155mm Howitzer Battery. On our first night in the tents, I had stowed my gear and laid down for a good rest when kaboom!! The tent shook and I fell out of my cot onto the floor of the tent. I was confused at first, thinking we were under a rocket attack. As I started to run to the nearest bunker, I noticed men standing around looking at me with a questioning look on their faces. Before I got to the bunker, I was stopped and asked what I was doing. I explained and they all laughed. Great fun for them but I doubt that any of them had ever experienced a rocket attack on troop tents before. As for me, I was taking no chances, been there done that! That "kaboom" was from the 155mm Battery just down the way. When those things went off, it sounded like a freight train had crashed into a brick wall and sent pieces of wall flying out into the world at large. They were nothing like the 105's we had on that mountain firebase in August. What a horrible place to put combat troops, but we were just grunts and had to suck it up. Welcome to the 5th Marines. Luckily, I didn't spend much time there since I was in the bush most of the time.

As I had written in my letters, the 5th Marines in An Hoa were mostly "boot camps" as far as I was concerned. After being whittled down so badly, 2/5 was refurbished with an influx of new replacements along with the few of us who had survived in the 27th Marines. What bothered me was that all that inexperience could get the Marines in our platoon killed or injured, including me. From the viewpoint of the few experienced men in Golf Company, Lopez, Thomas and I were at first looked upon as no better than replacements and we were treated as such, but things would change quickly when our squad leader went on R & R and I became the temporary squad leader, with Thomas as the temporary number one team leader/gunner and Lopez as the number two team leader.

Actions recorded from the records between September 10th to the 14th state:

> At 101500H, a squad combat patrol from Company G was searching living structures at AT896504 when 3 Vietnamese males were observed. Upon seeing the Marines, the Vietnamese ran and refused to halt as instructed. The patrol fired S/A and A/W killing 1 VC. The remaining enemy fled to area. Results: 1 VC KIA.
>
> At 101850H, a Company G OP, at AT910485, received 150 rds of S/A and A/W fire from an estimated 5 enemy at AT915492. Another Company G unit maneuvered to aid the OP, and a Marine detonated a booby trapped 60mm rd with trip wire. The enemy, seeing the reinforcements, broke contact. Results: 3 USMC WIA Evac.

> At 110900H, a squad from Company G found several fresh graves at AT900508. The graves contained 8 VC bodies dressed in black pajamas, killed by fragmentation. Results: 8 VC KIA
>
> At 130710H, a platoon from Company G searching a village at AT89550 observed 20 VC fleeing the area in all directions. The platoon fired small arms and automatic weapons and searched the area. While searching, a Marine detonated a booby trapped M-26 grenade with trip wire. Results: Two USMC WIA Evac and Five VC KIA.
>
> At 130930H, a platoon escorting two VC bodies and several detainees detonated a booby trapped 60mm round with trip wire at AT895500. Results: One USMC KIA and two USMC WIA.

A search of the Wall in Washington, DC, indicates that the most probable casualty in the incident on September 13, where a 60mm booby trap was detonated, is PFC James D. Wardlow. He is listed as an 0311 rifleman serving with Golf Company, 2nd Battalion, 5th Marines. Cause of death is listed as an explosion.

More from the records:

> At 131800H, a platoon from Company G, searching in the area of AT895500 after an artillery mission had been fired, found three Vietnamese males, one wounded by shrapnel. The wounded man died of wounds. Interrogation revealed that all three were rice carriers for the NVA. Results: One VC KIA and two VC POW.
>
> At 140730, a platoon from Company G at AT897503 observed seven VC, some with weapons, carrying the bodies of four VC at AT89550. The platoon fired small arms and the enemy dispersed. Results: Four VC KIA.
>
> At 141015H, a platoon from Company G on a search and clear mission found one VC body, dressed in black shirt and brown pants at AT895500. Results: One VC KIA.
>
> At 141050H, a Marine from Company G was wounded at AT894500 by a sniper round from the vicinity of AT 895500. Results: 1 USMC WIA Evac.

Unlike the 27th Marines, the reports of 2/5 do not always identify units lower than company level. At this time, 3rd Platoon was in An Hoa providing security on Hwy. 1 and Liberty Bridge. My memories of this time are bleak, but our Company was operating together, minus 3rd Platoon, with 1st and 2nd Platoons and the Company CP acting in concert. The booby trap problems were really taking their toll, primarily due to inexperience.

In a letter dated September 14, 1968, I wrote:

Dear Folks,

Well, here I am and there you are. Now what do you think of that! I am [finally] situated as the acting squad leader of the 2nd squad Machine guns in the Second Plt. The squad leader is on R & R and when he comes back I'll be the first team leader. But actually I'm having to run most of the military strategy in the Plt., in a [roundabout] manner. There are only about 8 of us who have been here in country over 6 months and in fact the majority of the people have only been here 1 or 2 months, plus the fact that these boots haven't seen any action yet either. So I've a job to do for sure.

I'm out in the bush, about ¾ of a mile East of An Hoa, and will be here until they bring us in, when ever that will be. ... Everything seems to be alright on a whole. Things are real petty back at An Hoa, but out here in the field things seem to be fairly well up to par as far as living in the bush is [concerned]. I can't say much for [our] military greatness because it is a boot Plt. but if tradition holds true this plt. [ought] to be okay.

With all my love, Chuck

Continuing the reports from the records:

> At 150900H, a Marine from Company G on road sweep security detonated a booby trapped M-26 grenade with friction pull device at AT910486. Results: One USMC KIA.
>
> At 151100H, a platoon from Company G, at AT899501, observed three VC at AT890495. Tanks attached to the platoon fired two rounds HE of 90mm. Search of the area produced one body. Results: One VC KIA.
>
> At 151645H, a Marine from Company G detonated a booby trapped fragmentation grenade, with unknown type detonation device, at AT898499. Results: Four USMC WIA Evac.

Third Platoon was still operating as security along Hwy. #1 and the road sweep patrols were no piece of cake either. AT 150900H a Marine hit a booby trap. One USMC KIA. The Marine that died that day was PFC Timothy James Melville. He was in 3rd Platoon, Golf Company 2/5.

The reports of booby traps continue:

At 162000H, a Marine from Company G detonated a booby trapped M-26 grenade with trip wire at AT904516. Results: 1 USMC WIA Evac.

At 171000H, while moving into OP #4, at AT910496, a Marine from Company G detonated a booby trapped M-26 grenade with trip wire. Results: 1 USMC WIA Evac.

At 180200H, a squad ambush from Company G found 1 SKS near their ambush site at AT891515. Results: One (1) SKS captured.

The records are silent for Golf Company from the 19th to 27th, with the exception of the G-3 patrols along Hwy. 1. We were still in the bush and on September 22nd I wrote:

Dear Mom,

Well, I got your letter today, and believe you me, it was like a gift from heaven. Both yours and Dad's [letters] got here, so I guess I'll write you both.

First of all, about my personality piece. Believe it or not, some of the fellas in my team have been kidding me about my mustache, saying I look like [Groucho] Marx. Tom Thomas, who is my gunner, and who has been with me ever since Staging [Staging Battalion in early February] keeps saying, "Just tell 'em Groucho sent you." Wow, what a blow. Oh well, I'll keep it any way, just so you all can have the pleasure of watching me shave it off. But, believe it or not, it kind of fits my frame of mind right now. Namely all fuzzed up. It still hasn't grown out like I want it yet, but by the time I get home it should be looking pretty good. But enough on that.

As you already know, I'm in the field again. I've been out here about a mile or so east of An Hoa for about 2 weeks now and there is no telling how much longer I'll be out here. But it doesn't really make that much difference, because like we say over here, no matter what happens, the clock won't stop running. Pretty soon I'll be home and this will all be over for me. The Lord willing. So far I have been an off and on Squad Leader and Team Leader. But now I am the first Team Leader for good until the squad leader, who just came back from R & R, goes home or gets hurt. I've got 4 men under me, which is more men than I had in my squad when I left the 27th. There are 2 teams to a Gun Squad, and this squad has 10 men plus a squad leader. I only had 3 men left plus myself when I left the 27th. So actually I'm better off, but it sure would be nice to be with the 27th. This unit is practically all boot, even the Plt. Com-

mander and Plt. Sgt. It sure is hard to take [orders] from men who don't know what they are doing, but what can you do in the service.

Oh well, things could be worse. I'm glad that you all are starting to get something done with the V.A. I sure hope everything goes for the best. …

With all my love, Your Son, Groucho?

P. S. Just tell 'em Chuck sent you!

I remember one encounter clearly during this time. We were running patrols in the Arizona and I had, once again, the dubious honor of leading a daytime patrol. As we were moving across the rice paddies, approaching a tree line, ahead and to our left front, sniper fire range out. Everyone hit the deck and ate some dirt along a convenient dike. Everyone but me, that is. With a boot patrol on my hands, I had to make sure they stayed safe. I remember the Marines closest to me telling me to get down, as I was standing over them watching the area that I believed the rifle fire had come from. Not very bright on my part, but by this time I had truly lost all concern for my own life, with even a touch of death wish thrown in. I was so haunted by the deaths of Decker and Richee.

My reason for standing was to determine where the sniper was. I knew that we would just be sitting ducks if we got up to continue the patrol without first taking out that sniper. In my mind, this was a typical encounter. Alone, scared, and not able to hit the broad side of a barn, I could just see in my mind, a lone VC facing a patrol of Marines coming his way. It appeared that this VC was alone. So far, there had only been one shot fired. While everyone else continued to hug the dirt, I waited and sure enough, another shot rang out. I could not detect any hits near where we were, but I did get a range and azimuth for the enemy location. It was only then that I knelt down by the radioman and reported having received incoming small arms fire. I asked for fire support and was told that an 81mm mortar was available for a F/M (fire mission). I gave the coordinates for my position, followed by a range and relative bearing to the target. Soon a WP (white phosphorous) round came in, exploding in a puff of white smoke. I adjusted the fire from the point of first impact and once I had the rounds on target, I called in for a set of six rounds of HE (high explosive). Once the smoke cleared, I waited a while to see if there would be any more enemy fire. Before long, I got everyone up and we went to the area of the sniper attack. We could see the damage caused by the mortars, but no evidence of VC were discovered. A normal patrol. We continued on our way.

I must have seemed crazy or fearless to my men through all this, probably the former, but the facts were that I always tried to face the enemy whenever possible. Turning your back on an assailant would only get you killed. Couple that with my understanding of the enemy by this time, I felt confident that the best way to survive this war was to take the fight to the enemy. It also helped to bolster the confidence of the men in their patrol leader, which is paramount in this business. Of course, that was not why I acted as I did, it was just a positive side effect.

Again, on the 22nd, I wrote:

Dear Dad,

Well, well, well, so you think I look like old Fidel Castro, egh. Well don't forget that I'm more or less in his field of work, and so I might as well present the proper image, right? But believe me, that isn't near as bad [as] Groucho Marx! I know, why don't you all call me [Genghis] Kahn. That is much more flattering. Besides, the mustache helps present the image of the big, green, mean, Marine. Of course I don't need a mustache for that anymore, but you would be [surprised] how it helps with the new men.

Seriously! In Viet Nam the mustache is a symbol of combat experience and a certain coolness in action. The new men know that you have been in Nam a while and are more willing to listen and take orders. It is a small thing, but it helps. Well, so much for that.

I've already explained in Mom's letter what my job is, so I'd like to tell you a little, just a little of how I feel. It would be impossible to put all my feelings down, so I'll just say this. I am so tired of fighting and killing and of war in general, that at times I almost get sick to my stomach just thinking about it. And do you know what the one thing that I can picture in my mind which calms me and gives me a great incentive to get home? Well, I'll tell you. It's that ugly puss of yours. Yep, Dad, I look forward more and more each day to seeing you again. Of course I want to see the rest of the family too. But to sit with you and talk over a good cup of coffee will be all the home coming I will ever need. I provide that kind of strength to my men as much as possible. But I'm not perfect. My strength comes from the Lord I know. But at times I sure look forward to being with you and the strength you [emanate]. I just hope I can provide my sons with the same strength and courage with which you inspire me. Maybe the reason I am saying this now is because I am so tired mentally and physically …

Well, you take care, write soon, and keep up your good work. Oh, and good luck with the V.A., give 'em hell.

With all my love, Your Chuckie Boy

P.S. There's nothing like having a killer for a son is there. Believe it or not Dad I'm sick of myself for the things I've done and pray constantly that the Lord will forgive me. I can't tell you about these things yet, but I hope you understand. Pray for me Dad, I need it! I just thought about it, and I guess I'm just feeling sorry for myself.

Our job in the Arizona with 2/5 was similar to what I did in Duc Ky with 2/27. I'm sure that the memory of incidences in Duc Ky and in the Arizona prompted me to open up a bit to my Dad. That letter was very telling, with some of my anguish coming to the surface.

Just so the reader can understand my relationship with my Dad, I'll try to relate in a short form who and what he was. Richard J. Van Bibber, that was his name. His friends called him Dick. He was a rancher's son from Colorado. The Van Bibbers had homesteaded a ranch in the Gunnison country of Colorado that eventually would be home for 3 generations of Van Bibber's; Henry, who homesteaded the place in the 1880's; Jess, born in 1890, who ran the ranch till the depression hit, and my dad who was born there. Dad was a WWII veteran. He was a bulldozer operator for the Army Engineers in the Philippines. He was in combat for about a year and a half. Eventually he would be sent home in 1945, shot in the knee. He had displayed extraordinary courage when he volunteered to take a bulldozer and cut a road through the jungle so that tanks could knock out enemy artillery that was housed deep in caves along a ridge in Northern Luzon, Philippines. The gun emplacements were too far for our guns to reach them and too deep in the ridge for air power to knock them out. For this action, he received the Silver Star:

15 November 1945

Dear Mr. Van Bibber:

It is an honor to inform you that, by direction of the President, the Silver Star Medal has been awarded you by the Commanding General, Twenty-fifth Infantry Division. The citation relating to this award is as follows:

For gallantry in action against the Japanese forces at Kapintalan, Luzon, Philippine Islands, on 8 May 1945. Private First Class VAN BIBBER, a bulldozer operator, constructed a road 150 yards to the top of a knoll in order that tanks could give close-in support to the

> infantry. Upon reaching the crest of the knoll, the bulldozer operated by him was bracketed by 10 rounds of direct fire from an enemy 47mm gun on an adjacent ridge. Fully realizing the danger of operating the bulldozer, with complete disregard of his own personal safety in full view of the enemy who were firing at him, he completed the road. Private First Class VAN BIBBER's gallant actions and devotion to duty were an inspiration to all who witnessed and were in keeping with the highest traditions of the military service.

The first dozer he had was a fully armored one, but that soon got blown up by incoming artillery rounds. The Japs had seen what he was up to and they were having none of it. Not injured by the blast, Dad went back and got another dozer, this one not armored. Soon it would be blown up too. As he progressed in making the road, he would have to hold up the blade of his open-faced dozer to deflect the machine gun fire that started to come at him. He would do this two or three more times, before an artillery round came in and hit a mahogany tree which crashed onto his open faced bulldozer, striking him in the head and giving him a concussion. The road had been completed far enough that the tanks did come up and fire directly into the caves, knocking out the guns there.

About three years after the war was over, Dad started having severe headaches and soon went into a coma. I was about three years old at the time. Hospitalized in the V.A. Hospital, it was determined that he had a blood clot on the brain from the concussion he had received in the Philippines. He had two brain operations, where the clot was removed and a metal plate installed. There was only one complication. He was left blind and an epileptic. After regaining his strength, Dad went to the Heinz rehabilitation facility for blinded solders in Pennsylvania. He was classified as a 100% disabled veteran.

Dad never gave in to his blindness. He had to take medications for his epilepsy, and often went days suffering with grand mal seizures, but he would recover and go on about his life. From my earliest memories of him, I could see the strength of will that kept him going, along with the love for his family. Dad went on to have five children and supported us as best he could on his pension. As soon as he could, he moved us to a small ranch in Texas where we lived off the land and loved it. We all thrived from his love and strength and the care given by my saintly mother Becky. We had a great life growing up in the Texas Hill Country outside of Fredericksburg, Texas, the home of Admiral Nimitz.

So there it is, part of the strength I needed to fight in Vietnam came from him. He like to died when I enlisted in the Marine Corps, knowing that I would probably go to combat in Vietnam. He knew what jungle fighting was all about. Even though he was displeased with me for doing that, he supported me completely, as did all of my family, and it was only to him that I could open up as I did in that letter.

Yes, I was at the point of no return. Self-loathing would get me nowhere, so I just stuffed it down and went on with my job. The records continue with the actions we were in:

271725H CO G 2/5 PLT S&C LOC AT898487. LVT MOVING THROUGH HEAVY BRUSH HIT TREE: TREE FELL INJURING ONE USMC. MED-EVAC CALLED. RES: 1 USMC NBC EVAC.

272000H CO G 2/5 PLT DEF POS LOC AT899495. UNIT REC'D S/A FIRE FM ENEMY LOC AT895500. UNIT RET'D S/A FIRE AND CALLED MARINE 81MM MSN OF 10 RDS HE. WILL SEARCH AREA AT FIRST LIGHT.

281530H CO G 2/5 CO S&C LOC AT 905487. UNIT FD 600 LBS OF RICE. FORWARDED TO REGT CP.

290800H CO G 2/5 CO S&C LOC AT 898494. UNIT FOUND 18 BUNKERS AND 2 TONS OF RICE. BUNKERS TO BE DESTROYED AND RICE WILL BE FORWARDED TO REGT CP.

291300H CO G 2/5 CO S&C LOC AT 887509. UNIT OBS 15 ENEMY MOVING SOUTH LOC AT880509. ENEMY CARRIED RIFLES. INITIATED CONTACT WITH S/A FIRE. RES: 2 VC KIA. REMAINDER OF ENEMY OF ENEMY UNIT BROKE AND FLED SOUTH.

At 291300H, Company G on a Search and Clear mission at AT875509, observed 15 enemy at AT874505. The Company fired 150 automatic weapons and called a 30 round HE 4.2 mortar mission. Results: Two VC KIA.

301350H CO G 2/5 PLT S&C LOC AT882501. USMC DET M-26 GRENADE RIGGES [*sic*] AS SUR EXPL DEVICE. RES: 3 USMC WIA EVAC.

> At 010900H October 1968 2nd Battalion, 5th Marines came under the operational control of the 7th Marines and terminated participation in Operation MAMELUKE THRUST II.
> 302400H SEPTEMBER 1968 OPERATION MAMELUKE THRUST
>
> 2/5 (-) AT FIRST LIGHT CO E, CO G AND THE BN CMD GRP MOVES BY FOOT TO LZ ALAMO (AT90705) TO BE HELILIFTED TO HILL 65 (AT878577).
>
> 2/5 (-) ON ARRIVAL OF BN CMD GRP AT HILL 65 CHOPS TO SEVENTH MARINES.

And so the month ended and the stage was set once again for another major action. Of course, none of us in the squads had any idea of what was to come. I guess it's better that way. If we knew what was coming, who would be wounded and who would be killed, we may have some trepidation about going into battle. Thankfully, no one can see the future, so we just "charged" ahead and did our best to defeat the enemy and survive at the same time. Some wouldn't make it. I was now a "Real Combat Marine." Gone was my anger toward the Corps. I did have problems with my Platoon Commander and some of the others in the platoon. But I had learned to embrace the Corps and the efforts to support me in my mission.

Lastly from the records for 2/5 in September:

> The Battalion joined 5 officers and 145 enlisted men during September. The Battalion transferred 8 officers and 108 enlisted during the same period. Casualties during this period were:

BATTLE				NON-BATTLE		TOTAL
KIA	WIA	DOW	WIANE	NBD	NBC	
18	77	3	33	1	8	140

DOW stands for Died Of Wounds
WIANE stands for Wounded In Action – Not Evacuated
NBD stands for Non-battle Death
NBC stands for Non-battle Casualty

The numbers of Battalion personnel were advancing to the rear in true Marine Corps fashion. Having transferred 116 officers and enlisted, joined 150 officers and men and lost 140 casualties, the numbers show that 2/5 was in the hole by 106 men for September.

Chapter 12

October 1st had arrived and I now found myself with Golf Co. as well as Echo Co., attached to the 7th Marines, part of a move to assist a Special Forces Camp in Thuong Duc which ran along the Song Vu Gia river. They were receiving heavy fire and were in danger of being overrun. From the 1st to the 5th we would be involved in moving to Hill 52, which was our staging area. Fox Company and Hotel Company had already been put under the control of 1st Battalion, 5th Marines between September 23 and 25 to continue participation in Operation Mameluke Thrust II.

Again, the *U. S. Marines in Vietnam: The Defining Year 1968*, by Gary Jarvis PhD, Chapter 21, gives the overall view:

> The Special Forces camp at Thuong Duc was nestled in a valley at the confluence of the Song Vu Gia and the Song Con, [Song in Vietnamese means river] where "Green Berets" trained and advised CIDG [Civilian Irregular Defense Group] troops recruited from the local villages. By controlling these two river valleys, the Special Forces soldiers and their CIDG counterparts forced the enemy to move troops and supplies bound for the Da Nang area along far more difficult routes through the mountainous jungle. Additionally, they denied the enemy access to the source of food and recruits located in the populated area along the rivers.
>
> Near the end of September, the Communists were ready to strike. III MAF [Third Marine Amphibious Force] intelligence officers identified elements of two NVA infantry regiments surrounding the camp: the 21st from the 2nd NVA Division and a new 141st Regiment. The 368B Rocket Regiment was in support. In a predawn attack on 28 September, the enemy overran and occupied two of the camp's outposts, seriously threatening the main compound. With bad weather hampering normal close air support operations, a Marine Tactical Air Control Party flew into Thuong Duc in the

late afternoon. Using a radar beacon, the forward air controller directed 18 sorties of Grumman A-6A Intruder all-weather attack aircraft against the enemy force. By the afternoon of the 29th, the enemy troops occupying the two outposts withdrew, their position rendered untenable by the A-6A Intruders of the 1st Marine Aircraft Wing.

With Thuong Duc temporarily safe, but still surrounded, General Youngdale Commanding General (CG) 1st Marine Division moved to lift the siege, assigning Colonel Beckington's 7th Marines the task. For Operation Maui Peak, Youngdale gave Beckington control of the 7th Marines' own 3rd Battalion and BLT Battalion Landing Team 2/7 (still the SLF Special Landing Force battalion, but temporarily under the operational control of the 7th Marines), and the 2nd and 3rd Battalions, 5th Marines. General Cushman CG III MAF placed one brigade of the 1st Air Cavalry Division on six-hour standby to reinforce, and General Lam Vietnamese I Corps Commander assigned four ARVN battalions to operate in coordination with the Marines.

On 1 October, the 2nd Battalion, 5th Marines was conducting operations along the southern bank of the Thu Bon River in the An Hoa sector and Company G had engaged a small enemy force near the river edge. Lieutenant Colonel James W. Stemple Battalion CO, 2/5 later related that in the middle of this firefight he received orders from the 5th Marines that he was being attached to the 7th Marines for a new operation and that he should prepare his battalion for immediate helicopter movement to Hill 65, about 15 kilometers east of Thuong Duc. Immediately detaching from the engagement, the battalion consisting of Companies E and G, and Company A from the 1st Battalion, 5th Marines, arrived at Hill 65 about 1300 hrs. At that point, Stemple remembered he was told to report to Colonel Beckington at the 7th Marines command post on Hill 55. After some delay to obtain a jeep, he arrived in time to attend the 7th Marines briefing for the operation. Stemple later observed that he was not too inspired when one of the briefing officers remarked, "I don't know how we are going to support this operation; I guess we'll play it by ear."

According to Stemple, the concept of operations called for his battalion to secure not only Hill 65, but also Hill 52, only six kilometers from Thuong Duc, before nightfall. Upon his return to Hill 65 and maintaining an outpost there, the battalion moved out in a

> column of companies following Route 4. With an attached engineer platoon from the 1st Engineer Battalion assisting in the detecting and clearing of antipersonnel, antivehicle, and antitank mines, the battalion arrived at Hill 52 about 1630. In taking the hill, the Marines captured one prisoner from the 141st NVA Regiment.
>
> While the battalion gained a measure of control over Route 4, which was the only road available for ground resupply, Lieutenant Colonel Stemple vaguely recalled that an enemy road mine accounted for at least one Marine vehicle. During the next four days, artillery units of the 3rd Battalion, 11 Marines and Army 175mm guns of the 4th Battalion, 8th Field Artillery took up firing positions at Hills 65 and 52. The 3rd Battalion, 7th Marines moved into the area between the two hills, guarding the road and freeing the 2nd Battalion, 5th Marines to direct its efforts westward, toward the enemy.

On October 3rd, I wrote home in one of the few letters from that month:

Dear Folks,

Well, here I am and there you are. I'm now on hill #52 not more than 10 miles from the [Laotian] Border, in the mountains west-north-west of An Hoa. I don't know how long I'll be here, or even what I'll be doing. With all the V. C. in the area, we might just be getting ready for another operation. I mailed my check yesterday, let me know when you get it. …

There isn't a whole lot to say about the "Nam", I'm fine and the clock is still running, and I guess that that is about all that can be expected. I'm enclosing a copy of the Sea Tiger with some news of the 27th. Enjoy it in good health. …

I'm constantly on the go now in the 5th Marines. I've never seen such a pushy outfit. I'm really tired of it, and might ask for a transfer if things get worse. But enough about that.

All my love, Chuck

I was still brooding over my transfer from the 27th Marines and taking it out on the 5th. By now, I was leaving out any battle descriptions from my letters, and of course, I didn't have much time to write anyway. It would be over two weeks before I would write again. Looking back, a number of things stood out about the 5th Marines. First, I must admit that I judged them incorrectly. It wasn't that they were "gung ho" so much as it was orders, and someone loved to put the 5th Marines in harm's way. Understandable now, given the outstanding job they did up at Hue during the Tet

Offensive of 1968, and given the fact that 2/5 (-) was given the orders to pull out of contact with the enemy and go to Hill 65 for the start of Operation Maui Peak. Rather, my feelings were based more on the condition of 2nd Platoon. As I have said, it was a "boot camp" platoon, with even the platoon commander and platoon sergeant new in country. In September, even before the Lt. and SSgt. came in, the other men in the platoon had started to look to me for direction, especially when my machine gun squad leader was gone. So after the Lt. and the SSgt. arrived, the men still looked to me for information in setting up a perimeter, designating fields of fire and other things, where only experience would do. The Lt. took offense at this and tried to counter my every move. I tried to get the Lt. to move at night after setting in at dusk, as Lt. Jones had done in the 27th, that little trick which had worked so well to keep us protected. He was having none of it, and in fact he started to assign me to many night ambushes, more than was justified, which in my mind was his way of getting rid of me. As a result, the Platoon CP was hit by mortars and small arms almost every night while we were in the field. He pushed and pushed and had no idea what he was doing. He was a short, loud, red-headed "90 day wonder" straight from OCS (Officer Candidate School - which usually lasted three months as opposed to academy grads who took four years to become an officer). This harassment by my Platoon Commander would continue until he left the Platoon.

Another thing about the 5th Marines and my Platoon in particular, was that, being "boot camp", no one knew how to spot booby traps. I tried to teach the men, but with the Lt. countering my every move, I just couldn't get the information out in time. As stated before, in a Marine manual on booby traps:

"Experience has shown that an alert Marine, aware of what to look for and where to look, is the most effective detection device."

Records for Golf Co. in September show a total of 1 Marine KIA and 15 WIA's due to booby traps, and all but one of these killed or wounded were from the 1st and 2nd Platoon. 3rd Platoon on road sweeps only had one KIA - far too many for the Company in my book. When I was with the 27th we learned to detect and either dismantle or blow up booby traps, and what few casualties we had from those explosives were usually by new guys. Therefore, I constantly got in hot water with my Platoon Commander over my efforts to teach what I knew. He even went so far as to scream loudly in my face as I stood at attention, right there in front of the men. Some of the other NCO's also took exception with my efforts and in fact, once my squad leader returned from R & R, he would move me from one job in the squad to another rather than leave me as the number one team leader. Part of that may have been because the Lt. seemed to have it in for me and was using me to run one night ambush or patrol after another. Maybe my squad leader wanted a man that wouldn't get moved so often to be his number one team leader, I don't know. As a result, by the time we started Operation Maui Peak, I was more of a floater, carrying the gun sometimes and the M-16 at other times, as the situation arose.

At the start of Maui Peak, which was a break-off operation from Mameluke Thrust II, the recorded estimate of enemy forces we were up against were:

> General Situation.
>
> Maui Peak.
>
> Elemennts of the 21st Regiment, Battalions of the 141st Regiment, one Battalion of the 368B Regiment (NVA Artillery) one Battalion 68B Regiment and 31st Regiment QuanDa were reported in position to interdict Route #4 (Dien Ban to Thuong Duc) and harass friendly units in the area. POW's and documents taken after ground contact indicated that the 1st Battalion 141st Regiment (Artillery) was reported to have 140mm rocket capability. This unit is believed to have fired two of the 140mm rockets on the 2nd Battalion, 5th Marines Command Post on 6 October 1968.

Again, the actions of the various units involved are described from *The Defining Year, 1968*:

> On the morning of 6 October, attack aircraft and B-52s began bombarding landing zones in the hills surrounding Thuong Duc. Colonel Stemple remembered that several bombs from one of the B-52s, "fell short of their objective with two bombs landing in the E/2/5 area to the rear of Hill 52." Fortunately, there were no Marine casualties and the rest of the errant bombs fell harmlessly into the river. At the same time, the 2nd Battalion, 5th Marines stepped off in the attack westward along Route 4 toward the Special Forces camp. This was to be a feint to distract the enemy from the landing of the helicopter-borne elements. Soon after crossing the line of departure, however, the Marines became decisively engaged with the NVA 1st Battalion, 141st Regiment, and Colonel Beckington canceled

> the plan for a feint and ordered the 2nd Battalion to clear the enemy from the battlefield.
>
> While the 2nd Battalion, 5th Marines mounted the hills overlooking Route 4 and came to grips with the enemy, other units joined the operation. At that time, there were only 2 rifle companies from 2/5 involved in those hills, Echo and Golf. At 1030, 1st Marine Aircraft Wing helicopters, carrying the 3rd Battalion, 5th Marines, swooped down into LZ Sparrow, four kilometers south of Thuong Duc. The preparation fires had ended at 0730, after severely pounding the LZ and surrounding area. If the fires had hurt the North Vietnamese units in the vicinity, the enemy commander apparently made good use of the three-hour break between the end of the preparation and the landing of the helicopters. As the first wave of aircraft touched down in the landing zone, a hail of heavy machine gun fire filled the air. Unable to complete the mission against such stiff resistance, the helicopters turned away, carrying the 3rd Battalion back to An Hoa.
>
> At 1100, BLT 2/7 and two ARVN battalions landed unopposed in LZ Vulture and LZ Hawk, seven kilometers north west of Thuong Duc. While the rest of the battalion remained at the LZ with Battery W, 3rd Battalion, 11th Marines, Companies E and G, 7th Marines struck out for the high ground overlooking Thuong Duc from the north. The terrain was extremely challenging. At times, the Marines needed lifelines to negotiate steep hills covered by a thick jungle canopy and dense undergrowth.
>
> Back on Route 4, the 2nd Battalion, 5th Marines was still involved in a heated battle against North Vietnamese units in the hills overlooking the road. At one point, where the road passed along a very narrow gap between the river and a large, steep hill, the enemy put up a spirited defense, beating back the Marines' first two assaults. After a third pounding by supporting arms, the battalion attacked and captured the hill, gaining control of the vital pass.

It is interesting how they take the human element out of the picture. This isn't a criticism of the *Defining Year* mind you, it's just an observation of how the Marines grunts are reduced to ants in the big picture. Normal I suppose. When they talk about the "Battalion," they are actually talking about two rifle companies, and when they say the "... battalion attacked and captured the hill ..." the truth is that it was only Echo Company that attacked that hill, 2nd Platoon, Golf Company had already taken the hill on the other side of that pass. The temporary Battalion HQ (head-quarters) was stationed on Hill 65.

A brief account of the Operation is given in the records:

> The first contact was at 060930 October 1968 in the saddle in the vicinity of ZC197561. This contact was light and involved about a platoon which held the high ground west of the saddle. The platoon was in shallow fighting holes and was overrun. The second contact was at 071600H in the vicinity of ZC190561 and was heavy. The contact was with a company size unit and was carried into the next day. The enemy company was well dug into the base of the hill at ZC190561. The elements at the base defied air preparation and turned back the first attempt to take the hill. The next day more direct fire was aimed at the base of the hill as well as the peak, and the remaining elements of the NVA company were overrun. The enemy company received some supporting mortar fire as the Marines moved up the hill, but it was light and ineffective. Marines remained on the high ground for the rest of the operation. The Marine units took light harassing fire from mortars and light line probes with only one counterattack which was stopped. The NVA units did maintain anti-aircraft positions in the area and used it on supply aircraft and close air support in the area. As the weather changed, the enemy avoided any other significant contact in this area of the operation in the latter days of the operation.

The unit fighting in the saddle at ZC197561 was Golf Company, 2/5, with 2nd Platoon in the lead. The second contact with the enemy at ZC190561, who were dug in at the base of that hill, was Echo Company, 2/5.

It was October 6th, and we were ordered off of Hill 52 and moved across the Vu Gia River onto Hwy. 4. As we started our march, we met up with a tank and some self-propelled artillery pieces, 105mm guns. By noon or so, we began to receive enemy fire from above us in the hills that rose just above the road. We then were told to assault those hills and take out the enemy that was up there. We were also told that the enemy was in fact "Mr. Charles," the term used for NVA soldiers. I was back to being number one team leader at that time, and my buddy Tom Thomas was put in as number 2 team leader, with David Lopez and Lockett as his gun team plus another two ammo humpers. We attacked as a company, with second platoon in the lead. It was a dreadful hill we climbed, very steep and overgrown with jungle. A first aid station was set up at the base of the hill close to the road and it already had plenty of customers. Our sister company, Echo Company, continued down the road, bypassing us as we took the hill.

As I was climbing up the hill, I slipped and hit my right knee on a rock and when I tried to walk, I felt severe pain. My squad leader told me to go down to the first aid station. I couldn't walk, so I slid down a trail that was made to carry out the wounded. Once I got to the station, the Doc massaged my knee and told me to rest a bit and see how it was. I knew what the problem was, but I never told anyone for fear of being kicked out of the Marine Corps. Complain as I did, I loved the Corps. The problem was a growth that had formed under one of the ligaments in my right knee. It happened just a month before I joined the Corps when I was involved in a car crash. In that crash, I cracked my pelvis and injured my right knee. The month before I went to boot camp, I was laid up in bed at home letting my knee and back heal. I had already enlisted before the accident and couldn't miss my bus from San Antonio, Texas to MCRD (Marine Corps Recruit Depot) in San Diego, California if I wanted to be a Marine. It hurt some in boot camp, but I managed and it hadn't given me any real problems until now. (I finally had it removed in 2002 when it again got lodged and would not move back in place.)

As I lay there, I grew more and more anxious about my men and the assault up that hill. As soon I could I stood up, tried my knee, and found that it was working okay. The massage had pushed the growth back to the spot where it lived in my knee, and I was back to normal. Filled with adrenaline, I grabbed my M-16, climbed back up that hill and continued the assault with the rest of the company. My squad, being in the advance, was way ahead of me and near the top but I was able to catch up with them. Soon, I would be just behind Thomas close to the head of the assault. There were NVA everywhere, in foxholes and lying dead along a path up to the top of the hill. I received rifle fire from time to time and returned fire whenever it was prudent to do so. I had to watch out that I didn't accidently shoot our own men. Occasionally grenades came tumbling down the hill, smoking like a chimney (the Communist 'Chicom' grenades were like that), and would explode or just fizzle out. The men at the top were pinned down by heavy enemy fire and as they dropped to return fire, the rest of us caught up with them, so it became a ticklish situation, with everyone bunched up.

Tom Thomas was one of the first men to hit the top. There were only about four men with him and they took several grenades before clearing the hill. Tom remembers an officer hollering loudly at him to take the hill. I believe that that officer was our "90 Day Wonder" and that he eventually was overcome by the heat and was evacuated, leaving only Captain Poole to run 2nd Platoon and the hilltop position. I arrived soon after that and was up there with Tom as we started to clear the dead NVA off the top of the hill. Some men continued the assault partway down a small ridge that led to the small stream running east to west at the base of our hill. Another hill just north-north-west of us would be the target for Echo Company. The rest of us, especially the machine guns and mortar teams, continued to clear the hill and set up our own defensive positions while the riflemen swept the area around the hill.

There were NVA bodies all over the place and Thomas and I started to remove them from the hilltop. We picked them up by the hands and feet and swinging the body between us, releasing it in time to send it down the hill. Good job you might say, but there was a real problem. Except for a cleared area on top of the hill, the slopes were filled with jungle brush. The bodies would hit the area where the heavy jungle started and just stay there, maybe 50 feet or less from the top. Soon the hill was ringed with the dead and it began to stink like crazy, flies everywhere and maggots galore. I remember one such body in particular that Tom pointed out to me. Besides a few hits to the body, the head took most of the damage. The face was completely blown out, and as it lay on its back on the ground, all you could see was the back of the skull riddled with bullet holes. We laughed and remarked that it looked like a human sieve. I remember someone taking a picture too. Oh no, we weren't too jaded, were we! Tom remembers that we might have had members of the press with us and perhaps one of them took the picture.

Taking that hill resulted in many casualties and changes in our machine gun squad. Thomas as team leader and carrying the M-16 and having a lighter load, managed to reach the top faster than the rest of us with myself not far behind. Lopez, being smaller struggled with the climb, but eventually made it to the top. It wasn't so important in an assault like that to get the machine gun up, as it was to make the mad dash and take the hill, which was pretty hard to do when you are carrying your pack, canteens of water, ammo and a 23 pound machine gun as well as sundry gear like the .45 and it's ammo. I believe that LCpl. Lockett was carrying the gun for 2nd team and he arrived some time later. He had been with Golf since May or June and was there on August 18 when the 3rd Platoon platoon sergeant, SSgt. Williams was killed. Being lead by the Company Commander, Captain Poole, rather than any platoon leader, we were dispersed around the hilltop. Since it was mainly 2nd Platoon on the hill, with a mortar team and enough other platoon members to fill in the perimeter, the Captain placed the machine guns, one on each end of the hilltop. My end with LCpl. Weber and Pfc. Scroggins was were the ridge dropped down to the river facing the hill on the other side of the pass. Thomas, Lopez and Lockett were on the end facing the saddle we had just traversed to reach this hill which was the third in the line of hills and the highest in the chain. The Captain then placed one of the other platoons on the middle hill, which was connected to our hill by the saddle and split the other platoon between the two hills. It was important to keep the high ground if we were going to have any chance at all up there.

Captain Poole set up his command post in the middle of the hilltop, placing the mortar team close by and the rest of us on the perimeter. The "vital pass" that is talked about in the *Defining Year*, was actually a small stream bed that led to the Vu Gia River. The ridges leading up to their respective hills were very steep and effectively blocked anyone's view from the road to the hills beyond. Once we were set in, we started to dig our fighting holes which became almost impossible because of the hard-packed hilltop, but we did our best. I managed to dig a shallow "mortar hole" about five inches deep that I could lie in, which would protect me from a mortar round unless I took a direct hit. I also started on a deeper hole on the very edge of the hilltop where the earth seemed a bit softer, but for tonight this would be enough. My squad leader, Mike Copeland, had removed me as Team Leader, not understanding the problems I had with my knee, and positioned the gun team at the access route from the ridge with myself set in just to the right of the gun position. From my hole, I could clearly see the hill to the north that Echo Co. would attack in the following days and a clear line of sight to the stream below.

The Captain called in for resupplies, c-rations, ammo and water, while the rest of us dug. Soon a yellow smoke grenade was lit in the middle of the area that was determined as a landing zone, and Ch-46 (Sea Knight) helicopters dropped nets full of stuff we needed to survive. The Sea Knights were much like the Ch-47 Chinooks; both were the banana shaped helicopters. That resupply was all we would have for several days. Later, when the resupply resumed, a chopper carrying a net of water cans dropped their load early and when it landed, the water cans broke apart and left a mess with water everywhere. Due to the weather and enemy anti-aircraft guns set up in the mountains on the other side of the valley, resupply seemed hopeless.

Arc Light runs (Arc Light was the name given to B-52's dropping 2,000 lb. bombs) would help some, but they were few and far between. Still, when they hit everyone knew it, because the whole hill would shake from the air strikes many clicks away. Meanwhile, those who ate most of their food that first day suffered later when there was none left. A trash pit was started where Marines tossed unwanted things like packets of coffee, cream and sugar, since most Marines didn't take the time or have the taste for c-ration coffee. Over the next several days, those same Marines would scrounge the trash pit for those packets. Pouring the contents into a canteen cup with a touch of water forming a paste, which is the best chow ever when that is all you have. Luckily, it rained every day and we collected water in our ponchos that were spread across our foxholes.

After the first day on top of that hill, things got progressively worse. We got mortared three or four times day and night, along with squads of NVA overrunning our positions like crazy men, throwing grenades and firing AK's. One or two might have made it all the way to the other side of the hill, but that was all. The rest would lay dead on top. Most of these overruns occurred late at night, so each morning we would have to, once again, toss the dead off the top of the hill, which meant more bodies stacked up around the perimeter and more flies and even more maggots. I started to call the place "maggot hill" because of all the maggots wiggling around on top of the hill. You couldn't lie down, sit down, or stand still without maggots crawling all over you. Soon it became a lost cause and we ate what we had along with the maggots. It was either gag on a few maggots or starve. The rain came in about 1500 hours, we collected our water, and it helped some to wash the maggots away. One thing I learned on top of that godforsaken hill was that there is no end to maggots: stomp on them, bury them, wash them away, they were always with us. Finally, we took to standing up to eat and then changed to walking around while we ate. In the end, nothing worked and we just had to endure. Nighttime was particularly nasty because on top of the incoming mortars and overruns by the NVA, you would inevitably awake with a start when the maggots crawled into your ears, nose, and mouth as you slept. Any wonder why I called it "maggot hill?"

The Marine Corps records for 2/5 on 6 October record the following:

Mission. Initially occupy Fire Support Base at Hill 52 and be prepared to attack on order to relieve friendly elements at Thuong Duc Special Forces Cam.

Concept of Operations. Second Battalion (-) Rein attack to the Northwest along Route #4 to seize the high ground vicinity Hill 100. Establish blocking positions along high ground from ZC194561 along line to ZC203564.

0907H	Co A 1/5 Position at River
1045H	Co G departing hill 52
1100H	Co G is in contact, receiving S/A from ZC200550
1215H	Co G 3 WIA, Med-Evac chopper receiving fire
1230H	Co G While attacking hill, received A/W fire and B-40 rockets from ZC195561.
1315H	Co G ¼ Fixed wing on station to support Golf
1400H	Co G 5 WIA's Med Evac complete
1520H	S-3 ¼ Med-Evaced 6 WIA's and 2 KIA's
1600H	Co G Has 3 Emerg Evac heat casualties
1630H	Co A 1/5 Discovered 1 Viet body in grave at ZC197558
1705H	Co G Evaced 30 USMC's
1800H	S-3 Units secured day act and commenced night defensive positions and acts
1930H	Co A 1/5 Night positions set in

In addition, the after action reports state:

At 060930H, the point man of a Company E patrol detonated a "tomato can" type explosive device rigged with trip wire at AT890491. Results: 2 USMC Evac.

At 061315H, while assaulting a hill at ZC198559, Company G received automatic weapons and B-40 rocket fire from an estimated platoon of NVA. Air strikes and 60mm HE were called in. Utilizing its units for a base of fire, Company G successfully took its objective on the third assault. Results: Two USMC KIA, 16 USMC WIA-Evac and 12 NBC Evac, nine NVA KIA and capture of two AK-47 rifles, one B-40 rocket launcher, ten ChiCom grenades and assorted military gear.

Helicopter Support Teams attached to each company and the Battalion CommandGroup coordinated all resupply for Operation

> MAUI PEAK. Resupply was made by helicopter and motor vehicle from the LSU at Hill 55.

As I have mentioned, the 6th was the last resupply for Golf Co. until several days later. We took a licken' taking that hill, with 2 KIA, 35 WIA and 12 NBC on that day. Forty-nine men out of action meant that we had lost over one third of the men in Golf Co. – the equivalent of one whole platoon - in taking that hill. That was why Captain Poole had to split our forces the way he did. Still, later, many men would question the wisdom of the layout of the positions on our hill, especially the machine gun positions. Be that as it may, it was what it was. The casualties in Echo Company in their efforts to take the hill just north of us a few days later would be equally heavy, if not worse.

The story of Echo Company, 2/5 on operation Maui Peak is one of blood and more blood. I remember watching their progress with others from my company as they attacked their hill. It was about a click (1,000 meters) away, probably more. We could see the E Co. Marines move up the hill through thick brush under a devastating hail of lead. Tom Thomas remembers the Captain telling him to take the machine gun and provide covering fire for Echo Co. He pointed out to the Captain that the range was too far for any accurate shooting, and that if he did open fire, he stood as much of a chance of hitting our own Marines as he did the enemy. So all we could really do was watch. Still, we did as ordered and Tom and I aimed our machine guns at such an angle as to pepper the top of that hill with lead.

The VC would wave at us, show their asses and taunt us, one hill to another. The hill was all bare dirt, much bigger than the one we were on, with bunkers dug in deep. We could see the VC come out of their bunkers, fire down on our Marines and then retreat back into their bunkers. It was awful to witness, helpless as we were to help. It wouldn't be long though before the AO (Aerial Observer) on our hill got set up and started calling in air support for Echo Company. They bombed the crud out of that hilltop, but it still took Marines on the ground to accomplish the task. Echo Co. finally took their hill after their third assault a few days later.

Back to Golf Co. and 2nd Platoon, the 7th and 8th were spent with continuing efforts to dig in more and handle the mortar, machine gun and AK-47 fire that was with us day and night up there at one time or another. The records give a quick glimpse at the action:

> At 070405H Company G in defensive position at ZC195561, was attacked by an estimated two squads of NVA supported by B-40 rockets and 82mm mortars. As the enemy closed, the defensive position returned small arms and automatic weapons fire, grenades and 38 rounds of 81mm mortars, and called for and received a spooky gunship. At 070550H the enemy broke contact. Results: Five USMC KIA, Four USMC WIA Evac, Three NVA KIA and capture of two AK-47 rifles and one SKS.

Later that morning, we would have another man severely wounded by mortar fire. He would be listed as KIA after his medevac. The Marines killed on the 7th were all from 2nd Platoon with the exception of Pfc Colgan:

Pfc. Daniel P. Colgan 0311
LCpl. Richard A. Dudek 0311
Pfc. Hilton Hayes Jr 0311
Cpl. Sheldon D. Hoskins 0311
Pfc. Carrey E. Scoggins 0331
LCpl. Gregory J. Weber 0331

With another ten men dead or wounded, Golf Company was now down by 59 men, almost half of the Company, with 2nd Platoon taking the brunt of the casualties. In the early morning of the 7th we were in two-man foxholes, with one-on and one-off, trying to get some much-needed sleep. For some reason I was placed in a position by myself. The gun team was positioned to my left, covering a likely avenue of approach. Weber, a long-time member of Golf Co., was with Scroggins, who had only been in Vietnam for 37 days. The VC hit us like a sledgehammer, and although the machine gun seldom opened up at night due to the tracer rounds, (one in 5 in the ammo belt) they had no choice. Tracer rounds had a bullet that had a pyrotechnic charge imbedded in the rear of the slug. Ignited by the burning powder, it burned brightly as it traveled to the target. A dead giveaway for the gunner.

Mr. Charles was all over the gun team and all they could do was return fire. I think the gun position was hit by grenades or maybe a satchel charge, killing everyone there. I could just see the advancing NVA to my left front and I threw grenades and fired my M-16 trying to stop the gooks. I didn't even notice when LCpl. Weber got the gun going again. No one could move for fear of being shot by our own men. We returned fire at anything that moved on top of the hill and killed three of them. The hill was in total chaos and stayed that way until first light, when the Company Gunny and the

Platoon Sergeants got things back in order. After that attack, I wound up with the M-60 again. After a detailed cleaning and test fire on the area across the little stream, the M-60 was back in action and remained with me for the duration of the operation. I kept to the holes I had dug, learning the lesson from that night attack, and was able to cover all avenues of approach which we cleaned up, throwing more bodies down the hill and cutting down more brush to create an even wider clear area. That allowed me to cover the side of the hill, with interlocking fields of fire to my right. The rest of the day and every day afterwards I dug on my hole hoping to make it deep enough to give me some real cover. I never saw the actions of the gun team or Cpl. Hoskins. They were all beyond my line of sight. The "old guys" like Mike Ervin and Mike Copeland took Weber and Hoskin's death hard. They had been with them since December of 1967 - more short-timers getting wiped out.

From a memorial for LCpl. Gregory John Weber, KIA October 7 1968:

> We Nam Brothers pause to give a backward glance, and post this remembrance to you, one of the gentle heroes and patriots lost to the War in Vietnam:
>
> Slip off that pack. Set it down by the crooked trail. Drop your steel pot alongside. Shed those magazine-ladened bandoliers away from your sweat-soaked shirt. Lay that silent weapon down and step out of the heat. Feel the soothing cool breeze right down to your soul ...
>
> and rest forever in the shade of our love, brother.

Another long-time member of Golf Co. that died on the 7th, Cpl. Hoskins, was honored for his heroic acts by Charles (Mike) Ervin and with the Silver Star as quoted below:

> Charles Ervin, Served in same platoon. To set the record straight – information on "The Wall" indicates death as being attributed to Artillery, Mortars, etc. This is erroneous. Cpl. Hoskins was killed (Small Arms) when we were partially overrun at night at about 0200. We were overrun twice in a period of two days and lost approximately 6 Marines in all. Mike Ervin, 2nd Platoon, Golf 2/5 Operation Meade River Maui Peak.

Silver Star:

> The President of the United States of America takes pride in presenting the Silver Star (Posthumously) to Corporal Sheldon

D. Hoskins (MCSN: XXXXXXX), United States Marine Corps, for conspicuous gallantry and intrepidity in action while serving as a Squad Leader with Company G, Second Battalion, Fifth Marines, FIRST Marine Division (Rein.), FMF, in connection with combat operations against the enemy in the Republic of Vietnam. In the early morning hours of 7 October 1968, during Operation MAUI PEAK, Company G was occupying a defensive position on a hill near Ha Nha Hamlet in Quang Nam Province when a sector of the perimeter was assaulted by a large North Vietnamese Army force utilizing automatic weapons and hand grenades. During the initial moments of the fierce attack, every Marine in one of the forward machine gun emplacements was seriously wounded and the friendly perimeter was in danger of being penetrated by the enemy. Completely disregarding his own safety, Corporal Hoskins unhesitatingly left his covered position and maneuvered across twenty meters of fire-swept terrain to the silent machine gun. Ignoring the hostile rounds impacting near him, he fearlessly commenced directing a heavy volume of fire against the North Vietnamese soldiers who had advanced to the edge of the perimeter. Continuing his determined efforts, he resolutely expended his ammunition against the hostile force and was reloading his weapon when he was mortally wounded. His heroic and timely actions inspired all who observed him and were instrumental in his unit repulsing the enemy assault. By his courage, bold initiative and selfless devotion to duty, Corporal Hoskins upheld the highest traditions of the Marine Corps and of the United States Naval Service. He gallantly gave his life for his country.

The reports show that Alpha 1/5 also had their hands full as they attacked the high ground from their river positions:

Company A called for and received extensive preparation fire on a hill at ZC190560. After the fire was lifted, the 2nd platoon came under intense rifle and automatic weapons fire and B-40 rocket fire from an estimated two reinforced NVA platoons in numerous fighting holes and fortified bunkers. Company G, providing supporting fire, came under heavy semi-automatic and automatic weapons fire from vicinity ZC195561 and ZC189562. Due to the heavy volume of fire from enemy emplacements, Company A pulled back and called

> for additional supporting fires. Results: 12 USMC WIA, 27 NVA KIA by Marine Air and 15 NVA KIA by assaulting infantry.

Even when the resupply choppers couldn't get to us, the blessed medevacs kept going, fair weather or foul. They even brought in things like ammo and chow whenever there was a mission for us. Interesting, though, is the lack of reporting of many events, including medevacs, in the records. Continuing on to the 8th:

> At 081610H, immediately after an artillery prep fire, Company E began to assault its objective at ZC190561. As the lead elements, supported by four 90mm tanks, maneuvered to the base of the hill, they came under moderate small arms fire from across the Song Vu Gia River, vicinity ZC193553. At 1700H, two platoons on line from ZC190558 to ZC192558 assaulted the hill. At 1715H, the lead elements reached the crest, and by 1730H, the Company had secured the hill.
>
> During the advance, the assaulting units received three rounds of incoming 82mm mortar fire from ZC192567 and ZC194544. A counter mortar mission of 130 rounds 81mm and one flight of fixed wing aircraft were called, and both mortar positions were silenced with a secondary explosion observed at ZC192567. The small arms and automatic weapons fire received from across the river during the assault was suppressed by artillery fire.
>
> Company G, supporting the assault troops by fire, received incoming small arms and 50 caliber machinegun fire from ZC192566. An 81mm and 60mm mortar mission silenced the enemy guns. Results: One USMC KIA, eight USMC WIA Evac, one USMC WIA Non-Evac, and 37 NVA KIA.

The KIA on the 8th was from Echo Co. His name was:

LCpl. Pierce Malmquist 0311 Rifleman

Of the WIA's from the 8th, Golf may have had one or two, the rest would have been from E Co.

I recall my involvement in that action. As described in Johnnie Clark's book *Gun's Up!*, Alpha 1/5 came onto Hwy. 4 with tanks on Oct. 8. They caught hell trying to get beyond the hills where we were and where Echo Company was. At one point, Clark describes having to fire at an enemy machine gun up on a hill to his left front and that as he was returning fire, a machine gun from the hill to his right front opened up on that same enemy machine gun. That was me on the hill to his right. Alpha Company had made it as far as the gap between the hills, with a tank in tow. The narrow pass was formed by the hill on the left that Echo was on and the hill to the right that Golf was on. My machine gun position was just above where Clark was. Two things happened there. First, I saw the enemy machine gun or at least the tracer rounds coming from across the gap between our hills. It wasn't up on the top of the hill where Echo was; rather it was much lower and closer to me. I took it on, not noticing any fire from below from Alpha Co. As I was firing on the enemy machine gun, we started to get some incoming mortars. I could see the muzzle flash of the mortar tube, but it was too far for me to have any effect on it. Captain Poole came over to my position and asked me to take it out, but I explained about the distance and he went back to his CP. The mortars continued and the Captain came back and told me that he had a tank on the horn (the term horn was used for the radios, like the PRC-25) and said that the tank would help us but they couldn't see the mortar muzzle flash and had no point of aim. That was the tank that was with Alpha Company at the pass. I told the Captain that I could spot the mortar with the tracers from the machine gun and asked if the tank could see that. I fired a few bursts in the direction of the mortars and the tank came back and said yes, that they could see my tracers.

Now I had learned to pop the tracers out of belts whenever I could and as a result, I kept a small belt, maybe 50 or 60 rounds wrapped around my waist for situations like this. I didn't want to waste the rounds, but I also didn't want them in the belt I used for night watch. Anyway, I pulled out that belt, loaded it up, and told the Captain to tell the tank to watch the arc of my tracers. I started firing short bursts of all tracers which made a nice red line in the sky, and fell in the vicinity of the muzzle flashes. The rounds probably fell short, but at least the red line pointed in the right direction. Then, like a Hollywood movie, one of the last tracers heading out was swallowed up by a bigger object and it looked like they went in together and blew up the mortars. That was the 90mm from the tank. There was a large explosion and many secondary explosions and the best part was that the mortar attack stopped. I remember men standing around me jumping up and down hollering:

"Hurray, hurray!"

Now that is my memory. However, as shown below, the reports say that the weapons used to take out those mortars were 81mm mortars and rounds from a 105 inch howitzer. Tank or howitzer, it got the job done.

The 9th of October is described best by the Marine Corps Records:

0315H	Co E Defensive posit received Enemy fire from ZC189568
0400H	Co A 1/5 Received enemy fire from ZC198562
0425H	Co G Defensive posit received S/A fire fm ZC196563
0445	Co G Def posit received probing Enemy fire from vicinity ZC198563
0830H	Co G Observed 10 NVA heading South
1250H	Co G USMC wounded by air strike at ZC196568

At 090400H, Company A, in defensive positions, came under a coordinated enemy probe consisting of mortars, B-40 rockets, grenades and small arms fire. Results: Two USMC KIA, three USMC WIA-Evac, one NVA KIA and capture of one AK-47 rifle.

At 091130H, Company A observed one automatic weapons site. Artillery was called and one body was seen blown into the air. Results: One NVA KIA.

At 091250H, an AO working with the Battalion, observed a group of NVA at ZC188568. A fixed wing napalm strike was called with excellent coverage. Results: Ten NVA KIA.

At 091534H, Company E at ZC189560 received one incoming 82mm mortar round from ZC192567. Air strikes were called. Results: One USMC Evac and seven USMC Non-Evac.

At 092010H, Companies E and G received 40 rounds of incoming 60mm and 82mm mortars. Returned fire on suspected enemy mortar sites consisted of 69 rounds of 81mm mortars and 36 rounds of 105mm artillery. Air strikes consisting of 40,000 pounds HE and 48 napalm pods were called on an enemy concentration of approximately 16 NVA with excellent coverage. Results: Seven USMC Evac and 16 NVA KIA.

Along with more dead and wounded, the 9th of October would be another hard day for Golf Company. The men lost to Alpha 1/5 that day were:

Pfc Wardell L. Armstrong 0331 Machine gunner

Pfc Paul M. Kolenda 0311 Rifleman

And 3 more WIA

A more detailed account of Alpha 1/5's action during Maui Peak is given in the well-written book by Machine Gunner, Johnnie M. Clark in his book *Guns Up!*.

Echo 2/5 would have 8 WIA, one medevac and 7 walking wounded.

Golf would catch the brunt of the October 9th attack, with 3 KIA:

Cpl. Joe E. Arnold 0311

Pfc. George M. Johnson 0311

LCpl. Raymond J. Stevens 0311

And 10 WIA medevaced.

Loosing another 13 men from 2nd Platoon meant that we were down by a total of 10 KIA and over 24 WIA, almost 75% of the Platoon and the Company was now down by 55% from the original assaulting force. As we got whittled down, the Captain would call for more men from the other hill to fill in the lines. Of those killed in Golf Co. on the 9th, Cpl Joe "Little Joe" Arnold, another long-time member of Golf Company, is remembered by Mike Ervin in his striking account of combat in Vietnam and the memories of a good friend and buddy:

"Little Joe Arnold"

> It's September 1999, and I sit here gazing at the different icons on this Compaq system's CRT and begin to scroll through the little window boxes of my past. One might wonder what has stimulated me to this point, as mundane as starring at a computer screen might seem, but if you were to watch my eyes you could possibly detect that I'm into a different time zone.
>
> If you know what I'm talking about then you know the look. It's that distant gaze that takes me back, far and away, to unanswered questions of betrayal, to youthful warriors, and to the death of superman. One visit to the Vietnam Memorial would produce untold stealth veterans, standing like shadows in the foreground, still unable to touch the ebony stones engraved with so much blood. Their nightmares still rage most likely bordered by two thoughts: If I had only….. and WHY?
>
> I'll be fifty-three this December. You might think that after thirty-one years some things might fade. You might suppose that feelings stemmed by long ago memories should be dulled. However, from where I sit, a memory like the texture of torn flesh now resembling jello keens sharply. I feel I haven't really talked with anyone

that might understand how I feel. Maybe that's the real issue for me. I want some one to be me. Then I'd know they understood.

My first wife, who lost a brother to Vietnam, never really knew or understood. And I can't say I imparted any real information to her that would have promoted a better understanding. But, to give her full credit for whatever she did feel, she did tell me about the time we were separating that she didn't think I had it all that bad. I felt sorely vilified. And she further related some war story of some other vet she knew and expressed genuine sorrow at his plight. I think his name was Jody.

My second wife has read different passages of my life as I've placed much in written form. However, whenever I reach a certain stage with respect to past Vietnam issues, she begins to ask questions, not of the war itself but of me; my psyche. My instinct is to pull away. I feel like she trespasses. I am able to relate a story but I can't relate a feeling other than this instinctual sense of trespass.

I think my problem really resides with my ego. These memories are all mine. No one knows how I feel. No, not what I've experienced, but how I feel inside! That piece of me that even I can't touch. That part of me that I can't give away. That part of me that I can't share. That part of me that still says I'm to blame.

In talking about the Vietnam experience, I've seen other people, like myself, whom I felt and believed to be really "out of it". However, rationally I've come to understand that maybe their grief was something I've put aside. Mine just leaks out, literally leaks out, one drop at a time. And then, again, I set it aside until, like tonight, when I accepted an invitation to a Vietnam Veterans function and, as the guest speaker details his personal experiences, I begin to relive an earlier life.

There are several people that stand out in my life during my Vietnam experience. There was Barney Wayne Barnes from Birmingham, Alabama. We hung tight the whole tour. We even found each other stateside and we visited my home although I never had the opportunity to meet his family. I've lost him for the time being but I'm still looking. Then there was Don Davis, Bob Setlak and Michael Chubby Hale from Chicago, Michael Witt, Salvatore Albano from Springfield Mass, and Little Joe Arnold from Chicago. Three of these men would come home in body bags. The rest would come back stateside. Whether they have ever been able to make it home,

I can only pray. Although I have memories of them all, and more, one of them still piques at me when I least expect it.

My 395 day tour of South Vietnam spanned the period of November 1967 through November 1968. I was a grunt marine attached to 2nd Platoon, Golf Company, 2nd Battalion, 5th Marine Regiment, 1st Marine Division in some little spot on the map called An Hoa, which was 24 miles southwest of DaNang. On my flight there, looking down on the pock-marked countryside, I now believe some of the craters in the rice paddies below may have been bigger than An Hoa.

Our area of operation in I Corps spread from Antenna Valley on Operation Essex to as far north as the Provincial Capital of South Vietnam, Hue City, during the Tet Offensive of 1968. There were 14 operations in all with my last being Operation Mameluke Thrust. My last official role was watching my entire unit, what friends were left, board the CH46s, and liftoff in search of Charlie.

As most of you probably remember, friendships were developed early on. FNGs became friends with other FNGs. The old Salts hung to themselves and really only took time to personalize with other Salts. One didn't know it at first but you made close friends and you lost close friends. Eventually you stopped making friendships. It didn't hurt as much when someone you didn't really know went down. I remember a Boot Lieutenant who was there maybe nine days and took a round. I am not sure if even his Platoon Sergeant knew his name!

Little Joe came into my platoon within weeks after I arrived. I'm not sure how we ever became friends. And, it might have just been my own prospective that we were but I, along with others, loved Little Joe. Of course, I say that now! I understand it's full meaning, now too! Back then, we would just say we were tight

Little Joe was an imp: a real clown. Not a show-off but a funny impish, clown. He was about 5 foot 4 inches tall and maybe weighed 140 pounds with two, one hundred round bags of gun ammo strapped to his waist. He was missing a digit of his small finger right hand. As to how it got missing, I think he related some story of childhood mischief in black Chicago. He also had a scar across one of his shoulder blades. I don't know if that was pre or post entry to Vietnam. It could have been the wound scar from the 1968 Tet Offensive in Hue City.

The Marines still used the same field marching pack from WW II and Korea. So it was a good guess there was more "stuff" lashed to the outside of the pack then what was inside. Socks, olive drab in color, carried stores of C Rat cans. Then there was the E Tool that wasn't worth a shit other than as a anchor but then couldn't find one when you needed it ,however, used properly they could make a heck of a weapon. Then there was a least one strand of gun ammo, a 60mm mortar round, a LAW, a gas mask, and maybe balanced out with a Claymore. We all knew we carried our body weight in some form of armament.

Little Joe was about the size of nothing. A small marine flak jacket was like a barrel around him. To watch him beat feet under fire was like watching a bucking pack horse shedding all paraphernalia not securely lashed down. He'd be holding onto his helmet with one hand, rifle with the other, with a periodic grab at his cartridge belt which would inevitably slide down because he wore is loose and low, and all this stuff swaying, flapping, and bouncing helter-skelter made you wonder how he ever remained upright.

Little Joe was for some reason always right around me at some hot times. He was right behind me as I danced to the tat-tat-tat-tat of Chicom 7.62 dust busters walking across a porch rail right beside me as I zigged zagged for a doorway. I believe he bled that day. He was with me when Chubby and Witt bought the farm. He was with superman when he caught his kryptonite bullet.

Thirty-one years ago this coming October on a dismal, dreary, rainy pre-dawn morning somewhere north of the Song Thu Bong River, 40 clicks west of DaNang, on a hill overlooked by Charlie Ridge, Victor came to call. Little Joe was on the roll. When I found his body, I knew he hadn't suffered. There were two points of entry: chin and sternum. I cradled his body in my arms sitting him on my knees, shifted his weight to my right shoulder, and carried off the hill. And then I wept! Later I would be asked if I was injured. When I asked why, I was told I had blood all over the back of my flak jacket. It was still wet.

I wrote to Little Joe's mother. She even wrote me back. What amazed me about this entire episode was a Louisiana Marine named George Washington. He didn't have time to really know Little Joe but when he found out that I wrote his mother, and got a letter back, he was astonished. How could a white man care for a black man. If only he knew!

He doesn't remember that it was I who set up the perimeter, positioned the foxholes, and inspected the fields of fire. He doesn't know it was I who was enjoying the safety of the perimeter being a squad leader and slept while Little Joe stood lines. He didn't know, like myself, that when you sat down in Little Joe's foxhole you couldn't see over the rim of the hill. Positioned three feet further over the rim and he might have seen the enemy in time.

Every once in a while, like tonight, I see his face, that impish face smiling, and I start to leak again, one drop at a time. I sometimes wonder why. And there is a periodic nagging of if only I had....

Cpl. Charles M. Ervin, USMC
2350632

An eloquent statement of what we all feel. Mike Ervin condenses the real Vietnam experience in a few well-written paragraphs and mirrors much of my own experience. I am privileged to have served with him and honored to include his statement in this story.

To date, Golf Company had lost approximately 72 men on that hill; most of those were from 2nd Platoon.

Yes, the 9th was hard. They hit us early in the morning, well before dawn. The main assault came from the saddle and directly at David Lopez's gun position. Tom Thomas was in his hole just a few yards away, with Little Joe in his hole opposite Tom's position. Out of nowhere, rounds were fired at Lopez's position and others around him. Before he could react, the attacking NVA tossed a grenade into his hole. His right leg caught the brunt of the explosion. Lopez knew he was severely wounded and with his buddy, LCpl. Lockett, gone, he call for the "Doc." "Corpsman, Corpsman," was his call and it was echoed up and down the line, as other Marines would be targeted that morning. Even though severely wounded, Lopez continued to fire off a Claymore Mine to defend his position until help arrived. Thomas tried to get to Lopez to help, but the incoming fire was just too great. All Lopez could do was wait and hope that the doc would get to him before the enemy did. Meanwhile, the assault continued. It finally petered out, leaving several more NVA bodies to be tossed down the hill, adding to the maggot population. I was fortunate enough to be on the far end of the assault this time and it was over before any NVA got to my position. A medevac came in shortly after dawn and loaded up the dead and wounded. That was the last time I saw David Lopez. I thought he had probably died from his wounds, bleeding to death even as the chopper was taking him away. It was only years later, in 1988, that I went to the Wall and found no evidence of his death. Through a process to get in contact with the families of Marine KIA's, I was able to contact Mrs. Ruth Decker and through her, I found out that Lopez was alive and well, minus one leg. Lopez and I have been in regular contact ever since.

I believe the whole picture that night also included an attack on the remainder of Golf Company on the hill behind us. Several of the casualties from that night were not from 2nd Platoon and I can envision a split attack up each side of the saddle by the NVA. All the KIA's were from 2nd Platoon, but some of the WIA's were from what was left of Golf Company. Thank goodness, we had the high ground.

I have talked much about my friend and combat buddy David Lopez. He is a quiet, unassuming, gentle man. As a Marine, he carried on, loving the Corps and doing whatever was asked of him and more often than not, giving more of himself than was expected. He is reliable and steadfast and I trusted my life in his hands, knowing that he always had my back. I could go on and on about him, but I think you have the picture. He has his own story about the hill we took on Operation Maui Peak. I am proud to share that story with you:

"The Lopez Story"

> As our company was going up this hill, we all could see it was going to be tough. The brush was thick as ever, as I remember we had to use our machete's to cut through the brush and we could hardly see the guy in front of us as we marched up the hill.
>
> Finally, we got to the top of the hill. It seemed like it took forever, but it probably took 3-4 hours to reach the top of the hill. We set perimeter around the top of the hill and digging up two man foxholes and setting claymore mines in front of our foxholes. We all were Gung-Ho as we were so ready for a firefight.
>
> The first night was fine, no incoming mortar fire and no small arms fire from the VC or NVA. The next day was not the same as we all felt something was going to happen. Well, we were right!
>
> Sure enough, that night we got hit. The enemy hit us; they walked mortar fire on top of us, as enemy walked behind with small

arms fire. We were over run. Time of attack was about 2 o'clock in the morning, no moon out and dark as hell!

As I jumped into my foxhole, I hit someone that was not my marine buddy (Lockett). Instead it was a gook (enemy), how I knew was when I jumped in the hole, he jumped out quick and ran to the front line. I had my M-16 in hand and opened fire. I also pressed the plug on my claymore mine; hoping to hit anyone coming up the hill. As all hell was breaking around us, I felt something hit my face hard, it hurt bad. It felt like being hit by a big stick.

After a few seconds, everything blew from under me. Must have been as the gook (VC) ran from the hole, he threw back at me a chicom grenade, and that's what hit me. As I lay at the bottom of the fox hole, I felt this warm water flowing from my leg. Had to be the blood coming out of my leg, and it was.

Laying there thinking of my life passing by me, I could see my family - my dad and mom, and all my brothers and sisters. I have 2 brothers and 6 sisters. For sure I thought I was going to die. As I was calling out "corpsman, corpsman," I heard no one and all I could hear was incoming mortar fire and gun fire. Right then I knew we were getting over run. So I said to myself I better be quiet so the enemy can't hear me.

I prayed and I asked God if it was my time to take me. I also prayed to God to take care of all my fellow marines that were left to fight to the end.

Just when I heard someone call my name "Lopez! Lopez!" I answered "over here!" It was dark and all I could see was sky and the stars. I kept yelling "over here!" Finally, he got to my hole and it was Lockett. I said "get me a corpsman," and he answered back "give me your rifle." I'm saying to myself "what?" I searched around the hole and I finally found my M-16, the stock on the rifle was gone. As he left I said to him "Take care."

It seemed like I was in the fox hole with my leg hurting for a long time. Not knowing how badly I was hurt, I was still conscious and I knew what was still going on and I was still praying. Then I heard someone again "Lopez! Lopez!" "Over here," I said. It was Lockett again and he brought help. They pulled me from the hole and dragged me to the other side of the hill.

Still hurting and praying, I still could hear all the gun fire around me. Just then someone said "How you feeling Lopez?" I said "Not so good."...it was the corpsman. The corpsman put a flashlight to my face and he said "you're doing fine Lopez. Hang in there!"

Still not knowing how bad I was, I laid on the ground waiting for the chopper to come. Probably shot up with Morphine, I felt better. Finally I hear the chopper from a distance. As it got closer I said to myself, as I lay looking to the sky and prayed to God to get me through this. As the chopper came down, I don't think it landed on the ground because of the heavy brush. I think it hovered above the ground. They threw us in the chopper. I remembered being thrown in, and then someone came in and landed on my leg. I yelled "my leg, my leg. It hurts!" By that time everyone was on. I felt the chopper start going up. I kept praying "Lord help us all!" Then the machine gunner on board started firing his gun. Please let us not get hit and the chopper was on its way to Da Nang naval hospital.

As the chopper landed at Da Nang naval hospital, I looked out of the chopper and everything looked bright white. I thought God was taking me home. When I heard someone ask for my serial number, I gave it to him. When I woke up I was in this room. There was a corpsman sitting at the end of the bed. As I looked under my sheets I saw that I had lost my right leg above the knee. I thought I was dreaming and I asked the corpsman "Did I lose my leg?" and he said "yes." Later that day there was this loud commotion in my room across from my bed. Another marine came in and was in very bad shape. I thought I was in bad shape, but this marine lost two legs and an arm. There were a lot of high brass marines in this room for this guy. Come to find out later, it was Chester [*sic*] Puller's son.

I stayed in Da Nang naval hospital a little over a week. I then went to Japan to stay in a hospital there for a few days, and then I went to Alaska, then to Fort Dix for a day.

Then I was bussed to the Philadelphia naval hospital and stayed there from October 24th 1968 to May 1969.

While I was at the Philadelphia naval hospital, a marine buddy that was in Vietnam with me was also there. His name is James Seabolt and he also lost a leg. I've kept in touch with him and he's doing fine.

Also while I was at the hospital, a wonderful lady mailed me a care package and wrote me letters while I was there. It was Al Decker's mom. She knew I was with Al when he was killed. We've kept in touch with her family and ours for the last 40+ years. It was because [of] Ralph Gibson that Mrs. Decker found out I was at the hospital.

A few years later, another fellow marine called me and it was fellow machine gunner by the name of Chuck VanBibber. It was VanBibber and I that have been together from the time we got in Vietnam, with the 27th Marines and the 5th Marines. And until I got hurt, VanBibber was on the same hill I got hurt and he was taking care of business.

I also keep in touch with him and yes he's doing fine also. Semper Fi!! I too am doing fine!

I am married to a wonderful lovely wife for 45 years, her name is Linda and I have three great sons, David Jr., Thomas Edward and Timothy John. I also have two lovely daughter-in-laws, Amy and Janelle and two beautiful, wonderful grandchildren, Gabriella Korin and Easton Edward.

Tom Thomas also has his own story. Here is his account:

"The Thomas Story"

The taking of those hills to the east of the road that ran along the river Song Vu Gia was one tough job. Initially we had marched through Hill 55 to get to Hill 52, where we arrived by October 3rd. On the morning of October 6th, we were choppered off of Hill 52 to a road leading to a Special Forces camp. We had some self propelled artillery and tanks with us and we were told that we were going to march up this road Hwy 4 to save some Army Special Forces who had been getting their butts kicked at their camp. It was hot and getting hotter.

Some time before noon, we started to catch fire from some NVA in the hills above us and we were told to assault those hills. We did ok until we hit a saddle between one hill and another. As we crossed the saddle, we started to get hit by a large volume of fire which slowed us down. The area we were in was very heavy with jungle brush and trees and moving up from the saddle, the hill became very steep. As we continued to move, many men, mostly the new guys, would drop out from heat exhaustion. At times I thought I was going to die from the heat myself.

Besides the heat, we were catching AK-47 fire and grenades coming from the top of the hill. I saw one Lieutenant stand up hollering for his men to move forward and the next thing, he got shot in the chest. Our platoon was in the lead and I wound up in front of everyone. There was another guy with me, a Sergeant, and together we tossed grenades up the hill, moved a little and tossed more grenades. The Gooks had their holes dug by bushes and they were very hard to spot. We had to stop from time to time when the firing got bad, but eventually, the Sgt. and I made it to the top. Van Bibber, my buddy from the 27th was close behind and once we were sure the hill was clear, Van Bibber and I started tossing the dead bodies down the hill. There was still shooting going on, but it was mostly from the men still moving up, pumping rounds into the dead bodies just to make sure they were dead.

Captain Poole finally arrived and set up his CP and walked the rim of the hill with our platoon sergeant, setting the lines. He placed Van Bibbers gun on the far end of the hill top and my gun at the end facing the saddle. He put the gun hole down the slope a little, with some riflemen above it. I was in a hole to the right of the gun. I didn't think about it then, but that gun was way too far out which we would all learn a few days later.

I remember one day when we had been getting some air support, and this pilot went down. Captain Poole asked for volunteers to go get the pilot and I volunteered. We started to get ready, when the Captain changed his mind since it was getting dark and not a good time to make a long patrol through enemy territory. Another memory is when I spied an enemy soldier down by the stream below us. I took the M-60 from Lopez and took out the NVA. His body landed in the water and Lopez jumped up and down hollering "You got him. You got him." Before anyone could verify the kill, the body floated out of sight around a bend in the river. But I got him and Lopez was my witness.

The resupply on that hill was awful, and we went hungry for a long time. All of us were scrounging for food anywhere we could find it, as well as having to fight off the maggots that had taken over the hill.

Early in the morning on October 9th, probably around 0400, we got over run and they came right at me and at Lopez's hole. The start of the assault was with Lopez taking a grenade in his hole, blowing off his leg. I tried to reach Lopez, but couldn't leave my hole because not only were the Gooks trying to kill me, but the guys above me were firing over my head at the advancing NVA and I just couldn't lift my head. A chicom grenade landed in front of my hole but when it finally exploded, it was a light with little to no damage. For a while, all I could do was put the barrel of my M-16 on the rim of my hole and hold the rifle so the rounds would go down the saddle, hoping to keep the Gooks from blowing me up too. A hole or two down from me also caught grenades and AK fire, killing two Marines. [That was Little Joe Arnold's position]

All this time, Lopez was calling out that he was hit and that it hurt and he needed a Corpsman. Soon, the Corpsman came over and the fire above my head stopped, and the Corpsman and I hauled Lopez out of his hole. When we got him to the staging area for the dead and wounded, the Corpsman shot Lopez up with morphine and as the morphine set in, he kept saying to me "Don't leave me Thomas! Don't leave me." I asked the Doc how his leg was and he said that the only thing holding his leg on was the pants leg. Doc cut off the pants leg and put a tourniquet and we waited for the Medevac. When it came in, I helped Doc and others to load the chopper with the dead and wounded. I thought Lopez had probably died since he looked really bad and had lost a lot of blood. Just recently, Van Bibber got in touch with me and told me that he was still alive.

After the 9th, things got worse, not so much from the Gooks, but from the weather. Resupply was getting bad again and the rain was getting worse every day. Some days, I thought we were getting hit by a hurricane. Wet, tired and hungry, I often felt hopeless up there. My feet were killing me from jungle rot and I was feeling all alone with Lopez gone. I didn't get to see Van Bibber much as he was at the opposite end of the hill perimeter. We often caught mortar or rocket rounds during the day and the night was owned by Charlie, so we got even less sleep than usual. A few hours in 24 was good if you could manage it.

Our platoon was devastated and if it weren't for a resupply of guys from the other platoons, we would surely been wiped out. I remember the B-52 strikes across the valley and in the mountains above us. One guy caught a large piece of shrapnel from one of those explosions. They had told us to get down in our holes because of the danger but still that Marine got hit. There were mostly new guys up there, as the "salts" Marines with over 6 months in Vietnam were getting wiped out left and right.

Another incident that happened was when a Marine convinced the Captain that he could short fuse grenades. The Captain gave him the go-ahead for the purpose of setting out some booby traps against the enemy. Well, he had an accident and wound up getting killed along with others getting wounded. The devastation just didn't stop.

One day, I saw two helicopters collide and crash to the ground. It was awful. As we started to run out of men, we went back to back in one long trench, preparing to defend ourselves to the last man.

Finally the choppers were able to come in and take us off that hill. Echo Company had secured their hill and the NVA were in retreat. The weather was still bad and getting worse, so it was a good thing we got out of there.

After getting back to An Hoa, I found out that my Mother was dying of cancer and I was going home. Copeland told me he was rotating out too and within a few days, both of us were gone from G 2/5 and Vietnam. I hated to leave because the guys I fought with needed every man for the operations to come, but family matters took precedence.

I remember seeing Van Bibber after he rotated out in March 1969 and we had some fun and even double dated together. Van Bibber got transferred and I lost touch with everyone. I picked up my life and went on from there. I have no regrets about my service in Vietnam, but certainly wouldn't want to do it all over again.

Of those Marines killed that day, Cpl Joe "Little Joe" Arnold, a long time member of Golf Company, is remembered in a memorial written by Barney Barns, originally a 2nd Platoon squad leader and later 3rd Platoon platoon sergeant who had transferred back to the States around the 1st of October:

"NEVER FORGET"

Posted for: JOE EDDY ARNOLD:

Little Joe,

I found this photo of you from June 68 while at HAI VANN PASS. I wanted to share it with others who come to visit this site. I wanted to let them know just what an excellent MARINE and true friend you were. I miss you Little Joe. Just once I'd love to hear you say one more time again, "Barney, you got a lot of soul for a CHUCK DUDE!"

REST IN PEACE, BROTHER...you are not and will not be forgotten by your GOLF 2/5 Brothers.

Posted by: Sgt Barney Barnes

The "Old Breed," those who were with the Company since November/ December 1967, were further reduced that day. I understand the feelings of the surviving "Old Breed," as I experienced that same thing in August when our Platoon in Fox 2/27 lost so many men. But now, with the medevac of David Lopez, I was cold inside and closed off to the deaths that were piling up around me. I wish I had been able to feel something then. Maybe this book is my way of finally grieving. Another long-time member of 2nd Platoon to get wounded on the 9th, was Cpl Don Davis. Davis would eventually rotate out and remain in the Corps, retiring as a Top Sergeant.

October 10th could be considered a "normal" day, with mortar attacks and nighttime attempts to overrun us. At 10:20 p.m., we received some small arms fire. Echo 2/5 and Alpha 1/5 had their share of the action as well. One unique incident occurred on our hill when an Engineer accidently detonated a grenade. He had told the Captain that he could short-fuse grenades so that any booby traps set around the perimeter would detonate almost instantly when tripped. The Captain gave him the okay and while in the process of doing this, the grenade went off causing a large explosion, rendering the Marine into pieces.

Our booby traps were of two kinds. First were ready-made booby traps, like the "Bouncing Betty," which was a self-contained unit that, when tripped, would send an explosive up in the air and explode with an air burst. The other type was detonated with grenades on a tripwire. Sometimes the only explosion would be the grenade itself, others would include other explosives like mortar rounds or blocks of C-4 or Claymore Mines set next to the grenade. The problem with these setups was the delay in the fuse of a standard grenade, which was 5 to 7 seconds. Short-fusing the grenades would fix that, and it was only the Combat Engineers that could do it.

Mike Ervin remembers the incident as well. He recounts that he had just walked past the Marine who was short fusing the grenades when the ground erupted and there was a large crater where the Marine had been. Mike remembers the Marine holding a Claymore Mine before the explosion happened. The best guess is that he was setting a booby trap using a short-fused grenade with a Claymore Mine and the grenade exploded, setting off the Claymore, creating the large explosion.

A search of the records gives the following entry for October 10th:
1750H Co G Marine accidently detonated a grenade, ZC195561

As a Combat Engineer, the Marine would have all the credentials to do the short fusing, but he had only been in Vietnam since August 24th, 1968. Forty-seven days isn't much time to get good at things like that. Still accidents happen, and it may not have been his fault at all. I think it was very brave of him to do all this to help save his fellow Marines from attack and give an early warning system. He knew the risks and went about his job anyway. That is true courage, to be fearful and do the job despite the dangers. He is a real Hero of the Vietnam War.

October 11th would be another horrific day. We received much-needed resupply while Echo Co. got some incoming small arms fire along with their resupply. Other than that, our job was to continue to clean up "Maggot Hill" and get ready for more mortar attacks and overruns, as had been the norm since we first took our hill. On the evening of the 11th, Mike Ervin was lounging in a hammock he had rigged when he got hit by something, knocking him senseless for a minute. He was evacuated that evening, another "Old Breed" leaving the hill.

The horrific part of that day would occur when there was a mid-air collision of two helicopters carrying troops and supplies. We witnessed the accident from our hill and were shocked by the destruction. Detailed personal accounts have given the clearest picture. These accounts may not always agree, but that is normal, since every individual will always see things slightly different. These accounts may be redundant for the most part, but each one provides a slightly different eyewitness viewpoint and are worthy of recounting here.

Memoriam for 1st Lt. William Thomas Hale, co-pilot of the CH-46A (Sea Knight), twin bladed helicopter, similar to the CH-47 (Chinook):

William Thomas Hale, First Lieutenant
HMM-265, MAG-36, 1ST MAW (HMM, Marine Medium Helicopter)
(MAG, Marine Aircraft Group)
(MAW, Marine Aircraft Wing)
United States Marine Corps

29 July 1944 – 11 October 1968

On 11 Oct 1968 four CH-46As from HMM-265 were engaged in resupplying Marines at Hill 52 north of the Song Vu Gia River in Quang Nam Province. The weather was good, described as "a clear, sunny day with a few scattered clouds high in the sky" although there were "some threatening heavy clouds off to the northeast towards DaNang". As CH-46A BuNo 151917 lifted off from the landing area at the base of Hill 52 it climbed into the flight path of a UH-34D, BuNo 148802, from HMM-362. From the ground the collision appeared to be limited to rotor strikes, but both aircraft shed their rotors, caught fire, and plunged vertically to the ground, impacting on a sand bar in the river. The UH-34D was entirely consumed by post-crash fire, while the CH-46 was demolished on impact but had only limited fire. All aboard the two aircraft died:

CH-46A 151917, HMM-265, MAG-36:
1stLt Jeffrey W. Rainaud, South Hadley Falls, MA, pilot
1stLt William T. Hale, Big Spring, TX, copilot
Sgt Marvin Wesley, Guin, AL, crewman
Cpl Gary D. Kemski, North Hollywood, CA, crewman
UH-34D 148802, HMM-362, MAG-36:
Capt Steven W. Martin, Wolfeboro, NH, pilot
1stLt Peter E. Schryver, Fort Lauderdale, FL, copilot
LCpl Lantie L. Harris, Shrewsbury, NJ, crewman
LCpl Lawrence C. Kleinhans, Honeoye Falls, NY, crewman

Passengers, E Co, 2nd Bn, 5th Marines:
Cpl Benny J. Hicks, Pensacola, FL
Cpl J D. Walters, Dayton, OH
LCpl Willie C. Ferguson, Oklahoma City, OK
LCpl Thomas F. Hankins, Pittsburgh, PA
LCpl Brian T. Heaver, Peoria, IL
HN Ivan L. Heller, Geneseo, IL (H&S/2/5 with E/2/5)

Bill Tom started his tour in Vietnam on September 11, 1968. He was assigned to the HMH-265, 36th Marine Air Group in Da Nang. On October 10, 1968, Bill Tom was the co-pilot of a CH-46A helicopter. He was operating as a part of a group of four CH-46As who were flying re-supply missions to the 5th and 7th Marine Regiments, operating in/around Hill 52 about 5 miles west of An Hoa in the Quang Nam province. The Marines of Mike Company / 7th Marines had been taking heavy fire in and around the L.Z. where aerial re-supply was underway. Two previous CH-46As had landed at the L.Z. and completed their re-supply and had taken off. Bill Tom's aircraft, tail number 151917 then landed and off loaded their supplies and took on passengers, 5 marines and a navy corpsman (this appears to be in dispute). Two other ground marines, the commanding officer and sergeant major of an artillery battery supporting Mike Company / 7th Marines also attempted to get on the craft before it took off, but were waived off by the crew chief. As the CH-46A then began to ascend out of the L.Z. and at a height of about 1500 feet, the aircraft collided with an UH-34D helicopter, tail number 148802, operating in the same area. The UH-34D were operating with a crew of four. Upon impact, the UH-34D exploded and the CH-46A (Bill Tom's aircraft) lost its main rotor and both aircraft and debris came crashing to the ground. The four crewman and passengers on the CH-46A and the four crew man on the UH-34D were all killed. All but two bodies were recovered. The remains of the other two were recovered in 1973.

The subsequent investigation concluded that the area was congested with many helicopters flying personnel and supplies in and out. There were low level clouds and cloud breaks. Although the ground visibility was good, the aircraft at higher altitudes were flying in and out of cloud banks. It was concluded that the CH-46A upon take-off did not see the other aircraft due to blindspots [*sic*] and the overcast conditions. The other aircraft the UH-34D apparently flew out of a cloud bank as the CH-46A was ascending. The area was under heavy fire and although there was no evidence that either craft took any hits from hostile forces, it was classified as hostile due to nature of the area. There seems to be some confusion as to which aircraft was actually carrying the passengers. In documents released and reviewed, the passengers are shown to have been on one or the other aircraft. One witness statement states the CH-46A took off without passengers, another witness states that he was not sure as to why the CH-46A had passengers as their role had been only re-supply."

From a memorial for Lantie Lawrence Harris Jr. LCpl:

Notes from The Virtual Wall: Although there is confusion regarding some details of this incident, there is no doubt about what happened: there was a mid-air collision between a CH-46A and a UH-34D above Hill 52 southwest of Danang. Fourteen men aboard the two aircraft died as a result.

The following synopsis is drawn from the Pop-A-Smoke site:

On 11 Oct 1968 four CH-46As from HMM-265 were engaged in resupplying Marines at Hill 52 north of the Song Vu Gia River in Quang Nam Province. The weather was good, described as "a clear, sunny day with a few scattered clouds high in the sky" although there were "some threatening heavy clouds off to the northeast towards DaNang". As CH-46A BuNo 151917 lifted off from the landing area at the base of Hill 52 it climbed into the flight path of a UH-34D, BuNo 148802, from HMM-362. From the ground the collision appeared to be limited to rotor strikes, but both aircraft shed their rotors, caught fire, and plunged vertically to the ground, impacting on a sand bar in the river. The UH-34D was entirely consumed by post-crash fire, while the CH-46 was demolished on impact but had only a limited fire. All aboard the two aircraft died.

As noted above, there is some confusion in detail, specifically about which aircraft was carrying the Marines from Echo 2/5. The USMC/Vietnam Helicopter Association (operators of the "Pop-A-Smoke" web site) places the six passengers aboard the CH-46A, while the Vietnam Helicopter Pilots' Association (VHPA) puts LCpl Ferguson and Hospitalman Heller aboard the UH-34D - and by inference, so too the other four men from Echo 2/5. One eye-witness description on the Pop-A-Smoke site very specifically states that the CH-46A took off without passengers - but another eye-witness states that it was the UH-34 which lifted off and climbed into the CH-46, an account which is clearly mistaken.

In one sense it makes no difference; the passengers died in the crash. While the 1993 casualty database indicates that the bodies of all 14 men were recovered, another source indicates that the remains of LCpl Ferguson and Hospitalman Heller were not recovered and identified until early 1973 - an indication they may well have been aboard the UH-34D, which was reduced to a smoldering pile of ash by the post-crash fire.

From a memorial for Brian Tracy Heaver LCpl 0341 (Mortarman) Echo 2/5 and Ivan L. Heller HN (Hospitalman) Corpsman E 2/5

I was standing near the top of Hill 52 at the 3/7 CP. The CO and SGT MAJ of the arty battalion supporting us had gone down the hill to catch a ride on CH-46 # 151917 which was in the LZ just below. As they ran up the back ramp, the crew chief on the CH-46 motioned for them to get off. They turned around and departed the aircraft. I watched as the CH-46 took off, without any passengers, and began climbing out in a steep ascent with its nose pointing south toward An Hoa. It was a clear, sunny day with a few scattered clouds high in the sky. At about 800-1,000 feet, the CH-46 came up underneath UH-34 #148802 which was flying overhead on a similar heading. It appeared that each helicopter was in the others blind spot and that no visual contact had been made between them. I don't think the two fuselages actually collided but they chewed off each other's rotor blades.

An orange fireball and black smoke erupted from the rear of the CH-46. A series of quick clacking sounds and a muffled explosion reached us on the ground as the blade parts were sent flying in every direction overhead.

The two aircraft, momentarily, just hung there. Then the CH-46, its aft end burning and smoking, began tumbling end over end toward the ground. The UH-34 simply nosed over, the weight of the big radial engine in its nose causing it to plunge straight down like a dart.

Clearly visible, standing at the open forward hatch of the CH-46, a crewman somehow managed to keep his position as the aircraft somersaulted downward. As the UH-34 hurtled down, I saw three passengers dive out the starboard loading hatch. One of them assumed a spread-eagle position, like a free-falling skydiver. The others just tumbled.

Thunderous noises echoed across the valley floor as the aircraft impacted on a sandbar which extended out into the Vu Gia river. Thankfully it was on our side of the river. The other side belonged to Charlie.

The UH-34 hit first, sending up a towering eruption of bellowing fire, white smoke, and streaking shards of red flame.

The CH-46 quickly followed, close by, on the same stretch of sand. The aft section, with the engines, split away from the forward half of the aircraft and was a burning heap. Black greasy smoke plumed high into the sky. The forward section did not catch fire.

I ran down to the crash site and found Marines from Mike Company 3/7 pulling the bodies of the pilot, co-pilot, crew chief, and crewman out of the CH-46.

Three crumpled bodies, those who dived out of the UH-34, rested on the sand in the immediate vicinity of the UH-34 wreckage. The Mike Company Marines spoke of a fourth individual who had dived out and had landed in the river. I could not verify it.

The UH-34 was burning white hot; so intense that it was impossible to get near it. Within a few hours the wreckage was reduced to a surprisingly small mound of gray ashes, making the retrieval or identification of human remains virtually impossible. This remains one of the sadder days in my life.

Submitted by Frank Powell, S-3, 3/7.

Personal Narrative:

I witnessed the air collision between the H-34 and the H-46. The former UH-34D exploded and burned. The H-46 CH-46A went down like a brick. Both aircraft crashed on a nearby beach. We took part in the recovery of the deceased. The collision occurred just off the LZ. I would estimate 300-400 feet off the ground. I was with Mike 3/7 at the time. We were operating off Hill 52 (north of Song Vu Gia River, Quang Nam Province) with other companies from the 5th Marines. The LZ was below the hill ? some units were departing - much helicopter activity--I was near the summit of the hill. My recollection was that the H-34 was ascending, the H-46 coming in. I heard the explosion first and then saw the aircraft going down. The H-34 burst into flames almost immediately. The H-46 just went down like a brick. The crew chief or gunner (starboard side of the helo) stayed at the hatch all the way down. His conduct, from my perspective, was something unforgettable.

My platoon assisted in the recovery of the dead. We got to the scene(s) of the crashes pronto. I do not know if either aircraft took enemy ground fire. I do not recall any sniper fire incoming, although it was a noisy time with all the traffic. I always have had an enduring appreciation for the good men that flew in the Corps. I dreaded hot LZs, but have many fond memories of looking upon helicopters as my safe haven out of the bush. I'm pleased I was able to get the names of those men, rather than remember them as anonymous Marines. Semper Fi.

Submitted by David Bruneau, M/3/7, USMC witness on ground.

Personal Narrative:

I was the co-pilot and Dick Upshaw was the aircraft commander of the 4th CH-46A from HMM-265. Jeff Rainaud was the 2nd section leader in the flight of four that left Phu Bai and went to Da Nang and then to Hill 55 to take external supplies to a unit West of Hill 55 and drop the supplies at Hill 52. When the four CH-46A's finished the resupply, we were to go to the air field at An Hoa for a new mission. The first and second CH-46 dropped their loads at Hill 52 and departed to An Hoa for a new mission. Jeff Rainaud and Willy Hale in A/C # 3 successfully dropped their external load into Hill 52. Dick Upshaw, crew and I were orbiting approximately 1500 AGL feet above ground level to the West of Hill 52. We were watching A/C # 3 come out of the LZ and climb as we were aligning for our approach in A/C # 4. I was watching A/C #3 climb out and I initially saw a large explosion and I thought they had been hit with some type of rocket or artillery, which I told Dick Upshaw, the HAC. I watched the blades of the CH-46 separate as it tumbled end over end and impacted on the river bed below. Seconds after it impacted, I saw another impact on the river bed nearby, which I later saw was the CH-34. There were a few clouds moving between Hill 55 and Hill 52. The two A/C hit each other and that was the explosion I saw. Jim Cahill, pilot, HMM- 265 identified the crew. Our log books , unfortunately, do not have the rest of the crew members listed. CH-46A serial number 152547, mission 1R9, 6.3 hrs flying time."

Submitted by Sam C. Kelly III, Wingman, HMM-265, co-pilot 4th A/C.

Personal Narrative:

I was aircraft commander in a flight of four H-46s; Sam Kelley was my co-pilot and Jeff Rainaud and Bill Hale were flying on our wing. We were the second section of two aircraft in a flight of four. Major Yanke, our squadron XO, was our flight leader.

At the time of the mid-air, Sam had the controls as we were circling overhead of Hill 52, which we were resupplying. I remember the weather had some threatening heavy clouds off to the northeast towards DaNang. We were at an altitude of 2000 feet MSL and we were in a wide left turn as our wingman was coming out of the LZ. I don't remember why he was carrying troops because, as I remember, our mission was resupply; seldom did we pick up troops on resupply.

Suddenly Sam, who was setting in the left seat looking over his left shoulder and could see the aircraft below, let out a loud shout over the intercom. He had witnessed the midair and I can't remember exactly what he said, but I'll never forget the rush of emotions that flashed through my heart. It was devastating. Major Yanke descended to witness the crash scene on the ground and to verify the conditions of our squadron buddies.

The rest of the flight continued on to An Hoa where the Major rejoined us later with the dire results. We all knew that there would be no survivors, especially in the H-46. Those opposite rotating front and aft tandem blades, once damaged in flight, always exploded into shattered debris as they thrashed each other and demolished almost everything and everyone nearby. I had not seen any H-34s in the area, and at the time it was my impression that he had come out of the clouds and hadn't had time to locate any of our flight. Certainly Jeff wouldn't have had time to see him.

Jeff and Bill, crew chief Sgt. Wesley, and gunner Cpl. Kemski were all excellent at their respective jobs. Their loss was a tough nut to crack for our squadron, and that day will remain vivid in my memory forever.

Submitted by Dick Upshaw, Section Leader, HMM-265.

Personal Narrative:

I witnessed the mid-air that destroyed a 34 and a 46 on 681011. At that time, I was on top of Hill 52 and saw the 46 at a height lower than the hill top fly from my right and around. The next thing to happen was the mid air and I looked up to see the 34 without blades in a nose-down attitude. There was fire coming from the nose completely covering the front of the 34.

I saw one individual either jump or fall from the 34 at about 350-500′. The 46 was also falling nose down and slightly turned to the right. The 46 had no rotor blades on the front. I thought they might make a hard but safe landing only to see the46 explode in flames when it touched down. Both the 34 and 46 landed on a sand bar of the river Song Vu Gia.

My unit was assigned the task of going to the scene of the accident and securing the area. There were no survivors. We recovered the bodies and noted that the wreckage consisted of just molten metal; a very horrible and sad day for all.

I really salute the heroes of our USMC helicopter squadrons. On two separate occasions you flew into the hot LZ and by doing so I am able to provide you my comments on the incident of 681011.

Submitted by John H. Valentine, Platoon Cmdr, Mike/3/7

Personal Narrative:

I was the crew chief on the forth a/c, piloted by Dick Upshaw; co-pilot Sam Kelly of HMM-265. My recollection of this incident is as follows: as we were waiting our turn to land in the LZ, I was sitting on my jump seat when I heard one of the pilots say something over the IC, something like, OH MY GOD! I immediately jumped up and looked out the windshield between the pilots and saw a large fireball directly in front of us, I was initially confused as to what was happening but I quickly realized our wingman hit something or was hit by something and then I was able to see a CH-46 (our wingman) falling away. I stepped back to my door for a better view and I could clearly see the rotor blades popping off the a/c. I remember in an instant wondering if we were going to be hit by the flying debris but quickly returned to the horror of watching as our wingman and crew fell out of the sky and exploded in a giant fireball when it hit the ground. At first we didn't realize what caused this to happen but quickly came to see that there was another a/c involved. I remember speculation that it was a RVN H-34 but later found out that, to make matters even worse, it was a Marine CH-34. These are my recollections of that sad day.

Submitted by Lowell Lyman, crewchief *sic* on CH-46 in the operation.

Personal Narrative:

We were operating off Hill 52, getting supplies and having some wounded taken out. At the time I was the 1st platoon radio operator, so I was keeping an eye on the birds coming in and out of the LZ. I recall the H-34 lifted off and was at about 500 feet AGL when it hit almost head on into the H-46 that was on approach to our LZ.

The H-34 exploded and fell to the beach on fire, and the H-46 was throwing rotor blades and debris over a 300 meter area. I was part of the recovery team that removed the KIAs. The H-34 was burned to ashes, and the H-46 was totally destroyed upon impact. It was a devastating site, and one I will never forget. I would like to take this time to thank all the pilots and crews for all their help in getting our wounded out from hot LZs and removing the grunts to safety. Semper Fi.

Submitted by Doug Hilton, M 3/7 USMC, witness on ground.

On the "Wall" in Washington, DC, there are 16 Marines and one Navy Corpsman listed as being killed on October 11, 1968 in Quang Nam Provence, Vietnam. Fourteen of the seventeen were from the crash described above, including the Navy Corpsman. Horrific indeed!

Chapter 13

October 12th was another hard day for Echo Company. The records tell the story:

> At 120400H, Company E in night defensive positions, came under a well-coordinated mortar and ground attack from an estimated NVA company. Under a barrage of 40 rounds of 82mm mortar fire, the enemy attacked with small arms, automatic weapons, grenades and B-40 rockets. Company E returned fire with small arms, automatic weapons, grenades and claymore mines. Artillery missions totaling 26 rounds of 8", 249 rounds of 155mm, 300 rounds of 105mm and 438 rounds of 81mm mortars were called in on troop concentrations and suspected mortar sites. Results: Eight USMC KIA, nine USMC Evac, one USN Evac, ten USMC Non-Evac, 46 NVA KIA, one NVA POW and capture of nine AK-47 rifles, one AK-50 machinegun and 47 ChiCom grenades.

I remember the 12th for two reasons. First, it was the day I took out two NVA down by the river below my position. I had gained a lot of skill with the M-60 and I was able to fire it like a rifle by locking the bi-pods into a sandbag or mound of dirt. Getting in a real steady position with my sights adjusted to what I thought the range was, I pulled back the bolt, loaded a belt of ammo, took the gun off safe and just brush the trigger, allowing one round to be fired.

Accounting for the drop in elevation, I adjusted the sights to 800 meters aimed high and fired. The first round went into the dirt close to the enemy soldier. I quickly adjusted my point of aim and fired again. Down he went before he could figure out what had happened, dead before he hit the ground. I think the second shot got him before he heard the sound. As the second NVA started to react I fired again, this time with three or four round bursts and down he went. For years I have questioned my memory thinking maybe I just made it up, but someone must have seen what occurred and made a note of it, because it is not only recorded in the 2/5 monthly reports, but it is also mentioned in my personnel records. I had been at this for a while and the M-60 was real comfortable in my shoulder. Still taking out that first NVA was probably more luck than skill, but it gave me the confidence to take out the second NVA as well. Mr. Charles stayed clear of that stream from then on, at least the part where I could see them.

The records from 2/5 record that incident:

> At 120730H, a Marine from Company G observed two NVA crossing a stream bed at ZC196563. He opened fire killing both. Results: Two NVA KIA.

I wasn't the only one with this "talent," Tom Thomas did a similar thing off of his end of the hill. I am not sure what the date was, but he recently told me about it. Seems like he also observed one NVA down by the river, set his sights and took him out. This may have occurred before the ninth, because he said that Lopez had witnessed the shot, but before anyone else could verify it, the body had floated around a bend downstream and out of sight.

The second thing that everyone remembers on that day, was an attack on Echo Co. which was set in on the hill to the north west and just across the small stream. That hill seemed to be slightly below us and we had a real good view of the fight there. It started around 0400 hours, the time almost all of these early morning attacks started and we could see the muzzle flashes and hear the reports of the weapons being fired. There were numerous explosions which we assumed were mortars, since we had been receiving our share ever since we took our hill. As it turns out, there were also B-40 rockets being used against us. There was really nothing we could do without endangering the Echo Co. Marines in the process. All we could do was watch and pray. Overall, Operation Maui Peak took the lives of 34 Marines and Navy corpsmen, with 175 known NVA dead.

The records tell it this way:

> Company E, 2nd Battalion, 5th Marines received the only sizeable counter attack which it turned back, but the Company did take one POW and documents indicating the 1st Battalion, 141st Regiment was the unit in contact. At the start of the operation, the unit received incoming 140mm rocket fire, indicating the 3rd Battalion, 368B Regiment was within its stated area of operation northeast of Second Battalion's position. No contact was made with any other unit reported to be in the Battalion's TAOR.

A remembrance from "The Wall" in Washington D. C. records the following about Echo Company:

"A Note from The Virtual Wall"

In the fall of 1968 North Vietnamese Army units were attempting to cut road access to the Thuong Duc Special Forces camp on the Thu Bon River just west of Ha Tan, about 35 kilometers southwest of Danang. The US response was Operation MAUI PEAK (06-19 Oct 68), a multi-company operation under the control of the Commanding Officer, 2nd Battalion, 5th Marines. He was ordered to move west along Route 4 into the Thuong Duc Valley and clear away any NVA units that could be brought to battle. Elements of the 21st NVA Regiment, three battalions from the 141st NVA Regiment, one battalion from the 368th NVA Regiment, an artillery battalion from the 36th NVA Regiment, and elements of the 31st QuanDa Regiment (VC Main Force) were believed to be in the mountains around the Thuong Duc Valley.

MAUI PEAK began 06 Oct and had limited contacts with the NVA for the first two days. That changed when the Marines left the valley floor and moved to the hilltops, which the NVA defended with some vigor. The NVA also attacked night defensive positions (NDPs) on several occasions. The most severe of these attacks involved an assault by the 1st Bn, 141st NVA Regiment on Echo 2/5's NDP:

At 120400H Company E in night defensive positions came under a well-coordinated mortar and ground attack from an estimated NVA company. Under a barrage of 40 rounds of 82mm mortar fire, the enemy attacked with small arms, automatic weapons, grenades and B-40 rockets. Company E returned fire with small arms, automatic weapons, grenades and claymore mines. Artillery missions totaling 26 rounds of 8", 249 rounds of 155mm, 300 rounds of 105mm and 438 rounds of 81mm mortars were called in on troop concentrations and suspected mortar sites. Results: Eight USMC KIA, nine USMC WIA evac, one USN WIA evac, ten USMC WIA non-evac, 46 NVA KIA, one NVA POW...

The eight Marines who died in the attack were:

LCpl Wiley L. Martin, Cleveland, OH

LCpl David A. Pietraszak, Toledo, OH

Pfc Adolfo M. Bejarano, Port Isabel, TX
Pfc Henry J. Kuykendall, Los Angeles, CA
Pfc John E. Metzler, McKees Rocks, PA
Pfc Luis F. Saavedra, Forest Hills, NY
Pfc James L. Thomas, Beech Grove, IN
Pfc Michael L. Wasserman, Boise, ID

> Overall, Operation MAUI PEAK cost the lives of 34 Marines and sailors, with 175 known NVA dead. The most severe loss of American lives came on 11 October, when 14 men died as the result of a mid-air collision between two Marine helicopters, one supporting MAUI PEAK and the other supporting a 3/7 Marines operation.

October 13th was relatively quiet. With the weather getting progressively worse, even the NVA were hampered in their assaults. The one thing that they had going for them were mortar and rocket attacks. It seemed like we got hit every day by some type of harrassing fire.

The records from the 13th through the 19 report the following:

> At 131005H, Company G snipers at ZC195561 observed three NVA at ZC191568. The enemy were taken under fire. Results: Two NVA KIA.
>
> due to heavy rains and reduced visibility throughout this period helicopter resupply of units engaged in maui peak was not attempted. additionally the msr [main supply route] supporting the operation is rapidly becoming impassable to vehicular traffic. cross country mobility of foot troops is seriously hampered. further heavy rain will seriously effect the support of this operation.
>
> intermittant heavy rain and low visibility continued to hamper efforts to resupply units on maui peak. withdrawal of units from maui peak ao [area of operation] continues to be influenced by the weather. normal patrolling activity in the taor [tactical area of responsibility] has been curtailed due to widespread flooding.

14Oct68	0630H Co G Units were supported by 1 flare ship firing on suspected enemy position and on ZC185564.
15Oct68	1310H Co E Search of area at AT860481 produced 2 NVA bodies
	1435H Co A Patrol completed without incident

16Oct68	0510H Co A Defensive posit received enemy fire from ZC201562
17Oct68	0800H Co G Sniper observed 1 NVA in hole at ZC191567

With the weather setting in, the attacks by enemy soldiers slowed down but the mortar attacks continued. By the 19th we were out of there and on to other operations around An Hoa. I am not sure of the exact day that we were lifted off that hill, I think it might have been on the 18th.

Mike Ervin, one of the "old breed" from Golf Co, wrote his own account of what happened in Operation Maui Peak:

> Maui Peake [*sic*] started in early October 1968. Golf 2/5 was on the standard S&P ops in the My Loc area of Quang Nam Province out along the Song Fu Bong. There wasn't much going on except for an occasional sniper throwing a round here and there plus the normal booby-traps. We had a couple of Dinosaurs (Amtraks – amphibious assault vehicles) with us which was unusual. However they could carry a lot of ammo and supplies. Only real problem was if they slung a track in a paddy. We did have a machinegun open up on the rear of the column but I have no idea what the guy was shooting at. I happen to turn around just as the enemy opened up from a corner of a hedgerow and watched the burst of smoke from the gun barrel but the guy only hit air.
>
> Anyway, we walked about 12 clicks a click is 1000 meters back to Liberty Road about mid point from An Hoa and Phu Loc 6 just to be picked up by CH-53s Sikorsky Sea Stallion, heavy-lift, single blade and were flown to the other side of the river almost adjacent to where we'd been 3 hours earlier. That made real sense to me: walk 10 miles just to be flown 11 miles but only about 1 mile from where you'd just come from.
>
> Maui Peake [*sic*] started from about this point along the road from Hill 55 in 1/5's TAO toward a Special Forces camp up in Elephant Valley. Golf 2/5 spread out on line and walked another 5 to 7 clicks up along the river towards an area where the foothills adjacent to Charlie Ridge converge on the river and make a very narrow passage thru the parallel mountain ridges that follow the river. There were 4 of these foothills all of which were approximately 150 feet high. The first hill is separated from the other 3 by about

5 hundred yards and a small stream where the other 3 sit grouped as chess pieces with the nearest one being the smallest and the furthest being the largest. The one in the middle is connected to the first with a saddle like passage which dips below the crest of both some 50 feet.

G 2/5 made its way to the nearest hill and, on first inspection; it looked as if the hill had been overrun by the enemy. Old ordinance was everywhere strewn around on the ground and in many cases half buried by the weather. The watch tower was blown half way over and most of the bunkers were in shambles. We hadn't been there very long when Charlie welcomes us with a 122 rocket. I was sitting on the east wall of a fighting trench and just happened to be looking right at the launch site. I saw the rocket come off the side of the mountain and I think I yelled "ROCKETS" before it cleared the treetops. Then I watched it streak for the landing area where at least two CH-46s were parked unloading and reloading men and supplies. The nearest 46 lifted just as the rocket hit – right under underneath it. Other than noise, there was no damage. That was the last rocket I saw fired by NVA while in country.

G 2/5 started making little sorties into the surrounding area with no contact. Heavies (Mobile 155 battery) started showing up and they started airlifting in a battery of 105 howitzers, 106 recoilless, 81 mortars. It became evident that G 2/5, the company, was growing into 2/5, the Battalion.

Charlie was making his presence well known. We watched from our box seats as an F-4 got shot down. The crew bailed out just off the apex of Charlie Ridge and floated down about 300 yards from the top. Huey gunships were right on station to recover the pilots. From our vantage point we could hear a small firefight develop as the choppers maneuvered to pick up the down pilots. And then they were off to the races. As for our participation: the 105 battery tried to put holes in the downed pilots' parachutes but could only get close. G 2/5's 106 team hit the target on first try.

The only real casualties taken the first couple of days were from mid-air collisions although we must have been taking some ground casualties because one of the choppers that collided was a medivac CH-33 [*sic*]. The 33 [*sic*] took off from the LZ, I presume, with wounded destined for DaNang. It lifted and started a tight clockwise circle to get altitude before making the down river run for Da-

Nang. There was an incoming 46 probably filled with personnel and supplies circling counter-clockwise down. The 46 sat down on the 33 [*sic*] at about the 150 foot level and a ball of fire erupted. We saw bodies spilling out of the falling wreckage but any hope for survival rested with landing in the river. There were no survivors. Between the 46 and 33 [*sic*] there were a least 7 crewmen. As for the people in the choppers, I have no idea. I do remember after we left this area that I saw a rotor head, the part that holds the rotor blades to the shaft of the engine, about a half mile down river from where the crash took place. That was about the biggest piece they ever found.

2nd Platoon made a recon of the 2nd hill. It showed much evidence of prior activity. We even walked down into the saddle between the 2nd and the 3rd hill but turned around and went back to the base camp. The following day, we went back up on the 2nd hill and proceeded to the 3rd hill via the saddle and we found Charlie. He was well dug in.

The 3rd hill was a tight conical type hill with very thick vegetation all around the sides with the exception of the side facing Charlie Ridge. That side was rocky, very steep, and with only head high type underbrush. The rest of the vegetation was much like what I remember about the thick locust groves in Hawaii: the trees are about 2 inches thick and about 12 feet high and you can't move thru them without making a lot of noise.

Anyway, Golf 2/5 walked into Charlie's trap at point blank range. These guys were very good a disguising their foxholes. They'd dig down right beside a bush and pile all the loose dirt around the bush or somewhere else. You couldn't really tell where they'd pop up unless you saw the hole which you really never did until it was too late. Well, we kick them off the hill after about an hour fire fight and lost about 10 men in the process. I don't remember that anyone was killed. Sgt. Lamb probably got it the worst taking a round thru both legs at the knees. This was his 2nd tour and they shipped him back with only 7 months left in the Corps.

I pulled a recon around the hill after most of the gun play was over. I only found one dead NVA. His body lay out there on the side of the hill for several days and bloated up lick [*sic*] a tick. We'd throw rocks at it to see if it would burst. Not sure what we did with the body but we probably had some FNG drag it off the side of the hill so we wouldn't have to smell the stench.

The night belonged to Charlie. He didn't call the first night but he made two successful calls two nights in a row. We lost several men during these assaults. One of those was a good friend of mine Little Joe Arnold. The night Joe was killed I remember seeing a man crawling thru where I was moaning and groaning. I couldn't understand what he was saying so I bent down to get closer and he was missing his lower jaw. During these assaults, Puff or Spooky were called on station. These were Flare Ships equipped with mini-guns. They popped flares for the rest of the night and, if needed, used the guns. I always like watching the guns in action. The gunner would sort of wave the weapon around and, at night, the tracer rounds looked like a long thin tongue of fire from the plane to the ground being waved sic by the wind. The tracer was every 5th round.

Golf 2/5 also got much support from the air wing. Those guys could really jockey a jet. I remember seeing one of these guys come down and insert himself between Hill 4 and 3, sweep around the back side of 3, and then swoop up thru the saddle between 3 and 2. I swear this guy's right wing tip was dragging through the tops of the trees in the saddle. I actually didn't think he would make it. He was dropping napalm at about dusk. So, with the reflection of the fiery explosion, the time of day, the angle of his assent up thru the saddle's gap, the near side of the F-4 looked as if it was on fire. I even think I could read "US Marine" on his helmet. I'm pretty sure he was checking his shorts when he got back to base.

During the more dull moments of Maui Peake [*sic*] people were trying to occupy their time with trying to figure out ways to booby trap the side of the hill where Charlie kept infiltrating. One person doing this was an Ordinance man. He had taken apart a Claymore Mine and was trying to short fuse the blasting cap. I think Don Davis and I had just spoken to him and were watching but had drifted about 30 yards down the saddle from him was when, all of a sudden, there was a white flash and a tremendous blast. Where the guy had been sitting on the ground was just a smoking hole and the bush behind him looked like it was covered with rags on one side. Two people ran to where this was and I remember the cringed look on their faces. There was no Ordinance man to be found.

During the course of Maui Peake [*sic*], I think it was Echo 2/5 that eventually took the 4th hill. Golf 2/5 was situated on the 3rd hill; I have no idea who was on the 2nd Hill. Anyway, Echo tried to take this hill on 3 different times on 3 different days and every time with the same result: Charlie wouldn't vacate. We called in artillery. We called in air support. We called in mortars. About the only thing we didn't call in was for Pizza. Finally, they told us to get into are [*sic*] foxholes: they were calling for 1000 pounders. The top of Hill 3 was only about 300 years from the top of Hill 4. Well, we all got down in our foxholes and the jets came on station with the big ones. Echo took the hill and, like Golf, got harassed at night by Charlie. We actually had one casualty on Hill 3 from the 1000 pounders. One guy took a good size chunk of steel in the leg. He was hollering more from the heat of the metal then the blood from his leg. Capt. Poole was our CO at the time and I could never figure out, after loosing [*sic*] all these people, why in the hell we never prepped this hills before we spent all these (people). Ordinance must cost more in the long run than human life.

Mother Nature decided that everyone had had enough and it started to rain. And it continued to rain. We even had problems with resupply because of rain. I remember a 46 coming in at dusk with a basket full of jerry cans of water and they wouldn't come below 50 feet. They eventually dropped the basket which broke open all the water cans. Most of us wanted to shoot the SOB Pilot and Crew Chief for being such chicken shit Rat Bastards.

I ended up leaving the theater of battle via some type of ordinance that blew up right beside me and threw me out of a homemade hammock. It must have rattled my brain because my eyesight wasn't right. I was evaced to DaNang. Along the way I ran into Lt. Pace and I told him about Little Joe. When I got back to An Hoa I was wearing Glasses (At least to read).

Cpl. Charles "Mike" Ervin was wounded late on October 11, and medevaced out that evening. After being treated for his wounds, he returned to Golf 2/5 until the middle of November when the Freedom Bird (nickname for the civilian jets that transported troops back to the U. S.) took him home.

The records differ slightly, but the after action report for 2/5 lists the following:

> During the period 1 October to 19 October 1968, the Second Battalion (-) (reinforced) was under the operational control of the 7th Marine Regiment. During the period 6 October to 19 October, the Battalion in coordination and cooperation with ARVN and other Marine units participated in Operation MAUI PEAK. The primary mission of the Battalion was to conduct a diversionary attack by maneuvering west along Route #4 toward the Thuong Duc Special Forces Camp. On 6 October, the Battalion made heavy contact as Company G was sweeping the high ground North of Route #4. The Battalion mission was then changed to search and clear. Operation MAUI PEAK terminated on 19 October and on 23 October 1968, the Battalion began participation in Operation HENDERSON HILL.

Counting the men from Echo Co. that died in the helicopter crash, the actual total KIA for 2/5 was 28, 16 from Echo and 12 from Golf and H&S (headquarters) Co. Ten of the 12 from Golf were from 2nd Platoon.

The number of enemy KIA's vary between the 2/5 and 7th Marines reports. I believe the 7th Marine reports are more accurate since it was the 7th that was in charge of the operation. That report gives a total of: 52 VC KIA, 316 NVA KIA, and 6 POW.

We got back to An Hoa somewhere between the 18th and the 19th, for a brief rest and resupply of newbies, beans and bullets. To me, the most egregious statement in the records for 2/5 in October was:

> Treatment of Casualties and Hospitalization:
> There were no significant problems encountered during Operation MAUI PEAK.

I think that speaks for itself, and from the point of view of the ordinary grunt, it's nothing less than what was expected from our leadership. If I could say anything to the Officers at the top, I would say:

"Try telling that to all the Marines who were killed or wounded, with horrible pain and loss of limbs. Like the fourteen men killed in that terrible helicopter crash or the ten men from our Platoon that were killed on Maui Peak or David Lopez with his leg blown off or Chesty Puller's son, struggling to survive from wounds and lost limbs."

"No significant problems encountered," indeed! I guess I wasn't the only one who had turned numb in the face of all the combat. Still, how much combat did the writer of that statement really experience? Had he really become that jaded? In his defense, I guess he was just reporting the facts as he saw them. The god of war is a real cold-hearted bastard. Looking back, I'm very glad I didn't know at the time what the Battalion really thought of us. Yet, what could be said when the normal state of things were dead and severely wounded Marines and the business of the Corps was Death.

The brief rest was over. Some of our wounded had returned to the Platoon, one of which was Mike Ervin. It was October 23rd, and we were starting out on Operation Henderson Hill. Absent from my machine gun squad were Tom Thomas, who had received word that his mother was dying of cancer and he was going home to be with her. And of course, David Lopez, my good buddy who lost his leg on Maui Peak. Mike Copeland, who was rotating back to the states, also left. Mike did a hell of a job as the machine gun squad leader and he was lucky to have made it out alive. I took over the machine gun squad and prepared for Henderson Hill. I was also assigned as the machine gun section leader in Weapons Platoon.

The members of my squad were not green newbies anymore and some had even seen action in the August 18th fight, where Golf lost several men. Therefore, with that fight and Maui Peak under their belt, I was confident in most of them. They still had much to learn, but by now, they had gained a appreciation for the things that might save their lives and the lives of their brothers in the Platoon. There was some dope smoking in the squad and in the Platoon before I became squad leader and I made sure that the men knew that would not be tolerated in my squad, period. With Thomas and Lopez gone, I reorganized the Squad for what I hoped would be the best results. The squad consisted of the following:

Myself as Squad Leader
1st Gun Team: LCpl. Reyes - 1st gun team leader and gunner
Pfc. Parker - A-gunner
LCpl. Lockett - Ammo Humper
Pfc. Hornfeck - Ammo Humper
Pfc. Ho - Ammo Humper

2nd Gun Team: Pfc. Marsh - 2nd gun team leader and gunner
Pfc. Warner - A-gunner
Pfc. Dawes - Ammo Humper
Pfc. Cannady - Ammo Humper

I was really lonely these days, especially with Thomas and Lopez gone. All my "old breed" were killed, or sent to other units, or wounded and sent home. It was a real strange feeling. If it hadn't been for my responsibility of the machine gun squad, I don't know what would have happened. As it was, I sucked it up, took charge and "Marined On." Still, that dead spot in me was growing ever larger. I cared for my men, but I never again had any close buddies and have found it difficult to have close friends ever since.

Back to my squad, LCpl. Reyes was wounded during the August 18 firefight. He got shot and the bullet cut a groove across his right forearm from his wrist to his elbow. He would return to the squad during Operation Henderson Hill and show off his scar, which was a puffy line of skin with the holes from the stitches still visible. He was one great Marine as was his counterpart in the 2nd gun team, Pfc. Marsh. Marsh was a Native American and we all called him "Chief." One of the few Marines I knew with a nickname. Most of the men in the squad did a very good job, and I remember them well, but have been unable to contact them in these after years. As Johnnie Clark wrote in his book *Gun's Up!:* ".... I never knew any 0331's in the Fifth Marines who were not killed or wounded." Yep, being a machine gunner was a very dangerous job.

On October 21st, I wrote:

Dear Mom,

Well, I'm back off of that operation finally. The name of it was [Maui] Peak and boy was it a dilly. There's no use going into the operation itself, you should be able to read about it. From what I understand, it was the only operation going on in Nam at the time, and naturally the 5th Marines was it. It has been raining and windy ever since the 1st of Oct., and up on the hill we took we were all constantly wet and cold. I've got some jungle rot from it and have been a little under the weather, but everything being taken into consideration I'm all right. There is no telling when I'll be out in the field again, all I can do is take advantage of the time my company has here in the rear and hope we don't go on any more opp's. The Monsoon Season has really set in now and everyone is suffering from it. But it will be over around January, and it won't be too long after that till I'm home. So much for the front. ...

Oh, I got your package and Cathy's and Chris' all when I got off that operation and boy have I been chowing down. That chili sure hit the spot, plus all the other goodies. Cathy sent some cookies and soda water. That pop sure was an inspiration on her part, let me tell you. ...

Oh, before I close, I might as well let you know that I am up for Corporal again. The reason I didn't get it in the 27th was because they weren't making any more Corporals after June, so that was that. But I stand a good chance of getting it this time, God willing. …

With all my love, Chuck

October 22nd seems to have been letter-writing day. First I wrote:

Dear Chris,

I bet you have been wondering when this dirty old Marine was going to write again weren't you. Well, I have been busier than a cat on a hot tin roof since I came to the 5th Marines. I just do have time to get an occasional letter written to the family. So please excuse me.

Now let's see, first of all I want to say thanks so much for your monthly package. I always get a real lift and laugh out of those funnies and the Mad magazine. …

If you have any buddies who are wondering about what to do as far as the military service is concerned, just tell them that it is 100% better to go in the Service for only 2 years and then make their way in the world. Of course I'd hate to see any of the boys back home come over here, especially you, but everyone should do their part and hopefully this war will be over by the time you graduate from high school. …

Your Pal & Brother, Chuck

I also wrote:

Dear Dad,

Well, Dad, it looks like I've finally gotten [around] to writing you; last, but surely not least. I hope I can get this written before we move out again. So far the word is that we are supposed to go out again any day now, for some kind of opp in the [Arizona] Territory which is about 5 miles due north of An Hoa. There is supposed to be an [awful] lot of N.V.A. there and I suppose that we will be expected to wipe em all out. Good old Gungy Golf. It sure would be nice to stay out of the shit for a while, but "fight" is the 5th Marines pet word. Oh well, what can I say.

I'm glad that something is being done about your trouble with the V.A. I know it may be a while before things get cleared up but it is sure worth the fight, egh. I know I sure hope the V.A. will take care of me if anything happens over here. I'm giving a year of my life and I figure that they should be able to give a little money. …

Say, that sounds like a great idea about that book. Believe it or not I have had that same idea in mind now for quite some time, but I just never

get around to it. I guess I'll have to wait till I'm an old man, egh! You know, like a year or so from now. …
With all my love, Your Son, Chuck

These were the last letters I wrote for about a week or so. We kicked off Operation Henderson Hill shortly after writing these letters. Once again, my evaluation of Golf 2/5 was based upon the little guy looking up the chain of command. We all griped like hell about all the operations we were on. Of course the main reason for our discontent was the constant combat and exposure to near-death experiences. We just couldn't get a break. At the same time, we looked forward to contact with the enemy because once that happened, all other thoughts disappeared and we could just concentrate on fighting. Not too mixed up, egh!

Another look at those letters and I realize that there was no mention of the actual combat that I had been in since the 6th of October. I just couldn't write about that any more.

Operation Henderson Hill is best described in an overall view in *The Defining Year 1968*:

> Operation Mameluke Thrust ended on 23 October, after five months, with the participating units reporting 2,730 enemy killed, 47 prisoners, and 8 ralliers [ralliers were VC who had turned themselves in using the Chu Hoi Program, turning VC into friendly forces]. As the 5th Marines closed Mameluke Thrust, it opened Operation Henderson Hill in the same AO [Area of Operation]. The net result of this was a continuation of the same operation, in the same area, under a new operational codename. Lieutenant Colonel Stemple remembered that the 2nd Battalion, 5th Marines had returned to the An Hoa sector after Maui Peak, and on the 23d , his battalion command group and two of his companies were patrolling the area east of Liberty Road, when he received word to disengage. The Marines boarded trucks and returned to An Hoa where Stemple was met by Major General Youngdale and several members of the 1st Marine Division staff. According to Stemple, the division commander told him that a new NVA regiment, the 90th, was suspected of having moved into the Arizona Territory and that there had been numerous sightings of enemy troops in the area. After a quick aerial reconnaissance, Stemple and the MAG-16 helicopter coordinator selected a primary and secondary landing zone. While

enemy small arms fire prevented the landing in the primary zone, the Marine battalion reached its assigned objectives in the Arizona before nightfall, but no indication of the reported large numbers of North Vietnamese troops. In a series of sweeps as part of Henderson Hill during the next few days, both the 2d and 3d Battalions of the 5th Marines developed little enemy contact, but captured a 24 page document describing the enemy's proposed "Winter-Spring 1968-69 Campaign." The operation then continued in the An Hoa and Go Noi Island sectors into November. ....

By the records, the casualty count for Mameluke Thrust, which ended on 23 October was:

Results

These figures reflect cumulative figures for Operation MAMELUKE THRUST:

USMC Personnel

133 USMC KIA, 2 USMC NCB KIA, 744 USMC WIA EVAC, 147 USMC WIA MINOR, 1 USMC MIA, 61 USMC NBC EVAC, 4 USMC NBC MINOR

From *The Defining Year 1968*:

In Operation Henderson Hill, the 5th Marines surrounded and attacked the NVA *1st Battalion, 36th Regiment* at the familiar battlefield of Chau Phong, site of so many earlier engagements. Uncharacteristically, the enemy did not defend, but rather attempted to escape, the NVA troops donning disguises, hiding their weapons, and attempting to slip through Marine lines in the dark.

On 16 November, the enemy went on the offensive around Da Nang, conducting ground attacks and firing 122mm rockets at Da Nang Airbase and the port, one of which scored a direct hit on the deep-water pier, killing 2 people and wounding 16 others. Within the city, several small firefights erupted, in which Free World non-communist security units captured seven prisoners claiming to belong to the *Q.91 Special Action Sapper Unit*. North of the city, near the Song Cu De, North Vietnamese forces overran and annihilated a seven-man ambush team from the 1st Battalion, 26th Marines. The dead Marines all suffered bullet wounds to the head inflicted at close range, in execution fashion. At the opposite end of the Da Nang TAOR, at the Vinh Dien Bridge north of Dien Ban, elements of the NVA *36th Regiment* attacked ARVN bridge security units and a Combined Action platoon. In heavy fighting that lasted through the following day, the Marine command reported 305 North Vietnamese dead.

The enemy offensive around Da Nang continued for several days. In an indirect fire attack during the night of the 19th, 13 rockets fell on the Force Logistic Command, and another 12 struck the city. At Marble Mountain Air Facility, mortar fire also struck the NSA Hospital. On the morning of the 21st, 10 rockets hit the 1st Marine Division command post, killing 2 American soldiers and destroying a helicopter and 2 jeeps.

During the night of the 21st, an enemy battalion attacked An Hoa. Supported by fire from 82mm and 60mm mortars, 57mm recoilless rifles and B-40 rockets, North Vietnamese and Viet Cong troops advanced against the base's eastern perimeter. When the attack began at 2200, Marine tank and artillery crews on the perimeter began direct fire against the advancing enemy, using "Beehive" [Each "Beehive" projectile contains thousands of tiny darts, called flechettes, which are expelled and thrown forward at high velocity, spreading in a deadly pattern] antipersonnel ammunition. Amphibian tractors arrived and added the weight of their machine guns to the battle.

CAP Combined Action Platoon 2-9-1, positioned in the hamlet of Mau Chanh, about a kilometer east of the base, lay in the path of the attack. The CAP Marines and their PF Popular Forces counterparts took the enemy flanks and rear under fire, calling for air and artillery support. At 2330, the Communist troops fell on CAP 2-9-1. AC-47 gunships held back the enemy while a platoon of Marines mounted in amphibian tractors, with tanks and helicopter gunships escorting, attacked east from An Hoa to reinforce the hamlet and bring an ammunition resupply.

The battle raged for five hours, during which the Marines threw back four waves of attacking NVA and VC. At 0330 the shooting died down. Despite the heavy fighting, friendly casualties numbered only three Marines and a PF with minor wounds. Marine sources listed 21 dead Viet Cong in the area.

The enemy offensive reached a crescendo on the night of 24-25 November. Communist rocket and mortar fire fell on Da Nang Airbase, Marble Mountain Air Facility, the 5th Special Forces Group compound in east Da Nang, and Hoi An. Enemy company-sized

> units carried out ground assaults against Dien Ban, Liberty Bridge, and three bridges spanning the Song Cau Lau and the Song Vinh Dien along Highway 1. U.S. Marines, Korean Marines, and South Vietnamese soldiers fought off the enemy attacks, and 25 November dawned with all of the enemy's objectives still in friendly hands.
>
> The attacks of the 24-25 November were the last gasp of the Communist November offensive. Fifteen kilometers south of Da Nang, in the infamous Dodge City Area, the 1st Marine Division had begun an offensive of its own, the largest "County Fair" operation conducted up to that time: Operation Meade River.

My participation in Operation Henderson Hill, would be limited to the Arizona Territory. The Marine Records for the 5th Marines in October reveal the following:

> At 231200H October 1968, 2nd Battalion (-) (Rein) was helolifted into the Arizona area. There was no initial contact. After one week of extensive patrolling, the Battalion was lifted back to An Hoa and subsequently moved to the vicinity of Go Noi Island. Alternately establishing blocking positions for sweeps by ARVN, ROKMC [Republic Of Korea Marine Corps] and other Marine units, the Battalion attacked to seize and search pockets of enemy resistance.

After we went back into the Go Noi area, we found ourselves by a blown up railroad bridge. We were hot and very dirty, so several of us decided to get a bath in the river. "Chief" Marsh set up his machine gun on the high ground where the bridge had fallen into the river. The whole area was overgrown with high grass and brush, so it was important to have someone on watch at all times. The new guys wanted to jump right in, but I stopped them and told them that this wasn't a swimming hole. They could undress and get in at the edge of the water, wash up and get out. They grumbled about not getting to go deeper in the river, but when I told them that they could only go in knee deep because if they submersed their private parts in the water, they stood a good chance of having a leech crawl up inside their penises, they made sure that that wouldn't happen. It was funny to see the guys that were already in the water. They hopped out of that river like a snake had bit them. After my little advice, no one went in more than ankle deep. I had had plenty of experience with leeches, they had probably sucked out half of my blood by now. I knew of men who had little leeches go up their penises, and they were fully clothed when it happened. Those that wanted to got their baths and we were soon on our way again, back into Go Noi Island. Back to night ambushes and patrols.

Given the losses that 2nd Platoon had received to date, we were top heavy in new guys, including our Platoon Commander and Platoon Sergeant. With most of the experienced squad leaders gone, I was left holding the bag and the Platoon Commander knew it. He hadn't participated in Maui Peak that I know of and no one I have talked to remembers him being there either. I believe he was medevaced as a heat casualty. He was still green as Chinese tea. Whether he had looked at my records or not, I was chosen to run night patrols and hopefully teach others how to set in night ambushes and return without unnecessary losses. From the point of our return from Maui Peak, that Lt. required me to go out on all the patrols where my guns were involved. With two gun teams and one of me, I was kept hopping. Luckily, the VC had chosen to hide rather than fight.

The minimal reports from the rest of the month tell the following:

24Oct68	0630H	Co G Night ambushes returning to CP
	2030H	Co G All night ambushes set in

One incident during this time is remembered by me and Mike Ervin, not long before Mike rotated out of Vietnam. Probably during the first part of November, we were in this grassy clearing with jungle all around and a stream running along the boundary between the brush and the open area. We were there taking a break during Operation Henderson Hill. Even when resting, we were always alert and I had made sure that the machine gun teams had good positions before stopping to rest. They always complained about that, but I had learned my lessons the hard way. In combat, you had to have eyes everywhere, including the back of your head and be ready to fight in an instant. In the States they may call that PTSD, but in Vietnam, it's called Survival, especially against booby traps or unexpected events.

This would be one of those unexpected events. We were all "set in", which meant a place to fight from, and we rested. This was no squad patrol; this was a platoon patrol. Unlike the 27th Marines, Golf 2/5 operated mostly as a whole company, with platoons assigned to different positions in the line of march or sweep. So we were with the whole platoon. Suddenly, like a deer, this VC appeared at the edge of the stream in the open area. He had some Chieu Hoi pamphlets and was waving them over his head. These pamphlets were supposed to be "tickets" for VC to give themselves up. They were written in Vietnamese, Chieu Hoi meant "open arms," and told of the goodness of coming over to the South Vietnamese side. But VC-Charlie and NVA had also learned to use these pamphlets to lure Marines to their death. Most of the platoon was ignorant of all this, being so new in country.

Mike Ervin remembers that there were two Chieu Hoi's - the first one was taken in custody, with the second appearing early the next morning. I don't remember the first one. What I do remember is the hairs going up on the back of my neck and my "combat sense" going off like a fire alarm when the second VC, which I was watching closely, was constantly looking behind him and had this spooky look on his face. Mike remembers seeing me standing tall with my hands on my hips, staring at this VC.

Keeping my eyes on the VC, I told my gunner to get ready to fire and take out that VC at my word. The VC wouldn't come any closer but kept hollering:

"Chieu Hoi, Chieu Hoi."

Suddenly he tried to dart away and after hollering for him to stop, I told the gunner to fire. The gunner was good and took that VC down before he could escape. We didn't receive any incoming fire but we could hear a rustling in the brush like many men running away. A couple of men brought back that VC, who was shot up pretty good. Everyone could see that he wouldn't last long. He was medevaced after being treated by the Corpsman. It had become late in the evening and the Lt. finally decided we would stay and make this our night position.

Our stupid "boot" Lt. came over and asked what all the shooting was about, and started to get in my face about shooting the VC that had run. I had to turn away to keep from flattening him right there. I went to the brush on the other side of the stream, did a little recon (reconnaissance) and returned. I told him that there were signs of several men having been in the brush, and he could go look for himself. It was common for the NVA to set traps using VC as bait and I was sure that the rustling in the bushes was NVA didi-ing (di di mau, a Vietnamese term for "go quickly") out of the area. There was no way to explain all this to the "newbie" Lt. so I just went back to my gun teams. Everyone around, even the new guys, understood the danger we had been in and realized that their bacon was saved, everyone but the angry new lieutenant. Mike and I both knew new guys who just couldn't or wouldn't learn about combat in Vietnam, and we both had carried their bodies off the field of battle in ponchos. Curiosity and/or booby traps usually got them.

These events are recorded in the October records of 2/5 for Operation Henderson Hill:

241700H FOLLOW UP CO G 2/5 CO S&C LOC AT807477. 1 DETAINEE CLASS BY ITT AS 1 NVA RTNE.

At 241700H, while setting into night defensive positions at AT807488, Marines from Company G were approached by a Vietnamese male calling "Chieu Hoi". The Vietnamese was later classified as an NVA. Results: One NVA Chieu Hoi.

At 250705H, an NVA soldier came toward the Company G Command Post at AT807477 in an apparent attempt to Chieu Hoi. He was within 150 meters of the friendly position when he broke and ran in the other direction. He continued to run although ordered to stop, and at the last possible moment the Marines opened fire with small arms. A search team found the NVA wounded near a treeline. Results: One NVA POW.

At 251115H, a platoon from Company G found four bodies estimated to have been dead for a week at AT806466. Of the four, two were VC wearing khaki uniforms over black pajamas. Results: Two VC KIA.

26Oct68 1930H Co G G-1 & G-2 ambushes departing CP

On October 28th, I was able to get a letter off:

Dear Folks,

Well, here I am and there you are. And where am I? Well, I'm back out in the bush on another operation. This one is called Henderson Hill. We left An Hoa on Oct. 22 and there's no telling how long we will be out here. So far so good, we haven't run into anything but a few snipers who can't hit the broad side of a barn. So now you know my situation. Now, how about you all. Is everything [okay]? I hope you all appreciate my efforts in writing everyone individually. That won't happen too often, the way the 5th Marines [operate].

Oh, it stopped raining [around] the 20th, and we have had dry weather now since then, except for a few showers at night. So I don't know if the regular Monsoon season is here yet or not. Oh well, I've got about 4 ½ months to wait for it.

Did my buddy Tom Thomas get to call you all yet? I asked him to call you all collect if he could, to let you know for sure that I'm alright. He is a real good friend of mine, we have been together ever since I.T.R. Infantry Training Regiment. He had to go home on emergency leave because his mother has cancer. …

With all my love, Chuck

Then on October 30, 1968:

0700H	S-3	Bn (-) E, G, H, to be lifted to An Hoa

At the end of October, the Battalion would continue Operation Henderson Hill and start Operation Meade River. The personnel and casualty count in 2nd Battalion, 5th Marines for the end of October was:

The Battalion joined 4 officers and 232 enlisted men during this month. The Battalion transferred six officers and 153 enlisted during the same period. Casualties for the month were:

BATTLE					NON-BATTLE		TOTAL
KIA	WIA	DOW	WIANE	MIA	NBD	NBC	
30	108	0	42	1	0	12	193

The running total since September is:

KIA – 48, WIA – 185, DOW – 3, WIANE – 75, MIA – 1, NBD – 1, NBC – 20, Total – 333

Again, the numbers of Battalion personnel were advancing to the rear. Having transferred 159 officers and enlisted, joined 236 officers and men and lost 193 casualties, the numbers on a whole show that 2/5 was in the hole by 116 men for October and a grand total loss of 222 men since the first of September. It was no wonder that we had so many newbies.

Chapter 14

Operation Meade River started on November 1st, but our participation wouldn't happen until the 20th. From the 1st to the 20th of November, we participated in the end of Operation Henderson Hill.

The monthly reports help to piece the picture together:

> During the period 1 November to 13 November 1968, the Battalion continued its participation in Operation HENDERSON HILL. Alternately establishing blocking positions for sweeps by ARVN, ROKMC and other Marine units, the Battalion attacked to seize and search pockets of enemy resistance uncovering large caches of rice and capturing 11 prisoners.
>
> On 20 November the Battalion under operational control of the First Marines began participation in Operation MEADE RIVER.

> Operation HENDERSON HILL moved to the Northeast part of the 5th Marines TAOR in the opening days of November when Intelligence from S-2, 5th Marines reported elements of the 36th NVA Infantry Regiment working from the west end of Go Noi Island. Light to heavy contact was maintained throughout the period 1 to 12 November. The 2nd Battalion, 5th Marines used as a blocking force, took fourteen detainees, seven of whom under interrogation, established that they were from the 1st Battalion, 36th Regiment, 308 Division (NVA) or support units and had been part of the rice gathering efforts in the area. Intelligence taken in the first days of the sweep of the area indicated that the 2nd Battalion, 36th Regiment was in the east end of Go Noi Island. Flooding of the Go Noi area by monsoon rains reduced the effectiveness of friendly sweeps in the Island. The 2nd Battalion, 5th Marines sweep back to An Hoa Combat Base netted a large amount of rice and assorted documents.

By the 1st of November, we were placed back in the Go Noi Island area where Operation Allen Brook had occurred just a few months earlier. We were still in Operation Henderson Hill, just a different phase.

As stated in the reports, "2nd Battalion, 5th Marines sweep back to An Hoa Combat Base netted a large amount of rice and assorted documents." I contributed to the captured documents.

I had gone out on a night ambush with about ten men. I had one gun team with me, but not from my squad. As section leader I often took a gun team from other squads with me, primarily aimed at breaking them in. Golf Company was still picking up new guys, and they needed to get in the fight too.

It was a night with no clouds and enough moon and starlight to make maneuvering through the jungle just passable - and enough to light you up in the rice paddies. I had done enough night ambushes to have several plans of action. In this case, I chose to skirt around a village we had come upon by first moving across the north side of the village on a well-trod trail, then moving silently through the brush along the west side of the copse of trees that surrounded the village. After stopping for a break, to let the quiet set in, I took the squad along the outer edge of the village along the south end, moving at the edge of the rice paddies that bordered the trees on all sides.

I set up the ambush at the very corner of the trees, just inside the tree line, with the machine gun set up at the point of the ambush facing north. The machine gun position allowed for an unobstructed field of fire for 270 degrees covering the ditch and the rice paddies around us.

The main point of interest was the north-south ditch coming from the village toward the machine gun. I placed the rest of the ambush along a line that ran from the point of the ambush alongside of the trees 90 degrees from the ditch. I positioned myself along with the radioman close to the M-60, with the others spaced out facing in alternate directions so they could cover our back and anyone moving through the trees. One last preparation was to have the machine gunner take all the tracer rounds out of his first belt to prevent the enemy from immediately pinpointing his position. That gave him the edge of having almost 100 rounds to fire before the tracers started up from extra ammo, if it was needed. Reminding everyone to be quiet, I had the radioman turn down the volume on the radio before settling down myself. It was common procedure for an officer or NCO to track our progress at night. Periodically, they would call asking our status. We replied by squeezing the talk button on the handset - one squeeze for yes, two for no.

No other voice communication would occur unless it was necessary, mainly for calling in artillery or mortars.

All settled in, the quiet and still of the night set in and the wait was on. I had previously informed the men of my ambush rules, which were: no smoking, breathe softly, relax but stay alert. If they felt sleepy, I told them to just imagine a gook sneaking up on you and slitting your throat while you slept. That last one usually did the trick. I concentrated on the gunner and told him not to open up unless he knew for sure that someone was coming toward him, and focus on that ditch. With the moonlight the way it was, the ditch I was focused on was in shadow and all we could do was go by sound.

I was tired and fighting off sleep. The night wore on and on. Every once and a while I would touch the man next to me and he would repeat that touch down the line. Even if someone was napping, that touch in the dark would wake them up, afraid that Charlie had found them and was fixing to cut their throat. It was hard to be alert, but we were making progress. It wasn't like we got to sleep in before we went out at night. I preferred the short ambushes on a night patrol. Everyone stayed awake on patrols.

Another problem on ambushes like this was how to deal with bodily urges. Taking a crap usually wasn't a problem because we normally didn't have anything in our stomachs. Besides, our nerves kept things tightened up pretty good. It was having to take a leak that posed a real problem. The only way to solve that was to take small sips on your canteen when absolutely necessary, or suck on a rock to keep your mouth from drying up. If you really had to pee you had to kneel in place, scoop out a little hole, relieve yourself and cover the hole back up. In the mountains and rocky areas, all you could do was just pee and get it over with. The main thing was to do all that as quietly as possible. Sound travels like a beacon at night and if you give away your position you can be ambushed yourself.

The night wore on.

I was getting sleepy.

Several hours later, about 0200 hours, I was again fighting sleep, when the machine gunner suddenly touched my shoulder. I instantly lost my sleepiness and passed the touch down the line. As I was busy alerting the rest of the ambush, the gunner opened up. He was firing straight up the ditch with several bursts from the gun. No incoming rounds were fired at us, so I signaled the gunner to cease-fire. He was so high on adrenaline that he kept firing another burst before he eased off the trigger. He was as wild eyed as anything I had ever seen in Vietnam. He said:

"I got 'em, I got 'em!"

What to do now? If we got up to leave or tried to go back to the CP in the dark after having pinpointed our own position, we would certainly have a fight on our hands. One thing for sure, we couldn't stay here.

I gathered the squad around me and explained that we had to move, but very quietly. We couldn't go into the trees, because we would be expected to do something like that. The only place to go was into the rice paddies. I was hoping to find a place to hide in plain sight. I didn't give the squad time to figure it out, I just told them to crouch down and follow me.

I took them out 90 degrees from the main ditch into the rice paddy. It was not in use and the stubble from the rice was still there. About 75 yards into the paddy, I found what I was looking for. My feet detected a depression in the ground and I had everyone lay down in the stubble. I formed them in a circle, flat on their stomachs, facing straight ahead from their positions. Like the spokes of a wheel. I had the gunner set up facing the tree line that we had just left, watching for anyone moving in the ditch.

Hide in plain sight! It had worked before and hopefully it would work again. The key was silence, absolute silence. I passed the word around that every other man could get some sleep, with a rotation of half an hour. I had to get the men to relax, but still be ready. They all got the message loud and clear and performed beautifully. I don't think anybody slept at all that night. I turned to the radioman and told him to turn his radio off. He didn't want to at first, but I told him that even the click of the handset could give us away. We agreed that he would make a quick, quiet call to the CP, telling them that we were turning the radio off. Click, that was that. We could always turn the radio back on if we needed it.

I had been in similar situations before, and the powers that be in the CP would always bug me to death wanting a sit rep (situation report). That was when I found the courage to turn the radio off. A big no-no, but my life and the lives of my men meant more to me than appeasing some officer in the rear.

Before early dawn we heard some noise in the trees, but no movement in that ditch. The VC never even thought to look in the rice paddy. Laying there in the pale light, not moving, it would be hard for anyone to spot us, if they even bothered to look our way. The depression we were in kept us just low enough. The rest of the night passed quietly. The movement in the trees faded out and we waited for dawn to arrive.

Sucking on rocks, staying as still as possible, I waited. As the first rays of light shone down on us and the trees, I could see that everything was still quiet over at the ditch. Charlie must have been really confused about our whereabouts, and probably thought that we had somehow melted back into the woods. At any rate, once dawn was in full bloom, I had the men ready themselves for an online assault to the ditch. I told the radioman to turn on his radio and call in and explain what we were doing, but cautioned them not to call us. We were way overdue from the ambush return time, and I didn't want anyone to come bulling their way through the bush looking for us. All that would accomplish was the possibility of them running into a VC ambush.

With weapons at the ready, we approached the ditch. Once there, the machine gunner went right to a spot where he thought a body should be, unless the VC had hauled it off. He was real close, I mean real close and it wasn't long before he found the body. There was only one body there, but a couple of blood trails could be seen leading into the trees. I had this sense that the VC had left, so I had a few men track the blood trails, but not go too deep into the jungle. They returned and said that the trails had ended. Someone must have hauled them off. Security was still important, so I formed a perimeter around the ditch.

Turning back to the body, I flipped it over and noticed that this was no VC. He was way too tall and muscular to be a Vietnamese. He was oriental though. Searching his clothes, I came across some papers and even a photograph of what looked like his wife and kid. I didn't feel anything about that, I just put it with all the other papers and put them in the pockets of my jungle shirt.

This was something different. My guess was that he was Chinese. I decided to take the body back with us to the CP. I had a couple of guys cut a stout bamboo pole about 10 feet long and we strung him on the pole by his arms and legs, using lengths of cloth that we had cut from his clothes. The body was very heavy. Dead weight. I assigned two men to carry the body and on the way back we rotated on the pole. It was difficult to carry the body and try to be quiet on our way back. I rarely took bodies back from an ambush, it was just too difficult. However, in this case I made an exception because of the Chinese connection.

Trying to keep our progress as safe as possible, I took the squad off the trails and through the bush. At times it was hard going, but much safer. As we neared the CP, we stopped and I had the radioman call in. He made contact, and I told the CP that we were coming in at coordinates that were different from the original route of the ambush. They acknowledged and we moved out again. Before entering the CP, I got on the horn again and told them that I would pop a red-white-red flare combination from our position, and for them not to shoot us.

The gooks must have been really spooked by the "phantom ambush", because we had no problems returning to the CP. Once inside the Company Command Post, we turned the body over to the officers as well as the documents we had recovered. Tired to the bone, we went back to our positions in the line and fell asleep. The captain or somebody must have had some pity for us, because we didn't move that day. The following day, we were surrounded by our buddies, asking all kinds of questions. We answered as best we could, as we squared away again waiting for orders to move out. I don't remember any "well dones" from any of the officers.

This incident is not in any records that I can find, and I believe that it was kept quiet because of the Chinaman we had killed. Everyone knew that the Chinese had "advisers" in Vietnam, but it was not officially acknowledged because of the fear that China would get involved in the war more that they were. So, our accomplishment passed into the annals of history, not to surface again until written about in this book.

The activities of Golf Co. 2/5 is reported in the daily reports:

> DTG 011537, G 2/5 Co S&C Loc AT960506. USMC Det M-26 Grn Sur Expl Dev . Res: 1 USMC WIA Evac.

Translated, it reads:

On Day Time Group, 1 November, at 1537 hours, Golf Co., 2/5 on a Search and Clear operation located at map coordinates 960506, a Marine detonated an M-26 grenade surprise explosive device. Result: 1 Marine WIA was evacuated.

Continuing with the November reports:

> At 011510H, while attacking Northwest at AT966506, Company G received small arms and automatic weapons fire, seven B-40 rockets and eight 60mm rounds from an estimated platoon of NVA in a fortified village. Company G returned small arms, automatic weapons and M-79 fire and 24 rounds of 60mm HE. Four flights of fixed wing aircraft and a 105mm artillery mission of 17 rounds HE supported the company. Results: One USMC WIA Evac and three USMC WIA Non-Evac.

011510 (FOLLOW UP) 2/5 CO G CO S&C LOC AT966506, BECAUSE WOUNDS WERE SUSTAINED DURING CONTACT WITH ENEMY UPDATE TO READ: 1 USMC WIA EVAC VICE 1 NBC EVAC.

011537 Co G 2/5 Co S&C Loc AT960506. While conducting S&C OPNS, USMC det M-26 grenade set with trip wire as Surprise Explosive Device. Med-Evac called. Res: 1 USMC WIA Evac.

At 012030H, Company G at AT976510 received seven rounds of 60mm HE. Returned fire of 36 rounds of 105mm HE resulted in three secondary explosions at AT071517.

020125H 2/5 Co G Co def posit loc AT987510. Unit had 60mm rd to fall short on friendly posit wounding 3 USMC. Rd was apparently defective as it was 8th of 10 rd volley. All other rds on target. Unit called Med-Evac. Res: 3 USMC NBC Evac.

020125H (follow up) 2/5 Co G Co def posit loc AT987510. Because wounds were sustained during contact with enemy update to read: 3 USMC WIA Evac vice 3 NBC Evac.

021229H 2/5 CP loc AT971507. While sweeping area, unit found 7 tons rice and 1 NVA SP [Special Purpose] Pack. Rice destroyed because unit was pursuing enemy.

Golf was operating with the Battalion Command Post and it was during this time that many more discoveries were made. Continuing information from the records:

030745H 2/5 CP def posit loc AT976523. VN male walked into CP claiming knowledge of VC/NVA movement in the area. Man to be forwarded to Regt S-2. Res: 1 male detainee.

031700H Co E, F, G, 2/5 Co's S&C loc AT975514. At AT975514, units found 1 M-14 SN#425234 and 1 bolt action IWC of unk type. Also found 1 NVA Pack, 3 cases Korean beer, 500 lbs of sardines and canned meat, 50 pints can milk, 2 five gal water cans, 100 lbs blasting cps for chicom grenades, 89 chicom grenades, 1 M-26 grenade, 11 chicom grenades without blasting caps, 30 chicom stoppers, 100 ft NVA time fuse, 1 chicom grenade pack, 1 NVA song book, and 2200 lbs rice. Fwd to Bn S-2.

031720H Co CP 2/5 Co S&C loc AT987507. While resupply with 81mm ammo being unloaded, CH-46 helo released net before pallet reached the ground. Pallet rolled down side of hill striking 1 USMC. Man Med-Evaced on CH-46 to DaNang. Res: 1 USMC NBC Evac.

After three days of Search and Clear (S&C) operations, it was obvious that we were making progress in rooting out enemy supplies. It also shows the unknown dangers from our own evolutions, like mortar attacks against the enemy and simple resupply operations. There was just no safe place anywhere in Vietnam.

Continuing on with reports from the records:

> 040600H 2/5 – Co G and Co E attack north from Chiem Son (3) (BT0157) to Song Chiem Son (BT015523).
>
> 051530H Co G 2/5 Co S&C loc BT015519. While conducting S&C opns, unit found 1500 lbs of polished rice loc at above coord. Will fwd to Regt CP.
>
> At 051600H, a Marine from Company G detonated a booby trapped grenade with pressure type detonator at BT015518. Results: One USMC WIA Evac.
>
> 051810 Co G 2/5 Co S&C loc BT013510. While sweeping area, unit found 5000 lbs rice loc at above coord. Fwd to Regt CP.
>
> 2/5 – Co F and Co G attack north to destroy enemy forces in Regt Obj Twelve (BT000545)
>
> At 061715H, a Marine from Company G detonated a booby trapped ChiCom grenade with trip wire while clearing fields of fire for night positions at AT980525. Results: One USMC WIA Evac.
>
> 2/5 – Co E and Co G maintain blocking positions from At9854 along south bank of Song Thu Bon to BT0250 in support of seventh Mar opns.
>
> November 7th: 2/5 – Co G blocks south of Song KY Lam from AT980540 east to BT020550, front north, in supp opt of 7th Marines.

Once again, the SFDs (Special Firing Devices) and SED's (Special Explosive Devices) were haunting our company as well as all those involved in this operation. Given the monthly influx of new men into the company and an obvious lack of experience in detecting these devices, more casualties ensued.

On November 7th I managed to send another letter home:

Dear Dad,

Well, here I am and there you are, but once again I bet you don't know where I am. That operation Henderson Hill ended for us on the 31st and the next day we were back out in the bush. I don't know the name of this opp, but it is in the same place that operation Allenbrook was in. Your letter was the first one I've gotten in a good week or so, so I decided to try and get a letter off to you so you could relax your fingers for the few minutes it takes to read this letter. But cross 'em back right after you are through, because I only have about 118 days left, and anything can happen.

Say, that description you had of me was sure accurate, but you left out one thing, SCARED. With a little less than 4 months left to do I am really watching my p's and q's.

That idea about the rock in the boot sounds real good, and believe you me, the shorter I get the more ideas I get on how to get out of the field. But I am now Section Leader & Squad Leader with a bunch of "boots" to take care of, so I figure it will be at least 2 more months before I can see my way clear to try and stay in the rear. I've got a job to do so I might as well do it. Besides, I've got the Good Lord on my side so I needn't worry too much. …

Well, I guess I've just about talked myself out, so I'll sign off, but before I do let me mention one thing. You were talking about how bad the wet weather can be, and of course I agree wholeheartedly. But you do remember saying that the [mildew] keeps the tents bullet proof. Well, let me fill you in on something. I haven't built a tent in 2 months. We move everyday almost and can't put up a tent, because the tent just gives the position of our fox hole away. You must remember that here in Viet Nam we get hit from any and all directions. That's why we set in in a circle so we can watch all sides. So take away the tents and wrap up in a leaky poncho that is too short and that's how I live in the rain. It's been so long since I've had a roof over my head that I'll probably sleep outside when I first get home. Yea, I MIGHT, But I Kinda DOUBT IT.

Well, Dad, I guess I will go now. I just want to let you know that I sure enjoy your letters and get just enough extra strength from them to keep going. Till the next time,

With all my love, Your Son, Chuck

In the confusion of moving around all the time I hadn't realized that when we entered the Go Noi Island area, we were still on Operation Henderson Hill. I couldn't say for sure if being Section Leader and Squad Leader kept me steady or not, but I did take the job very seriously. As Section Leader, I had about 27 men to look after - my own squad and two others, which were assigned to the 1st and 3rd Platoons. Mainly I looked after them when we were in the rear, or when I was needed for some reason. I didn't interfere with the other machine gun squad leaders unless I needed to advise them on tactics while we were operating with the whole company. However, whenever possible, I would take out as many new guys as I could to give them some of my experience, which was the case when my ambush got that Chinaman. My squad was with me at all times and I worried over them like a mother hen. I don't guess they knew how I anguished over their safety, but they didn't need to, that was my job. Part of that responsibility meant that I stood up for them at all times, usually to the displeasure of my platoon commander.

One such incident occurred during Operation Henderson Hill. We were set in close to a graveyard. The Vietnamese buried their dead in the Buddhist fashion, sitting up, so the graves were mounds of dirt over the bodies with prayer sticks stuck in the tops.

Without any other thoughts, I placed the number one gun team at a large grave and told them to dig it out to form a horseshoe position, leaving as much dirt in front as possible. The gun was placed with the bipods down on top of the rim of the grave/foxhole. No one complained. This was live or die and we all wanted to live.

Pfc. Parker, LCpl. Reyes' A-gunner, was the gunner in that position. I don't remember where Reyes was, but I have a picture of him at that blown-up railroad bridge so he must have been gone for some other reason. Anyway, Parker was new on the gun and nervous, which could be expected. The gun team numbered four men who dug positions out of the graves around the gun. The rest of the Platoon was in a circle around the graveyard and the number 2 gun was placed about 180 degrees from the 1st team.

Our position was by a small swift river, which was the boundary of our area. We had no way of crossing the river so any VC shot over there stayed there. The number 1 gun team faced the river and the number 2 team faced the open area beyond the graveyard.

Our platoon leader had not said that he planned to spend the night there, so the riflemen didn't bother to dig holes. At least the newbies didn't. The more experienced men dug shallow fighting holes, myself included. The Platoon Commander and radioman were checking lines when a sniper cut loose on our position. When I looked in the direction the shots came from, I could see the top of an old pagoda sticking up above the trees on the other side of the river, and figured that that was where the shots came from. The sniper didn't hit anyone and he did more to shake up the Lt. than anything else. Before I could move, the Lt. ran over to Parker's machine gun position and screamed at him to take out the sniper. Parker, being new on the gun and shook up by the Lieutenant's screaming, tried to direct some fire on the pagoda, but he was too nervous to be effective. It takes some terrible lessons to learn to be cool under fire and Parker just wasn't there yet, at least not with the gun. The screaming didn't help either.

I arrived at the gun position shortly after the Lt. did and watched Parker as he fired. The sniper must have figured that he had it made because he popped off another round and when he did, I could see a small movement at the top of the pagoda. Suddenly, the Lt. turned on me and hollered, "Why can't your guns hit anything?" or something like that. Actually, what he said must have been much worse, because it caused me to grab the M-60 out of Parker's hands and take a bead on that pagoda. The next time I saw movement I fired some bursts. You could see the top of the pagoda give off little puffs of dust as the rounds struck home. The sniper fire stopped and most people breathed easy. I handed the gun back to Parker not saying a word and stomped off to my hole.

I couldn't believe that that stupid little red-headed shrimp of a Lt. could get me to do that. I felt terrible about taking the gun from Parker, knowing that I may have just ruined any self-confidence he had with the gun, and I was determined to apologize to him in front of everyone to help him gain his self-respect. I was beyond any care for my own image. What could they do, "Send me to Vietnam?"

As I stewed behind a bush by my hole, I spied the Lt. and radioman moving across my front and the next thing I knew, the radioman running behind the Lt. had his antenna shot off. I heard the call, "Sniper! Sniper!" but I knew that that was no sniper shot. I came back to myself only to realize what had happened. I knew that that son-of-a-b Lieutenant had pushed me too far. As a result, I swore to myself that I'd never let anyone push me into taking a gun from a gunner or react in anger, no matter how much I might want to. I did apologize to Parker and my men and told them that that would never happen again. Still steaming, I walked away and the matter was over. My men had my back and that was enough for me.

This was the first time in Vietnam where I lost it like that. I had lost it before against the enemy and attacked them like a mad dog, but never our own men. All this really sobered me up and the memory stayed with me and helped me keep calm during other similar times in the future.

I'm not condoning my behavior, and I understand the necessity for strict obedience to orders in the Corps, but I also know that I have a right to speak up if those orders are not conducive to accomplishing the mission at hand or unnecessary danger to my men. I also think that it's the job of officers to lead Marines, not push them unnecessarily. I was an experienced combat Marine after all, not some private in Boot Camp.

November 8th through the 10th would find us on blocking force duty and on the 11th, we started to make a sweep from AT9851 to AT9550. Note that when map coordinates only list two sets of two numbers as in AT9851, it is understood that the first set of two numbers it the longitude and the second set is the latitude.

November 11th would be a busy day. The records report:

> 110920H 2/5 Co G Plat S&C loc AT975503. Unit found 4 M-26 gren rigged with trip wire as surprise explosive device. Unit destroyed in place.
>
> 111015H 2/5 Co G Co S&C loc AT971516. Unit found 66 hundred pound bags of rice. Rice to be forwarded to An Hoa.
>
> 111300H 2/5 Co G Co S&C loc AT971516, 964515, 963507. Unit found 74 hundred pound bags of rice at above loc. Unit will forward to An Hoa.
>
> 111600H 2/5 Co G Co S&C loc AT971516. Unit found a total of 301 hundred pound bags of rice at above loc for 11 Nov. Rice awaiting trans to An Hoa.
>
> 111900H 2/5 Co H&S Co def posit loc AT875483. USMC rec'd wounds from blasting cap of claymore mine. USMC treated at BAS.

That last note from the records sure struck home. I remember the incident or one just like it very well. We had stopped for the night and were setting up a perimeter. My hole was just behind one of my gun positions and close to the perimeter line. I saw this Marine go out with a Claymore in one hand and a blasting cap and wire in the other. My view was such that I could see both the Marine going out and his buddy still at the foxhole. I glanced at the Marine placing the Claymore and suddenly, there was a small explosion. The blasting cap had gone off in his hand, blowing off most of his fingers and part of his hand. It was a bloody mess.

Quickly, I looked toward the foxhole and saw that the Marine there was holding the jack-box with the wire attached, looking shocked. The jack-box, or squeezebox, was a small electrical generator that would produce an electrical charge capable of igniting a blasting cap at the other end of the wire. It was small enough to be handled with one hand. The normal procedure when setting out a Claymore mine was to first take the Claymore and the blasting cap and wire out to the position to be defended. Unfolding the legs on the Claymore, it would be stuck in the ground with the outside of the curve facing the enemy. The blasting cap would be pushed on the end of the wire and placed into the Claymore. The last step would be to unroll the wire, laying it on the ground and covering it with dirt until you reached the foxhole. In the foxhole, the wire would be split and the ends attached to the jack-box, making it operational. All that had to be done then was to squeeze the box, setting off the Claymore. For safety sake, we usually left one wire off of the box until nightfall, and if not used that night, we would again take a wire off of the box in the morning. In daylight, it was easy enough to re-attach the wire for use.

My best guess as to what happened is that the Marine in the foxhole was a newbie. Not thinking, he attached both wires to the box and then he either thought to test it, which would have meant he was fresh out of the States or, after attaching the wires, he tossed the box into the hole and it hit just right to cause a charge to be sent to the blasting cap. Luckily, the cap hadn't been placed in the Claymore yet. If it had, probably the only thing left would have been the fingers. Of course, had the Marine who took the Claymore out also taken the wire with him, as prescribed, none of this would have happened. Combat is a dangerous profession, not only from the enemy but also from friendlies. Mistakes happen all the time.

Additional reports continue:

> At 121300H, a Marine from Company G detonated an unknown type explosive device with trip wire at AT965514. Results: One USMC WIA Evac.
>
> 121320H 2/5 Co G Co S&C Loc AT961510 to AT971517. Unit found 4 ½ to 5 tons of rice at above Loc. Unit destroyed 600 Hundred Pounds. Other to be sent to An Hoa.
>
> 2/5 – BN CONTINUES SWEEP SW ALONG HIGHGROUND VIC AT920460. RETURNS TO AN HOA TO REHAB AND PREPARE FOR FUTURE OPNS.

The booby traps continued. At this point there was a "rehabilitation" of our battalion - we had to shave all facial hair and have good old "high and tight" haircuts. We were re-outfitted with some new gear and marched and treated like we were stateside Marines in ITR (Infantry Training Regi-ment). Part of this rehabilitation involved doing boot camp style drills and exercises. It seemed like there was no consideration given to Marines like myself who by this time had lost at least 20% of our body weight, suffered with jungle rot and trench foot and had been living in rags, which is the best description of the ripped, torn and dry-rotted uniforms we fought and died in. What we really needed was a lot of rest. Yet our leadership didn't see things that way and so we never got "rehabilitated." We just got more tired and more angry.

One perfect example of this was the time we were told that the Battalion was going on a forced march up this hill behind An Hoa, and a steep one at that. I am almost sure that it was the whole Battalion, because I remember this long long line of men, four abreast, marching up and down that hill, with one group coming down as another was going up. I got real tired and didn't try to push it like they wanted, I just didn't have the energy. In fact, most of us who had been in Nam for a good while were in such poor shape that we should have been in bed resting instead of hiking up and down a hill. When I left the States for Vietnam, I weighed 170 lbs and was strong and healthy. When I left Vietnam, thirteen months later, I weighed 140 lbs and was physically worn out.

The newbies, fresh from the States, had no problem, in their clean dungarees and new polished boots. Anyway, myself and many other of the "old guys" fell behind and decided not to be pushed around. We wound up at the tail end of the march and caught hell for it, but the body can only do what the body can do. I don't remember any Senior NCOs who had been in country as long as we had that participated in the march. My main misfortune was that I wasn't an NCO yet. I was a Lance Corporal, given the position and responsibility of a Sergeant, and wouldn't be considered an NCO until I made Corporal. It was just like the training in the States with healthy "gung ho" NCOs running the march. We eventually came down off that hill and went on about our business. Didn't help much if I wanted to make Corporal but at the time I couldn't do better. The one thing that the bright guy that thought up this training failed to understand was "adrenaline." In battle, we always kept going, as fast as we could, our adrenaline was up and our lives were at stake. I never knew any Marines who wouldn't do whatever it took to get the job done in combat. Part of that was pride, part fear and part anger. Often, if we faltered, we died. But this hill hump wasn't combat in any shape or form, it was just misery for no apparent reason.

I understand the problem in the Battalion having a large input of green Marines who hadn't learned to be mean yet. In my humble opinion, everyone would have been better served by treating the combat Marines with more consideration and given the NCO's who knew what was going on in

Vietnam a better chance at training their own troops instead of taking on the job at the Battalion level.

I guess I have gone on about this long enough, but I hope someone in the Marine Corps understands this and treats the troops with more respect. My feeling is that they do and that the current batch of young combat experienced Marines in Iraq and Afghanistan are better served than we were.

We stayed in An Hoa from the 12th through the 19th and on the 20th, the Battalion was attached to the 1st Marine Regiment to participate in Operation Meade River.

On November 15th, I wrote:

Dear Chris,

Well, believe it or not, it's me again. I just got out of the field [finally] yesterday and it looks like we may be here a day or two, so I decided to try and drop everyone a line. ... I got your package while I was out on that opp, but didn't get to read them until the other day. I sure worked hard to keep the funnies and all dry, and it sure was worth it. I especially liked the stories in that Boys Life. They were real good, did you read the one about the fullback who didn't want to hurt anyone? It sure was good.

Here it is the 16th, and I'm bound and determined to finish this letter. Right now, we are busy getting cleaned up, getting all our weapons checked to make sure they are in good working order, and to do all the crazy things the Marine Corps can dream up to keep us busy; like getting practically all our hair cut off, shaving off our mustaches, and a million and one little things that really get under our skin. Chris, take my advice, and don't come in the Marine Corps. It just isn't what it used to be. They still treat us like recruits, and here we are combat veterans. Boy, the day I get out will be the happiest day in my life. ...

With all my love, Chuck

As evident from my letter I was really upset, worn out, sore, tired and hurting from constant battles with jungle rot. One must understand the situation to understand the anger. Deep down I loved the Corps and still do to this day. The spirit and training I received before combat as well as the strong attachments to other Marines served me well in Vietnam. However, it was the experiences I had in Fox 2/27 that provided me with the tools for survival in combat, not humping up and down hills with no objective in sight. I was probably spoiled during my time in the 27th. I was treated like a Marine and given the responsibilities of a Marine. Lt. Jones, my Platoon

Commander, had led from the front and simply expected us to do our jobs. That trust and treatment kept us going, especially during the hard times. Also, the constant parade of night ambushes and patrols had put my nerves to the point of breaking and except for actual combat, anger was the only outlet.

Perhaps it was the high casualty count in the 5th Marines with a constant influx of new men to fill the holes left vacant by dead and wounded Marines that resulted in the "rehabilitation" that we went through in An Hoa. All that would soon change when we went out on the 20th for Operation Meade River.

On November 16th I wrote:

> *Dear Mom,*
>
> *Well, it's little old me, [finally], I've got a lot to tell you, but most of it is so involved that I'll just have to give you the brief outline. First of all, Golf Co.; 2nd Battalion; 5th Marines is undoubtedly the most messed up outfit I have ever seen. No one in higher authority knows what they are doing here in Viet Nam, so they treat us like we were still in training in the States. ... And! What tops it off, they won't listen to those of us who know about this war. Here's one example! The Lt. of 2nd Plt. with which I am attached wanted to put one of my machine guns in a position where, first of all they could be killed easily and second, they wouldn't be useful. He and I had it out, the Captain found out, and boom!!! I have to wait another month for Corporal. There is a lot more that happened, all petty [stuff], but it's too long to go into. But I'll just tell you that I sure am [disgusted]. Then again, it looks like we will be leaving either tonight or tomorrow. Wow, we had a real rest didn't we! Oh well, that's the way it goes I guess. But on a whole I'm doing fine and am counting the days just like you are. ...*
>
> *Take care for now and oh, have a happy Thanksgiving Day.*
>
> *With all my love, Chuck*

The Commander's analysis of Operation Henderson Hill is provided in the records:

> The Battalion conducted operations in two areas. The first, the Arizona Area, found the local population very poor, lacking in food, and in extremely bad health. The second, near and on Go Noi Island, resulted in the capture of 10 prisoners and large rice caches. Again, as with Operation Sussex Bay monsoon rains terminated sweep operations on Go Noi Island. Discovery and recovery of rice

> caches deprived the enemy of a much needed food supply. Enemy prisoners provided substantial intelligence information concerning the 36th NVA Regiment. Both areas of Operation sadly reflected the lack of GVN [Government of Vietnam] presence.
>
> The lack of operations on Go Noi Island since September has resulted in an extensive VC oriented population buildup in that area, particularly West of the railroad berm. If not in fact now, the area will soon be developed to provide an extensive staging area and safe haven for VC/NVA forces operating within the DaNang TAOR. The rapid re-vegetation of the area will complicate further friendly operations on the island and is presently aiding the illegal civilian population buildup.

The records for November 20th record the following:

> 2/5 and 3/5 Chopped to First Marines at DTG 200800 November 1968.

The casualty count for Operation Henderson Hill through November 21st was:

> CUMULATIVE CASUALTIES:
>
> 34 USMC KIA, 218 USMC WIA EVAC, 36 USMC WIA MINOR, 1 USMC NBC KIA, 14 USMC NBC EVAC, 3 USMC NBC EVAC, 1 USN WIA EVAC, 1 USA WIA EVAC, 4 VN FORCES KIA, 4 VN FORCES WIA EVAC, 1 VN FORCES WIA MINOR.
>
> 341 NVA KIA, 6 NVA KIA DISC, 13 NVA POW, 5 NVA RTNE, 159 VC KIA, 1 VC KIA DISC, 4 VC POW, 1VC POW, 1 VC RTNE, 72 DETAINEES, 34 INN CIV, 11 CIV DEF, 41 NWC

The Defining Year 1968 talks about the new operation named Meade River:

> Early on the morning of 20 November, seven Marine battalions, under the control of the 1st Marines, began moving into prearranged positions to form a ring around part of Dodge City.

I remember being on a patrol around Dodge City and came upon a little wood shack where two Vietnamese women were selling fifths of American whisky. Loving bourbon, I was tempted when I saw a bottle of Jim Beam, but when I remembered the tales of booze from Dodge City being contaminated with things like ground-up glass, and also being the patrol leader, I turned down the offer and we all moved out. Still, it sure was tempting. I know why combat soldiers and Marines drink, to blot out the world they're living in. That problem stayed with me for many years later.

The records give a good short version of Operation Meade River:

> Background. The An Hoa AO covers an area of some 364 square kilometers. The entire AO is served by a secondary road 10 kilometers in length. The road runs north to south from Liberty Bridge to An Hoa. The AO stretches 12 kilometers south of the terminus of the road, and 13 kilometers east, and 13 kilometers west its axis. The only means of resupply or movement through 96% of the AO is by foot or helicopter. The current concept of helicopters in general support severely limited the reaction capability of the Regiment. The long and cumbersome means for communicating plans through several layers of command, and the daily commitment of ever changing helicopter crews unfamiliar with the tactical situation leaves much to be desired.
>
> During the period 14 through 19 November, the Battalion was in Regimental Reserve. Classes were conducted on tactics and general military subjects. Familiarization firing was conducted with all individual and crew-served weapons with emphasis on weapons safety.
>
> The 2nd Battalion, 5th Marines continued participation in Operation HENDERSON HILL. On 20 November, the Battalion under the operational control of First Marines began participation in Operation MEADE RIVER.
>
> Initial Intelligence for Operation MEADE RIVER indicated that elements of the X-16 Local Force Company, the Q-82 Local Force Company and the R-20 Main Force Battalion were within the Operations area. Also, it was known that the area contained a large number of VCI [Viet Cong Infrastructure] who provided tactical, logistical, and intelligence support for transient units; consequently, there existed a strong possibility of unknown units of up to battalion size harboring the area. During the first phase of the operation, the Battalion expedited the removal of a large number of indigenous personnel from the hamlets in close proximity to its positions for screening by higher headquarters. The Battalion also captured one detainee who claimed that his unit was the R-20 MF Battalion which had been located shortly before in the operations area and

> which was trying to exfiltrate in small groups. A number of documents were also found on enemy the Battalion had killed.
>
> Personnel from Battalion Supply and S-4 were sent to Hill 55 with the necessary gear and vehicles to support the Battalion from that location. All personnel and gear being sent between An Hoa and the Battalion had to be routed through Hill 55.
>
> Helicopter resupply from Hill 55 was supplemented by motor vehicle convoy and the use of two Otters [M-76 "Otter" Amphibious Cargo/Troop Carrier] attached to the Battalion.
>
> A quantity of 800 rainsuits [*sic*] were received and issued.

Since it was monsoon season, we were issued rain suits. Similar to many other bright ideas for combat troops in Vietnam like the "rubber ladies," the rain suits were terrible. With the hot climate, wearing them meant that you couldn't dry out. They may have been okay keeping the rain out, but they also kept the sweat in. You could never be dry in them in the heavy rains in Vietnam. Water would trickle down your back and front from the neck area, and seep past the elastic band on your pants to hit your private parts, giving an instant chill that was hard to take. They were very bad when going on patrol, as the noise that was made when brush scrapes across plastic was a dead giveaway to anyone in the area. We were wet and miserable before the rain suits, and soon we realized it was best to stay that way. Fighting with those suits on was often a fatal mistake since they covered things like pistols, ammo and first aid pouch.

We would eventually discard those suits, keep everything we needed to stay dry in plastic baggies, and go back to the wet-dry-wet cycle we were used to. From the worst to the best, the old poncho and poncho liner was the trick. The poncho was used for all sorts of things, from carrying dead bodies to building hooches, to raincoat and ground cover when sleeping. The poncho liner kept you warm at night, trapping body heat even when wet, and when worn over the shoulders with a poncho on top it kept you pretty dry, preventing the cold rain that seeped through the poncho from reaching vital parts. For fighting, the poncho and poncho liner could be tossed off in a second, leaving you free to maneuver your arms and exposing all the necessary fighting gear. Ponchos had their down sides too. They were too short, which meant that your lower legs and boots got drenched. They sweat, which meant that moisture would seep through. With the hood up, which hampered hearing, the rain ran around the front and down inside. With the hood down, the rain ran down the inside from the back of your neck to your butt. All considerations in mind, I still would choose the poncho. So, poncho or rain suit, the best solution was just get wet and cover up only when in stationary positions.

As our 2nd Battalion, 5th Marines started on Operation Meade River, the base at An Hoa came under heavy fire. The description given in the records tells the tale:

> On 20 November 1968 the Fifth Marines CHOPPED the 2nd and 3rd Battalions to the First Marines to take part in Operation MEADE RIVER south of Danang. With only four rifle companies of the Fifth Marines left in the whole An Hoa AO the enemy began infiltrating back into the area attempting a buildup of forces around the An Hoa Combat Base. On 21 November 1968 at 2100H an enemy battalion made a coordinated ground attack against the Combat Base. Employing the fires of 82mm and 60mm mortars, 57mm recoilless rifles, B-40 rockets, and M-79 grenade launchers the enemy force attacked from the east to west against the base's eastern perimeter. The battle raged for five hours with the enemy sending in assault forces armed with grenades and AK-47's. Tanks firing beehive 90mm cannister [*sic*], artillery firing direct lay 105mm canister , and LVT's firing machineguns broke up four separate waves of NVA and VC. CAP 2-9-1, in the path of the attack performed outstanding service by taking the attackers under fire from the flanks and rear, and directing artillery and air strikes. The enemy effort was a complete failure resulting in maximum enemy and minimum friendly casualties.
>
> Following the massive attack the enemy forces withdrew and continued to harass with ambushes, mines, and mortar attacks. On the night of 22 November 1968 an enemy ambush attacked an unarmed German medical missionary vehicle killing one German civilian and wounding a second. The vehicle was clearly marked and identified by a flashing red light and appropriate painted symbols.

November 22nd brought on a different type of attack. From the records:

> On 22 November 1968, at 2215H a German hospital vehicle, while moving north on Liberty Road with flashing red light on, was attacked by approximately nine Viet Cong (VC).
>
> The attack consisted of a possible satchel charge, a B-40 rocket, and small arms and hand grenades.

Attack was of short duration; no attempt was made by the VC to exploit the results of the attack. Both occupants of the vehicle, German Nationals, were left where they fell following the vehicle's abrupt departure from the road.

A reaction force of one Marine amphibious tractor (LVT) with one rifle squad and two hospital corpsmen, and covered by fixed positions along the route, was dispatched to recover the wounded. The two Germans were taken to the nearest Battalion Aid Station at An Hoa Combat Base, where a Navy doctor saw the wounded and called for emergency medical evacuation.

The two wounded, one with severe head wounds, the other with light shrapnel wounds, were moved to the Regimental Aid Station at once, where they were picked up by the emergency medical evacuation helicopter and transported immediately to the Army Station Hospital at Danang, where a neuro-surgical specialist was available.

The search of the area of the ambush resulted in recovery of the following:

Two home-made Bangalore Torpedo explosive devices with friction fuses, tied together by heavy vine.

Moderate to light attacks on isolated outposts and An Hoa combat base continued through the end of the reporting period. At the close of the reporting period, the Q81 LF and the 38th NVA Regimental Headquarters were possibly located in the northeastern sector of the AO. Elements of the 21st NVA Regiment were reported located in the northern Arizona area, center mass AT8453, with the 1st Bn, 36th NVA Regiment plus the 36th NVA Regimental Headquarters reported vicinity AT9739. Acute food shortages among enemy main and local forces were also reported.

At 2210, 22 November 1968, two German Nationals on the staff of the Knights of Malta German Hospital were brought to the BAS for aeromedical evacuation. Both men were injured when Viet Cong insurgents attacked their jeep ambulance. Identified as follows: Otto HEISS suffering from a sucking chest wound and Gzoslaw DIXA suffering from penetrating wound of the head and sucking chest wound. Both men evacuated by helo to USA 95th Evac Hospital.

At 221300H, while on a sweep through a village at BT047579, Company G found a Vietnamese/English translation book, medical gear and 245 NVA dollars.

> At 240015H, Company G set in night defenses at BT047580 received 10 incoming 60/81mm mortar rounds. Results: Negative

This night mortar attack on our position was common in the 5th Marines and to my mind, unnecessary. While with Fox Company 2/27th, each platoon formed their own perimeter and the Company CP joined with one platoon or another when on Company sized operations. Practicing Lt. Jones' method of moving the platoon after dark to a new location, we were spared the mortar attacks that other units experienced. I often wished we could do this in the 5th Marines, but that was not to be and we had to suffer the mortar attacks, which in this operation happened often.

The next day, on the 25th, the records report:

> 2nd Bn, 5th Marines and BLT 2/26 commenced PHASE III of Operation MEADE RIVER on 25 November. In a coordinated advance to the CO CA RIVER where a relief of the ARVN Forces was executed, the Marines of 2nd Battalion, 5th Marines and BLT 2/26 made extensive use of metal probes. Their probing while laborious and time consuming, unearthed extensive bunker complexes and caches, to include 8 tons of buried rice, several bounding mines [a bounding mine is a "bouncing betty" which is shot into the air and then explodes], heavily laden packs for sustaining infiltration troops and such diverse items as rolls of Comm wire and a Hell Box [a machine for setting off multiple explosions] for command detonation of SFD's. These finds, coupled with the capture of a VC Supply Officer in the area, confirmed our long standing suspicions that THANH THONG was, indeed, a haven for the VC infrastructure and a major station on the infiltration route to DANANG. Having conducted a thorough and exhaustive search of this area, both Battalions passed through the ARVN positions to the CO CA River and assumed their blocking mission on the East side of DODGE CITY on 28 November.

On November 25th, I wrote:

Dear Mom,

I got your letter from the 14th about 4 days ago, but haven't had the time to answer. Everything here is [Okay]. We left the 20th for this operation we are on and the way it looks, we will be out here for a while. We have a battalion of NVA [surrounded], along with 2/7, 1/1 and the 51st ARVN's. But we are getting hit both from within and without our big circle. So it looks like we might clean this area up for a while I hope. …

Well, well, well, here it is the 29th and I finally have a few minutes to sit down and write again. I got [yours] and Dad's letters Mom and I must admit that up until yesterday when I got those two letters, I was feeling pretty low. Very little mail, Very much rain, [too] much digging, and not enough sleep, plus a million and one other things between me and this Boot Lt., have all had the effect of getting me down. I was fighting hard, but depression was slowly stepping in. Then I got a letter yesterday from Dad then one from Mom, yesterday the 28th, Thanksgiving Day. Well, I sat down and relaxed a bit last night and read those two letters by Marine Light (flares). I took a good look at myself again, set my thinking straight once again, Made my peace with the Lord, and am now ready to go home in 105 days approximately. So all is right here in Viet Nam, and from the sounds of things, everything seems to be shaping up real good at home. This operation is just about finished, but there is [a] rumor going around that we have 3 more opps in a row yet to come, so like always I'm in the dark about what I'll be doing next, and so I can guess where that leaves you. But, that's the way it is over here. Maybe this will help you. Whenever you hear about 2/5 doing something, I'm in it. Because 99% of our operations are on a Battalion sized level. We're not horsing around with [Mr.] Charles Any More! But then he's not horsing [around] either. ...

With all my love, Chuck

The records from the 29th report the following:

> At 291100H, while sweeping through the area at BT005590, a Marine from the Battalion Command Group was wounded by sniper fire. Results: One USMC WIA Non-Evac.
>
> Company G searching at BT022590 found one 4.2 inch round and three bunkers. Results: All destroyed in place.

Lima Company, 3rd Battalion, 5th Marines was also deeply involved in Operation Meade River. My good friend Dan Nordmann, who had been transferred in September to Lima 3/5 had just returned on November 28th, after his recovery from a gunshot wound to the neck, which he received shortly after being reassigned from Fox 2/27 to Lima 3/5. He came back to his unit with some Thanksgiving cheer and hot chow for the troops. Everyone was happy to see him and he resumed his place in the machine gun squad. Two days later, on November 30th, he was wounded again, this time from incoming mortars. He was medevaced and eventually sent home.

Our Thanksgiving, in Golf Company, was spent in the field, with C-rations and C-ration coffee. We were thankful to be alive and hoped things would stay that way.

During this time I had a problem with my poncho. Having stated the pros and cons of the humble poncho, and realizing that most of the time spent in the field, the simple poncho tent wasn't used due to enemy activity, the best one could do for resting was to just wrap up in the poncho liner and poncho and try and get a couple of hours of sleep. One night we were spread out on a low ridge running across a hillside, as a blocking force. At night we manned the lines with two-man foxholes, using one-on and one-off every four hours. Sometimes it would be adjusted to two hour watches.

It was my turn to try and get some rest, and I moved downhill at the back of the position a few yards, I checked the weather (smell the air, feel the air and look skyward) and decided to cover with the poncho. Since the ground was damp from previous rains, I had the bright idea to roll up in my poncho/poncho liner with my head pointing to the top of the ridge. That way I'd have ground and top cover. I used my flak jacket as a pillow, putting my head on the inside and covering with the other side.

Ah, the beauty of it - I'd stay dry if it rained, my bedroll was positioned so I wouldn't roll down the hill, and I'd be surrounded with warmth. It was November after all. Not so! During the night, the rains returned. It was heavy, but I was snug in my little cocoon. Suddenly, I couldn't breathe! I had water-boarded myself. Water was pouring down around my head and shoulders and out of the bottom of my poncho. I had created the perfect human pipe. Struggle as I might, I couldn't seem to be able to get out of that pipe. I was disoriented and didn't know how to get out of this. I must have been hollering, because someone came over and helped me get unraveled out my self-made trap. Once I got out I started cussing up a blue streak, stomping around looking for my gear, especially my rifle. Eventually I got it together and since I was awake anyway, I went back up the hill and relieved the other man in my hole. Although I have a list of my squad and some few memories of them, without any close connections, the Marine with me will always remain nameless. Needless to say, I never tried that little trick again. I don't know which was worse, the water pipe I found myself in or the inability to get out and get to my weapon. Lesson learned: keep the poncho and poncho liner spread out and sleep with your weapon, which I usually did anyway.

As if that wasn't enough to appease the rain gods, a few days later, as the rains continued, and being soaked to the bone anyway, I decided to get a shower. I couldn't remember the last time I was able to get clean, so with the rain coming down I stripped off my clothes, every stitch, and got my little piece of soap out of my pack and began to lather up. I was safe enough on the back side of this ridgeline with the whole company set in as a blocking force.

Oh, the silky feel of the soap as it removed all but the most stubborn grime. With the fresh rain water, slightly cool but soothing nonetheless, I was beginning to have a new outlook on life. Maybe that was my mistake. Maybe I wasn't supposed to feel good in a war zone. For whatever reason, just as I got really soaped up and ready for a good rinse, the rain stopped. That's right, not a drop, and the soap was starting to dry. I waited a while, but the soap only got harder on my skin. Finally, convinced that I had better do something, I did my best to remove the soap from my skin using my Marine green towel. I got dressed in my dirty jungle utilities, dirty socks and worn out boots and I began to itch from head to toe. No amount of scratching would help. It was bad, really bad, I felt like my skin was shrinking and trapping me in a straight jacket of rawhide.

So what happened about an hour or so later? Still trying to get past the itch from the soap, I started a C-ration meal. I got the C-4 burning and the can of chow on the C-ration stove when it started to rain like hell. Not only did I get completely soaked, with soap oozing out of my clothes, the C-ration can stove got filled with water, putting out the C-4, which had just started to catch fire, and ruined my C-ration meal. I was back in the mud again, soaked to the bone and needing a bath, only this time I was also hungry, with a ruined meal in front of me. That is, can you really ruin a C-ration meal any more than it already is coming out of the can? I did strip again and let the rain wash the rest of the soap off of me and soak my clothes so I could squeeze the soapy residue out of them too. Not perfect, but better than before. By now, evening was coming on and there was a little chill in the air, which meant I was also cold. You know, 75 degrees is pretty cool when you have been acclimated to 90-degree temps and above.

Finally, fully clothed but still wet, I huddled under my poncho, holding it out over a new C-4 fire and the water-logged meal (not enough food at hand to let it go to waste) with another C-4 fire heating water (rain water that I caught in my poncho) for C-ration coffee. I must have looked like a vulture squatted over his meal with wings outspread trying desperately to eat in peace. I ate quietly and returned everything except the poncho to my pack.

I took my place on the line and gave someone else a chance to eat before it got too dark for a fire.

Just another day in the life of a grunt. Those who have been there know. If you want to enjoy the same wonderful experience, just go into your back yard with the same artifacts, wait for it to rain, and go from there. Good luck!

Our company was spared during Operation Meade River. We moved often, keeping the circle closed. During the month of November our only casualties were 11 Marines WIA, mostly from booby-traps. At the same time, our "boot camps" were wising up and began to locate and destroy booby-traps they discovered.

One day when our company was on a sweep and had come close to a superior force of NVA, we moved to another position to form a blocking force until other units arrived to help. A Marine in my squad had trouble keeping up with the swift march to get out of there. I couldn't leave him behind and the rest of the company wasn't stopping for him to catch up. He was short and roly-poly and not up to the rigors of combat. Our forced march was very hard on him. I believe that he had only been in Vietnam a month or so, and still hadn't been able to get in shape.

My machine gun squad lagged back to help him catch up with the rest of the company, but I ordered them to keep going as I went back for him myself. No point is getting all of us killed. He had stopped again about 50 yards behind me, bent over and out of breath. I got to him pretty quick and told him that the gooks were right behind us and he needed to move it. He panted:

"I can't."

"You are going to move or I'm going make you sorry you were ever born. I'm not going to die because of you," I said.

And, with those words I pulled out my Ka-Bar knife and poked him in the butt. Startled, he jumped and started to move toward the company. From behind him, I urged him on, poking him in the butt once more when he started to slow down. It wasn't long before he got the message. Fear crept in and adrenaline started flowing. I kept looking to the rear the whole time, expecting the NVA to pop out and shoot us down. The area we were in was a flat open field with clumps of tall bushes scattered around. Not liking the openness of the place, I urged him on even more. Whenever he stopped, I threatened him again. And, once again he would jump with a start and move out. Fearing me more than anything else, he slowly made it back toward our lines.

Eventually, what seemed like an eternity, ended. The corpsman treated him for exhaustion but didn't call in for a medevac. No one said anything about him to me. I was still fuming and just needed to be left alone for a while. Later, when we got back to An Hoa, he was removed from the company. I have to give it to him - he never gave up, no matter how much he wanted to. He persevered and he made it back under extreme circumstances. This recollection is not to belittle him, but rather to acknowledge his bravery, overcoming his physical limitations to carry on.

Operation Meade River would result in a total NVA/VC KIA of 442.

From the Marine Corps records, the casualty figures for the month of November were:

The [2nd] Battalion joined 87 enlisted men during the month. The Battalion transferred 1 officer and 162 enlisted during the same period. Casualties sustained for the month were:

BATTLE					NON-BATTLE		TOTAL
KIA	WIA	DOW	WIANE	MIA	NBD	NBC	
15	57	2	4	0	0	39	155

The running total since September is:

KIA – 63, WIA – 242, DOW – 5, WIANE – 117, MIA – 1, NBD – 1, NBC – 59, Total – 488

For the third month in a row, the numbers of Battalion personnel were advancing to the rear. Having transferred 163 officers and enlisted, joined 87 men and lost 155 casualties, the numbers show that 2/5 was in the hole by 231 men for November and a grand total loss of 453 men since the first of September. The worst part was that the number of replacements had greatly diminished.

Chapter 15

December 1st found us in Phase IV of Operation Meade River, still in the field and closing the circle around the enemy. A description of this phase comes from the records:

> The second phase of the operation yielded no specific intelligence. During the third phase of the operation, the Battalion encountered minor resistance and found little information of intelligence value. As the fourth phase was initiated, it became evident that an unknown unit was harboring in the Dodge City Area. As the Battalion blocked along the Eastern edge of this area, psyops psychological operation units were used extensively in Chieu Hoi appeals. On 3 November, one Hoi Chanh was taken claiming that he was from the 3rd Bn, 36th Regiment, 308th Division and that his unit was in the path of adjacent sweeping units. Also during this phase of the Operation, the Battalion found a minor amount of assorted enemy equipment and documents. All enemy documents, equipment and weapons were forwarded to 1st Marines Forward Command Post. Close liaison was maintained to expedite the flow of intelligence information acquired.

Reports from December 1st show:

> At 011120H, Company G in defensive positions at BT015594 received small arms and automatic weapons fire from a treeline at BT012588. Company G returned fire with 60mm mortars, 3.5 rockets and automatic weapons. Results: One USMC WIA Non-Evac.
>
> At 011845H, while setting in night positions at BT015594, Company G received sporatic small arms fire and grenades from BT012588. Company G returned fire with small arms with undetermined results. Results: Two USMC WIA Non-Evac.

More examples of attacks in night positions, oh what I wouldn't have given for Lt. Jones to come back.

I had caught some small pieces of shrapnel from an incoming grenade thrown from the other side of the river. Our "Blooper Man" returned fire as well as several riflemen. The Blooper was another name for the M-79 grenade launcher, which fired a 40x46mm explosive round with an effective range of 383 yds. It was a minor wound, the corpsman patched me up, and I went on about my work. I guess I was one of the WIA Non-Evac.

Also around this time, I was given the dubious honor of running another night patrol and this time I had some ARVNs with me, a total of ten men. It was a fairly large patrol, because Mr. Charles was all over the place. The moon was up but it was cloudy, so although it was lighter than normal, there was still a haze in the air.

I followed our patrol route closely, but in a slightly different way. I hurried everyone along for a while and then stopped and set up a simple ambush before moving on to the next checkpoint. This method had many benefits. First, I was on the given route so I didn't have to worry about being in the wrong place. Second, it allowed me to ambush anyone that was following my patrol. Thirdly, it gave us a chance to rest and gain a heightened sense of awareness. Often, night patrols would just stroll along from one checkpoint to another. Any loss of attention on the route could cause someone their life. Keeping a keen edge while patrolling in the dark was hard to maintain and anything that would help was a potential lifesaver.

I noticed several trails leading out into a large grassy area, where the grass was about four feet tall. So I took the patrol out there to set up an ambush. I could feel a slight depression on the ground and stopped the patrol. Setting the men in a line, facing in alternating positions, I formed the ambush. I maintained a middle position with my radioman and the senior man from the ARVNs. I gave everyone the reminders to stay quiet, no smoking and wait for me to touch off the ambush if we made contact.

It must have been about a half an hour later and just about the time to move on, when I spied a line of heads wearing what looked like Marine helmets, bobbing up and down and moving right across the face of my ambush. Since no Marine patrol was supposed to be in the area except mine, I knew it had to be the enemy. The VC often used that trick at night, wearing captured U. S. helmets, hoping to be taken as a Marine patrol. I alerted my men and instantly the adrenaline hit us and we were ready to fight. Just as

I was fixing to kick off the ambush, the senior ARVN stood up and yelled loud enough for all to hear:

"No VC, no VC, ARVN, ARVN!"

As soon as he did that the heads went down and disappeared. I tried to catch sight of them in the tall grass but they had hunkered down and left the area as fast as they could.

When that VC patrol scurried out of there, I learned two things. First, that was no ARVN patrol. If it was, they would have come over to our position and the ARVN in my patrol would have talked to them. Second, my ARVN counter-part was probably a VC. Although we didn't have any success on our patrol/ambush, we had avoided the attack that was surely coming up behind us. Having experienced the VC coming up behind me on patrols before, I had developed my technique to turn the tables on the gooks if they were indeed creeping up on me – and it worked.

I was hopping mad. I called that ARVN/VC every name in the book. But it made no difference to him, he just kept saying:

"No VC, ARVN."

I calmed down and tried to put everyone at ease. Yet at the same time, I cautioned everyone to stay alert, because the gooks might know our patrol route and have an ambush set up somewhere ahead of us. Most of those with me on that patrol trusted me and I believe that helped them get their bearings.

I continued the patrol in the same method as before with no results, and we came back into the CP without incident. I reported what happened to my Platoon Commander and Platoon Sergeant, but I had no confidence in that redheaded horror of a Lt. I did what I could, and after turning in my report, I went to the other patrol leaders and told them what had happened and advised them to watch out. It wasn't long, maybe a day or two, before the ARVNs (Army of the Republic of Viet Nam) were detached from our company.

I never did trust the ARVNs and had many reasons to question their loyalty and their willingness to fight. I never, ever, trusted my back to an ARVN.

On December 3rd, I wrote:

Dear Mom,

Well, here I am, 100 days short. It's time for the count down, and I just wish the days would go by as fast as I can count. But, they don't, so I'll just keep plugging along and come March I'll make my bird. It's getting dark, so I'll have to finish this tomorrow if I have time. But while

I can I'll just sit here and chat. I was just thinking about the way the house looks and how it will probably look for Christmas. You all will have some decorations up again this year won't you, and my deer and Santa up on the TV set, and all the little trimmings that remind one of Christmas. …

Hello, it's me again, at about 8:00 in the morning. I just got some good flicks of some air strikes this morning. That napalm really does the trick. I sure hope the pictures turn out, I think you'll like 'em. … Dad, we have the same problem here that you all had in the Philippines. The gooks are in cement bunkers and deep trenches and artillery and mortars and rockets and even [napalm] aren't doing much good at all. That's why we brought in 750 lb. bombs plus [napalm] this morning. I sure hope we can blow those gooks out rather than have to go in and get them out like we usually do. Well, so much for the war. …

Well, things are beginning to pop a little [around] here again, so until next time, just remember that I love you all and wish everyone a Very Merry Christmas. …

Well, we flushed the gooks out, so I've really got to run.

With all my love, Your Son, Chuck

Confirming the accuracy of my letter, *The Defining Year 1968* states the following:

> With continuing heavy resistance, the Marines again called upon air and artillery, using 750-pound bombs, napalm, and "danger close" supporting arms.

Phase four of Operation Meade River is further described in the records:

> MEADE RIVER. Phase four of Operation MEADE RIVER found enemy forces confined in the area known as Dodge City. Enemy forces identified were the 3BN, 36th Regiment; elements of the R-20 Bn, V-25 Bn, T-89 Sapper Bn, 577 Arty Bn, and the 573 Arty Bn, Q-82 LF/Co, Q-89 LF/Co, and Q-90 LF/Co, as well as local guerrillas. Enemy forces located in the cordon elected to defend the area from reinforced, mutually supporting bunkers located vic BT014587 and BT007607 and conducted the defense of their positions to the last man. It is believed that the 3rd Bn 36th Regiment was annihilated as a result of Operation MEADE RIVER.
>
> PHASE IV commenced on D+9 (30 Nov 68). From midnight on, a heavy volume of artillery fire pounded the area inside the dimin-

ished cordon. At 0600 until 0700 the enemy was offered an opportunity to CHIEU HOI. They chose to fight. At 0700 a heavy air and artillery prep fire commenced.

Three phase lines had been established to control the 3rd Battalion, 5th Marines during the attack. As they moved through phase line ALPHA, heavy small arms, and automatic weapons fire caused several casualties. It took all of D+9 to secure phase line ALPHA.

On D+10, the 3rd Bn, 5th Marines took even heavier fire including 82mm and 60mm mortars, but managed to reach phase line BRAVO by late afternoon.

The 2nd Battalion, 5th Marines analysis of Operation Meade River is stated in the records:

Commander's Analysis. Initially assigned a sector of the Regimental Cordon, the Battalion took part in a successful helolift which trapped the enemy within the cordon. With this type of operation it is essential that the search and sweep be conducted in detail and with the patience required to thoroughly cover the area. Unique and sustained alertness especially during the hours of darkness is required and resulted in containment of the enemy within the cordon and destruction of forces attempting to escape and capture of documents and personnel of substantial intelligence value. Close coordination of supporting arms with other friendly units in close proximity compounded operations. This close proximity of friendly/enemy units as the cordon was tightened unduly restricted the use of heavy ordnance; resulting in casualties from enemy fire which might otherwise have been avoided. Visits by the regimental commander and his staff officers to the field materially facilitated coordination between adjacent commands and accomplishment of assigned tasks on a timely basis.

The participation of 2nd Battalion 5th Marines in Operation Meade River was cut short when on December 6th, we returned to An Hoa, spending just enough time there to again move out on Operation Taylor Common. The Marine Corps reports put it this way:

During the period 1 December to 6 December 1968 the Battalion 2/5 continued its participation in Operation Meade River. At 1800 on 6 December operational control of the Battalion was returned to the 5th Marines. During the period 7 to 8 December the Battalion as part of a larger force executed a combat sweep from Phu Loc (6) to the An Hoa Combat Base as Phase I of Operation Taylor Common.

In order to assist the 5th Marines in securing its AO with the forces available, the Americal Division [23rd Infantry Division, USA] commenced operations in the Eastern Regimental AO and continued operations in that area throughout December. During this period, units of Americal discovered bodies of over 300 of the enemy apparently previously killed by air and artillery in support of the 5th Marines.

Additional assistance in securing the AO was provided by the 1st ARVN Ranger Group under the command of LtCol HUY. The Ranger Group was composed of the 21st, 37th, and 39th ARVN Ranger Battalions.

Operation Henderson Hill terminated at 062400H December 1968. A highly successful operation, Henderson Hill ended with a total of 435 NVA KIA and 267 VC KIA.

Operation Taylor Common under the command of Task Force Yankee (BGen DWYER) commenced on 070001H Dec. At 070830H, BLT [Battalion Landing Team] 2/7 landed in LZ Champagne in the Arizona Area to begin the attack. With BLT 2/7 providing the blocking force, the 1st ARVN Ranger Group attacked SW through the Arizona Area toward BLT 2/7's positions. Upon completion of this phase, ARVN forces continued to conduct S&C operations in the Arizona Area. During the month of December, the 1st ARVN Ranger Group with the aid of FWF [Free World Forces] Supporting Arms killed 492 NVA and 38 VC while sustaining 69 ARVN KIA and 273 wounded.

No significant enemy contact was made in the AO at the onset of Taylor Common which commenced at 070001 Dec 68. However an increasing number of booby trap and terrorist incidents have occurred during the reporting period. Terrorist activities included firing M-79 rounds into the Duc Duc Refugee Center, the slaying of an innocent civilian on Liberty Road, and the assasination [*sic*] of the Sub-Hamlet Chief of Mau Chanh (2). There were indications that the enemy morale was quite low in the east-northeast portions of the AO. Four enemy from this area Chieu Hoied in the second half of the reporting period. The general state of morale was reported as low, due to Marine air and artillery strikes, and the lack of adequate food and medical supplies.

> On 7 and 8 December, 2/5 and 3/5 (-) returned to opcon of the Fifth Marines and in conjunction with 1/5, conducted a two day Regimental sweep of the area between Liberty Bridge and An Hoa. While the number of enemy killed was relatively small for the maneuver, enemy operations in the area were noticeably disrupted and the area stabilized prior to the departure of 2/5 and 3/5 (-) to opcon of the Third Marines.

During the 7th and 8th, my platoon, was positioned on a high ridge overlooking a wide plain with a river meandering through it. At the bottom of one side of this ridge, looking out toward the plain was the Battalion Headquarters and the rest of Golf Company. On the other side was a large wooded area that led down to Alligator Lake, which was all VC country, just outside of An Hoa. Several things happened up there.

On the 7th, our Platoon was helo-lifted to the top of the ridge and we formed a perimeter. They put us on an open spot with good views all around. I placed my machine guns at the opposite points of the ridge top, providing interlocking fields of fire for either side of the ridge. I reminded them to pop the tracers out of some belts for use at night and made sure that they had clear fields of fire. I was down to nine men in the squad after the roly-poly Pfc. was transferred out and LCpl. Reyes had returned, leaving me with 2 four-man gun teams and myself. Reyes was a great gunner and team leader and I was glad to have him back. My gun teams had gained experience and I left them on their own while I placed myself in the middle so I could support either team as necessary. It also left me able to defend the Platoon CP.

After we were all set in, but well before dark, my redheaded Platoon Commander told me that he had orders to run a reconnaissance patrol down the Alligator Lake side of the ridge to determine any enemy activity, and he wanted me to take both of my guns and run that patrol.

My blood came up instantly and I simply said, "No."

Machine guns are not used for reconnaissance patrol and besides, they were needed on top of the hill because of their firepower. I could see the blood rise in the Lt. as his face turned as red as his hair.

"Are you refusing my direct order?" he said.

"Yes," I answered.

Before I could state my reasons for keeping the guns on the ridge top, he grabbed the radio hand set from the radioman and called down to Battalion to speak with Captain Poole, our Commanding Officer.

It wasn't long before Captain Poole came on and the Lt. said to him:

"I have a machine gun squad leader up here that has refused my direct order."

Now this was a serious charge, since orders were orders and obedience to orders was paramount in the Marine Corps, at least, that was what the Lt. learned in Officer Candidate School. However, either they failed to teach him or he failed to learn that that was only true for lawful orders. Since I didn't see his orders as lawful but stupid beyond belief, I was forced to disobey, not for me or my men, but for the mission we were assigned to acccomplish. Not very smart of me, but I had a job to do and that was to protect our position and the back door to the Battalion's CP as well as the responsibility to not waste Marine lives unnecessarily.

"Let me speak to that squad leader," I heard Captain Poole shout over the radio.

Now, I don't know if he remembered who the squad leader was for guns in 2nd Platoon, so I took the handset that the Lt. shoved in my face but before I could say anything the captain hollered:

"Who is this?"

"Lance Corporal Van Bibber, Sir, section leader and squad leader for machine guns."

"Hey Van Bibber," like he suddenly remembered me, "What's going on up there?"

He remembered me alright, since we had crossed paths several times, from Maui Peak to my promotion to section leader/squad leader.

I told him that my Lt. had ordered me to take both of my guns on a recon patrol on the Alligator Lake side of the ridge and that I had refused him. I told him that my guns were the only automatic firepower up here between Battalion and the gooks on the Alligator Lake side of this ridge. I also told him that if he, the captain, ordered me to do that, then I would do it, but with reservations. He told me to hand the handset to the Lt.

I did as he ordered and handed the handset to the lieutenant. Well, I'm not exactly sure what the captain said to him, but the lieutenant's face turned even redder than before. The Captain must have really given it to the Lt. because all he did after that was to hand the handset back to the radioman and walk away. Needless to say, I didn't send the guns out on that patrol, but I sure caught hell from that Lt. After that incident, he would assign me to every dirty ambush or patrol he could. More than usual. Even the men noticed his vendetta against me. I was convinced now that he was trying to get me killed. We had had run-ins before but nothing like this, and I knew I had to really be on my toes or he'd surely get me killed. This all continued through December until one day he was gone and a new Lt. came to take his place. I have no recollection of him actually leaving or what happened to him, but when he was gone, the whole platoon gave a big sigh of relief. Friction among leaders is never welcomed in a fighting unit. My guess is that, having lost control of his Platoon, the Lt. was reassigned elsewhere. Otherwise, I would have wound up being transferred or in the brig. Of course, he could have been wounded (not necessarily from the enemy) and then transferred.

The next day, December 8th, we all witnessed a terrible turn of events. I happened to be near the radioman and heard a company by the river calling in for Air Support. We saw what looked like Phantom aircraft come in for a strike and just as it released a load of napalm, we heard:

"Abort, abort, friendlies, friendlies!"

Soon after that, the radio crackled to a deathly silence. It was too late. As we looked on we saw the napalm hit and eventually the radio crackled again with requests for medevacs. From what we heard and saw, we determined that Marines were being fried by our own napalm. Not pleasant to hear and for the Marines involved, not pleasant to experience.

The Defining Year 1968 relates the story much better, having access to the broader view:

> At 1120 on the 8th, the 3rd Battalion, 26th Marines attacked to the north with five companies abreast. The 2d Troop, 4th ARVN Cavalry, which had arrived the previous evening, consisting of 12 armored personnel carriers (APC's), reinforced the Marine assault. In their path, the Marines reported 79 dead North Vietnamese near the site of the previous day's battle. When Company H 2/5 reached a rice paddy a few hundred meters from their starting point, Communist troops hidden in a treeline [*sic*] suddenly opened fire, trapping Marines in the paddy. For 30 minutes, the Marines returned fire individually, then began moving in small groups toward a larger bunker which appeared to be the linchpin of the Communist defenses. Just beyond the bunker and treeline [*sic*], they could see the Song La Tho, on the other side of which the 1st Battalion, 1st Marines remained in its blocking position.
>
> The Marines requested air support. Because of the proximity of the 1st Battalion, 1st Marines, the aircraft had difficulty attacking targets without endangering friendly troops. In one instance, a napalm bomb impacted directly on Company H 2/5, but miraculously

bounced safely away before detonating. Captain George B. Meegan, the Company L, 3rd Bn 26th Marines in another sector, recalled that a "napalm strike landed" by his 1st Platoon and that several Marines sustained minor burns. Neither the airstrikes nor mortar and 3.5-inch rocket fire overcame the enemy resistance.

When supporting arms failed to silence the enemy in the bunker facing him, Captain Drez H 2/5 requested Lieutenant Colonel Roberson 3/26 to provide him with some of the ARVN APCs. The APCs arrived, armed with recoilless rifles, and halted in the rice paddy. According to Drez, however, the ARVN refused to help. Instead, Drez had his attached combat engineer, Private First Class Michael A. Emmons, jerryrig [*sic*] a satchel charge consisting of C-4, hand grenades, two 3.5-inch rockets, and a five-second fuze. With the assistance of another Marine, they carried the satchel charge to the top of the bunker where Drez lit the fuze and Emmons flipped the charge through an embrasure. When the others ran, Emmons momentarily remained atop the bunker. The explosion tossed him into the air, but he landed unhurt. The blast smashed the bunker, killing all but one of the North Vietnamese inside. The Marines reported 39 enemy dead and 1 prisoner in the vicinity of the bunkers. Emmons was later awarded a Silver Star Medal for his action.

The 7th and 8th for the rest of the company also had its dangers. With 2nd Platoon up on the ridgeline to provide security for the rest of the company and for Battalion Headquarters staged in the same area, the other two platoons were tasked with security patrols around the Battalion CP.

From the records, the following reports were made:

Date 07 Dec 68
0810H, S-3, Battalion leaving Phu Lac (6)
1110H, S-3, Battalion commences sweep along river
1747H, S-3, Battalion set in night activities
1942H, S-3, All companies' activities set in

Date 08 Dec 68
0815H, S-3, Battalion commenced sweep
1200H, CoG observed enemy at 970495
1315H, CoG found 1 VC KIA and 3 detainees
1700H, CoG detonated booby trap at 928469: 2 USMC WIAE

Date 09 Dec 68
0755H, CoG detonates booby trap at AT922462: 2 USMC WIAE [WIA Evacuated]

On 9 December 1968 at 1800 Operation MEADE RIVER was terminated. Units were returned to their parent organizations after 20 days of vicious, intense fighting. The 1st Bn, 1st Marines took over and mopped up the NORTHERN BUNKER COMPLEX for two more days. During this post-MEADE RIVER period, 1/1 found additional bodies and killed some NVA remaining in bunkers, refusing to come out. A total of 50 enemy KIA were accounted for. They also recovered numerous additional enemy individual and crew served weapons.

The 9th through the 13th was spent being resupplied for the next operation, Operation Taylor Common. On my birthday I was busy setting up an ambush. What more would you want than to be able to shoot people on your birthday. I had fallen down the rabbit hole and couldn't find a way out.

My little blood stained wheel book gives an idea of what we would be facing at Hill 214. The notes state the following:

Going to Hill 214 stay there 2 weeks
Be at BAS [Battalion Aid Station] 0800
No one will drink local water
Helmets strapped and buckled
1800 Gooks in area
Carry weapons, flack jackets & helmets when moving anywhere

The records state:

On 13 December the Battalion was helolifted to Hill 214 southwest of An Hoa, vicinity ZC 1945. The Command Group, Company G and two batteries from the 12th Marines began establishment of a Fire Support Base. The remaining rifle companies conducted extensive combat patrols within a 2,000 meter radius of the base.

Also, from the records of the 3rd Marines:

On December 13, upon their arrival at An Hoa, OPCON of 1st Battalion 3d Marines was passed to the 3d Marine regiment. The 3d Marines received OPCON of 2nd Battalion 5th Marines also. One platoon (-) of B Company 3d Engineers with one platoon of 1st Force Recon were helilifted to Regimental objective 2, for the construction of a landing zone. The 2nd Battalion 5th Marines was helilifted to objective 2 upon completion of the landing zone. With one company of 2nd Battalion 5th Marines providing security, construction of FSB [fire support base] PIKE was commenced.

Fire Support. Two firing batteries were in direct support of the Battalion, Battery A 1st Battalion, 12th Marines and a provisional battery of 155's from the 12th Marines from 13 December to 31 December 1968.

General support was provided by two platoons of 155 howitzers.

Significant Fire Support Events. Ammunition resupply in the early phase of Taylor Common was considered inadequate to support a Fire Support Base. Harassing and interdiction fires could not be fired because of low ammunition stocks on position. The only missions that could be fired were known enemy targets and contact missions. Additionally night defensive fires could not be registered for isolated companies. Insufficient helicopter were available to establish and resupply the Fire Support Base. Three other battalions were also in the field supported by the same helicopters. Later in the month, as the seriousness of the problem became apparent, additional helicopters were provided. At the end of the month stocks of ammunition had reached acceptable, if not ideal levels.

On December 14, 1st Battalion 3d Marines conducted their rehab at An Hoa. OPCON of 3d Battalion 3d Marines was passed to the 3d Marines upon their arrival at An Hoa. The 2nd Battalion 5th Marines began search and destroy operations in the vicinity of FSB PIKE. (4) 155 Guns were helilifted to FSB LANCE, and (2) to FSB PIKE.

From the 2/5 reports for 15 December:
1800H G2 ambush left friendly lines.

This was my "birthday" ambush. Never a break.

The first few days on Hill 214 were better than tromping through the bush all day. We had our patrols and ambushes, but we could set up poncho tents and heat our chow. When not on patrol, we worked on fortifying our positions, which meant deep holes, covered with sandbags. Hard work for worn-out bush bunnies.

One incident happened up there that I will never forget. After eating my C-rations and coffee one evening, I went to my little one-man tent that I had rigged using my poncho. I slept on the ground in my clothes. We always slept fully clothed with the exception of our boots, which we removed to air them out as well as relieve our sore feet.

I didn't have any patrols or ambushes that night and I was looking forward to getting some much-needed sleep. I would awake every couple of hours or so and walk lines to check on my men and return for some more sleep. The moon was out that night and a dim glow flooded my tent as I laid down with my left arm as a pillow.

It must have been later on toward morning when I was brought awake by something touching the middle finger of my left hand. When I awoke, my head was resting on my left arm, which was stretched out straight down a line of sight from my eyes. I didn't move, I just opened my eyes. I had learned to come to a complete state of wakefulness in an instant and not move until I knew it was ok.

As I looked down my arm, I could see this large rat with his mouth around my middle finger. Not wanting to get bit, I moved just a little and he ran off. I guess he must have thought that I would be a tasty treat and was trying to haul me off to Rat Land. He sure got a surprise when he found me looking right down his throat. Just another rat encounter. We lived with them or them with us at all times in the bush, and this hilltop would be no exception.

Well, I certainly was awake now, so I got up and heated myself some C-ration coffee and went to check lines. All was well, and I returned to my tent to heat up some breakfast: C-Ration eggs, scrambled, with crackers and peanut butter and jelly - a certified treat. Thank goodness that we had a ready supply of C-rations up here on this firebase. Just another day in Vietnam.

From the reports of the 16th:

(2) 105's [howitzers] were inserted at FSB PIKE.

The routine set in and from the 15th to the 24th of December, it was a constant process of setting in LP's (Listening Posts) used at night, OP's (Observation Posts) used during the day, as well as day and night patrols/ambushes. I usually caught the night patrols/ambushes.

The 3rd Marines and 5th Marines, supported by the artillery on our Fire Base, were busy flushing out the enemy. The records report:

On December 21, F Company 2nd Battalion 5th Marines discovered a battalion size enemy base camp. Upon entering the camp F Company was taken under fire by an automatic weapon. F Company overran the weapon killing one NVA. K Company 3d Battalion 3d Marines found an extensive base camp with 30-35 hooches which appeared to be about one year old. I Company 3d Battalion 5th Marines while conducting search and destroy operations found an enemy village. The village consisted of 37 dwellings, a large classroom, a bakery, a hospital for twenty people and twenty-five well constructed bunkers.

On December 22, M Company 3d Battalion 5th Marines was standing by to be utilized for a bald eagle [quick reaction force]. K Company 3d Bn 3d Marines while on patrol found a small enemy harbor-site. E Company 2nd Battalion 5th Marines discovered what is believed to be an enemy R&R center. No bunkers or fighting holes were found.

Sounds like the same experience we had while I was in the 27th Marines on Operation Allen Brook. Enemy base camp, hospital and R&R center. The same discoveries we had on Go Noi Island in the June/July time frame.

On December 24th I wrote:

"Christmas Eve" (75 days)

Dear Mom, Dad, Granny, and Family,

Merry Christmas to you all. I hope that everyone is well and enjoying the holidays, and that you are all full of the Christmas spirit of joy and thanksgiving. Although I am not with you in person, I am still with you in mind and soul. May the Lord grant us Peace on Earth and Good Will toward All Men. …

Over here, one day is just like the other, only at Christmas we get a little U.S.O. packet and maybe an extra C Rat meal. Wow! I haven't gotten your package yet, but mail is real slow getting out here where I am. I should get it though.

You mentioned Operation Meade River. Well, I was on it all right. The last I heard, there was over 1000 confirmed NVA and VC dead from that opp. You should have [known] better [than] think I was wounded, because if I am, you'll be notified right away, so don't worry needlessly.

Right now I am about 5 miles South West of An Hoa, in the mountains . We've been here 2 weeks now, and this is the first time I have had the chance to sit down and write. I don't know the name of this opera-

tion, but it is sure a big one. So far we have been working on top of Hill 214, setting in an [Artillery] Battery. Reports are that we may be out here till the middle of March. So if that's true, then this will be my last operation, [Alleluia]! Only about 2 ½ months now and the days are going by just like clockwork. It seems like my birthday was just yesterday. I'm doing just fine, no better no worse. Just trying to ride this thing out till March. I'll try to write more often now if I can, but we are working all day every day. And then, the only connection we have with An Hoa is by [helicopter], so when it rains we don't get any resupply at all. So just keep your faith in the Lord and don't worry….

With all my love, Chuck

Uncanny how my mom detected that I had been wounded on Operation Meade River. I denied it of course in my letter on the 24th, no need to have her worry about a minor wound. I never did tell her. A truce was called for Christmas, but it didn't get anywhere.

The records report about the Christmas truce:

> The 24 hour Christmas truce became effective at 241800H and within 10 minutes the first of seven violations initiated by the enemy occurred. Violations were responded to with decisive and overwhelming force.

Christmas Eve was a welcome sight for me. We were still on Hill 214 and looking forward to a resupply with mail and packages. The 5th Marines brought us back to the base in An Hoa for one day, one platoon at a time. So we were choppered in and got a hot meal, taken in shifts, as we lounged near the landing pads for the helicopters. With all our gear staged for a quick load up on the choppers that would take us back to the hill, we opened our mail and boxes and had a good old time. However, before the Christmas goodies and our long-awaited packages could be accessed, we had to clean our weapons and get the area organized. Having accomplished all that, we dove in.

Someone had received a package with a small aluminum Christmas tree and it was standing tall (about one foot) in our area. It brought a smile to the lips every time I saw it. With the packages and letters we received, and full of what Christmas spirit we could muster, we enjoyed our brief stay at An Hoa. The next day we were on the helicopters headed back to Hill 214. Unfortunately, we didn't get to participate in any Christmas services or sing some Christmas carols or get too excited over Christmas because for us, it was just another day in Vietnam.

The security of Hill 214 continued until the end of December, with the same routine of patrols and ambushes.

The reports state:

The remainder of December was characterized by small unit offensive operations throughout the AO as 1968 came to a close.

From the Marine Corps records, the casualty figures for 2/5 in the month of December were:

The Battalion joined 7 officers and 165 enlisted men during the month. The Battalion transferred 4 officers and 152 enlisted men during the same period. Casualties sustained during the month were:

BATTLE					NON-BATTLE		TOTAL
KIA	WIA	DOW	WIANE	MIA	NBD	NBC	
14	62	0	57	0	0	14	147

The running total since September, 1968 is:

KIA – 77, WIA – 304, DOW – 5, WIANE – 174, MIA – 1, NBD – 1, NBC – 73, Total – 635

For the fourth month in a row, the numbers of Battalion personnel were still advancing to the rear. Having transferred 156 officers and enlisted, joined 172 officers and men and lost 147 casualties, the numbers show that 2/5 was in the hole by 131 men for December, even with a greater influx of replacements. The grand total loss since the first of September was 584 men.

Chapter 16

On January 5th we were still on Hill 214, providing security for the artillery. That day I wrote:

Dear Dad,

Say, [pardner], it sounds like our Uncle really tried to do you in. I'm sure glad that you were able to put up with it all. I have my own troubles with some of Uncle Sam's people, so when I get home we ought to have plenty to talk about on that subject.

I wrote you all at Christmas, thanking you for the package and cards. I got the package on Dec 25, Christmas Day, and boy was I glad to get it. …

Well, here it is the 9th and I'm still trying to finish this letter. It has been raining for 4 days straight now, but the sun is peeping out so maybe I can stay half-assed dry and get some work done, besides finishing this letter.

You know Dad, there was one thing in your letter that really made me feel good, and that was when you talked about us raising some hell together in a few weeks. Yep, 59 days left, only a few more weeks and I'll be home. It is really hard to believe that I'll be home in 2 months, about 8 weeks. I get so happy just thinking about leaving Viet Nam, that I am a total loss for words. …

With all my love, Your Son, Chuck

We were still on Hill 214 at Fire Support Base (FSB) Pike. The reports from 2nd Battalion 5th Marines make it simple to understand:

> During the period 1 January to 31 January 1969 the battalion continued search and clear operations on the ONG THU Slope 7 ½ miles west of An Hoa on Operation Taylor Common under the operational control of the 3rd Marines. Three rifle companies conducted extensive patrols in the battalion A. O. with one company

> providing security for and improving the defenses of Fire Support Base Pike. Although contact with the enemy was largely that of chance meeting engagements the battalion continued to uncover enemy base camps and supply points disrupting his logistic support. On 23 January the battalion was ordered to disestablish FSB Pike and prepare to move to a new A. O.
>
> The bulk of intelligence collected and disseminated during January was received from 3rd Marines, Duc Duc District Headquarters, CAP units and the local populace in addition to the normal intelligence sources available to an infantry battalion.

I remember the constant patrols in the Duc Duc area and how hard it was to control the area. I like to think that the work we did in Duc Duc while I was in the 27th Marines paid off, causing the area to be more favorable to U. S. interests and of use in future operations.

More information from Marine records:

> Enemy contacts, because of heavy vegetation and narrow trails, tended to be at very short range and of short duration. Enemy positions were usually placed so that flanking them was extremely difficult or where the few defenders could bring fire on the trail and then withdraw rapidly in defilade. On 25 January a male Caucasian about 69 inches tall, blonde hair, wearing jungle utilities was seen near ZC167484. Upon being sighted, he immediately ran north along a trail. One Marine shouted at him but no effort was made to stop him since he was thought to be one of the members of the company in the area.
>
> There were fifty-five cases of malaria treated. This large increase of malaria is thought to be due to the area where the Battalion is operating. A vigorous campaign of preventive measures including the use of chloroquine primaquine tablets and repellent is in effect. There were five cases of venereal disease from the Battalion seen this month.
>
> There were six Marines treated for rabies.

As the records indicate, there were many opportunities for injuries besides the enemy. Some men partook of the local "ladies" in An Hoa and the surrounding area. Many of them came down with all kinds of venereal diseases. It was said among the troops that there was a venereal disease that couldn't be cured, causing "crotch rot" forever. Rabies was also easy to contract from dogs, rats and any number of wild critters that we lived with every day. However, the worst disease and most contagious was malaria. I lost one of my men that way. My little book lists Pfc Hornfeck as one of the men at the BAS (Battalion Aid Station).

I remember clearly when he came down with malaria. We were on a long sweep around the base of Hill 214 and one of our checkpoints was by this large mountain river. It looked real nice, like the rivers back home, and some of the new men drank from it, thinking it would naturally be clean water. Although they had been warned, they drank anyway. What they hadn't learned yet was the fact that there were no clean rivers in Vietnam. In fact, there was no clean water at all, unless you found a spring and drank from the very point where the water came out of the earth and even then you need to boil it. Even wells were off limits because some had been poisoned by the VC. That was the primary reason I boiled all my water and made coffee with it. Boiling wouldn't help with poison so I chose my water carefully most of the time.

Well, a Marine from my squad drank from the river even after being told not to and before long, he came down with chills and fever. It may not have been from the water, but we all thought so. The corpsman did what he could and we carried him in a poncho stretcher back to the CP. Malaria was nothing to mess with. We were supposed to take a pill every day to help prevent catching it, but not even those pills worked all the time.

My squad roster by this time was:

Myself as squad leader	
LCpl. Reyes	1st team leader and gunner
Pfc. Marsh	2nd team leader and gunner
Pfc. Parker	1st team A-gunner
Pfc. Warner	2nd team A-gunner
LCpl. Lockett	1st team ammo humper
Pfc. Dawes	2nd team ammo humper
Pfc. Cannady	1st team ammo humper
Pfc. McFetridge	2nd team ammo humper

Life had become good for Golf Co. 2/5. Our assignment to be the security for FSB [Fire Support Base] Pike was as close to a break as we could hope for. Yes, we ran patrols and OPs during the daylight hours, LPs and ambushes during the nights. But we also got to go to An Hoa every so often to get a shower and a hot meal and any personal items we needed. A list in my bloody wheel book gives a typical resupply mission to An Hoa. The list was mostly for cigarettes with some other items such as writing materials, cashews, paintbrushes (for cleaning the machine guns), C size batteries for the flashlights and some Vienna sausages. Each man pitched in the money needed for his request and I would shop from the list, to ensure everyone got what they wanted. It was as close to an In-Country R&R as I could hope for. The best part was that as long as we were on that hill, I didn't have to contend with that little redheaded Lt. In fact, I don't remember him being around once we were on Hill 214 or after that time either. He may have been transferred out once we manned the firebase. Or something else happened to him to remove him from our platoon.

I had become used to the idea of taking out patrols often and with the other two platoons there, the rotation for patrols and ambushes was spread out among the whole company. Of course there was always the chance that we could be caught napping by the enemy.

One occasion on the hill reveals the tension we lived under. My machine gun squad was placed at the far end of the hilltop, on a finger that dropped off into the jungle. Having learned the lessons from Maui Peak, I placed each gun on the side of the finger with interlocking fire across the best avenue of approach up to the top. We were there long enough to dig some really good holes and managed to scrounge up some sheets of tin, plenty of sandbags and empty ammunition cases from the artillery guys. We dug a deep hole for the machine gun position, built in the shape of a horseshoe with the open end facing out toward the enemy. That way, we could move around the horseshoe shape and have a 180-degree field of fire. Attached to the back of the horseshoe was a square hole with the tin roof and ammo crates to sit and sleep on. We had dug plenty of grenade sumps around the lower perimeter of the position. A grenade sump is a hole dug at a slant into the dirt where the floor meets the dirt sides. This enabled us to kick a grenade into the sump if we had one thrown into that position. The earth would absorb the explosion and shrapnel - at least that was the idea. Fortunately, I never had to try out that trick. This was the number one gun position and mine as well. The number two gun was placed on an opposite side of the finger and built the same as ours. I also had them pop out the tracer rounds from the ammo belts that were used at night. Lessons learned.

We filled plenty of sandbags and lined the rim of the hole with them about two deep and two high, bringing the lip of the hole to an armpit height. We had also stacked up sand bags around the back hole at three or four sandbags tall with the tin roofing on top of them and held in place by more sandbags. There were two windows, one on each side, formed by an opening between the sandbags and a small log across the window top, which was covered by the tin roof and sandbags.

I had everyone dig similar holes to their own tastes, but not requiring the horseshoe shapes. We had flashlights with red lenses for movement in the dark, and maintained a "No White Light" policy in the positions. Any letter writing had to be done during the day, or by moonlight. We felt pretty secure there, but we still watched diligently. By this time everyone had been in enough fire fights to know what could happen if we let our guard down. All the holes were two-man positions. Since the VC knew where we were, I allowed smoking as long as it was done in one of the holes in the rear of the lines.

The finger we were on dropped away steeply from the edge where we had our positions and we were constantly cutting down the jungle on those slopes in front of us, to create an area with no cover for any enemy advancing on our positions. One last tool at our disposal was a Starlight Scope. This was a large scope used by sniper teams to spot the rounds fired when delivering a strike at night. They could also be used on a rifle for night operations. The scope amplified light so unless it was pitch black out, it worked okay. It was hard to get used to, because the images in the scope all tended to be a greenish grey, blending into the background, also a greenish grey.

Depth perception and distance were very hard to determine and any movement would throw the focus off. They worked well enough, and gave us Marines on the lines a sense of added safety.

One night, sometime around midnight, one of the men on watch in the horseshoe position awakened me. He quietly told me that he thought he saw a gook squatted down in the tree line in front of our position. I quickly turned two, slipped on my boots without bothering to tie them up and took a look for myself. By golly, there he was. I could see him with the starlight scope. He was squatted down by a log, with his conical VC hat covering his head. I could see the hat clearly. I didn't want to give away our position so I called up to the Company CP and asked for some 60mm illumination over our position. I first had to talk to the Officer on Watch to get the okay. Permission given, I gave my position and the approximate distance to the VC from my machine gun hole. The flare round from the mortar popped overhead and we all stared hard trying to see the gook by the light of the flare. Nothing could be seen. However, when the flare went out and we looked through the starlight scope, we could see him for sure. Several men looked and verified that they could see him too, so the next step was to ask for a WP (Willie Peter/ White Phosphorus) round as a spotting round. By this time the whole line in our area was awake and waiting to kick ass. I asked for the WP round and we could hear the mortar 'bloop' as the round left the tube and waited to see where it landed. It was off some and I called in adjustments until they were right on. During this whole time, the VC didn't move an inch. One tough VC I thought. Once the WP rounds were on target, I called in for a set of four HE rounds to follow. (HE is the term given to High Explosive rounds full of shrapnel).

In came the rounds and everyone took cover in case of a short round that could fall on us and blow us away. Explosions and then dust filled the area where we had seen the VC. After the last round hit, I called in giving an "on target" and waited for the dust to clear to give the mortar guys a damage report. As things became clear enough to see with the starlight scope, I looked and, "WHAT?"… that VC was still there, in the same position. Thinking we must have missed, I called in for another four rounds of HE, fire for effect, and the same procedures were repeated.

Again, that VC just wasn't moving. I called the mortar pit and told them that we would investigate at first light. That VC never moved all that night. Our lines stayed on alert - who could sleep after all that noise? The mortar pit kept asking for a damage report and all I could do was put them off and wait until dawn.

Later, as dawn broke, I took a small team with me and called to the CP that we were going down. Once the all clear was given, we went to the spot where the VC was spotted. Things looked so different in the daylight that it was hard to get my bearings. Having checked the spot with my starlight scope once more in the dawn light, I saw nothing but tree limbs scattered around where we had cut back the jungle.

We made a good show of it all, searching the tree line, but it was no use. That "starlight VC" was nothing more than a stump. So much for the starlight scope. I was getting short and feeling the pressure to get home without some VC blowing me away, and my men were spooked as well by the constant patrols and thick jungle, not knowing where the VC might be. My men conspired with me on making a report to the mortar team that we had found a blood trail and that was that. The CP and mortar team were satisfied, and everything went back to normal. There were plenty of quiet jabs and jeers among us all, each one of us pointing to someone else and the others pointing back saying:

"You saw him too, ha ha ha."

As the tension was released, we all had a good laugh about all that, and the guys would say:

"Hey Van, see any gooks down there?"

I may have been embarrassed but I put that to rest and again took charge of the situation. We all make mistakes, but that was a dilly. I simply attributed my error to being a short-timer.

In addition, the reports from the 3rd Marine Regiment, to whom we were attached, reveal the following:

> Significant Fire Support Events. Overall fire support during the month of January was good. Occasionally when bad weather hampered resupply, harassing and interdiction fires had to be reduced to a minimum to conserve ammunition stocks for contact missions. Two companies were operating out of 81mm mortar range of FSB PIKE. 105mm howitzers fired all missions for those companies.
>
> A problem area existed with helicopters transiting the AO from An Hoa to FSB Pike requesting "Check Fire" upon leaving An Hoa control. Air sentries maintain close watch on helicopters approaching the gun target line and "Check Fire" as helicopters approach. Closer coordination between the FSC [Fire Support Coordinator] and FAC [Forward Air Controller] alleviated the problem.
>
> Mine and booby trap incidents increased during January, and they were not limited to any particular area as they were in December. This was one indication that the enemy no longer considered any part of Base Area 112 safe from our incursions. Another indication of this realization was that the enemy was caught unaware less frequently. Enemy troops walked trails at sling arms and talking during December. For the most of January, he moved quietly and at the ready.

Another incident on FSB Pike happened to one of my men. He was also getting short and spooky and he had a little problem.

It was shortly after first light when my man came running over to our position and almost out of breath said:

"There's a rat in my hole! There's a rat in my hole!"

"Why don't you just shoot that rat," we teased.

"No sir, I looked at that rat and that rat looked at me and I said, 'Mister Rat, you can have my hole.'"

Well, a few of us went over to see his rat and sure enough, there was this very large rat in his hole. I told one of the men to shout "fire in the hole" several times, after which I took my M-16 and shot that rat. I went down in his hole, grabbed that rat by the tail, and brought it out. It was very heavy and very long. So long that with my arm stretched straight out from my side, parallel with the ground, and holding that rat by the end of the tail, it's nose just touched the ground. I remember someone getting a picture of me holding that rat. Later some said that it wasn't a rat but rather a nutria. However, a nutria is a rat-like creature that lives around water, in marshes and streams, not on the top of mountains. Whichever the case may be, it was one huge rat.

There have been many disbelievers who have heard the "Rat Story," but I researched rats and found that there is a species called the Giant Norway Rat. I have seen pictures of it and in one picture, a man is holding the rat by the tail while the nose touches the ground. THAT is my rat. So, as we said in Vietnam:

"There it is."

From the records of the 5th Marine Regiment:

> Operations. During the month of January all operational activities of the Fifth Marines were included in Operation TAYLOR COMMON.
>
> Situation. Enemy: Historically, Go Noi Island has served as an enemy staging area and as a point of departure for attacks on the Da Nang TAOR. During the 1968 Tet Offensive, the island served as headquarters for the 1st and the 21st NVA Regiments. The low-lying terrain largely consists of rice paddies and in heavy rains the area for the most part is inundated. It is marked by sporadically defended fortified villages employing bunker, trench, and tunnel complexes. Intelligence sources indicate the presence of the forward elements of Front 4 National Liberation Front or VC on the island. Various reports also suggest the remnants of units contacted during Operation MEADE RIVER have sought refuge in the area. These possibly include the V-25 and R-20 main force battalions and remnants of the 2nd Bn/35th NVA Regiment. The island has always been suspected as a retreat area of the Q-81 Local Force Battalion when Marine units sweep the northwestern section of the 5th Marines AO.

This brief analysis confirms what all of us who fought in and around the Go Noi Island area knew from the constant operations in that area. No matter what we did, turn it into a parking lot or not, the vegetation would grow and the enemy would return and everything would be as it was before. There is no accounting for the number of dead Marines attributed to that area. It was like a dog chasing his tail. Gone was the concept of taking territory and keeping it. The sound concepts of warfare conceived as far back in history as the Chinese Empire. The war was progressing in circles, with no end in sight. The "Art of War" was lost.

It was January 17th, and I thought that my little brother Chris had just turned 16 on the 15th. I must have been pretty far gone because his birthday was actually on February 15th. In the letter home to him I wrote:

Dear Chris,

Pardner, let me tell you that your letter of Jan 2, sure was a welcome sight. I don't know why, but every time I get a letter from you, it makes me feel like I'm already home. …

So you are still wearing that hat [a Marine Corps utility cover] I gave you egh, I wish I had a good Stetson but each to his own I guess. I'll sure try to bring home some more for you. I don't know if I can get any of those "Bush Hats" (the round one) but I'll try. I lost mine, and let me tell you, they are mighty hard to get a hold of. Say, if you can, why don't you send me a picture of you with your hat on and all. I've got your school picture, but that's not the same thing. Oh well, I guess I can wait 51 more days to see your ugly face. …

Whoa!!! I almost forgot, HAPPY BIRTHDAY! Let's see, you are 16 now aren't you, and almost as good a shot as I am, almost!!! (Ha, Ha) That sure was fine shooting you did. I hope there is some venison left when I get home. If not, maybe we'll just go out and get some. I sure am hankern' for some venison when I get home. …

With all my love, Your Brother, Chuck

On January 20th, I wrote to my Mom:

Dear Mom,

Here I am, I don't exactly remember when I wrote last, but I think it was just before I got your package. …

It sounds like our family is up to it's old tricks again, with the flu going around. But thank goodness you and Granny haven't had it yet. I've been real lucky and haven't had a bad cold or anything, except a little piece of [shrapnel] in my arm. I'll tell you all about it when I get home. … But don't worry about it because it happened two months ago. …

It won't be [too] long before I'll be right there in person. I count 48 days from today and I'll be going to [Okinawa]. …

With all my love, Chuck

My letters home had lost the edge of combat. I was so used to it that, unless something major happened, I didn't waste the ink. A part of me was looking forward to going home, while the other part continued to keep me safe. No telling how my mom took the news that I had been wounded and had not told her until two months later. For me, it was just too minor to talk about.

On January 21st, I wrote to my dad. It was much the same as the other letters, talking about being home, but one part kept things in focus:

> *Dear Dad,*
>
> *[It's] getting close to dark, but I don't get much time to write, so I'm trying to get as much writing done as possible. …*
>
> *Well, you did make one good statement and that was my 8 Sundays left. But from tomorrow I figure I've only got 7 Sundays, only 46 days left in Viet Nam. Then I go to [Okinawa] then home. It may be less if I'm lucky, but I'm not counting on it. …*
>
> *(Time out while I fix a cup of C Rat Coffee.) Well, there, boy! When you think of having to fill your canteens, then pour half a canteen cup of water, take C-4 (plastic explosive like TNT) cut it into chunks to heat your water, heat the water, then take 2 C Rat Instant Coffees find a spoon some where stir it all together and whew! Sit down and enjoy it? That coffee pot sure [looks] good, I can't wait to get home for some of Mom's coffee. …*
>
> *With all my love, Your Son, (and proud of it), Chuck*

As January 23rd approached, which was the date for the disassembly of FSB Pike, we continued our patrols and ambushes. After the 23rd, we remained on Hill 214, continuing our patrols and helping to destroy the area. Yes, I said destroy. Not only did the process begin to remove the big guns and all their associated equipment, but also to remove all material from the hill. Our fighting holes had to be disassembled as well as all sand bags cut and holes filled in, leaving nothing that the enemy could use to establish his own base on that hilltop. That process took us up to the 1st of February, when we were sent back to An Hoa.

From the Marine Corps records for 2/5, the casualty figures for the month of January were:

> The Battalion joined 7 officers and 129 enlisted men during the month. Eight officers and 120 enlisted men were transferred. Casualties sustained during the month were:

BATTLE					NON-BATTLE		TOTAL
KIA	WIA	DOW	WIANE	MIA	NBD	NBC	
7	21	0	32	0	2	153	215

The running total since September is:

KIA – 84, WIA – 325, DOW – 5, WIANE – 206, MIA – 1, NBD – 3, NBC – 226, Total – 850

For the fifth month in a row, the numbers of Battalion personnel were advancing to the rear. Having transferred 128 officers and enlisted, joined 136 officers and men and lost 215 casualties, the numbers show that 2/5 was in the hole by 207 men for January. The grand total loss since the first of September was 791 men.

Chapter 17

February was here, but I wasn't out of the woods yet. The records report the following:

> Throughout the month of February [1969], the Fifth Marines continued to participate in Operation "taylor common" under the OPCON of Task Force Yankee, BrigGen Ross T. Dwyer, Jr.; Commanding 1-14 February, and BrigGen S. Jaskilka, commanding 15-28 February 1969.
>
> Land clearing operations were also conducted by the 1st and 2nd Battalions along the MSR [Main Supply Route] near Liberty Bridge and adjacent river banks, and in the Phu Nhuan area with TD-18 buldozers [*sic*]. This has proved effective in the detection of numerous VC hiding places, trenches, fighting positions, bunkers, supply caches and in the reduction of casualties from surprise firing devices.
>
> On 1 February 1969, the Battalion helilifted to An Hoa for rehabilitation and refurbishment. On 5 February, participation in Operation Taylor Common was resumed with the rappelling of one reinforced rifle platoon into the canopy 20 miles southwest of An Hoa. After clearing an LZ, a rifle company (-) helilifted in that afternoon, with the Battalion arriving the next day. Search and destroy operations were begun with the building of landing zones throughout the AO undertaken to insure ready accessibility to the area at a future date. Contact with the enemy was light throughout. On 17 February the Battalion began a helilift to An Hoa which was completed on 18 February for 3 days of rehabilitaion and refurbishment. On 21 February the Battalion was moved to Phu Lac (6) to Go Noi resulted in light enemy contact but numerous booby traps along the way. On 24 February the Battalion (-) was pulled out of Go Noi Island to search and clear the area in the Phu Nhuans, Chau Phongs and Le

Nams. The Battalion encountered light enemy contact and on 28 February commenced a land clearing operation east of An Hoa in the Phu Nhuans.

The first part of the month was characterized by the enemy employing harassing tactics throughout the AO, and conducting probing attacks at night against friendly positions. The enemy continued his employment of mines and booby traps along the MSR, trails, and high ground throughout the AO. The employment of large numbers of squad-sized night ambushes, hunter killer teams, and extensive use of H&I harrassment and interdection fires and employment of A-6 Beacon Strikes, artillery, 81mm mortars, and land clearing operations significantly reduced the enemy's capability to interdict the MSR main supply route, to set booby traps or to mass any large scale attacks. The enemy launched his 1969 TET Offensive 23 February and mortar and rocket attacks increased against the An Hoa Combat Base and Liberty Bridge Defense Sector (Phu Loc (6)). The effectiveness of these attacks was drastically reduced by counter-mortar fire. The enemy did not attempt any large scale ground attacks during this period, but on several occasions enemy company size units were engaged as they attempted to travel through the Regimental AO. In each case, massive casualties were inflicted on the enemy through the employment of aggressive sweep and block maneuvers, ambushes, and the employment of supporting arms. The employment of a variety of offensive tactics stressing mobile, fast-reaction forces, permitted the Regiment to engage the enemy almost at will, and to entrap large numbers attempting to escape. Aggressive pursuit of contact coupled with the liberal use of supporting arms allowed the Regiment continued success against the enemy.

Fifth Marines continued to participate in Operation TAYLOR COMMON (Search and Destroy) throughout the month and continues into March.

Fire Support. Fire support and fire support coordination was provided for normal 5th Marines operations and included support of BLT 3/26 and the 1st ARVN Ranger Group. The USS Jersey, USS Newport News, and the USS Oklahoma City fired a total of 796 rounds (138 – 16″, 642 – 8″ and 13 – 5″) into the Go Noi Island area.

During this time, there was a strong emphasis on the use of Hunter Killer Teams, which were similar to the Killer Teams that I was part of while in the 27th Marines. There were also squad sized ambushes that were employed. There seemed to be no limit to the number of VC or NVA that we faced, and I remember clearly a squad-sized patrol that I had. I had one gun team with me, not from my squad, but from another squad, new guys who needed some salt under their belts. The riflemen were much the same. Newbies, they would be the death of me yet.

I took out the patrol around 1000 hours and expected to be back about 1400 hours. Our route would take us by a village that was supposed to be empty of any VC. I never trusted reports like that, and always moved as if the whole NVA Army was after us.

My men had been on a few patrols with me and knew the basics of what to do should we get hit. I practiced my method of moving quickly toward our next checkpoint and then stopping to set up a short ambush in case we were being followed. As we neared this village, I could see that it was anything but empty. There were hogs and chickens and even a water buffalo wandering around the village, with ample evidence of human habitation, but no one in sight.

With the village in sight from the edge of the wooded area we were in, I set up an ambush. We were tired from the hump since our last check point and the ambush was a welcome respite. I watched the village for about 20 minutes, trying to detect any VC, but it seemed deserted. Finally, I got the men up from their positions and went toward the village to check out the hooches. We never got the chance.

As we walked down a trail that ran past a water buffalo watering hole, all hell broke loose. Instantly I hollered for everyone to jump into the large watering hole as the bullets zinged around us. A normal watering hole was about 8 to 10 feet in diameter at the bottom with sloping sides all around except for a dirt ramp that led down to the water. It looked like a large keyhole shaped funnel. Water buffaloes were bigger than most beef cattle in the States, and very unpredictable. For some reason it was left to the children to tend the buffalo, controlling it with a rope that was run through a heavy metal ring in the buffalo's nose. A tender area for the buffalo and when pulled correctly, the kids could easily control the beast. Because of all this, the watering hole was made large and the ramp open enough so as not to spook the buffalo. Spooked water buffaloes are nothing anyone wants to contend with. I had learned that lesson at the Battle for Cam Le Bridge.

We all made it into the hole okay while the bullets were pinging off the lip of the hole. We were trapped. The incoming rifle fire was coming from all directions, especially from the village on one side and from a large rice paddy on the other side of the hole. Everyone was shook up, but calmed down as I directed their fire. With no other alternatives, we were prepared to fight it out. I had a machine gun with the patrol and I had it set up facing the entrance area, which was our most vulnerable spot. We returned fire as we could to keep the VC at bay, but had to watch our ammo expenditure. This would not be a good time to run out of ammo. Fire control was paramount. Fortunately, everyone carried at least three bandoleers of seven loaded M-16 magazines, which is 420 rounds. I always carried four bandoleers.

Things were getting real scary. The gooks were not letting up and I was afraid that sooner or later the VC would charge our position. Grabbing the radio hand set, with the radioman at my side, I called in for help. Our Company had a CP set up in the area and that command post was our link to fire support. I hollered over the phone that we were pinned down and taking heavy small arms fire. I told them that I need some air support. I waited a minute and was just about to call again when the person on the other end told me there was no air support of any kind for us because everyone was busy blowing up the enemy elsewhere.

Crap. We continued to try and keep the VC's head down and still conserve ammo and do our best to survive. I called back and asked them if I could get some artillery support, and again the reply was negative, all arty was already engaged.

Crap. Crap. My mouth was dry as a bone and I took a quick sip of water before I tried again. With my next call I asked for 81mm mortars and again that was denied. That broke the camel's back. I hollered into the hand set that we were on the verge of being overrun by a force of unknown size, and I wanted some help now. I was real worried that the gooks would eventually work themselves around so they could fire into the hole from the direction of the ramp, which was completely open. Given enough troops and determination, we would be sitting ducks if they got around us to that position. I had kept the machine gun quiet so they wouldn't know we had that kind of fire power, but if they charged from that direction, the gun would have to open up.

For the first time that I remember, I felt that the time for my immediate death was near. Always before, I was able to take evasive action or call in fire support when faced with a superior enemy force. I was the hunter, not the hunted. Not this time. We were stuck like rats in a trap. A trap with no end but death. However, I also realized that panic was my enemy every bit as much as the VC around us. I had to calm down.

I took control of myself and calmly told whoever it was on the other end of the line that if they couldn't give us any support, we would probably be dead before anyone could get to us. I was getting desperate. I said:

"Give me anything, anything."

Finally they came back on the line. The firing all around us had increased and I knew that the gooks knew that without some fire support, we would die. It wouldn't be long before the lead would start coming in from the direction of the ramp. My call sign was Golf 2 Alpha.

"Golf 2 Alpha, Golf FO, over." the voice on the other end said - FO was the code for the Company Forward Observer who controlled fire support missions.

"Golf FO, Golf 2 Alpha, over." I replied.

"Sit rep, over." (Sit rep meant situation report.)

"Golf FO, we are surrounded. We are holed up in a water buffalo watering hole, but won't be able to hold out much longer, over."

"Roger that, the only thing I have is some 5 inch Naval Gun Fire Support, over." - The 5 inch was a Naval Gun that fired a 5 x 54 inch projectile with a 13 mile effective range.

"Roger that, but I need it now, over." I answered back.

I found the map coordinates and relayed that to him, and asked for a fire mission on our own position. I was feeling desperate. He replied:

"Golf 2 Alpha, I can't call a fire mission on your own location, give coordinates or range and bearing for fire mission, over."

The fire was starting to shift and I had the gunner get ready to fire on anyone or any muzzle flashes in his field of fire. I checked the map and called back and gave him a range and bearing since I couldn't find a suitable set of coordinates on the map, which only showed a flat area of rice paddies. A few minutes later he came back on the line:

"Golf 2 Alpha, Golf FO, over."

"Roger Golf FO, over."

"Golf 2 Alpha, stand by for fire mission. One round Willie Peter on it's way, over." - Willie Peter was the code for a white phosphorus round which put up a plume of white smoke.

"Roger that, over."

The WP round came in but was off a bit. Just then, the worst happened, the machine gunner opened up on some enemy troops trying to maneuver to a better location in order to fire into our hole. I quickly called to adjusted the fire support to that enemy position.

"Golf FO, adjust fire, left 200, add 50, danger close, four rounds HE, air bursts, fire for effect, over." - HE meant high explosive, the adjustments were in meters.

I quickly got the men together and had them huddle up under their flak jackets with their helmets on but not strapped down, because with explosive rounds that close, the blast could blow the helmet up causing the chin strap to act as a garrote. We must have looked like big green turtles, but it was all we could do. I had adjusted the fire extremely close to our position.

Boom! Boom! Boom! Boom! The rounds came in. They hit about 50 meters from us out in the rice paddies all around us. As the smoke was clearing, I told the gunner to fire on anything that moved. I got the hand set and called in.

"Golf FO, Golf 2 Alpha, adjust fire, left 100, on target, danger close, air bursts, fire for effect, over."

The rounds came in, falling so close to our hole that we got some shrapnel in the hole. No one was hurt, but it made a mess of the village. One round was very close, close enough to shake our earthen hole and pucker up some butt holes. When the barrage lifted, I peeked over the rim of our hole and there was nothing but dust and smoke. The VC got the message and got out of Dodge. Again I adjusted fire.

"Adjust fire, right 200, down 50, danger close, fire for effect, over."

This adjustment brought rounds on the village where we had received the initial incoming rounds.

The rounds exploded again as we hunkered down under our make-shift armor.

"Golf FO, Golf 2 Alpha, cease fire, cease fire, over." I said.

The radio crackled, "Golf 2 Alpha, Golf FO, damage report, over."

"Roger, wait one, over." I replied.

I had the men check out the area. Everyone was on edge. A couple of shots rang out as the men shot anything that moved. The village was a mess, with some hooches burning and dead hogs and chickens lying all over the place, even the water buffalo was blown to pieces. But no VC bodies were found. The same results were discovered out in the rice paddies, no bodies. There were a few blood trails, but we certainly weren't going to follow them. I just wanted to get us back to safety. I still had no idea how many VC we were facing. With the FO bugging the radio man for a damage report, I got on the line and reported:

"Golf FO, Golf 2 Alpha, over."

"Golf 2 Alpha, report, over."

"Golf FO, damage report, On Target. Mission a success, enemy positions eliminated, blood trails, over."

He repeated what I said and ended with;

"Roger that, will relay damage report to Navy. Are you going to check out blood trails, over."

"Negative, no telling how many VC are out here, will return to CP, out." Those thirteen 5 inch Naval Fire Support rounds reported in the records were the ones that saved our bacon.

I couldn't believe it, here I was SHORT and this had to happen. Still shaken by the close encounter with the VC, I got the patrol lined up and we headed back to our base. I always stayed close to the point man and as we went up the trail, moving through the open area of the village and into the tree line, I noticed a puff of smoke rising from the bushes. Immediately, I called out:

"Grenade!"... and hit the dirt.

Everyone was down and still nothing happened. After a few minutes, which seemed like forever, I told everyone to stay down while I checked things out. Gingerly, I crept forward, found the tripwire and looked to a spot in the brush where the ChiCom grenade sat, still smoldering. I quickly turned away and told the men to move it out, now! After we had gone about a hundred yards down the trail, I stopped the patrol for a rest.

We were all a jumble of nerves by now and I knew I needed to calm the men down and make a quick march back to the CP so we could get in before dark. I gathered the men together and explained about ChiComs. They often didn't go off and just smoked. It was a real crap shoot as to which would happen. I think they used black powder in the grenades and if it got damp, all you would get was the smoke. However, you never knew, so if you tripped one and it smoked, wait a minute and either go around it or blow it in place. You had to be careful because it could still go off when you least expected it.

Would you believe it, not long after I said that, the damn ChiCom went off. Everyone looked at me like I was a guru or something. It surprised me as much as it did them, but I didn't let on. I told them never to mess with unexploded ordinance on their own. Leave that to the engineers as much as possible. They nodded their heads, wide eyes going up and down. No one got hurt that day, but it was a close call. Too close for a "Short"' man.

I believe that I may have been on Go Noi Island when this happened. The reports indicate the following:

> From 1 February to 17 February the 2nd Battalion, 5th Marines continued participation in Operation TAYLOR COMMON, a multi-battalion sweep of the southwest sector of the 5th Marines TAOR. The sweep yielded no specific intelligence.
>
> On 21 February the Battalion moved by convoy to Phu Lac (6) vicinity AT9353 in preparation for sweep of Go Noi Island beginning the morning of 22 February. Contacts in the area were made with small groups and with snipers. A total of 19 booby-trapped grenades, known and unknown types of rounds and firing devices were detonated or destroyed.
>
> On 21 February the Battalion began operations on Go Noi Island. After the shelling and light probe of the An Hoa Combat Base on 22 February the Battalion (-) displaced from Go Noi to hill 42 vicinity AT9148 where extensive combat patrols were conducted.
>
> During Operation Taylor Common an unseasonal increase in malaria casualties was seen. Beginning in February a gradual rise in non-battle casualties was also noted and attributed to prolong exposure in the field. Casualties were evacuated to the Da Nang area and treated at either First Medical Battalion or NSA Hospital. With the Regiment returning to Third Marine Division TAOR, evacuation was to the Third Medical Battalion, Quang Tri, RVN.

Back to the first of February, we were still on FSB Pike, making preparations for our return to An Hoa. We made our final move to An Hoa on February 3rd for a couple of days of rehab. The rest of the battalion was already engaged in operations in the Go Noi Island area. The records report:

> 2/5: AT H-HOUR ON D-DAY IN COORD AND COOPERATION WITH 1ST ARVN RNGR GRP IN EASTERN GO NOI COMMENCE OPNS IN WESTERN GO NOI TO FIND, FIX, AND DESTROY EN FORCES THERIN AND PROVIDE SECURITY FOR ENGR ASSETS TO DESTROY FORTIFICATIONS IN ASSIGNED AO. ESTAB BLOCK VIC RR TRACKS
>
> 031010H 0937 G/2/5 HELILIFTED TO AN HOA COMPLETED
>
> During the period 5-17 February the Battalion operated in the jungle canopy 20 miles southwest of An Hoa. All resupply was made by helicopter from ISA [Installation Supply Activity] at An

> Hoa. During the period 21-28 February resupply was made by truck convoy from An Hoa.

On February 8th, I wrote:

> *Dear Folks,*
>
> *Well, here I sit with about 28 days left in Viet Nam. And where am I sitting? Somewhere on a hill south west of An Hoa deep in the mountains. That's right, they've got me out in the bush again. I think this opp is Taylor Common II. Anyway, I am close to a [nervous] wreck, knowing that in just a matter of 4 weeks I'll be on my way home and yet, any minute Charles might hit us and well, you can well imagine how I feel. Oh, well, things could be worse, I guess. Just keep the prayers aimed skyward and I will [too], and if the Lord wants me home, I'll be there shortly.*
>
> *I don't know when you will get this letter, because we are having one hell of a time getting resupplied, so just don't worry about me if you don't [hear] from me [too] often. Our reunion will be well worth the waiting. …*
>
> *I don't know what else to say, so I'll go for now. I hope to go back to An Hoa in about two weeks, and if I do I'll start getting the letters to you all again. …*
>
> *With all my love, Chuck*

By February 10th, we would be heavily engaged in the process of establishing a LZ (landing zone) for helicopters to support the operation we were on. Of course, the LZ had to be on the top of a hill and getting there would prove to be very difficult in the mountain canopy.

The records report:

> On February 10, Companies F and H, 2nd Bn, 5th Marines conducted search and destroy operations IAW [in accordance with] mission. CP and Company E, 2nd Bn, 5th Marines moved to Hill #305, and operated from same. Company G, 2nd Bn, 5th Marines prepared for crossing river while Company M, 3rd Bn, 5th Marines prepared security for 2/5 (-) river crossing.
>
> 11 Feb 69 — 0715 CoG is leaving CoM lines
> 0815 CoG at the river
> 0920 CoG at ford on stream
> 1000 CoG At ford building bridge
> 1450 CoG On other side of river

On February 11, Company E, 2nd Bn, 5th Marines attacked battalion objective F, while Company G, 2nd Bn, 5th Marines attacked battalion objective G.

12 Feb 69	0821 CoG is moving
	0935 CoG at 004338
	1030 CoG at 010336
	1127 CoG at obj 998339 starting external LZ
	1940 CoG 1&2 night activities set in

On February 12, Companies E and G, 2nd Bn, 5th Marines reached their objectives

13 Feb 69 1300H In the area of YC990344, a patrol of Co G, 2/5 found a grave with 1 body killed by artillery.

Valentine's Day! February 14, 1969 and I was still alive, if that was what you could call it. It had now been a year since I left the States and landed in Vietnam. A whole year, and what did I have to show for it? A dead soul, a skinny worn out body and a mind counting the days that the enemy had left to kill me stone dead. I had become a real wreck, and the only thing I had become good at was killing Vietnamese. I was cold and hard inside and literally incapable of shedding a tear for any reason. I had become what the Marine Corps trained me to be, a Deadly Fighting Machine.

I thought back to that other Valentine's Day, an eternity in the past, and remembered the young men I was with as we headed out to war. All gone now, either dead or severely wounded. Luckily, the men in my current squad in Golf Company, 2nd Battalion, 5th Marines, were doing okay. I had lost two due to sickness, and one badly wounded who had returned to the squad, and one transferred. Every day I was thankful that no one had been killed.

I was "short," with only a little over three weeks before I was due to leave Vietnam forever. It wore on the nerves to be short and still be in the bush. All my senses were on super high alert while at the same time keeping my cool so as not to overreact in dangerous situations. There was one incident around this time that sticks with me today. It wasn't a bloody battle, but it was a mess.

Being in the mountains with no clear areas for helicopters to land, meant that the only resupply we had was when a Sea Knight brought in a net load of "beans and bullets," dropping the supplies down through the trees, hoping we could get to them before the enemy did.

To fix this problem, we had hacked and blown out an area just off the crest of the hill we were on, to be used as an LZ. This was an area of extremely thick vegetation, mountain canopy. Soon a Sea Knight came in with supplies as well as an officer from Battalion. I think he was from the Operations Center. Anyway, the chopper came in and landed beautifully. The Sea Knight quickly unloaded the officer and our supplies. The officer talked with our captain while we were trying to remove the supplies from the LZ.

Before long, as we were still moving the resupply, the officer climbed back on the Sea Knight and the chopper took off. Up and up it went until it was about treetop level. Suddenly, some shots rang out and the Sea Knight came down. It came down like a rock. The blades struck the ground and pieces of helicopter blade went whizzing through the trees. As the Sea Knight hit the ground, several men were thrown out as the chopper started to roll off the LZ and into the trees. The LZ was on a finger leading down from our hill and except for the small landing pad, it dropped off steeply on two sides.

I was close to the LZ, in the line of men passing the resupply along to the Company CP. As the chopper hit and rolled, it came right at me. It was enough to make you crap your pants. Here I am, a "short-timer," and this hunk of steel and gas and rotator blades is coming right at me. All I could do was drop into a little rocky gully that led down the side of the hill. I lay as flat as I could and hoped for the best.

Once the crash-bang-swoosh of the crash ended, I got up, unhurt, and surveyed the area. Everyone seemed to have survived the crash with just a few cuts and bruises. The officer was hurt more than anyone else and a call went out for a medevac as well as a Sikorsky HH-3E helicopter that we called the "Jolly Green Giant," used to carry big equipment like artillery pieces and the bodies of downed helicopters.

Before long, the medevac came in and took out the officer and crewmen of the Sea Knight. Then the Jolly Green came in and rigged lines to lift the body of the Sea Knight and take it away. Fortunately, no more shots were fired, possibly because the 60mm mortar teams in our position had fired rounds in the vicinity that the original gun fire had come from.

Eventually we cleared the debris from the LZ and resumed our mission. Later resupplies had no other problems and it wouldn't be long before we abandoned the hill. That was the whole story in Vietnam. Take a hill, a village or an area, killing anything that got in our way. Then leave it all behind and go someplace else to do the same thing all over again. As we left, the VC would come back to fill the vacuum and use the things we left behind to make a stronger position for themselves. It was like chasing your tail and biting your butt as you did so.

On February 14th, I wrote:

> *Dear Dad,*
>
> *Say, I got your letter! It has been about a week and a half since we have gotten any mail, and almost that long since we have gotten chow. So as you can guess, this country is pretty rugged. But we have blown a landing zone and are now getting chow, water and mail. So far we haven't made any contact with Charlie, but the next ridge line we go to is supposed to be loaded with 'em, but that remains to be seen. I don't know when I will get out of the bush, but I figure about 22 days left in Nam, so hopefully I might get out in about 10 days, maybe. But taking everything in consideration I'm just fine. ...*
>
> *As far as our favorite subject is concerned, just remember that war plays hell with a man's [conscience], and in fact after fighting for a year and more, one's [conscience] seems to [disappear]. So I guess you know what I need most when I get home, awhat. Yea, a good cup of coffee, ha, ha. Well, so much for that. ...*
>
> *With all my love, Your Son, Chuck*
>
> *P. S. I almost forgot, I [finally] made Corporal. It's about time too. So it looks like I'll be wearing two stripes home after all. I am also section leader of machine guns, and so have all three machine gun squads under me. So I'm doing pretty good.*

After we cleared the LZ, we were joined by Company F to help secure the LZ for future use. There were constant patrols and night ambushes in order to keep the enemy at bay. On the 16th, a TET cease fire was called but as the records report:

> A TET cease fire was effected at 161800H and at 162120H, Company G, 2nd Bn, 5th Marines received incoming fire, returned fire with unknown results. This incident is in violation of cease fire.

Golf Company must have been a "truce breaker magnet." The truce was broken at Christmas when Golf got fire on and now again in February for TET.

February 17th would be our last day on Operation Taylor Common. As reported on that day:

1200 2/5 chopped OPCON to 5th Marines

1630 CoG helolifted to An Hoa

On February 17, 1st Bn, 3rd Marines (-) helilifted to Hill #55 to conduct rehab. 3rd Marines passed OPCON of 2nd Bn, 5th Marines and 3rd Bn, 5th Marines to Task Force Yankee. Upon the departure of 3rd Marines for Dong Ha, 1st Bn, 3rd Marines was chopped OPCON to Task Force Yankee. Third Marines submitted SitRep number 270 as the last SitRep of Operation Taylor Common. 3rd Marines departed An Hoa for Dong Ha.

After our return to An Hoa we were immediately sent back out into the bush in the Arizona area. Operation Taylor Common might be over, but the war still raged on. Once again, the reports tell the tale:

Enemy activity during the first three weeks of February remained at the level of the previous reporting period. The 23rd of February, however, saw the onset of a new Communist offensive which resulted in large contacts with enemy units in the Arizona portion of the AO, and a sapper attack on the An Hoa Base itself.

Just prior to 23 February, units OPCON to the 5th Marines began to make large contacts with the enemy in the Arizona area. The intensity of these incidents increased daily and reached a high point on the 26th and 27th of February when a total of 105 NVA were killed through the combined efforts of Marine ground, air and artillery.

230715H Co G 2/5 Co S&C [Search and Clear] Loc AT969549. Unit Fd 1 WP RD w/press det.

On 23 February 1969, An Hoa was the target of a major attack by NVA/VC forces. RAS [Rear Area Security] personnel augmented "A" Med personnel in receiving, treating and evacuating casualties through the medical bunker. In addition, RAS personnel were utilized as members of search and recovery teams. The RAS sustained minor damage caused by concussion and shell fragments. During the remainder of the month, rocket, mortar, and small arms fire frequently struck the base. On these occasions, RAS personnel were used to augment the medical team from "A" Med.

On February 24, I wrote:

Dear Folks,

Well, I guess you have been wondering where I have been, and what I have been doing. I don't really know where to begin, but if I remember right, I wrote you last from the mountains on [Operation] Taylor Common. Since then we have been making sweeps [around] An Hoa, and I have been stuck out in the bush. But I am now in the rear and will probably stay here till my flight date. So all I have to do is wait a few more days and I'll soon be on my way home.

Oh. This is important. It looks like my promotion to Cpl didn't go through after all, so don't forget to put LCpl down when you write. We haven't had mail for about 5 days now, so I really don't know what to say. ...

I am enclosing my W-2 form for my Income Tax. Could you fix it up for me and send it in? If not, just hold it till I get home. ...

With all my love, Chuck

You could get your head blown off, but be sure you paid your taxes!

We took a few casualties in February, mostly from booby traps. The men were gaining confidence in finding SEDs (special explosive devices) but detecting them all was nearly impossible. If you crossed paths with one and survived, you were either good or lucky with emphasis on lucky.

As February closed, I was back in An Hoa, transferred from Golf Company and attached to H & S Company (Headquarters and Service Company). I was put in charge of a portion of the perimeter, ensuring that the men kept on their toes, alert at all times. Since the attack on An Hoa on the 23rd, everyone was expecting another big TET Offensive against An Hoa. I may have been out of the jungle, but not out of the battle. Not yet.

The casualties for 2/5 in the month of February 1969 were:

The Battalion joined five officers and 146 enlisted men during the month. Three officers and 153 enlisted men were transferred. Casualties sustained by the Battalion during the month were:

BATTLE					NON-BATTLE		TOTAL
KIA	WIA	DOW	WIANE	MIA	NBD	NBC	
4	26	0	12	0	7	19	68

The running total since September 1968 is:

KIA – 88, WIA – 351, DOW – 5, WIANE – 218, MIA – 1, NBD – 10, NBC – 245, Total - 918

For the sixth month now, the numbers of Battalion personnel were in the red. Having transferred 156 officers and enlisted, joined 151 officers and men and lost 68 casualties, the numbers show that 2/5 was in the hole by 73 men for February. The grand total loss since the first of September, 1968 was 864 men.

The monthly increase of new men from the States prevented the Battalion from being nearly wiped out. The average monthly strength for the Battalion in February was 33 Officers and 1008 enlisted Marines, only a 123 man difference from the total casualties since the 1st of September, making that loss close to the equivalent of a complete turnover of the Battalion.

After six months, from September 1968 through February 1969, the Average Monthly Battalion strength during the time in Vietnam was 1135 USMC officers and men.

The percent killed/missing or wounded in the 2nd Battalion, 5th Marines after six months, was 81%, a marked increase over the results from the 2nd Battalion, 27th Marines which was 61% after 6.5 months.

Chapter 18

It was March 1969 and the war just wouldn't leave me alone. I had only days left before I was scheduled to depart this hell-hole, and still the enemy came at me. The records report:

> The month [of] March was characterized by the enemy conducting frequent rocket, mortar and recoilless rifle attacks upon the An Hoa Combat Base.

010040	AN HOA CMBT BASE REC'D 59 82MM RR & 82MM MTRS & 122 RDS RES IN 13 USMC WIAE, 10 USMC WIA(M). RET'D ARTY MSN AND 81MM MSN ON 10 ENEMY POSITS.
010040H	AN HOA CMBT BASE DEF POS LOC AT873473 (FOLLOW-UP). CHANGE CUM CAS TO READ: 9 USMC WIAE, 15 USMC WIA(M).
020230H	AN HOA CMBT BASE DEF POSIT LOC AT873473. UNIT REC'D 61 RDS 82MM MTR & R/R FIRE FM EN LOC IN 13 EN POSITS RES IN 4 USMC WIA(M). RET'D COUNTER MTR FIRE & OBS 2 SEC EXPL.
021935H	AN HOA COMBAT BASE RECD 15 RDS OF 82MM NEG DAMAGE.
030245H	AN HOA CMBT BASE DEF POSIT LOC AT873473. TANK A12 REC'D 1 RD RPG RES IN 1 USMC WIAE AND VIEWPORT DAMAGED TO TANK FM EN LOC AT879479. CALLED MAR 81MM MSN ON EN POSIT.
031040H	AN HOA COMBAT BASE RECD 10 RDS 122MM ROCKETS RES IN 1 USMC E AND 4 USMC (M)

March 4th, 1969 would be my last letter from Vietnam. In it I wrote:

Dear Folks,

Well, I guess this will just about be the last letter you all will [receive] from Viet Nam. My flight date is the 8th of March, so by the time you all get this letter I should be in [Okinawa], and I am not in the least bit sad about that, are you[?] Ha, Ha. I leave An Hoa on the 6th, and that alone is a blessing in itself. Needless to say, I am so damn happy I could laugh, cry, and blow my nose all at the same time. No telling what day I will get in the States, but it will be soon anyway. I'll probably either call from California or from San Antonio, depending on how fast I can get a flight home. Well, there isn't much else to say, except I'LL SEE YOU SOON! Give everyone my love,

With all my love, Chuck

I was "safe" back in the Battalion rear at An Hoa. Yeah, right!!! Thirty-four Marines wounded by incoming mortars and rockets between the first and third of March (RR and R/R are rockets; MTR are mortars), and me on the lines every day until the 6th, when I went to Da Nang to catch my flight out of Vietnam. Those gooks were after me right up until the end. No rest for the weary, and my tour wasn't over yet.

The last incident for me in Vietnam happened during the rocket and mortar attacks that we had been subject to since February 23rd. By March 3rd, 28 Marines were wounded by the barrage of enemy mortars and rockets, and everyone was nervous on the lines. My position was slightly to the rear of the lines so that I could see from one end to the other of my section of responsibility. I was beyond "short," I was NEXT, I was determined to stay alert and leave this place in one piece. We had all known someone who was so "short" that he couldn't see over the tops of his boots and at the last minute, a sniper round or a mortar or a rocket or a machine gun or a booby trap or a snake or a rat or even a tiger would come along and kill him dead. Being "short" was bad, being Next was nerve racking.

It was after a recent mortar attack where the rounds went over our heads and landed deep inside the compound. They say that you never hear the one that gets you, and I can say that that is true. Yet, even if you hear rounds passing over your head, there was always a good chance that one round could be a short round and drop into your hole before you know it, sending pieces of yourself flying around like a bunch of sticky confetti. I know, I've seen that happen.

There was a break in the attack and everyone was up in their holes watching for the next phase, when the sappers hit the wire with satchel charges (ready-made explosive charges in canvas bags), paving the way for enemy troops to run over the bodies of their dead and through the wire, focused on one thing: Kill Marines. The lines commenced firing, stopping the sappers in their tracks. All went real quiet after that.

Suddenly I heard a high pitched noise that sounded like incoming mortars to me, and as I hollered:

"Incoming, incoming!"

I hit the ground in front of me, holding my helmet on with both hands. It wasn't long before I heard a bunch of laughter, and at the same time, I was still hearing that incoming sound. I raised my head and I could see a bunch of Marines gathered around me. One guy looked down at me and said:

"What are you doing down there Marine?"

The sound had stopped and as I got up I realized what had happened. A mule, which was a four wheeled, four wheel drive, flat-bed cart with an open driver position and a small gasoline engine, had come up behind me, carrying ammo for the troops on the line. It made a high pitched sound, which to me sounded like an incoming mortar round. I'd been had. I laughed with the guys and said:

"Hey, I'm short, in fact, I'm next, so give me a break."

It was a funny thing, but I was still in knots waiting for the one with my name on it.

March 6th rolled around and I was on my way to Da Nang to catch my Freedom Bird. I had to turn in all my weapons to the armory in An Hoa, and so, except for a Bowie knife with a bone handle, I was defenseless. I had acquired the knife from a dead gook not long ago, and had stored it in my sea bag back in Battalion. I broke it out and wore it at my side for insurance.

My sea bag is a whole story in itself. It had been tossed and jumbled from the States to the Battalion Headquarters of 2/27 and then on to 2/5. It had a combination lock, but I lost the combination long ago and had to have the engineers break out some bolt cutters so I could use it. I had picked up things like the Bowie knife and NVA pack and buckle and put them in my sea bag, but the only thing that survived the sticky fingers of the "POGs in the Rear" was my knife, a fairly recent acquisition. "POG" was a term we used for office personnel in the rear, meaning -Personnel Other than Grunt. As far as my uniforms were concerned, they were ruined. Mold and mildew and moths had taken a toll on the fabric, especially the wool. The only usable clothes I had were the ones on my back, and they weren't in any great shape either. But it didn't matter to me, I would have left Vietnam naked if I had to.

With my worn out jungle utilities, worn out jungle boots, crumpled up utility cover, and Bowie knife at my side, I carried my sea bag and boarded the Freedom Bird. When it lifted up and away from the Da Nang airport, everyone on board whooped and hollered out of joy for having left HELL behind.

The casualty statistics for 2nd Battalion, 5th Marines in March, 1969 were:

174 enlisted men transferred. Casualties sustained by the Battalion during the month were as follows:

BATTLE					NON-BATTLE		TOTAL
KIA	WIA	DOW	WIANE	MIA	NBD	NBC	
11	53	0	33	0	2	58	157

The running total since September 1968 is:

KIA – 99, WIA – 404, DOW – 5, WIANE – 251, MIA – 1, NBD – 12, NBC – 303, Total – 1075

This running total of casualties in 2nd Battalion 5th Marines from September 1968 through March 1969 continues the same pattern as before. What can be said, the 2nd Battalion, 5th Marines suffered greatly during this time, but in spite of all they had been through since TET of 1968, the Battalion continued to do the job it was assigned. As much as I complained about the 5th Marines, I had to admire the grit and determination of the men to take the war to the enemy. I am proud to have served with the 2nd Battalion, 5th Marine Regiment. The "Devil Dogs" of WWI fame, the fighters of Guadalcanal, the "Old Breed" of Peleliu and Okinawa in WWII. Had the Marines in Vietnam been left to their own devices in conducting this war, it would have been over by the end of 1969 - in my humble opinion. For those who may doubt the ferocity of the Vietnam war, just look at the statistics and read the stories of the men who were there. For those who may doubt the ferocity of U. S. Marines, remember that we turned back every offensive that the enemy threw at us in 1968 and early 1969.

March wasn't over when I left Vietnam and neither was the war that I carried within me. We were taken to Okinawa and reintroduced to the State-Side Marine Corps. We were given cots in tents to call our bed, and then prodded and probed to determine our physical shape. We received one set of Marine Corps dress greens, which was the uniform of the day. In addition to one dress uniform, we were issued the equivalent of a boot camp issue of clothing and sanitary kit bag. Any other uniforms that we may want or need, had to be purchased at our own expense.

It was one line after another. You were just a number and treated as such. We marched to chow, marched to medical, marched to get clothing, marched to Admin to get our Service Records and the rest of the time we either went to the PX (Post Exchange) or slept in our cots. There was no liberty, no chance to see the local area. We had a schedule to meet and a plane to catch which would take us back across the Pacific to Marine Corps Air Station, El Toro, California.

My time there is a blur, but one incident spoke clearly of what I would be facing in the State-Side Marine Corps. I had carried my Bowie knife the whole time in Okinawa without any problems from the non-combat personnel that manned the base there, that is until I got ready to board my plane. A line of tables had been set up as we were checked by Customs (more non-combat Marines) for any contraband, - like explosives, or liquor over the given limit, or fruit, etc. Then there was also the five finger discount Customs. As I approached my table, the Marine behind it asked if I had anything to declare. Not understanding what he was talking about, I said no. He told me to empty my sea bag and put everything on the table. I did this and he looked through my things until he came to my Bowie knife. When he spied that, he picked it up and looked it over and told me that I couldn't take it with me. I asked him why not and he said that it was because the knife had a bone handle and might carry some disease. He said that I could take it if I broke the handle off of the knife. Nervous, and anxious to catch my plane, I opted to let him keep it. I had my original pack and a blood stained C-4 pouch, but he never said a thing about that. Smiling all the way, he helped me pack my gear in my sea bag and sent me merrily on my way.

I guess I should have let him break off the handle of the knife and taken the rest with me, but all I wanted at that time was the plane home. Once we lifted off and were bound for the States, I told one of the guys next to me about the knife and he told me that he hadn't had any problems with war souvenirs and that I had just been taken. Welcome to the Real World! I would be back in the States in a little over 13 hours.

Chapter 19

The plane landed at El Toro, California and we disembarked. Since there were all branches of the Service except the Coast Guard on our plane, we were herded into groups by type of Service and marched - yes, marched - to the terminal to receive our sea bags and then to a temporary barracks. We were assigned to a rack in the barracks and some clerks came around and gathered up our records, or rather what was left of them. I have no idea what survived the office fire when I was with 2/27 or another office fire in 2/5 when I was with them. Be that as it may, the whole purpose for turning in our records was to get us back in the state-side system and to get paid and cut us orders for a 30-day leave.

The only uniforms I had at that time were my old jungle utilities and boots, along with one set of Greens with black shoes, and a basic issue of green utilities, shorts, socks, etc. The shoes hurt. I did my best to keep my uniforms clean. After all, I was a Marine, and a Combat Vet at that. There in that little part of the Corps, I still had my pride and I was protected from what was happening outside the perimeter of the base. Within a couple of days, our orders were cut and we had just one more step to freedom. We had to go to a debriefing. Not one about combat, but rather a small effort to orient us with the world outside of the base.

We were told of some anti-war people, protests and such, and we were advised not to wear our uniform in public any more than we had to. Not understanding the reality of what I would be facing when I left the base, I let the briefing slide calmly over my head. I didn't want any more confrontation in my life. At the end of the briefing I was handed my 30-day leave orders and told to report back to California at the end of my leave for further duty, as well as whatever pay I was due to date plus a month's pay in advance to help get me home. Then the door was opened.

"Where am I?"

"What's going on?"

"Why are things so different?"

War had become a way of life, not just an experience.

I walked out into the light glad to be alive, glad that I had a country to return to and looking forward to seeing my family soon. I just stood there on the sidewalk outside of the base in the only clothes I had, my Marine Corps Greens. Still holding my sea bag, I waited for something to happen. Where was I supposed to go? How could I heat some water for coffee without any C-4? Where was my pack and most importantly, where were my weapons? I had a strong ghost feeling of my .45 hanging off of my right hip. Almost like the ghost feeling that men who have lost limbs feel, but certainly not as serious. Once I got started, that feeling should fade. Right? Not so. I carried that ghost feeling for many years, and still feel it from time to time.

I was lost. I didn't know where to go or what to do. What if I was caught in an ambush? Just a week or so ago I was being mortared in An Hoa. People were trying to kill me. How did I get here, on this sidewalk, watching the cars go by? Then the kids started in on me.

From across the street, there was an anti-war demonstration, which turned out to be an anti-Marine demonstration. They called me every dirty name in the book, plus some I was not used to, like "Baby Killer" and "Marine Bastard." Their words ran over my head and into my soul. I was in shock. What happened to my country? Where were the parades and welcome signs and people happy to have me back, even if they weren't family? How could the Corps tell us not to wear our uniform out in public when our uniform was all we had to wear?

As the crowd jeered, I took stock of what money I had. Enough for now. I just needed to catch a flight home.

By luck or design, a taxi pulled up next to me and the cabbie said:

"Hey Marine, welcome home, need a lift?"

I jumped in the cab, mostly to get away from the jeering crowd, and told him:

"I need to go get some civilian clothes."

I got the message from the crowd. Don't advertise your service connection, especially with the Marine Corps. The cabbie was a nice guy, former Marine with Korean combat behind him. He knew the ropes and filled me in on what was going on in the "Good Old U.S. of A." He took me to an out of the way store where I could get some civvies (civilian clothes) and I rushed in and got out of my uniform a quick as I could. I was proud of my service and proud of being a Marine, but I had to put all that in my sea bag for now.

After getting some trousers, a shirt and sweater – I kept my Marine Corps shoes - I had him take me to the airport. He asked if I wanted anything to eat, but I said no, I just wanted to get out of here. I could eat at the airport. So off we went to the Continental airport terminal. As I got out of the cab I glanced at the meter and as I was getting my money together, the cabbie said:

"On the house, Marine." and drove off - there were some real people after all.

Except for my high and tight Marine Corps haircut and my shiny Marine Corps shoes, and the haunted look on my ruddy face and the extremely tanned arms, not to speak of the Marine Corps sea bag that I was hauling around with me, I was a civilian, wasn't I? I managed to get my ticket to San Antonio, with an arrival time of midnight or so. I had a few hours before boarding time, so I got something to eat at the costly food court in the airport and then got my ticket and turned in my sea bag for the trip to San Antonio. Next, I went to the waiting area to wait for my flight.

I had plenty of Camel cigarettes and I smoked like a steam engine, anxious about all the stares I was getting and about the flight home. I was overwhelmed by everything, which was so far removed from the life I had led for the past 13 months that I didn't even call home to tell them I was coming. Besides, it was already late in Texas with the time difference and all. Some young protesters had come into the airport and were heckling men like me. What was their problem, couldn't they see that I was a civilian? Right?

My joy was gone. My security, formed by the Marines around me, and my own knowledge of how to live and act in combat was gone. There was no use for a Combat Marine in this airport or in the country, as far as I could see. I headed to the nearest bar, hoping for some relief in good old Kentucky Bourbon. Bourbon and Camels kept me alive. You had to be 21 to enter the bar, which shut out the protesters. I sat with my back to a velvet covered wall in the dimly lit room and drank and smoked and waited. I would probably have missed my flight if it hadn't been for an older man who roused me from my musings, asked my name, and what flight I was waiting for. When I told him, he said that they had just called my name and "last call" for that flight. Jumping up, I thanked him, and took off for the gate. They had actually held the flight a few minutes hoping I would board. There was some good left yet.

I was just in time. I wound up being the last person boarded on the flight. Whew, I better slow down on the booze. Once the plane took off and we were safely in the air, the stewardesses came around and asked if anyone wanted a drink while an evening meal was being prepared. I couldn't resist and ordered a double shot of Jim Beam bourbon. Before long the meal arrived, and I wolfed it down, not realizing how hungry I was. People started to look at me like I was a mad man. Like I had looked at that "lost" Marine long ago in the chow hall at the 2/27 compound in February, 1968, and they were right – I had that 1000 mile stare and don't mess with me attitude. The food helped with the bourbon and soon I was relaxed and savoring the flight. A nice stewardess came over and asked if I wanted anything, and of course, I ordered another drink. When she brought it back, she asked if I was a soldier returning from the war. I told her yes, that I was a Marine and I had just returned from Vietnam. She warmed up to me and told me that she had done a couple of flights to Vietnam on Continental Freedom Birds. That cleared the air and we talked for a while, enjoying each other's company. She said that she had a brother in the Army in Vietnam. Before she left to tend to her duties, I told her not to worry, think positive and pray.

Belly full, bourbon in one hand and a Camel in the other, I relaxed for the rest of the flight. The stewardess had warned me about drinking at high elevations, so after I had finished my drink I stopped, at least until I got to San Antonio.

It was very late when I arrived at the San Antonio airport, well after midnight. I retrieved my sea bag and headed for the toilet. Oh, yea, I had just started to adjust to the use of a toilet. No more digging a little hole in the ground, squatting over it to do my business, and wiping with a little piece of toilet paper, if I still had any. A little piece of heaven, being able to use a toilet with plenty of paper, whenever you needed it. I splashed water on my face - from a faucet, Wow - from a faucet! I still wasn't used to water that was safe to drink, coming out of a faucet any time you wanted it.

I looked around the airport, and war protesters were nowhere to be seen.

"Gotta love Texas," I thought.

However, I would face a different type of protest at home. I called home and my mom answered and was shocked that I was in San Antonio. She fussed at me for not telling her when I was coming in, but soon forgot about that in the joy she had that her son had come home. She offered to come pick me up but I said no, that I would catch the next bus to Fredericksburg and meet her at the bus terminal there. I knew she had a family to take care of and I didn't want to cause her any inconvenience.

It was late, probably 1 or 2 a.m., when I called the bus company to find out when the next bus to Fredericksburg would leave and found out that it left around 4 a.m.. I thanked them and caught a cab and went to the bus terminal. After I arrived, I bought my ticket and called my mom again and told her when I would arrive in Fredericksburg. The bus terminal was nothing like the airport. It was pretty dirty with all kinds of unsavory characters hanging around. I found a place to get some coffee and a wall to lean against, protecting my back, and waited for my ride. I was more than ready for any foul play. Fortunately, nothing happened and I hopped on the bus when it arrived and took the hour and a half trip to my home town.

The bus arrived a little early, just about dawn, so I waited for my mom to come pick me up. I don't know what I was expecting, but after the trip from California, I thought I was ready for anything. I didn't have too long to wait when my mom drove up, all by herself, and crushed me in her grasp. I could feel the tension leave her, at least some of it, her oldest son was home safe and sound. She said that she had to hurry because she had to go to work, so we climbed in the car and headed for the house.

As we arrived I noticed a star in the window, indicating that there was a Marine in Combat. I didn't see any sign of a welcome home, but when I stepped into the house, my little brother Bill, 10 years old, and my little sister Jeannie, 8 , were jumping up and down on the living room couch, so excited they couldn't stop. As I went over and hugged them, their tears of joy filled the room. Unfortunately, my tears had long ago dried up. Mom asked me what I would like, and the first thing I said was a good cup of coffee, followed by bacon and eggs if she had the time.

Sure enough, I got the coffee, but had to fix the bacon and eggs myself because mom had to go to work. I noticed the tension she was under, but I didn't have a clue what the cause was. I fixed enough food for myself and Billy and Jeannie and enjoyed some time with them before heading for my old bed for a long needed rest. I don't remember where my brother Chris was, but he had a car and was probably off with his friends.

As it turned out, my folks were getting a divorce. On my first night home, my parents called me back into their room and said that they were thinking of getting a divorce and asked me what I thought. I was dead inside and I just said:

"Do what you want to do, it doesn't matter to me."

My brother Chris was in a tailspin and my sister Cathy had recently married and was living in San Antonio. My dad was not living in the house, and after the young kids left for school on the bus, the house was quiet as a tomb, as was my soul. I couldn't believe it, this was my welcome home. After a little self-pity, I realized what a mess my mom was in and I was determined to help as I could.

There were no bars in the county, so you had to buy a bottle if you wanted liquor. I didn't want to bring that into the home, so I just rested and ate and rested some more. The only notable experience I had in Fredericksburg was at a class reunion, marking the 4th year since high school graduation. I found out about it by reading the local paper and decided that I would attend. It would be good to see some of my old classmates, or so I thought. On the evening of the reunion, I came in late. Everyone was already in the hall where the reunion was held and I was the last to arrive. As I opened the door, everyone just seemed to ignore me. No welcome home, no "So what have you been up to?" - no communication. They just ignored me. I got the message real quick and just wheeled around and left. I guess the war protest was here too, just in a different manner. Everyone knew where I had been, this being a typical small town, so there was no misunderstanding their message. This remembrance is not to judge the town or the people. There were many people in town who had supported me while in Vietnam, especially the Grandmothers Club, so the response from my class was even more confusing. This is the home town of Admiral Nimitz of WWII fame after all. Rather, it was just a sign of the times. The national disapproval of our fighting men had even invaded Small Town USA. and once that happens, beware. Take heed America!

After getting my finances together, I bought a used car and went to San Antonio for some R&R. There sure wasn't anything for me in Fredericksburg. On one occasion, I took my brother Chris to a "go go" bar. He was back home and happy to go to San Antonio with me. I was dressed in some hippie clothes - T-shirt, cut-off jeans and moccasins, hoping I could pull off the "look," but to no avail. I was still a Combat Marine where ever I went. In the parking lot at the bar, I got into a little altercation with a cowboy who thought he was tough and wanted to impress his girlfriend. I had accidently bumped his truck door when I got out of my car, and as I was walking away he hollered at me.

"Hey, you better watch out who's door you're bumpin'."

I apologized, but he was having none of that. He came at me and when he got close enough, it didn't take long to convince him to quit. My brother was jumping up and down hollering.

"Get him, get him!"

The cowboy finally went back to his truck and said:

"You think you're bad, don't you, well, I've got something in my truck for you."

I got real still, wound up like a steel spring, ready for action, and replied:

"What do you have in there, a goddamn gun? You think I've never been shot at before?"

He went in his truck, closed the door, rolled up the window and that was that. I was relieved he did so because I could feel the Marine I knew in Vietnam coming to the surface and I would have instantly charged his truck and eliminated the problem, if he had made any move toward me. I was lucky on that one, it could have proven to be bloody. I was trying to control my reactions and put my combat experience at bay, but having a difficult time with all that, to say the least.

After the incident at the bar, I once again returned to San Antonio. After arriving in town, I got a motel room and hit the town. I was lost and I guess I looked like it. One day I went into a bar with an oriental name. I moseyed up to the bar (this was Texas after all), and ordered a beer. They didn't sell hard liquor. I think I was in uniform, not thinking about any problems I might face and not having any suitable civilian clothes yet. Anyway, I got the beer and then looked around and what did I see, men dancing with men! Oh no!!! Just at that time someone came up to me and said:

"Can I help you soldier?"

I almost lost it. I put that beer on the bar, looked at the bartender and he just nodded. I then acted like Superman - "faster than a speeding bullet" I left that place behind.

It was getting late and I sure didn't want to make that mistake again, so I went to the only place I could think of that served booze and stayed open late, a striptease bar in downtown San Antonio. I wanted a drink bad. As I ordered a drink I noticed a girl sitting at a table by herself. I went over and introduced myself and ordered drinks for two. It turned out she had no place to go, having been kicked out of her apartment due to her inability to pay the rent. I offered to help and we left to get her stuff from her room, which turned out to be just that, a room, not an apartment. We headed to my motel room and the next day I helped her get another place. We were two lost souls hoping to find something good in life. For myself, I was very,

very lonely. I wanted someone to care that I had fought a war and come home. I wanted things that I didn't even know I wanted. I felt I had sinned against God, and for me even that avenue was closed. That letter to my dad explaining what I felt about myself and saying that there were things I couldn't talk about was all too real. There are things even today that I can't talk about. I can honestly say that she really tried to help me relax, and she was real good to me, but I just couldn't relax. I was just a jumble of knotted muscles. There was no hope in my life, no joy, I couldn't even appreciate real affection when it hit me. Still, besides my family, she was the only one to take kindly to a beat-up Combat Marine who was like the proverbial fish out of water. I'll always be thankful for her kindness.

The hardest part of this month's leave was the absence of my dad. My feelings for him had not changed, but I had to put them down and focus on my mother who was struggling to keep the family together. She had to work and raise my younger brother and sister, and help my brother Chris who was affected the most by my parent's breakup. At the time, I felt powerless to help. My leave was soon up and before I left, I signed over the car I had bought to my mom, since my dad had just recently taken the one car that we had. The return trip to California was a reverse of the arrival trip, with the exception that my mom insisted on taking me to the airport in San Antonio. We said our goodbyes and I told her that I would contact her as soon as I got to my new duty station, and that I would send her some money.

I checked in to the Marine Base at Camp Pendleton and while there, I looked up my buddy Tom Thomas. We double-dated a few times but the girls really didn't want to have anything to do with Marines. On one such occasion, my date asked me what my sign was and I told her I was a Sagittarius. She said:

"Oh no, not a Sagittarius," and the date ended.

Tom was lucky - he had already found the love of his life.

I finally got my orders to the Marine security force at Cecil Field, Florida. While I was there, I started to really disintegrate. My drinking got so bad that I was puking stomach bile on the beach and eating raw hamburger. I couldn't get a girlfriend to save my life, and I was sending as much money home as I could to help my mom. Finally, after a serious bout of sickness from the booze, the Good Lord woke me up and I realized that I was on my way to being a full-fledged alcoholic. Having the stigma as the barracks drunk didn't help either. I stopped drinking and took a part-time job as a night attendant at an all-night gas station, leaving only enough time to work on the base, get a few hours of sleep and then go back to work in town. The only fun I had was playing VC against the guys that were guarding the base. I was good at that at least, and they paid dearly for their inability to stop me and my friend Stony who was the only other Vietnam Vet on the base. I believe he was a combat engineer, the blow stuff up kind.

Finally, I had had it. I requested a transfer back to Vietnam and signed a time waiver, which was needed before I could go back there. At that time, no one could be sent back to Nam before a year had passed unless they volunteered and signed a waiver. It was the only place I knew where I could be effective and use the knowledge I had to maybe save other Marines. It was the only life I understood. The deaths of my friends haunted me day and night and I was determined to go back to Nam and give my mom my paycheck, with no thought of coming back alive this time. Only, it didn't happen. The Gunnery Sergeant in charge of the Admin. Department took me aside when my request crossed his desk and counseled me that if I went back, especially as a machine gunner, I probably wouldn't come back alive. I understood that but was beyond caring anymore. I had re-acquired the Vietnam "fuck it" attitude.

I had been promoted to Corporal while at Cecil Field, and the Gunny said he would give me a meritorious promotion to Sergeant if I would re-enlist and stay with him there at Cecil Field. The other option was that he could let me out of the Corps on an "early out" program that the Marine Corps was using to cut back on the number of Marines, which had been mandated by Congress. I decided to take my early discharge and go home and be there to help my family. There were some good POGs after all. In later years, my parents would reconcile and remarry, but for now the whole load lay on my saintly mother's shoulders. I couldn't let her down.

After my discharge, the nightmares began in earnest and at first I tried to drink them away. It didn't take long before I realized that that wouldn't work, and instead, I buried myself in family and work. The anti-war sentiment never stopped. As much as I tried to hide it I was still a Combat Marine, and proud of it. I missed the military. Civilian life seemed to be a road to nowhere.

Within the next two and a half years I would relocate my family to San Antonio, where my mom had better access to good jobs. I would get married, work a no-where job and try very hard to get it together. Still, my longing for the Corps persisted. I still felt that I should never have left Vietnam and I was mad at myself for not going back. One day I went to the Marine Recruiting Station with my DD-214 (my discharge paper) and asked what they would offer for me to re-enlist. I guess they weren't too anxious to re-enlist Marines, because all they could offer me was a cut in rank, back to Lance Corporal and my same MOS (Military Operational Specialty) 0331, machine gunner. With a baby on the way, I had to turn that down. Sounded like they didn't want me anyway. I tried the Air Force and they wanted to send me back to boot camp. I laughed at that one and went down to the Navy. Evidently the Navy actually needed men and offered me a program where I could choose the job I wanted to do, with a meritorious promotion to Third Class Petty Officer (E-4) after successful completion of a year-long school. This was the same level I had been at when I left the Corps, so that sounded okay, and the bonus was that I could take my family with me and live in base housing. All I had to do was sign up and take the oath, go to Charleston, SC and get my uniforms, then go to Great Lakes Naval Base outside of Chicago for my schooling.

To this day, when asked if I would go back to combat in Vietnam I always say yes. Most people are surprised by that, but those who have been there, who had good friends die in their arms amid the blood and the mud of serious combat, who lost their innocence in Vietnam as well as their ability to feel and care, who had lost the chance to mourn for the men we lost or help the men that were seriously wounded, would understand and would probably go back with me. When we left Vietnam, the job was not done. It was an unfinished page in our life and deep down we wanted to finish it.

For us, those who experienced combat in Vietnam, the war is not over, it rages in our souls, in our sleep, in everyday happenings that trigger memories by sight, sound or smell. We drive our families nuts with the war and only find relief when we're able to talk to those who "know." As fallen beings, war will always be with us in one form or another. The trick is to learn to live with it. We will always be faithful to the duty to fight for our Constitution and the country we love, and for our citizens, even when they don't appreciate it. Semper Fi

EPILOGUE

So, what happened to all those wonderful plans I wrote about in my letters? Nothing! I did have some wonderful children, but several failed marriages. I went on to join the Navy, and made it a career. However, initially, I tried my hand at civilian life and wound up with several failed attempts to get it together and do life in a "normal" fashion. My normal was far different from those who had never experienced war. I started hanging out at state parks, with my machete at my side, daring anyone to try and mess with me. Not healthy. Only with those who had "been there" did I find acceptance and understanding and only in the Navy did I find the order and discipline I needed. The coolness part persisted. It was a great asset in combat, which was one reason I was always sought after when patrols had to go out. However, even that changed to a numbness that still lingers in my soul to this day. As I look back and read these words, I'm forced to face the reality of my transformation from a 21 year-old naive, happy young man, proud to be a Marine, to a truly lost soul who had just seen and done too much killing. The only good thing that I can report about my tour of duty is that I don't remember any casualties in the hundreds of patrols and ambushes I led. No physical casualties that is. Also, none of the men in my machine gun squad in Golf Company, 2/5 are listed on "The Wall" in Washington, DC. My love for the Corps has never wavered, although it has wandered from time to time. Being a Marine has always been and still is one of the highlights of my life.

My heartfelt thanks to all those fellow Marines who shared their memories and written statements adding a greater understanding to the events written here. Semper Fi Brothers. Also, I wish to thank Tim Dalton for his valuable input in bringing this work to the printed page. As I neared the completion of my manuscript, I found myself at a loss trying to have my book published. Then Tim emailed me concerning a remembrance that I had left on the "Wall" years ago for Mike Dalton, Tim's older brother, who was KIA on May 14, 1968. In our conversation, I mentioned my book and shortly thereafter through the efforts of Tim and his family, this book came to print. The Lord works in mysterious ways.

Finally, here are some statistics assembled from the Vietnam Memorial Wall.

There are 58,267 names now listed on "The Wall":

8,283 were just 19 years old.

The age group with the most KIA's was the 18 year-olds with 33,103 listed on the Wall.

12 were 17 years old.

5 were 16 years old.

One was just 15 years old.

The statistics go on and on. However, it's enough to realize that 71% of those killed in the Vietnam War were nineteen years old or younger. Teenagers!

Is there anything we can say to truly honor those 58,267 deaths?

I ask only one thing, if you are so inclined. Make the time to hold a moment of silence to honor those who suffered and died in that far-off country. To quote John 15:13:

"Greater love has no one than this, that he lay down his life for his friends."

A "boot camp" Pfc Charles A. Van Bibber, (AKA "Van"), at the 2nd Battalion, 27th Marines main base, Feburary, 1968

At the 2/27 base camp, February, 1968, Back row – L to R Dan Nordmann, "Doc" Puckett, Al Decker, Rhoden Front row – L to R "Doc" Mac (MacLaughin), "Van", David Lopez, unk.

SSgt. Staggs driving the boat at the Ha Dong Bridge, March, 1968.

L to R Marked up with grease paint, Lt. Jones and SSgt. Staggs enjoying C-Rat can coffee while on a Platoon patrol in Duc Ky.

Typical jungle trail. Often the place for ambushes by VC and Marines alike.

The Ha Dong Bridge. Note bunker to far right, the machine gun position.

Beer Call! 2/27 base camp. Tom Thomas (Back-Left corner of table with dark rimmed glasses). Dennis Freer (Front-Right corner of table).

ARVN camp. Back, Dennis Freer. Front L-R, David Lopez, Cano, Sgt. Ledesma, Jim Seabolt.

Playing "Stretch" at ARVN camp. In background: upper-left corner, board for knife throwing contest and Dennis Freer playing stretch.

The "Greek," George Kyricos at 2/27 base camp. [KIA 8-23-68 near Cam Nam, Cam Le Bridge]

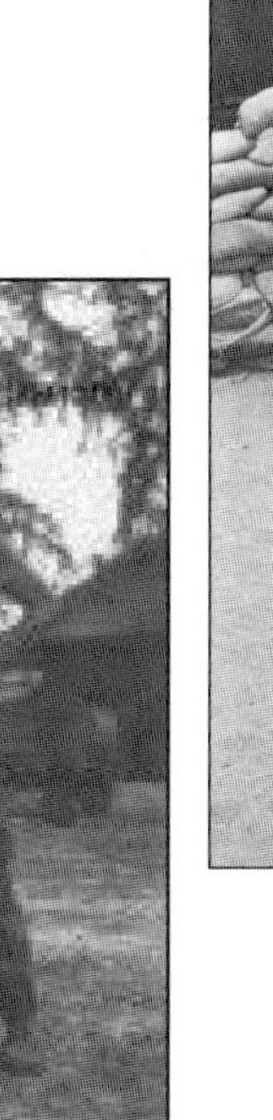

At 2/27 Base. Back row: L-R Tom Montie, Ralph Gibson, Sgt. Farmer, Howard, Al Decker. Front row: L-R unk., unk., "Moochie."

Michael F. Dalton at ARVN camp. [KIA 5-14-68 near Phong Luc (3)]

At a PPB (Platoon Patrol Base) Duc Ky area. My core squad (minus Lopez) Fox Co., 2nd Platoon. Back Row: L-R Dan Nordmann, "Van", Dennis Freer. Front Row: L-R Allan Decker, James Richee. [Allan Decker and James Richee KIA 8-25 at Qua Giang (2).]

F-2-D Night Patrol.

Dan Nordmann on top of the old Army Fire Base, 8-68.

At old Army Fire Base, 8-68. L-R Fox Co. Gunny; Fox Co. Commanding Officer Capt. Bill Collins; Lt. Jones and Lt. Frytown?

"Van" in An Hoa, after transfer to 2nd Platoon, Golf Company, 2/5, 9-68.

"Chief" Marsh at blown bridge on Go Noi Island, 10-68.

"Van" at 2/5 "rehabilitation" in An Hoa, 11-68.

Reyes on top of ridge, 12-7-68.

Medevac, Sikorsky UH-34, 12-68.

Air strikes against friendlies as seen from ridge, 12-8-68.

750 pound bomb strike, 12-68.

Napalm strike, 12-68.

"Van" wounded, 12-68, note the 1000 mile stare.

"Old Breed," at Phu Loc fire base 3-68. L-R George Doucette, Sheldon Hoskins. [Sheldon Hoskins KIA 10-7-68 near Ha Nha (4), Operation Maui Peak.]

Golf Co. 2/5, "Old Breed," at Liberty Bridge 11-67. Back, L-R Barney Barnes, Ted Harrison, Mike Ervin. Bottom, L-R Michael "Chubby" Hale. [Michael "Chubby" Hale KIA 8-19-68 near La Thap.]

"Old Breed," at Phu Gia Pass/Beach 4-68. L-R Lt. Pace, SSgt. Freddy Williams, Lt. Hancock, unk. [SSgt. Freddy Williams KIA 8-18-68 near La Thap.]

"Old Breed," at ARVN camp, Hai Van Pass 5-68. L-R Mike Copeland, Hector Quintana, James Fell, "Chubby" Hale.

"Old Breed," at ARVN camp, Hai Van Pass 5-68. L-R Forrest Burnette, "Little" Joe Arnold. ["Little" Joe Arnold KIA near Ha Nha (4), Operation Maui Peak.]

"Old Breed," Easter Sunday in mountains off Hwy 1. F-B "Chubby" Hale, Mike Witt, unk. [Mike Witt KIA 8-18-68 near La Thap.]